Romanticism and Illustration

This collection of chapters takes a fresh look at the important role of illustration in Romantic literature. The late eighteenth century saw an explosion of illustrated editions of literary classics and the emergence of a new culture of literary art, including the innovative literary galleries. The impact of these developments on the reading and viewing of literary texts is explored in a series of case studies covering poetry, historical texts, drama, painting, reproductive prints, magazines and ephemera. *Romanticism and Illustration* argues for a more detailed study of illustration which includes the context of a wider circulation of images across different media. The modern understanding of the word 'illustration' fails to convey the complex relationship between the artist, the engraver, the publisher, the text and the audience in Romantic Britain. In teasing out the implications of this dynamic cultural matrix, this book opens up a new field of Romantic studies.

IAN HAYWOOD is Professor of English at the University of Roehampton, London, where he is Director of the Centre for Research in Romanticism. His previous publications include *The Revolution in Popular Literature* (Cambridge, 2004), *Bloody Romanticism* (2006), *Romanticism and Caricature* (Cambridge, 2013) and two co-edited collections of essays, *The Gordon Riots* (Cambridge, 2012) and *Spain in British Romanticism* (2018). He is President of the British Association for Romantic Studies (until 2019).

SUSAN MATTHEWS is Honorary Senior Research Fellow in English and Creative Writing at the University of Roehampton. She is the author of *Blake, Sexuality and Bourgeois Politeness* (Cambridge, 2011) and has published widely on Blake, gender, politics and exhibition culture. She was the co-founder in 2011 of the Romantic Illustration Network.

MARY L. SHANNON is a Senior Lecturer in the Department of English and Creative Writing at the University of Roehampton, London. Her previous publications include the 2016 international Robert and Vineta Colby Scholarly Book Prize-winning work, *Dickens, Reynolds and Mayhew on Wellington Street: The Print Culture of a Victorian Street* (2015).

Romanticism and Illustration

Edited by

IAN HAYWOOD
University of Roehampton

SUSAN MATTHEWS
University of Roehampton

MARY L. SHANNON
University of Roehampton

CAMBRIDGE
UNIVERSITY PRESS

University Printing House, Cambridge CB2 8BS, United Kingdom

One Liberty Plaza, 20th Floor, New York, NY 10006, USA

477 Williamstown Road, Port Melbourne, VIC 3207, Australia

314–321, 3rd Floor, Plot 3, Splendor Forum, Jasola District Centre, New Delhi – 110025, India

79 Anson Road, #06-04/06, Singapore 079906

Cambridge University Press is part of the University of Cambridge.

It furthers the University's mission by disseminating knowledge in the pursuit of education, learning, and research at the highest international levels of excellence.

www.cambridge.org
Information on this title: www.cambridge.org/9781108425711
DOI: 10.1017/9781108348829

© Cambridge University Press 2019

This publication is in copyright. Subject to statutory exception and to the provisions of relevant collective licensing agreements, no reproduction of any part may take place without the written permission of Cambridge University Press.

First published 2019

Printed in the United Kingdom by TJ International Ltd, Padstow Cornwall

A catalogue record for this publication is available from the British Library.

ISBN 978-1-108-42571-1 Hardback

Cambridge University Press has no responsibility for the persistence or accuracy of URLs for external or third-party internet websites referred to in this publication and does not guarantee that any content on such websites is, or will remain, accurate or appropriate.

Contents

List of Figures [*page* vii]
Notes on Contributors [xi]
Acknowledgements [xv]

Editors' Introduction   [1]

PART I   ILLUSTRATING POETRY   [23]

1 The Ends of Illustration: Explanation, Critique, and the Political Imagination in Blake's Title-pages for Genesis   [25]
  PETER OTTO

2 'With a Master's Hand and Prophet's Fire': Blake, Gray, and the Bard   [47]
  SOPHIE THOMAS

3 Seeing History: Illustration, Poetic Drama, and the National Past   [70]
  DUSTIN M. FRAZIER WOOD

4 'Fuseli's Poetic Eye': Prints and Impressions in Fuseli and Erasmus Darwin   [94]
  MARTIN PRIESTMAN

5 Henry Fuseli's Accommodations: 'Attempting the Domestic' in the Illustrations to Cowper   [119]
  SUSAN MATTHEWS

6 Reading the Romantic Vignette: Stothard Illustrates Bloomfield, Byron, and Crabbe for *The Royal Engagement Pocket Atlas*   [143]
  SANDRO JUNG

7 Intimate Distance: Thomas Stothard's and J. M. W. Turner's Illustrations of Samuel Rogers's *Italy*   [171]
  MAUREEN MCCUE

PART II THE BUSINESS OF ILLUSTRATION [197]

8 Illustration, Terror, and Female Agency: Thomas Macklin's Poets Gallery in a Revolutionary Decade   [199]
IAN HAYWOOD

9 Maria Cosway's *Hours*: Cosmopolitan and Classical Visual Culture in Thomas Macklin's Poets Gallery   [221]
LUISA CALÈ

10 Artists' Street: Thomas Stothard, R. H. Cromek, and Literary Illustration on London's Newman Street   [243]
MARY L. SHANNON

11 The Development of Magazine Illustration in Regency Britain – The Example of *Arliss's Pocket Magazine* 1818–1833   [267]
BRIAN MAIDMENT

Coda: Romantic Illustration and the Privatization of History Painting   [288]
MARTIN MYRONE

Bibliography   [303]
Index   [323]

Figures

1.1 William Blake, Illustrated Manuscript of Genesis: First Title-Page (c.1826–7)   [*page* 27]

1.2 William Blake, Illustrated Manuscript of Genesis: Second Title-Page (c.1826–7)   [28]

1.3 William Blake, Illustrated Manuscript of Genesis: God the Father marking Cain's forehead (c.1826–7)   [43]

2.1 Thomas Jones, *The Bard* (1774)   [51]

2.2 Charles Hall and Samuel Middiman, after Phillippe-Jacques de Loutherbourg, frontispiece and title-page from Edward Jones, *Musical and Poetical Relicks of the Welsh Bards* (1784)   [53]

2.3 William Blake, *The Bard*; Page 2: Advertisement   [59]

2.4 William Blake, *The Bard, from Gray* (c.1809)   [63]

3.1 William Sherlock after Samuel Wale, *Edward the Martyr Stabb'd by Order of his Mother in Law*. From *New History of England* (1752)   [74]

3.2 William Wynne Ryland after Angelica Kauffman, *The Interview of King Edgar with Elfrida, after her Marriage to Athelwold* (1786)   [81]

3.3 William Dickinson after James Nixon, *Mrs. Hartley in the Character of Elfrida* (1779)   [82]

3.4a & 4b Frontispieces for Bell's British Theatre edition of *Elfrida* (1796), William Leney after James Roberts, 'Mrs Hartley as Elfrida'; and James Heath after Thomas Stothard, untitled scene depicting Elfrida, Athelwold, and the chorus of British virgins   [83]

3.5a & 5b Rennoldson after Samuel Wale, *King Edgar's First Interview with Queen Elfrida*; and Charles Grignion after Samuel Wale, *King Edward the Martyr treacherously Assassinated at the Gate of Corfe Castle by order of his Step-Mother Elfrida*. From Temple Sydney's *A New and Complete History of England* (1773)   [86]

viii   *List of Figures*

3.6 William Bromley after Robert Smirke, *The Treachery of Elfrida*. From Robert Bowyer's edition of David Hume's *History of England* (1806)   [88]

4.1 Henry Fuseli, *The Nightmare*. From Erasmus Darwin, *The Botanic Garden, Part Two: The Loves of the Plants*, 5th edition (1799)   [99]

4.2 Henry Fuseli, *Flora Attired by the Elements*. Frontispiece to Erasmus Darwin, *The Botanic Garden* (1791)   [102]

4.3 Henry Fuseli, *Fertilization of Egypt*, engraved by William Blake. From Erasmus Darwin, *The Botanic Garden, Part One: The Economy of Vegetation* (1791)   [104]

4.4 Henry Fuseli, Frontispiece to Erasmus Darwin, *The Temple of Nature* (1803)   [110]

4.5 Henry Fuseli, *The Creation of Eve*. From Erasmus Darwin, *The Temple of Nature* (1803)   [112]

5.1 Robert Smirke, *Elevation of one wall of Madame Recamier's bedroom, Hotel Recamier, Paris* (1802)   [129]

5.2 Richard Westall, *Paris Reclining on a Couch Looking up at Helen*. Etching and engraving by James Heath (1805)   [131]

5.3 Henry Fuseli, frontispiece to the first volume of Joseph Johnson's edition of *Poems of William Cowper* (1806). Engraved by Abraham Raimbach. Untitled proof version   [133]

5.4 Henry Fuseli, *A Dressing Room*. Engraving by Rhodes, published by Joseph Johnson (1807)   [135]

5.5 Henry Fuseli, *The Newspaper in the Country* (1807)   [137]

6.1 S. Gessner, Vignette 4, *Der Tod Abels* (1758)   [146]

6.2a Thomas Stothard, Vignette for January ('Round Euston's water'd Vale'), *Royal Engagement Pocket Atlas for the Year MDCCCII*   [152]

6.2b Thomas Stothard, Vignette for January ('A little Farm his generous Master till'd'), *Royal Engagement Pocket Atlas for the Year MDCCCII*   [152]

6.3a Thomas Stothard, Vignette for February ('With smiling brow the Plowman cleaves his way'), *Royal Engagement Pocket Atlas for the Year MDCCCII*   [154]

6.3b Thomas Stothard, Vignette for February ('A friendly tripod forms their humble seat'), *Royal Engagement Pocket Atlas for the Year MDCCCII*   [154]

List of Figures ix

6.4a Thomas Stothard, Vignette for July ('With bristles rais'd the sudden noise they hear'), *Royal Engagement Pocket Atlas for the Year MDCCCII*   [155]
6.4b Thomas Stothard, Vignette for July ('assembling Neighbours meet'), *Royal Engagement Pocket Atlas for the Year MDCCCII*   [155]
6.5a Thomas Stothard, Vignette for February ('the Ocean's miserable prey'), *Royal Engagement Pocket Atlas for the Year MDCCCXXV*   [160]
6.5b Thomas Stothard, Vignette for June ('Where loitering stray a little tribe'), *Royal Engagement Pocket Atlas for the Year MDCCCXXV*   [160]
6.6   Thomas Stothard, Frontispiece (The Siege of Corinth), *Royal Engagement Pocket Atlas for the Year MDCCCXVIII*   [163]
6.7a Thomas Stothard, Vignette for November ('Darkness'), *Royal Engagement Pocket Atlas for the Year MDCCCXVIII*   [164]
6.7b Thomas Stothard, Vignette for November ('Darkness'), *Royal Engagement Pocket Atlas for the Year MDCCCXVIII*   [164]
6.7c Thomas Stothard, Vignette for November ('The Prisoner of Chillon'), *Royal Engagement Pocket Atlas for the Year MDCCCXVIII*   [165]
7.1   J. M. W. Turner, *Venice* (1838)   [178]
7.2   Thomas Stothard, *Brides of Venice* (1838)   [183]
7.3   J. M. W. Turner, *Florence* (1838)   [187]
7.4   J. M. W. Turner, *Galileo's Villa* (1838)   [188]
7.5   Thomas Stothard, *Buondelmonte* (1838)   [191]
8.1   Francis Wheatley, *The School Mistress*. Engraved by J. Cole (1794)   [206]
8.2   William Hamilton, *The Antient English Wake*. Engraved by J. Chapman (1794)   [207]
8.3   Joshua Reynolds, *The Cottagers*. Engraved by Francesco Bartolozzi (1794)   [208]
8.4   William Artaud, *Mercy Stopping the Rage of War*. Engraved by Francesco Bartolozzi (1794)   [209]
9.1   Maria Cosway, *The Hours*. Engraved by Francesco Bartolozzi (1788)   [232]
10.1 The Newman Street area. From *Plan of the Cities of London and Westminster [...] Shewing Every House* (1792–9)   [247]

10.2   Approximate map of Newman Street (c.1800–1820)   [248]
10.3   25–28 Newman Street in 1956   [254]
10.4   Thomas Rowlandson, *The Chamber of Genius* (1812)   [255]
10.5   Thomas Stothard, *The Pilgrimage to Canterbury* (1809–17)   [257]
11.1   Title opening to volume IV of *The Pocket Magazine* (1819)   [268]
11.2   Title-page to volume VII of *The Pocket Magazine* (1821)   [269]
11.3   Robert Seymour, illustration from *The Pocket Magazine* (1826)   [270]
11.4   Double-page spread from volume II of the 'Robins Series' of *The Pocket Magazine* (1828)   [282]
11.5   Double-page spread from volume I of the 'Robins Series' of *The Pocket Magazine* (1827)   [283]

Notes on Contributors

LUISA CALÈ teaches Romantic period literature and visual culture at Birkbeck, University of London. She is the author of *Henry Fuseli's Milton Gallery: 'Turning Readers into Spectators'*, and co-editor of *Dante on View: The Reception of Dante in the Visual and Performing Arts* (with Antonella Braida) and *Illustrations, Optics and Objects in Nineteenth-Century Literature and Visual Culture* (with Patrizia di Bello). She has guest-edited special issues on 'Verbal and Visual Interactions in Nineteenth-Century Print Culture' for *19* (with Patrizia di Bello), 'The Disorder of Things' for *Eighteenth-Century Studies* (with Adriana Craciun), 'The Nineteenth-Century Digital Archive' for *19* (with Ana Parejo Vadillo), and 'Literature and Sculpture at the Fin de Siècle' for *Word and Image* (with Stefano Evangelista). Her current project, entitled *The Book Unbound*, explores practices of reading and collecting that question, subvert, or dismantle the book as a cultural form, with chapters on Walpole, Blake, and Dickens.

DUSTIN M. FRAZIER WOOD is Lecturer in English Literature at the University of Roehampton, and Librarian and Archivist of the Spalding Gentlemen's Society. His research is concerned with medievalism and antiquarianism in the literature and visual art of the long eighteenth century, and with the history of archives and manuscript publication. He has published articles on Anglo-Saxonist drama and politics, print culture, and antiquarianism, as well as the forthcoming monograph *Anglo-Saxonism and the Idea of Englishness*.

IAN HAYWOOD is Professor of English at the University of Roehampton, London, Director of the Centre for Research in Romanticism, and President of the British Association for Romantic Studies (2015–19). He organizes two research networks, 'Romantic Illustration' and 'Anglo-Hispanic Horizons', and has published widely on literary and visual culture in the eighteenth and nineteenth centuries, including the development of political caricature. His books include a 'trilogy' of monographs on Romanticism – *The Revolution in Popular Literature* (2004), *Bloody Romanticism* (2006), and *Romanticism and Caricature* (2013) – and two co-edited collections of essays, *The Gordon Riots* (2012) and *Spain in British Romanticism* (2018). His next book will be a study of radical caricature in the 1830s and 1840s.

SANDRO JUNG is Distinguished Professor of English at the Shanghai University of Finance and Economics and Past President of the East-Central American Society for Eighteenth-Century Studies. He is the author of *David Mallet, Anglo-Scot: Poetry, Politics, and Patronage in the Age of Union* (2008), *The Fragmentary Poetic: Eighteenth-Century Uses of an Experimental Mode* (2009), *James Thomson's 'The Seasons', Print Culture, and Visual Interpretation, 1730–1842* (2015), and *The Publishing and Marketing of Illustrated Literature in Scotland, 1760–1825* (2017). He co-edited the 2015 MHRA *Yearbook of English Studies* (on 'The History of the Book'), edited the 2013 *Essays & Studies* volume (on 'British Literature and Print Culture'), and is currently working on a new book, *Illustration and Literature*.

BRIAN MAIDMENT is Professor of the History of Print at Liverpool John Moores University and a past President of the Research Society for Victorian Periodicals. His most recent book is *Comedy, Caricature and the Social Order 1820–1850* (2013). He is currently completing a book on periodical illustration between 1820 and 1840.

SUSAN MATTHEWS is the author of *Blake, Sexuality and Bourgeois Politeness* (Cambridge, 2011). She is an Honorary Senior Research Fellow at University of Roehampton.

MAUREEN MCCUE is a lecturer in nineteenth-century British Literature at Bangor University, specializing in the interaction between visual art and literature in the Romantic period. Her monograph, *British Romanticism and the Reception of Italian Old Master Art, 1793–1840* (2014), was short-listed for the 2015 British Association of Romantic Studies First Book Prize. Her current project examines the ways in which the consumption and circulation of visual culture – such as prints, engraved portraits, and fashion plates – shaped a range of textual spaces, including novels, periodicals, and poetry.

MARTIN MYRONE is Senior Curator at Tate Britain, London, specializing in eighteenth- and nineteenth-century British art. He was curator of the Tate exhibitions *Gothic Nightmares: Fuseli, Blake and the Romantic Imagination* (2006) and *John Martin: Apocalypse* (2012). He has written widely on Blake, Fuseli, and on the transformation of history painting in the late eighteenth century, including *Bodybuilding: Reforming Masculinities in British Art 1750–1810* (2005). He is currently working on the topic of art education, the state, and artistic identity in the early nineteenth century.

PETER OTTO is Professor of Literature at the University of Melbourne, Director of the Research Unit in 'Enlightenment, Romanticism, and Contemporary Culture', and a member of the Australian Academy of the Humanities. His publications include *Blake's Critique of Transcendence* (2000), *Gothic Fiction: A Microfilm Collection of Gothic Novels* (2002–3), *Gothic Fiction: A Guide* (2003), *Entertaining the Supernatural: Mesmerism, Spiritualism, Secular Magic and Psychic Science* (2007), *Multiplying Worlds: Romanticism, Modernity and the Emergence of Virtual Reality* (2011), and *21st Century Oxford Authors: William Blake* (2018). He is currently completing a book on 'William Blake, Secularisation, and the History of Imagination', while also working on a project, funded by the ARC, on 'Architectures of Imagination: Bodies, Buildings, Fictions, and Worlds'.

MARTIN PRIESTMAN is Emeritus Professor of English at the University of Roehampton, London. He is the author of *The Poetry of Erasmus Darwin: Enlightened Spaces, Romantic Times* (2013), *Romantic Atheism: Poetry and Freethought, 1780–1830* (1999), *Cowper's Task: Structure and Influence* (1983), and a number of articles and chapters on Enlightenment and Romantic literature. He has edited *The Collected Writings of Erasmus Darwin* (2004) and an online edition of Darwin's *The Temple of Nature* (2006) and is currently co-editing an issue on both Erasmus and Charles Darwin for *Romanticism and Victorianism on the Net* (forthcoming). He has also published widely on crime fiction and edited *The Cambridge Companion to Crime Fiction* (2003).

MARY L. SHANNON is Senior Lecturer in the Department of English and Creative Writing, University of Roehampton. Her book *Dickens, Reynolds and Mayhew on Wellington Street: The Print Culture of a Victorian Street* (2015) won the 2016 Robert and Vineta Colby Scholarly Book Prize and she has published articles on nineteenth-century visual and print culture. She is on the steering committee of the Romantic Illustration Network.

SOPHIE THOMAS is Professor of English at Ryerson University in Toronto, where she teaches eighteenth- and nineteenth-century literature. She is the author of *Romanticism and Visuality: Fragments, History, Spectacle* (2008), and of articles and chapters that address the crosscurrents between literature, material culture, and visual culture in the Romantic period. She is currently completing a book on objects, collections, and museums at the turn of the nineteenth century.

Acknowledgements

This book emerged from the 'Romantic Illustration Network' (RIN) based at the Centre for Research in Romanticism at the University of Roehampton, London (https://romanticillustrationnetwork.wordpress.com). The editors would like to thank the Department of English and Creative Writing and its Head of Department Laura Peters for supporting RIN from its inception. RIN would not have been a success without the exceptional work of its former post-doctoral Fellows Mary L. Shannon and Dustin Frazier Wood, who are now both faculty in the department. Thanks are due to Chawton House Library, The House of Illustration, Tate Britain, The Institute for English Studies, and the British Academy for hosting RIN events. Thanks also to the University of the Third Age for being such enthusiastic participants in our workshops, and to all those colleagues who participated in our symposia and other events. We are delighted that Linda Bree, former commissioning editor of Cambridge University Press, agreed to take on this project. Finally, thanks to our editorial assistants Manuela Salvi for her excellent work in putting the book together and Jonathan Turner for his excellent proof reading.

Editors' Introduction

1 Illustration before Illustration

This volume is based on an argument: that we have lost the ability to fully understand and appreciate the place of illustration in the Romantic period, a time when large numbers of literary texts carried visual matter but in which the nomenclature and working practices of illustration familiar from the 1830s onwards were not yet established. The aim of this Introduction is to sketch out some new ways of thinking about the place and practice of literary image-making in Britain in the late eighteenth and early nineteenth century, and to outline the scope and significance of the chapters gathered together in this volume.

The first point to make is that the Romantic period saw an unprecedented rise in the numbers of illustrated books. According to William St Clair, the end of perpetual copyright in 1774 was followed by an 'explosion' of visual material within printed books: 'Of the millions of volumes which became cheap and plentiful, almost every one is illustrated with at least one engraving, and some with many.'[1] The most significant effect of this 'plentiful' expansion of engravings on literary history was the rise of the affordable, illustrated series of 'old canon' British writers.[2] This was a new phenomenon aimed squarely at providing standardized 'classics' for the middle-class reading public:

> The editions of the poets published by Bell, Cooke, Whittingham and most others, for example, often provided a portrait of the author, an engraved title page, and sometimes a frontispiece, and these were an intrinsic part of the book's design. We find illustrations too in the reprints of the novels, the essays, the conduct books, and Shakespeare.[3]

But there were also major consequences for art history, as illustration became the standard fare of most established painters:

> The reprint publishers thus opened up new opportunities for painters and engravers, and many of the artists who were later to become famous as painters of individual works, including Fuseli, Opie, Smirke, Stothard, Turner and Westall, reached their first viewers around 1800 when they were employed to provide illustrations to be engraved.[4]

This twin development does not seem to have been a response to new technology, such as lithography and the revival of the woodcut, which only began to dominate illustration in the 1830s and after. The established method of engraving images on metal and reproducing them on framed, separate pages remained in use: 'There was no change in technology which suddenly made illustrations cheaper in absolute terms, and newly published books continued, for the most part, to be unillustrated.' Nevertheless, there was clearly a large public appetite for illustration; large print runs kept costs low and the result was an unprecedented access: 'the explosion of reading of literary texts was accompanied by an explosion in the viewing of engraved pictures'. Given the scale and impact of this visual turn in literary culture, it is all the more surprising that, as St Clair notes, this change 'has not been noticed … nor its implications explored'.[5] Although St Clair's lament at the absence of scholarship on Romantic 'engraved pictures' is no longer quite so applicable, as this Introduction will show, this field of research is still at an early stage, and some fundamental epistemological questions need to be addressed.[6] As Cristina Ionescu and Renata Schellenberg observe, illustration still has an 'undefined place' in literary studies and there is 'no commonly accepted or universally used method for the study of the illustrative image'.[7] Literary critics, art historians, and historians of the book have struggled to identify a methodology for analysing and appreciating the plethora of small-scale images that accompany so many literary texts of the period; moreover, the link between these 'engraved pictures' and the world of displayed works of art needs to be part of any reassessment of Romantic illustration, not least because artists who designed for books did not consider themselves illustrators in the modern sense of that term.

Romanticism and Illustration starts from the assumption that terminology matters and that the absence of the word 'illustration' in its familiar meaning in the Romantic period is significant. To clarify this point, an ECCO search for illustrated texts for the years 1780–93 produces 1,003 results, but few of these books use the word 'illustration' to refer to their images. Instead, we find words like 'embellishment' and 'engraving', terms which imply that the image was not subservient or secondary to the text. One of the aims of this volume is to explore the possibility that illustration before 'illustration' carries meanings that have subsequently been lost to us. Before the modern meaning of the word (a picture commissioned to appear only in a book, representing a moment or scene from the text) appeared for the first time in 1817, and became dominant in the 1830s and 1840s, the concept of a pictorial accompaniment or embellishment suggested that an image was as much a product of art and visual culture as it was of the book. In fact the word 'illustration' in the eighteenth century was usually used to refer to text rather than image, signalling the presence of textual exempla or extracts. This can be confusing to the modern reader. For example, the use of the word 'illustrated' in editions of the Bible in the eighteenth century did not necessarily refer to pictures. In an edition entitled *The Sacred Books of the New Testament, Recited at Large: and Illustrated with Critical and Explanatory Annotations, Carefully Compiled from the Commentaries and Other Writing* (1739), the exegetical illumination derives from critical annotations, not images. Similarly, *A Philosophical Analysis and Illustration of Some of Shakespeare's Remarkable Characters* (1784) refers to the ways in which the tenets of philosophy 'illustrate' (throw light on, make real, exemplify) the plays. By the end of the eighteenth century, this earlier use of illustration as enhanced typification is carried over into the semantic field of Romantic visual imagery. Hence Thomas Macklin advertised his literary galleries in the 1790s as 'Pictures painted for Mr Macklin by the Artists of Britain, Illustrative of the British Poets, and the Bible'. The aim of this 'mode of illustrating the authors of our own country' is to exemplify the best qualities of British poetry, not simply to turn textual episodes into pictures. The printed images, which Macklin calls 'engravings' and 'embellishments', had a vital role to play in enhancing rather than serving their texts. The Royal Academy artists he employed need not have felt they were demeaning themselves or compromising aesthetic standards by designing images destined to be reproduced on the page. On the contrary, they may have agreed with Macklin's claim that he was elevating print culture into the sphere of exhibited, mainstream painting and fostering the development of a British school of art. This was a virtuous spiral, raising the standard of both text and image.[8] To see illustrations as exempla rather than mimetic reproductions makes their relationship with the text one of equals.

This dynamic relates to a second strand of the complex meanings of illustration in the Romantic period. The word also signified the action of making brilliant or distinguished, a meaning present in *Inquiry into the Wealth of Nations* (1776) when Adam Smith writes that in Rome, the law 'gave a considerable degree of illustration to those citizens who had the reputation of understanding it'. Behind this definition may have been a lingering consciousness of an earlier meaning of 'illustration' as illumination.[9] Did a reader encountering Charles Cooke's 1794 advertisement for his *Pocket Edition of Select British Poets* 'illustrated with SUPERB EMBELLISHMENTS' imagine light flooding from the text, a kind of early digital reader? Stothard's illustrations to Scott which appeared in *The Lady's*

Magazine in 1819 were intended to 'embellish' the accompanying short extracts from Scott. In the choice of visual details and the positioning of the characters they epitomize the plot of the *Waverley* extracts quoted in the magazine, and remind the reader-viewer of the narratives as a whole.[10] In this discursive formation, the picture enhances and elevates the text rather than simply visualizing its contents.

Indeed, in some cases the modern understanding of illustration was completely inverted. In this third genealogical strand, text became the 'illustration' or elaboration of the image. The growing enthusiasm for print collecting led publishers to commission written text for saleable and popular artists and genres. In order to cash in on the rage for all things Hogarth, John Boydell published John Ireland's *Hogarth Illustrated from his own Manuscripts* in 1798, in which Hogarth's unpublished words act as a glossary for the images.[11] As the Napoleonic wars drew to an end, Rudolph Ackermann scored a commercial hit with *The English Dance of Death* (1814–16), a series of caricature images by Thomas Rowlandson with an accompanying text by William Combe.[12] The close of the Romantic period saw another flourish of this collaborative publishing format in the middle-brow Keepsake volumes, where poets such as Letitia Elizabeth Landon were commissioned to write poems for high-quality engravings.[13] At the lower end of the market, Pierce Egan and the Cruikshank brothers collaborated on the illustrated serial *Life in London* (1820–1), a picaresque narrative where text frequently illustrates the images. Egan declares of one particular plate that:

> [It] is equal to anything in HOGARTH'S collection; it may be examined again and again with delight: and the author thinks, that his readers will agree with him, that he has not travelled out of his way to thank the artist for the powerful talents he has displayed in portraying such a scene of LIFE IN LONDON.[14]

Knowing London relies upon visual skills in this text; the plates are given equal and often primary importance to the letterpress, and indeed formed the basis of many of the theatrical adaptations which flourished in the early 1820s.[15] In the 1830s, this convention flipped ironically into its opposite when a young Charles Dickens was approached by Chapman and Hall to provide text for the satirical cartoonist Robert Seymour's wood-engraved images of sporting and rural life, otherwise known as *Pickwick Papers*. Seymour's tragic suicide after only two issues is thought to have been precipitated by a wrangle over the control over the illustrations, and Dickens's victory (as some conspiratorially-minded critics might see it) heralded the age of 'Phiz' and the rise of the professional illustrator.[16] In these quite different examples, words become 'paravisual', serving the image rather than controlling and defining it.[17] A similar process was at work in mainstream exhibited art. What might be called literary paintings often showed a scene such as a landscape, accompanied by a quotation from poetry, even though the two were not logically connected. In this case, the text conferred literary status on the image. According to Richard Altick, such paintings were 'detached forms of book illustration, in which were constantly assimilated the literary and artistic tastes of the time. They combined to produce a tertium quid, a new kind of imaginative activity in which the separate experiences of reading and beholding coalesced'.[18] This volume aims to locate new imaginative activity in illustrated Romantic texts.

These three semantic strands (typification, enhancement, and textual accompaniment) show that we must think of literary illustration in the Romantic period in new ways. As the examples adduced so far attest, it was not the case that the explosion of demand for the visualization of literature led straightforwardly to the rise of the professional illustrator who produced tailor-made small images for the printed page. The commissioned artist was usually at several removes from the text. According to the OED, the first appearance of the modern meaning of the word 'illustration' occurs in the title of *Westall's Illustrations to the Works of Walter Scott, Esq*. in 1817, but even here the title-page states that the illustrations are 'beautifully engraved from the Paintings of R. Westall, R.A.'.[19] The illustrated edition was part of a dynamic communication circuit which linked personnel (writers, artists, engravers, publishers, entrepreneurs, readers, viewers), products (paintings, designs, engravings, books, and other forms of printed merchandise), and venues (art and literary galleries, bookshops, print shops, the printed page).[20] As Sandro Jung notes, 'The illustrations added to editions serve both as intra-textual markers and as referents to an extra-textual economic and cultural world that anchors the subjects in the visual and material cultures of art, music, fashion and luxury objects, as well as practices of collecting and exhibition'.[21] The prestige and ubiquity of illustration derived from its complex semantic configuration, its vital role in the canonization of British literature, and its synergies with the art market and artistic institutions. The illustration was a locus of bibliographical, commercial, ideological, and aesthetic concerns, and a portal between the text and its cultural context. As Andrew Piper asks, without venturing an answer: 'how can the romantic engagement with the reproducible illustration be read as part of a larger engagement with the problem of reproducibility itself that was gradually shaping the romantic bibliocosmos?'[22] The rest of this Introduction will propose some ways to rethink the wider 'bibliocosmos' of Romantic illustration.

2 'Pictured Wonders'

It may seem counter-intuitive to stake a claim for illustration's importance in Romantic studies, given the scarcity of illustrated editions of the 'Big Six' poets and the major living novelists in their own time (the major exceptions are of course Blake and Scott). The most illustrated poets in the period were actually 'old canon' (Shakespeare, Milton and above all Thomson, whose long poem *The Seasons* was the most illustrated of all eighteenth-century literary texts), and we have to wait until the late 1820s and 1830s before the complete illustrated works of Scott and Byron appear.[23] Romanticism never saw an iconic collaboration between Wordsworth and Constable.[24] But as Altick and other scholars have confirmed, mainstream Romantic authors are unrepresentative of a broader visual turn in Romantic literary culture.[25] By the end of the eighteenth century, it is not an exaggeration to state that books were both seen and read. Many popular genres were illustrated, including history, travel literature, botany, and medicine. In the field of imaginative literature, children's books, classics and plays, as well as old canon poetry and fiction, were all published in illustrated editions.[26] As Fuseli announced in 1788, the role of illustration was to turn 'readers into spectators', a phrase that Calè uses as the subtitle of her book on Fuseli's Milton Gallery.[27] For a typical middle-class consumer in London, reading an illustrated edition provided visual pleasures that could be supplemented and reinforced by other forms of related cultural activity: a visit to a literary gallery and the purchase of its merchandise, a visit to Bell's or Cooke's bookshop to inspect Stothard's latest design for an illustration, or a visit to a print shop to purchase an engraving to insert into an 'extra-illustrated' edition.[28] An illustration in a book was 'an intermedial cultural object',[29] part of a dynamic economy of images that circulated throughout literary and artistic culture, eroding conventional distinctions between the original and copy.

Understanding this lost culture of illustration shifts the way we read the illustrated canon of the Romantic period. The publishers of illustrated editions offered the reader access to the work of the top artists, in effect turning themselves into 'grand impresarios' of art and converting the book into a miniaturized art gallery.[30] John Bell, for example, announced proudly that he had secured 'new engagements with the most capital artists in the kingdom'.³¹ Charles Cooke followed suit by claiming that he had hired 'the first artists in the kingdom' and had ensured that 'the arts are not only encouraged, but the taste and judgement of those who are disposed to cultivate them greatly promoted and highly improved'.³² Not to be outdone, John Sharpe vaunted that his volumes were an 'opportunity of possessing specimens of BRITISH ART, even to those whom expense has hitherto forbidden it'.³³ But even those artists who are now seen as central to the work of illustration, such as the immensely prolific and respected Thomas Stothard (1775–1834), were not illustrators in the modern sense of the word.³⁴ Stothard's obituary in 1835 praised the scale of his achievement, nothing less than heralding 'an era in British art' and 'a new taste in the public mind':

> Most of the embellished volumes published during the last half century have been illustrated by the inimitable compositions of this truly poetic painter, and they form a monument, not to his fame only, but to that of the country which gave him birth.³⁵

The older meaning of illustration as embellishment (enhancement, illumination) jostles with the newer one (providing tailor-made pictures for a book) in this tribute. Designs by Stothard and others for *The Lady's Magazine* appeared heralded by a similarly complex tribute:

> We beg leave to call the attention of our Subscribers to the beauty of the Plate which embellishes this Number; and we can confidently assure them that our future Plates will surpass rather than fall short of this one in excellence. It will, doubtless, be gratifying to the ADMIRERS OF THE FINE ARTS to be informed, that in future it is our intention to illustrate the most popular works as they are published, with highly finished Engravings by HEATH, from the designs of WESTALL, STOTHARD, CORBOULD, &c.³⁶

Stothard's plates were accompanied by extracts from Scott presented as 'explanatory' of the engravings, as much as the other way around.³⁷ When Charles Lamb wrote a sonnet to celebrate Stothard's contributions to Samuel Roger's poem *Italy* (1830), a volume Stothard co-illustrated with Turner and which is now regarded as a masterpiece of steel engraving,³⁸ Lamb found his own distinct vocabulary to express the aesthetic superiority of Stothard's work:

> Consummate artist, whose undying name
> With classic Rogers shall go down to fame,
> Be this thy crowning work! In my young days

> How often have I, with a child's fond gaze,
> Pored on the pictured wonders thou hadst done. (ll. 1–5)[39]

Though the poem is entitled 'To T. Stothard, Esq. On his Illustrations of the Poems of Mr. Rogers', Lamb refers to these 'illustrations' as works of art:

> Age, that enfeebles other men's designs,
> But heightens thine, and thy free draft refines.
> In several ways distinct you make us feel –
> Graceful as Raphael, as Watteau genteel.
> Your lights and shades, as Titianesque, we praise;
> And warmly wish you Titian's length of days. (ll. 9–14)

Compared to Turner, Stothard is all but forgotten today, but Lamb's eulogy is evidence of the aesthetic impact and reputation of illustrated editions in the Romantic period. Like Lamb, Leigh Hunt also had fond memories of illustrated poetry: Charles Cooke's volumes were 'books at once so "superbly ornamented" and so inconceivably cheap!'[40] Once again, the emphasis is on enhancement and beautification ('ornamented'), not fidelity, realism or accuracy. Reduction in scale, one of the key features of illustration, did not diminish artistic value. Indeed, miniaturization was part of the appeal and charm: 'I doated on their size; I doated on their type, on their ornaments, on their wrappers containing lists of other poets, and on the engravings from Kirk'.[41] Thomas Kirk (1765–97) is another forgotten master of pictured wonders, but his name evokes this flourishing collaboration between academic artists and commercial publishers. Purchasing an illustrated book was the equivalent of visiting the Royal Academy and acquiring a work of art, albeit on a reduced scale. By the 1820s, *Life in London* turns this into a snide joke, as Egan describes the textual and visual 'portrait' of his hero Corinthian Tom as one which, 'it is hoped, […] may bid defiance to the stare, the shrugs, the sneers, the ridicule, the grimaces, and the cant of criticism, whenever it has the honour of being placed in its "true light" by the hanging committee belonging to the Royal Academy'.[42] However, if Hunt and Lamb are to be believed, some of the more hyperbolic and self-serving claims of the publishers and entrepreneurs were not actually too wide of the mark: illustration was a democratization of British art, making its treasures available to the middle classes (though not yet to the working class, as this required the revival of wood engraving, as discussed below). On 13 December 1790, *The Times* printed a glowing endorsement of Bell, Macklin, and Boydell, concluding: 'let them therefore go hand in hand to the Temple of Fame, to enjoy in triumph and comfort the lasting rewards of their meritorious pursuits'.

It is for these reasons that the literary galleries of the 1790s can be seen as a particularly spectacular attempt to promote illustration as a nationalist cultural mission during a revolutionary and war-torn decade. Despite their commercial failure, the Shakespeare, Milton and Poets' Galleries brought together the 'ornaments' of British art and literature on a grand scale: the displayed paintings and the various forms of illustrated print (editions, designs, serialized instalments or 'numbers', single-sheet prints in black and white or colour) were mutually complementary. The galleries were sites of 'new configurations which crossed from display, spectacle and gallery into the reproductive print culture of the souvenir' and where it was possible to 'display history paintings but sell book illustrations'.[43] The word 'gallery' even referred to both the physical venue and the printed product: Macklin, for example, called his bookshop the Poets' Gallery and his exhibition The Gallery of Poets, a canny chiasmus. It was this combination of display and dissemination which distinguished the literary galleries from their most obvious competitor, the Royal Academy.[44] The Academy had an uncomfortable relationship with the commercial market and this explains its reluctance to exhibit prints and to legitimate the role and talent of engravers, only a few of whom were granted 'Associate Engraver' status.[45] Painters were generally not classified or regarded as illustrators. Hence an artist such as Francis Hayman, whom Altick describes as the first book illustrator to submit paintings to the Society of Artists, was exhibited as a painter of genre scenes, or as a history painter.[46] Kirk, Stothard, and other artists exhibited their painted designs for illustration in the normal way, but the prints and illustrated books were absent. Academic honours were given to watch-chasers and enamel painters, but not to engravers, who were perhaps too close to the mechanics of reproduction.[47] Even though engravings of its paintings were sold for profit, the Academy was rather curmudgeonly in the way it displayed prints in inappropriate rooms where they were unlikely to make much impact.[48] In the literary galleries, on the other hand, both in their actual (display space) and virtual (printed) form, 'the intricacies of engraving could be viewed to their best advantage'.[49] Engravers were conspicuous by their huge fees, in complete contrast to the public image of the Academy which downgraded their role.[50] In the event, the laborious pace of high-quality metal engraving was to prove an insurmountable obstacle to the commercial success of the literary galleries, but the inept economics reflected the fact that the whole point of the gallery was to appreciate the transfer of 'aura' from the so-called original to the engraving: in Christopher Kent Rovee's words, 'No painting existed in its own, original splendour, but only and always in tension with its reproductions'.[51] This 'seemingly endless recess of images', in Frederick Burwick's phrase, marks one of the unique contributions of the literary galleries to Romantic visual and literary culture.[52]

As considerable scholarly attention has been given to Boydell's and Fuseli's galleries, in this volume we concentrate on the understudied Macklin's Poets' Gallery.[53] Macklin is particularly interesting, as his aim was not to produce the ultimate illustrated edition of British poets to rival Bell and Cooke. Instead, he published a series of illustrated excerpts of poetry in a format ('Numbers') that resembled a periodical or magazine, and therefore moved illustration away from the bound volume towards the 'extra-illustrated' or more open system of collection and re-assemblage. In this respect, he overlaps with another important 'lost' cultural practice that is only now receiving due consideration from scholars.[54]

Extra-illustration or 'Grangerization' was initially restricted to wealthy collectors who added prints to books, binding them into volumes as they thought fit, but by the 1790s the hobby had embraced a wider clientele who may have been responding to the shortage of prints caused by the war with France.[55] The book trade, spotting a commercial opportunity, began to commission prints specifically designed to be added to existing books. Cooke offered purchasers differently priced packages, his cheapest being a 'Scenic Representation' which the purchaser needed to place in the correct location.[56] But the practice extended far beyond popular publishers. Bewick and Blake, the conventional champions of Romantic illustrated books, were also involved in the trade. Purchasers of Bewick's bestsellers *A General History of Quadrupeds* (1790) and *A History of British Birds* (1797) could assemble a version of the book that matched their individual taste. As Diana Donald explains:

> In successive editions of *Quadrupeds* and *British Birds*, many species and figures were gradually added, new tailpieces were introduced to fill up the extra pages, and old ones often changed position – the blocks being occasionally reworked … Buyers often made choices from among the unbound sheets offered to them – choices that reflected personal taste as much as the recognition of degrees of technical excellence.[57]

Illustrations became paratextual tools with which the reader, publisher, and author could create an evolving, personalized text. When Blake was commissioned by John Flaxman to produce a unique, extra-illustrated copy of Gray's poems for Anne Flaxman, he cut the text from a printed edition and pasted it beneath windows cut into his water-coloured pages, a brilliant example of text and image illuminating each other.[58] One way to think about Blake's famous illuminated books, each with differing colouring, selection, and ordering, is that they are authorial versions of this new mode of creating an illustrated book. But Blake's readers also repurposed his images: Copy D of *Europe* contains added marginal glosses in ink which allow the puzzled owner to view Blake's images as illustrations to familiar extracts from Bysshe's *Art of Poetry*.[59] This willingness to extract and repurpose images was characteristic of reading practices in the period, and representative of a culture of illustration significantly different from that which grew up later in the nineteenth century.

3 From Metal to Wood

The argument so far is that the ways in which illustration was conceived and practiced in the Romantic period is in many respects quite different from our modern understanding of the term. The 'explosion' of illustrated editions was a phenomenon that mobilized a larger visual infrastructure including the major institutions of British art and the riskier world of cultural entrepreneurship. Much more was at stake than fidelity to the source text. Illustration was the vehicle for some major cultural and ideological shifts. A whole 'rhetoric of improvement' was erected around the visualization of British literature, though – as the chapters in this volume will show – this discourse of national progress and redemption was open to appropriation, contestation, and subversion, and the advocacy of the moral benefits of consuming images often fractured along class, gender, and ideological lines.[60] As W. J. T. Mitchell has argued, there remained a residual Puritan resistance to image-gazing among many Romantic writers and intellectuals, and various accommodations had to be made.[61] In general, it was still felt that the mass circulation of images could be dangerous (unless, of course, these were authorized by the state, such as portraits of the monarch stamped on coins). Images were more immediate and provocative than texts, not least for the very obvious point that they could appeal to the illiterate and uneducated, hence their use in the conservative Cheap Repository Tracts in the 1790s. The revolution in illustration which this volume covers is essentially a bourgeois phenomenon, a widening of access to reputable art at a time when there were still no public art galleries (the Dulwich Picture Gallery opened to the paying public in 1817 and the National Gallery in 1824). Indeed, Altick credits the literary galleries as a 'half-way station' on the road the National Gallery.[62] Radical political movements, for reasons of choice or economics, used very little visual propaganda.[63]

In order to locate the moment when illustration expanded its social range, we need to turn to the most autonomous and subversive art form at this time: caricature. Though satirical prints were not in themselves illustrations, there is a moment of crossover between the two modes which marks an important staging post in the development of illustration in the Romantic period. In 1819, the radical publisher William Hone and the leading caricaturist George Cruikshank collaborated on an illustrated pamphlet which savaged the Tory government for its part in the Peterloo massacre. *The Political House that Jack Built* was phenomenally successful and established a new format for combining image and letterpress on the same page. The conservative popular educator Charles Knight later described the genesis of the pamphlet as a diabolical creation myth, the radical rebirth of illustration in a new, popular form:

> Three friends – fellow conspirators, if you like – are snugly ensconced in a private room of a well-accustomed tavern. Hone produces his scheme for 'The House that Jack Built.' He reads some of his doggerel lines. The author wants a design for an idea that is clear enough in words, but is beyond the range of pictorial representation. The artist pooh-poohs. The bland publisher is pertinacious, but not dictatorial … 'Wait a moment,' says the artist. The wine – perhaps the grog – is on the table. He dips his finger in his glass. He rapidly traces wet lines on the mahogany. A single figure starts into life. Two or three smaller figures come out around the first head and trunk – a likeness in its grotesqueness. The publisher cries 'Hoorah.'[64]

The key phrase in this spry re-enactment is 'wet lines on the mahogany', as it signifies the crucial shift in medium from metal to wood engraving. Wood was cheaper and more durable than metal, hence the pamphlet, which contained a dozen illustrations, sold for only sixpence. Unlike metal, woodcut images were produced by relief engraving (the parts to be inked protruded from the block) which enabled image and letterpress text to be printed on the same page simultaneously, further reducing costs. The democratic potential of Bewick's medium could now be unleashed, and the future of literary illustration was inscribed in wood.[65] For Bewick, 'the use of wood cuts will know no end, so long as the importance of printing is duly appreciated and the liberty of the press held sacred'.[66] Knight understood this only too well – 'It is essentially that branch of the art of design which is associated with cheap and rapid printing' – and his own career was driven by the desire to use wood to bring apolitical visual pleasure to the masses.[67] Of course metal engraving did not disappear overnight (as already noted, there was a flourishing of steel engraving at the end of the Romantic period), and until the mid-1830s lithography (engraving on stone) vied with wood in the popular market, but the 1820s marks a point when debates about the aesthetic, moral, and political agency of illustration (and visual culture more generally) began to be addressed to a much wider potential audience.[68] In his unpublished memoirs, written in 1828, Bewick looked back nostalgically to the cheap woodcut prints which were a common sight in the cottages of his rural community: 'These prints, which were sold at a very low price, were commonly illustrative of some memorable exploits.' If only similar prints could once again 'embellish almost every house', the beleaguered industrial working class would possess a handy, reassuring source of moral illumination.[69] This cluster of associations – typification, adornment, elevation, enlightenment – is an apt illustration (pun intended) of the complex issues that lay behind the illustration revolution in the Romantic period.

4 The Chapters

The chapters in this collection reflect the book's aims of asking some new questions about the place of illustration in Romantic literature and culture. The book is divided into two Parts, 'Illustrating Poetry' and 'The Business of Illustration'. The first section recognizes that, despite the ubiquity of illustration in print culture, it was in the field of poetry that the most significant, high-profile aesthetic and ideological work was taking place.[70] Recognizing his position as Romanticism's most famous and celebrated illustrator of (his own) poetry, we begin with two chapters on William Blake. Blake exemplifies the complex issues surrounding the status and practice of illustration. For most Romantic critics, his crowning success as an artist and poet was achieved in spite of his career as an engraver. For John Bender and Anne Mellor, in a groundbreaking essay first published in 1983, Blake's revolutionary breakthrough was to undermine the 'dependent' relationship of image and text: 'the inherited hierarchical tradition of *ut pictura poesis* effectively dies. Blake presents a new theoretical possibility concomitant with the French revolutionary era and the overthrow of the ancien regime … setting forth autonomous visual and verbal texts that are independent, equally valid, and irreconcilable'.[71] There is no doubting Blake's extraordinary imagination and maverick visual talents, but the argument of *Romanticism and Illustration* is that this exceptionalist view of Blake underplays the extent to which his images interacted with the wider culture of illustration. In their respective chapters, Peter Otto and Sophie Thomas explore Blake's attempts to work within and exceed the resources of different models of illustration. Otto's 'The Ends of Illustration: Explanation, Critique, and the Political Imagination in Blake's Title-pages for Genesis' considers Blake's title-page designs as an experiment in transferring divine aura into secular images in the context of the spectacular Romantic revival of the Biblical sublime, while Thomas's '"With a Master's Hand and Prophet's Fire": Blake, Gray, and the Bard' restores Blake to the commercial world of commissioned engraving and display in which he both excelled and struggled. Blake's unsuccessful, self-made exhibition of 1809 shows that he conceived of illustration as part of a continuum with public art rather than a privatized medium for the initiated.

Following on from the theme of Blake's interest in the remote past, Dustin Frazier Wood's 'Seeing History: Illustration, Poetic Drama, and the National Past' shows how history and literature authorized each other through the medium of illustration. An iconic example was the image of the Anglo-Saxon queen Elfrida which circulated through art galleries, frontispieces of editions of poetic drama and histories of Anglo-Saxon England, and all this at a time of major visual revivals of the national past such as Bowyer's Historic Gallery. The contribution of illustration to national enlightenment is also pursued in Martin Priestman's ' "Fuseli's Poetic Eye": Prints and Impressions in Fuseli and Erasmus Darwin' where the focus is on the cosmological and scientific imagination. Priestman argues that Fuseli's illustrations were an important element of the success of Darwin's poems, but not because they were mimetic renditions of key episodes. On the contrary, the images functioned like meditations on Darwin's complex ideas, embellishing and elevating the poems' themes, and evolving a new iconography of Romantic science. Fuseli, one of the most important Romantic artists, is also the subject of Susan Matthews's 'Henry Fuseli's Accommodations: "Attempting the Domestic" in the Illustrations to Cowper' which looks at how Fuseli responded to the challenge of working for commercial publishers of illustrated poetry. Fuseli's domestic interiors offer an ambivalent response to the changed circumstances of art viewing and consumption in the first decades of the nineteenth century. His small works respond to the commercial, ideological and imaginative failure of the Milton Gallery and discover in the illustrated book a new home for the imagination.

Perhaps Fuseli suffered more than his fellow artists in making the transition from the Milton Gallery to the illustrated edition, but as outlined above, book illustration was the standard fare of Academy painters, so we should be careful about romanticizing Fuseli's antagonisms. The prolific Thomas Stothard is more representative of the norm, and as Sandro Jung shows in 'Reading the Romantic Vignette: Stothard Illustrates Bloomfield,

Byron, and Crabbe for *The Royal Engagement Pocket Atlas*', Stothard's humble miniatures for this now-forgotten publication gave Romantic readers and viewers some of their first images of living Romantic poets and their texts. Jung elucidates the dexterity and power of the vignette, a form revived by the exquisite tailpieces of Bewick, in which a surprising degree of significant and often unexpected detail is contained in a very small space. In line with *Romanticism and Illustration*'s aim of bringing illustrators such as Stothard back to light, the final chapter in the first section is Maureen McCue's 'Intimate Distance: Thomas Stothard's and J. M. W. Turner's Illustrations of Samuel Rogers's *Italy*'. As noted above, this now neglected poem can be regarded as a crowning achievement of Romantic illustration, and McCue shows how the combination of Turner's landscapes and Stothard's human figures delivered to the reading public a highly attractive notion of Renaissance Italy that has endured to the present day.

The second section of *Romanticism and Illustration* is called 'The Business of Illustration' and its four chapters explore various aspects of the illustration industry. The two chapters on Thomas Macklin's Poets' Gallery aim to bring Macklin's achievement out from under the shadow of Boydell's more renowned Shakespeare Gallery. Haywood's 'Illustration, Terror, and Female Agency: Thomas Macklin's Poets Gallery in a Revolutionary Decade' shows how the serial publication of illustrated 'Numbers' produced configurations of images and texts that were and still are wide open to subversive interpretations, while Calè in 'Maria Cosway's *Hours*: Cosmopolitan and Classical Visual Culture in Thomas Macklin's Poets Gallery' focuses on the ways in which Maria Cosway's *The Hours* enhanced and elevated the English literary canon, even though her painting was retrofitted to Gray's text. These two chapters show that the literary galleries repay close reading and require further, more prolonged study. The final two chapters take us deeper into the infrastructure and later stages of Romantic illustration. Mary L. Shannon's 'Artists' Street: Thomas Stothard, R. H. Cromek, and Literary Illustration on London's Newman Street' uses the methodologies of cultural geography and network studies to map a fascinating community of illustrators in one London street. Shannon's case study is another example of the ways in which illustration must be rethought as a nexus of commercial, professional and aesthetic practices. Finally, Brian Maidment's 'The Development of Magazine Illustration in Regency Britain – The example of *Arliss's Pocket Magazine* 1818–1833' points the way to significant developments in popular illustration in the post-Romantic period. Maidment explores the ways in which relatively modest magazines like *Arliss's Pocket Magazine* adopted the revived technology of wood engraving in order to produce high-quality images of anonymous, serialized fiction for an enlarged readership and viewership, thus blazing a trail for the rise of the professional illustrator in the 1830s and beyond.

Romanticism and Illustration is only the beginning of what we hope will be a scholarly renaissance of work on Romantic illustration, but it is to be hoped that this volume is a worthy and interesting first step in what promises to be a lively, growing and engaging area of Romantic studies.

Notes

1 William St Clair, *The Reading Nation in the Romantic Period* (Cambridge: Cambridge University Press, 2004), 134.
2 The most important publishers were John Bell, Charles Cooke, and John Sharpe, though it was a crowded field. For a full survey of this development, see Thomas Frank Bonnell, *The Most Disreputable Trade: Publishing the Classics of English Poetry 1765–1810* (Oxford: Oxford University Press, 2008); see also John Buchanan Brown, *Early Victorian Illustrated Books: Britain, France and Germany 1820–1860* (London: British Library and Oak Knoll Press, 2005), 34–5. To date there has been little significant work done on the hundreds of illustrations in these volumes. One exception is Sandro Jung, *James Thomson's 'The Seasons': Print Culture, and Visual Interpretation 1730–1842* (Bethlehem: Lehigh University Press, 2015).
3 Ibid., 134.
4 Ibid., 134.
5 St Clair, *Reading Nation*, 134–5. According to James Raven, 'The commerce in prints and the illustrated book entered new territory' at this time (*The Business of Books 1450–1850* (New Haven, CT; London: Yale University Press, 2007), 253). It is worth adding that the rise of illustration was also facilitated earlier in the eighteenth century by the arrival of copyright in images in 1734–5. As John Pye remarked, 'print-shops were opened in various parts of the town; and, whilst the works they exposed to view, by drawing the attention of the public, aided in making artists known, and in diffusing taste for art, they constituted an entirely new characteristic of the metropolis of Great Britain' (*Patronage of British Art, an Historical Sketch* (London: Longman, Brown, Green, 1845), 42–3).
6 See Luisa Calè, *Fuseli's Milton Gallery: 'Turning Readers into Spectators'* (Oxford: Clarendon Press, 2006); Sophie Thomas, *Romanticism and Visuality: Fragments, History, Spectacle* (London: Routledge, 2010) and 'Poetry and Illustration', in Charles Mahoney, ed., *A Companion to Romantic Poetry* (Oxford: Wiley-Blackwell, 2011), Chapter 11; Gillen D'Arcy Wood, *The Shock of the Real: Romanticism and Visual Culture, 1760–1860* (New York: Palgrave, 2001); Theresa M. Kelley and Jill H. Casid, eds, *Visuality's Romantic Genealogies* (Romantic Praxis, 2014).

7 Cristina Ionescu and Renata Schellenberg, 'Introduction' to *Book Illustration in the Long Eighteenth Century: Reconfiguring the Visual Periphery of the Text* (Cambridge: Cambridge Scholars Press, 2011), 10, 29.
8 *Catalogue of the Third Exhibition of Pictures Painted for Mr Macklin* (London: T. Bensley, 1790), iv.
9 See the relevant OED definitions.
10 See, for example, *The Bride of Lammermoor*. Steel engraving. Stothard/Heath, *Lady's Magazine* August 1819, facing p. 339.
11 John Ireland, *Hogarth Illustrated from his own Manuscripts, Vol III and last, A Supplement to Hogarth Illustrated* (London: Boydell, 1798). See also Sheila O'Connell, 'Hogarthomania and the Collecting of Hogarth', in David Bindman, ed., *Hogarth and his Times: Serious Comedy* (London: British Museum Press, 1997), 58–60.
12 See Ian Haywood, *Romanticism and Caricature* (Cambridge: Cambridge University Press, 2013), Chapter 4.
13 See the Romantic Circles hypertext version of the Keepsake of 1829, edited by Terence Hoagwood, Kathryn Ledbetter, and Martin Jacobson, www.rc.umd.edu/editions/lel/index.html (accessed 5 January 2017).
14 Pierce Egan, *Life in London*. Illus. Robert and George Cruikshank (London: Sherwood, Neely, and Jones, 1821), 347.
15 See Charles Hindley, *True History of Tom and Jerry* (London: Reeves & Turner, 1890).
16 See Stephen Jarvis, *Death and Mr Pickwick* (London: Jonathan Cape, 2015). See also Gerard Curtis *Visual Words: Art and the Material Book in Victorian England* (Burlington, VT: Ashgate, 2002).
17 Ionescu and Schellenberg, 'Introduction' to *Book Illustration*, 34.
18 Richard D. Altick, *Paintings from Books: Art and Literature in Britain 1760–1900* (Columbus: Ohio State University Press, 1985), 3; see also 2, 23.
19 "illustration, n." OED Online, Oxford University Press, December 2018, www.oed.com/view/Entry/91580. Accessed 4 February 2019. BL has Walter Scott, Westall's Illustrations of the Lord of the Isles, etc. London: Longman, Hurst, Rees, Orme & Brown; Edinburgh: A.Constable [1815].
20 The theory of a communication circuit connecting author, publisher, printer, distributor, bookseller, and reader is most associated with Robert Darnton: see *The Business of Enlightenment* (1979), though he has very little to say about illustration. Roger Chartier, another key figure in book history studies, at least notes that illustration was one of the 'reading protocols' of the past (*The Order of Books* (1994), cited in Tom Mole, ed., *The Broadview Reader in Book History* (Ontario: Broadview, 2013), 258).
21 Jung, *James Thomson's 'The Seasons'*, 2.
22 Andrew Piper, *Dreaming in Books: The Making of the Bibliographic Imagination in the Romantic Period* (Chicago, IL; London: University of Chicago Press, 2009), 187.

23 Altick, *Paintings from Books*, 422–48. On Scott, see Richard J. Hill, *Picturing Scotland through the Waverley Novels* (Farnham: Ashgate, 2010), and Peter Garside, 'Print Illustrations and the Cultural Materialism of Scott's *Waverley* Novels', in Sandro Jung, ed., *British Literature and Print Culture* (London: D. Brewer/The English Association, 2013). On Thomson, see Jung, *James Thomson's 'The Seasons'*.

24 Philip James mused that 'of all the illustrated books which might have been one can think of none more truly and essentially English than Wordsworth's poems illustrated by Constable. This would have united all the English qualities; the literary bias and the romantic flavour as well as the love of natural beauty' (*English Book Illustration 1800–1900* (London: Penguin, 1947), 12).

25 In addition to the sources cited so far, see Ian Haywood and John Halliwell, eds, 'Romantic Spectacle', special issue of *Romanticism on the Net*, May 2007.

26 See Ionescu and Schellenberg, 'Introduction' to *Book Illustration*, for a very useful survey of the scholarship on illustration in the eighteenth century.

27 Calè, *Fuseli's Milton Gallery*.

28 Charles Cooke, *Plan and Catalogue of Cooke's Uniform, Cheap, and Elegant Pocket Library* (1795), 4; Anna [Mrs] Bray, *Life of Thomas Stothard* (London: John Murray, 1851), 105–10; Bonnell, *The Most Disreputable Trade*, 123–4.

29 Ionescu and Schellenberg, 'Introduction' to *Book Illustration*, 42.

30 Raven, *The Business of Books*, 253.

31 Cited in Bonnell, *The Most Disreputable Trade*, 114. Altick states that such illustrations 'opened the eyes of a generation of artists to the seemingly limitless artistic potentiality of English literature' (*Paintings from Books*, 41).

32 Cooke, *Plan and Catalogue*, 3.

33 Cited in Bonnell, *The Most Disreputable Trade*, 284.

34 Shelley M. Bennett, *Thomas Stothard: The Mechanisms of Art Patronage in England circa 1800* (Columbia: University of Missouri Press, 1988). Bennett cites a tribute from the publisher William Pickering in 1825 which comes closer to the modern meaning of the word illustration: 'Of all our artists who have applied their talents to the illustration of books, he is unquestionably the most original in composition, the most varied, refined and characteristic' (30), though Stothard is still an 'artist' who brings his talents to books. Anna Bray states that despite being the most engraved artist in illustrated books (he produced around 3,000 designs in his career, an astonishing achievement), Stothard never painted with the 'print shops in mind' (*Life of Thomas Stothard*, 143).

35 'Thomas Stothard, Esq. R.A. Librarian to the Royal Academy' pp. 230–247 in *The Annual Biography and Obituary* (Longman, 1835), XIX: 233.

36 *The Literary Gazette and Journal of Belles Lettres, Arts, Sciences*, Part 2, no. 134, Saturday 16th August 1819, p.528, an advertisement for Lady's Magazine for July.

37 See, for example, vol. 50, no. 10 (October 1819), 437.

38 David Bland *The Illustration of Books* (London: Faber and Faber, 1951), 249; Edward Hodnett, *Five Centuries of English Book Illustration* (Menstone: Scolar

Press, 1988), 126; Maureen McCue, *Romanticism and the Old Masters* (Basingstoke: Palgrave, 2014), Chapter 5. See also William St Clair and Annika Bautz, 'Imperial Decadence: The Making of the Myths in Edward Bulwer-Lytton's *The Last Days of Pompeii*', *Victorian Literature and Culture* 40 (2012): 359–96, 379.

39 *The Works of Charles Lamb*, edited by Thomas Noon Talfourd. 2 vols (New York: Harper and Brothers, 1838), 1: 418.

40 *Essays by Leigh Hunt* (London: Edward Moxon, 1840), 51.

41 Leigh Hunt, *The Autobiography of Leigh Hunt with Reminiscences of Friends and Contemporaries*, 3 vols (London: Smith, Elder and Co., 1850), I: 132–3.

42 Egan, *Life in London,* 51.

43 Morris Eaves, 'The Sister Arts in British Romanticism', in *The Cambridge Companion to British Romanticism*. Second Edition, ed. Stuart Curran (Cambridge: Cambridge University Press, 2010), 249.

44 Though it is worth pointing out that the literary galleries were also in competition with Bell and Cooke: for the price of just one of Macklin's prints (one guinea), the Georgian reader could purchase around 15 volumes of illustrated poems with at least 15 octavo images.

45 Sarah Hyde, 'Printmakers and the Royal Academy Exhibitions, 1780–1836', in David H. Solkin, ed., *Art on the Line: The Royal Academy Exhibitions at Somerset House 1780–1836* (New Haven, CT; London: Yale University Press, 2001), 217.

46 Altick, *Paintings from Books*, 38. See also David Solkin, *Painting for Money: The Visual Arts and the Public Sphere in Eighteenth-Century England* (New Haven, CT; London: Yale University Press, 1992), 149–56.

47 Hyde, 'Printmakers', 268. See also her comment that the Academy's display criteria of 'uniqueness, novelty and originality … conflicted with the very nature of contemporary printmaking practice' (224).

48 Greg Smith, 'Watercolourists and Watercolours at the Royal Academy', in Solkin, ed., *Art on the Line*, 200.

49 Hyde, 'Printmakers', 228.

50 Hans Hammelmann, *Book Illustrators in Eighteenth-Century England*. Edited and completed by T. S. R. Boase (New Haven, CT; London: Yale University Press, 1975), 9–10.

51 *Imagining the Gallery: The Social Body of English Romanticism* (Stanford, CA: Stanford University Press, 2006), 80, and see Chapter 2 *passim*. See also Stuart Sillars, *Painting Shakespeare: The Artist as Critic 1720–1820* (Cambridge: Cambridge University Press, 2006), who notes that critics of the Shakespeare Gallery have tended to ignore the engravings despite this aspect of the gallery having 'repercussions on the structures and devices used to transmit meaning and the ideological assumptions they enfold' (256).

52 Frederick Burwick, 'The Romantic Reception of the Boydell Shakespeare Gallery: Lamb, Coleridge, and Hazlitt', in Walter Pape and Frederick Burwick,

eds, *The Boydell Shakespeare Gallery* (Bottrop, Essen: Verlag Peter Pomp, 1996), 156.

53 For the Shakespeare Gallery, see in particular Rosie Dias, *Exhibiting Englishness: John Boydell's Shakespeare Gallery and the Formation of a National Aesthetic* (New Haven, CT; London: Yale University Press, 2013). On Fuseli's Milton Gallery, see Cale, *Fuseli's Milton Gallery*. For Macklin's Poets' Gallery, see Sean Higgins, 'Thomas Macklin's Poets' Gallery: Consuming the Sister Arts in Late Eighteenth-Century London' (unpublished PhD, London: Courtauld Institute, 2002); G. E. Bentley Jr, *Thomas Macklin (1752–1800), Picture-Publisher and Patron: Creator of the Macklin Bible (1791–1800)* (Lampeter: Edwin Mellen Press, 2016).

54 Lucy Peltz, *Facing the Text: Extra-Illustration, Print Culture, and Society in Britain, 1769–1840* (San Marino: Huntington Library Press, 2017); H. J. Jackson, *Marginalia: Readers Writing in Books* (New Haven, CT; London: Yale University Press, 2001), 186–90; John P. Klancher, *Transfiguring the Arts and Science: Knowledge and Cultural Institutions in the Romantic Age* (Cambridge: Cambridge University Press, 2013), 98–100.

55 Timothy Clayton, *The English Print 1688–1802* (New Haven, CT; London: Yale University Press, 1997), 207–82, 281–2 in particular.

56 Bonnell, *A Most Disreputable Trade*, 233.

57 Diana Donald, with contributions by Paul F. Donald, *The Art of Thomas Bewick* (London: Reaktion, 2013), 10. In his unpublished memoir, Bewick reveals that the text of both books was written by his business partner Beilby as an accompaniment to the images, an active use of one of earlier understandings of illustration; see *A Memoir of Thomas Bewick, Written by Himself* (London: Longman and Green, 1862), 145.

58 See the chapter by Sophie Thomas in this volume.

59 On the annotations to *Europe* Copy D (in the British Museum) see Susan Matthews, *Blake, Sexuality and Bourgeois Politeness* (Cambridge: Cambridge University Press, 2011), 157–64.

60 The phrase 'rhetoric of improvement' is used by Cale, *Milton's Fuseli Gallery*, 76. On the wider issue of art and politics in the Romantic period, see John Barrell, *The Political Theory of Painting: The Body of the Public* (New Haven, CT; London: Yale University Press, 1995).

61 W. J. T. Mitchell, *Iconology: Image, Text, Ideology* (Chicago, IL; London: Chicago University Press, 1987), 25, 151–4.

62 Richard D. Altick, *The Shows of London* (Cambridge, MA: Belknap Press of Harvard University Press, 1978), 109; Emma Peacocke, *Romanticism and the Museum* (Basingstoke: Palgrave, 2015), 91–3.

63 See John Barrell, 'Radicalism, Spectacle and Visual Culture in the 1790s', in Haywood and Halliwell, eds, 'Romantic Spectacle'; Marcus Wood, *Radical Satire and Print Culture 1790–1820* (Oxford: Oxford University Press, 1994).

64 Charles Knight, *Passages of a Working Life,* 3 vols (London: Knight and Co., 1873), 1: 245–6.
65 Sheila O'Connell, *The Popular Print in England 1550–1850* (London: British Museum Press, 1999), Chapters 7–8.
66 *A Memoir of Thomas Bewick*, 238. The memoir was completed in 1828, just before his death.
67 Knight, *Passages*, 2: 115, 3: 18–20; Valerie Gray, *Charles Knight: Educator, Publisher, Writer* (Aldershot: Ashgate, 2006), 157–8, 160–1.
68 See Brian Maidment, *Comedy, Caricature and the Social Order 1820–1840* (Manchester: Manchester University Press, 2013); Patricia Anderson, *The Printed Image and the Transformation of Popular Culture* (Oxford: Clarendon Press, 1991).
69 *A Memoir of Thomas Bewick*, 247.
70 For a useful discussion of the illustration of magazine fiction, see Leigh Grey Dillard, '"The Cheapest Work Ever Printed": Illustrating the Classics in Limbird's *British Novelist*', in Christina Ionescu and Ann Lewis, eds, *Picturing the Eighteenth-Century Novel Through Time: Illustration, Intermediality, and Adaptation*, Special issue of the *Journal for Eighteenth-Century Studies* (2016): 533–57.
71 John Bender and Anne Mellor, 'Liberating the Sister Arts: The Revolution of Blake's "Infant Sorrow"' *ELH* 50: 2 (1983): 297–319, 297–9.

PART I

Illustrating Poetry

1 | The Ends of Illustration: Explanation, Critique, and the Political Imagination in Blake's Title-pages for Genesis

PETER OTTO

> We no longer believe in a primordial totality that once existed, or in a final totality that awaits us at some future date … We believe only in totalities that are peripheral. And if we discover such a totality alongside various separate parts, it is a whole *of* these particular parts but does not totalize them; it is a unity *of* all those particular parts but does not unify them; rather it is added to them as a new part fabricated separately.
>
> Deleuze and Guattari, *Anti-Oedipus*[1]

In the last year of his life, Blake was commissioned by John Linnell (1792–1882) to produce an illustrated copy of Genesis, the Bible's book of beginnings. The result of his labours is extant on 11 unbound leaves, which include two title-pages and nine pages of text accompanied by illustrations, all of which are unfinished.[2] These pages renarrate and re-envision the story told in the first chapters of Genesis (1:1–4:15), from the creation of this world to the division of Adam and Eve from each other, their expulsion from Eden, and the murder of Abel by Cain, which together set the nightmare of fallen history in motion.

The manuscript can be placed in at least three ways. First as the culmination of Blake's ongoing dialogue with Genesis, which begins with his attempt in *The First Book of Urizen* (1794) radically to rewrite it. Second, in relation to the illustrated Bibles published in England in the late eighteenth and early nineteenth century, such as *The Protestant's Family Bible* (1780–1) and *The Royal Universal Family Bible* (1780–2), both of which contain plates engraved by Blake. And third, as a text strongly influenced by the growing recognition that Genesis is a historical document rather than the word of God – a view argued by Alexander Geddes (1737–1802) in works such as his *Prospectus of a New Translation of the Bible* (1786) and debated, in the late eighteenth and early nineteenth century, in the pages of *The Analytical Review*.[3]

After describing the manuscript's formal features and the iconography of the designs, most accounts of the illustrations move, without further ado, to an account of the views on art and religion they imply, in which Blake seems to have swapped his political engagements for a surprisingly conventional theology, out of kilter with views expressed in other works with which he was preoccupied at the time, such as his Illustrations to Enoch (1824–7) and 'הי [Jehovah] & his two Sons Satan & Adam' (1826–7). Damon writes, for example, that 'the most interesting feature of these illustrations is [Blake's] acceptance of the Trinity', which involves an about-turn in his assessment of God the Father, whom he had previously dismissed 'as the Evil Creator'.[4] According to Rowland, the title-pages show that '[t]he result of [Adam's and Eve's] disobedience is personal and social disintegration as creation degenerates and violence comes into the world'.[5] Turning from the Father to the Son, Nanavutty concludes that '[o]nly through the catharsis of suffering and the mercy of Christ can man liberate his spirit, his intellect, his senses and his body, thus attaining an eternal blessedness'.[6] Paley echoes this view when he writes that in these illustrations 'physical existence is viewed as entirely negative'.[7] And Crosby and Essick, arguing that Blake's representation of the triune God is inflected by his patron's Trinitarian views, see in the first title-page a deeply conventional chain of being, which descends from 'the Holy Ghost … at the top of the design' to 'the "firmament" … and its creator, and humanity and its creator/redeemer, then earth, and finally, if the flames above the figures at the bottom of the design are infernal, hell'.[8]

In contrast, this chapter takes a more circuitous approach to such matters, by mapping the ways in which the visual elements that comprise the two title-pages to Genesis (Figures 1.1. and 1.2.) are articulated with each other. In brief summary, it argues that the third of the contexts mentioned above conditions Blake's understanding of the roles played by illustration, in ways that radically disrupt the tradition of Biblical illustration to which the Genesis manuscript belongs. Rather than reflecting Blake's supposed turn from politics to religion, when read in this context the Genesis manuscript elaborates the political and artistic implications already implicit in *The First Book of Urizen*. In both works, revelation is replaced by critique; the sacred is realized in the profane; and the notion of a 'primordial totality that once existed' and of 'a final totality that awaits us at some future date' are dismissed. But in the later work, echoing *Milton* (c.1804–11) and *Jerusalem* (1804–c.20), the prophetic imagination is presented as a power able not just to illustrate (make clear to the mind) and to critique, but also to veer from the given – a triumvirate of capacities that, Blake's illustrations to Genesis suggest, in a society without gods, priests, and kings, would become evident each time we illustrate a text.

The Ends of Illustration 27

Figure 1.1 William Blake, Illustrated Manuscript of Genesis: First Title-Page (c.1826–7). Pencil, pen, gouache and watercolour on wove paper (34.1 x 23.9 cm). Courtesy of the Huntington Art Collections, San Marino, California.

28 PETER OTTO

Figure 1.2 William Blake, Illustrated Manuscript of Genesis: Second Title-Page (c.1826–7). Pencil, pen, watercolour and liquid gold on wove paper (33 x 23.5 cm). Courtesy of the Huntington Art Collections, San Marino, California.

'In the Beginning'

Genesis is the first of the five books of the Law (the Torah or Pentateuch) which were traditionally supposed to have been dictated by God to Moses.[9] It opens with an account of Creation that unfolds in eight steps, across six days, with the seventh day set aside as a day of rest (2: 3). This labour comprises three operations. The creation of space: the firmament is divided from the waters above and below it (Day 2) and the earth divided from the ocean (Day 3). The creation of living creatures to populate this space: birds, fish (Day 5), beasts, and finally Man and Woman, who, unlike the animals, are created 'in the image of God' (Day 6). And the creation of time: Day is divided from Night (Day 1); sun, moon, and stars are formed to measure days, years, and seasons (Day 4); and the Sabbath is sanctified, in order to mark the boundary between one week and the next (Day 7).[10] Inside this world, Man and Woman stand together 'at the apex of a cosmological pyramid',[11] with 'dominion … over all the earth' (1: 26).

This narrative is followed by a second creation story (2: 4b–3: 24), radically different from the first, according to which Creation occurs on earth rather than in a void; is the work of Jahweh Elohim rather than Elohim; and is effected by art rather than divine fiat. Ignoring the passage from chaos to order, this narrative is preoccupied by the journey from bliss to suffering.

According to this story, Creation begins after 'a mist [rises] from the earth' and waters 'the ground', causing plants and herbs to grow (2: 6). In this now verdant world, God's first act rather than his last is to create Adam, by moulding his body from 'the dust of the ground' rather than from nothing, before then 'breathing into his nostrils the breath of life' (2: 7). The Garden of Eden is created next, within which God causes trees to grow, including 'the tree of life … and the tree of knowledge of good and evil'; and this is followed by the Law, which is conjured by the command not to eat of 'the tree of knowledge of good and evil'. Only then are beasts and birds created, followed by Eve, who is formed from one of Adam's ribs (2: 21-2).

The Paradise this last act completes is soon lost, through events that simultaneously create the fallen world and draw life into it. The path to this end begins when the serpent tempts Eve, who tempts Adam, and they both eat of 'the tree of knowledge of good and evil'. They are consequently expelled from Eden and, to prevent their return, God employs Cherubim and installs a 'flaming sword' to block the entrance to Eden and make 'the tree of life' inaccessible (3: 24).

At this stage, the fallen world is still virtual rather than actual; but it rapidly becomes real, as described in the third chapter of Genesis, which turns our attention from the all-powerful acts of the first narrative and the human frailties of the second, to the politics of everyday life. Like the preceding narratives, it is concerned with creation, but of a kind shaped by male and female bodies rather than transcendent gods. The narrator reports simply that 'Adam knew Eve … and she conceived, and bare Cain … And she again bare his brother Abel' (4: 1–2). This begins the linear sequence of historical time, marked by generations, genealogies, and patriarchs, rather than the circular time of the first and second creation stories, which is measured primarily by days, nights, weeks, and seasons. But this new time is almost immediately marked by the murder of Abel by Cain, at which point Blake's transcription of Genesis breaks off.

Illustrating Genesis

Since the early nineteenth century, the Bible's first and second creation stories, now known respectively as the 'P' (Priestly) and 'J' (Jahwist) narratives, have been considered the work of different authors.[12] This view was first advanced by the German theologian Johann Gottfried Eichhorn (1752–1827), who regarded Gen. 1: 1–2: 3, Gen. 2: 4–25, and Gen. 4: 1–26 as the work of different authors. In Britain, Alexander Geddes reported these suggestions with some scepticism. In his view, the Pentateuch had been compiled from a mass of disparate documents, perhaps by Moses, probably by Solomon, and was therefore more fragmentary than Eichhorn allowed it to be.[13]

The mismatch between the first and second stories of creation was, of course, known to readers of the Bible well before the publications of Eichhorn and Geddes. For this audience, as Acosta remarks, '[t]o assume that' they 'were not divergent versions but different expressions of the same fact made perfect sense … The traditional exegetical question had been how best to integrate them and make them clearly complementary'.[14] And this was normally achieved by foregrounding one of the creation stories at the expense of the other. Nevertheless, the realization that the Bible's creation stories are not just different from each other, but are the work of different authors or, worse, an assemblage of fragments, extended the role of history and critique in biblical criticism, bringing it into accord with aspects of Enlightenment thought.

This did not mean, of course, that after Eichhorn and Geddes conventional readings of Genesis disappeared or that the Bible's accounts of creation lost all purchase on the present. Geddes argues, for example, that by dismissing the Pentateuch's claim to be divinely inspired, we can appreciate it as a human creation, which merits comparison with the greatest works of antiquity.[15] And at least part of Paine's animus against the Bible derives from the way its fictions continued to influence the present. Praise and blame are not normally related to each other, but in this case they had the same aim, namely to uncover the truth hidden by the Bible's fictions. 'It is time', Geddes writes, for 'the pure spiritual religion of JESUS [to] throw aside all the tawdry cumbersome load of exotic ornaments, borrowed either from Judaism or Paganism, … and reclothe herself in the white spotless robes, in which she was originally invested'.[16] And for Paine, once the Bible has been shown to be a fiction, we can turn to the Creation, 'the Bible of the deist', where we can read, 'in the hand-writing of the Creator himself, the certainty of his existance (sic), and the immutability of his power'.[17]

Blake rates the Bible still more highly, with regard both to its power as fiction and quality as literature, although the conclusions he draws from these judgements are quite different from those drawn by Paine and Geddes. He writes in the margins of Richard Watson's *An Apology for the Bible* (1797), for example, that the Bible is 'Poetry'; but then describes that poetry as 'inspired' (E617).[18] Similarly, in יה *[Jehovah] and his two Sons* he describes 'The Old & New Testaments' as 'the Great Code of Art'; but then adds that 'Art is the | Tree of Life' (E274). These collocations suggested to Blake that 'Tom Paine is a better Christian than [Bishop Watson]', arguably because he shifts our attention from Heaven to Earth, Law to Art, and being to becoming. And, as Blake goes on to say, it is therefore 'the Holy Ghost who in Paine strives with Christendom as in Christ he strove with the Jews' (E614). This shifts power from the supposed author of the Pentateuch, whether Moses or God, to its readers/illustrators, whose role now expands to include explanation, critique, and even revision of the fictions that govern our lives. Blake's illustrations to Genesis, although incomplete, are the most ambitious example of this mode of illustration, which begins by illustrating/re-visioning the topography of the world created by God.

The Architecture of this World

The first title-page (Figure 1.1) presents the viewer with four clearly defined realms, namely Heaven, Earth, Hell, and Chaos, which it holds in equilibrium with each other.[19] The first realm, seen in the upper half of the design, is ordered by the letters 'G', 'E', 'N', and 'E', with the first and second letters placed immediately above the third and fourth, so that together they form a large square. The square is, of course, a conventional symbol of Heaven's harmony and balance, which is repeated, for example, in the foursquare patterns prescribed for the altar of burnt offering (Exodus 27: 1) and the New Jerusalem (Revelation 21: 16). On the title-page, this ordered space is flanked on three sides by figures commonly identified as the persons of the Trinity. Beginning at the top and moving clockwise, they are the Holy Ghost, identified by his outspread wings; the Father, who is seen dividing the waters above from those below the firmament; and the Son, who leans out from a circle suspended in the air.

The fourth realm is evoked by the ocean, sketched near the lower margin of the design, the waves of which surge against a low rounded rock or hill. The rock is, one presumes, 'the fixed point around which, in the beginning', according to Jewish and Christian mythology, 'God had formed the earth', and beneath which swirl 'the subterranean waters, those forces of chaos that were for ever threatening to engulf the ordered world'.[20] The ocean is seen again at the top of the design, where it crosses from the left- to the right-hand margin, and then half-way down the page; but here it recalls the primal 'waters' from which the world was born.

Earth, the second in our list of realms, lies midway between the first and fourth, inside the ovaloid space outlined by the following elements: the vertical line of flames rising into the sky, which can be seen near the right-hand margin of the design; next, the lower boundary of Heaven, marked by the water beneath the feet of the Father and by the base and spurs of the letters 'N' and 'E'; then, near the left-hand margin, the cascade of water, represented by wavy blue-lines, falling from Heaven to Earth; and, completing the circuit, the upper boundary of Chaos, defined by the meeting of sea and rock. Although only lightly sketched, twin columns of smoke (one on the far left and the other on the far right) bracket this space as a whole, perhaps to cloak it in obscurity.

The enclosed space outlined by these elements contains the letters 'S', 'I', and 'S', arranged in horizontal sequence, which hang in the air, immediately above a horizontal line of flames, shaped like cloven tongues (Acts 2: 3), which hang in the air immediately above the primal rock mentioned earlier. At the centre of the space, a giant man, normally identified as Adam, stands naked, behind the letter 'I', which covers his stomach and genitals. He stands on the rock beneath him, in the middle of the horizontal line of flames that reaches up to his knees, while looking up towards and reaching with his right arm up into the heavens. Beneath him, on the margin dividing sea from land, four roughly sketched figures are attempting to rise from or struggling not to fall into the ocean.

As this survey of Earth's primary features has no doubt already suggested, it is divided into two domains, one of which is Hell. Most obviously, the narrow border between the base of the letters 'S I S' and the line of flames beneath them, divides it into upper and lower worlds, with the first aligned primarily with the Word/spirit and the second with the image/body. This division is intensified by the contrast between Adam, as upright-man, and the suffering crowd beneath him. But Adam is also divided, by the flourish that caps the letter 'I', which separates the upper from the lower portions of his body. If one focuses on the former, which is enclosed in a sphere or framed by a halo, he belongs to a circle that includes all three members of the Trinity. But if one turns to the latter, the lower extremities of which are in flames, he belongs with those beneath him, in the circle of the damned.

The kind of threat posed by the lower to the higher faculties/worlds is made explicit by the naked woman, standing amidst the flames, who is pressing her legs and stomach against Adam's right foot. She lifts her breasts up towards him, by bending her upper body backwards, in an attempt apparently to catch his eye. Hell, it seems, is a place on earth, with Adam the locale where Heaven and Hell pit their energies against each other.

In conventional Christian cosmologies, Hell is divided from Heaven and Earth by a vast distance. In contrast, on the first title-page, which is strongly influenced by Emanuel Swedenborg (1688–1722), Blake places these realms in intimate relation with each other – so intimate that Heaven lies immediately above Hell, while Earth is the cramped space (the border or line) between these realms. But for Blake this topography embodies a contingent set of social/psychological relations rather than, as it does for Swedenborg, an unchangeable reality.

The implications of this last observation become apparent if one steps back from the design for a moment, to view it as a whole. From this distance, Heaven, Earth, and Hell together take the form of a large egg, a form often used in creation stories to symbolize the chaos from which the world is born. But in this case the egg is itself the Creation – an amalgam of form and chaos that recalls the 'petrific abominable chaos' created by Urizen/God in *The First Book of Urizen* (3: 26, E71). In the Christian story, after Adam is created, he steps into a world that is perfect. It is only later that he 'falls', an event marked by the fig leaf that hides his nakedness. But in the design we are considering, Adam has already covered his genitals, suggesting that Creation and Fall are contemporaneous with each other. In contrast to most Bible illustrations, Blake's illustration of Genesis therefore leads back not to an omnipotent God but to a social/psychological system that frames the imperfect reality that is this world. The acts constitutive of this system become evident when we turn once again to the Word.

The Word and the Flesh

The 'Prologue' to the Gospel according to John identifies the Word (*logos*) with the Creator, who brought this world into being, and with Jesus, 'the Word made flesh', who teaches fallen humanity that we 'were born, not of blood, nor of the will of the flesh, nor of the will of man, but of God' (1: 13). And Blake's first title-page for Genesis seems at first to follow suit. Most obviously, it mimes the creative work of the Word, by arranging the letters G, E, N, E, S, I and S in such a way that each time we gather them into the syllables G-E, N-E, and S-I-S, and so into the word GENESIS, we move from the upper to the lower realms of the design, from the foursquare form of Heaven to the divided world of Earth. Indeed, in this design, each time we articulate the word 'G E | N E | S I S', we rehearse the actions that bring this world into being.

To begin from the beginning: the first syllable of GENESIS, like all syllables, is formed by acts of division and union: G is divided from *and* coupled with E. As if magnifying this process, the spread-eagled limbs and wings of the Holy Spirit, with his left foot immediately above the letter G and his right foot above the E, opens the gap between left and right (breadth) while simultaneously bridging it, as he runs/flies from the left-hand side of the page towards the right. This collocation of movement and stasis, opening and coupling, places the Spirit's genitals immediately above the abyss dividing 'G' from 'E', recalling Milton's description of the beginning of Creation, when, 'Dovelike', the Holy Spirit 'satst brooding on the vast abyss | And mad'st it pregnant'.[21]

Next, the first and second syllables of 'G E | N E | S I S' are collocated by acts of division and union, similar to those described in the preceding paragraph, which are represented by the empty rectangular-space that elevates 'G E' above 'N E', while binding them together in such a way that the foursquare form of Heaven is established. Immediately to the right, magnifying these processes, God the Father divides the waters above the firmament from those below it (Gen. 1: 7), while instituting the Law, represented by his cold watery body, that will henceforth hold them in a fixed relation to each other. Now that breadth and height have been created, light streams from the upper-right-hand corner of the design, passing between the right foot of the Holy Spirit and the right-hand of the Father, into the foursquare space of Heaven, which it divides into regions of light and of darkness.

Appropriately enough, the third syllable, which completes the word (Genesis), is added by the Word (Jesus), who is seen with narrowed eyes and dishevelled hair, leaning out towards the viewer from the surface of a large circle suspended in the air. He throws his left arm horizontally across the surface of the page, echoing the movement of the Spirit above him, while pointing to the Father on the other side of the design. At the same time, holding his outstretched right arm at 90 degrees to his left, he adds 'width', to the Spirit's 'breadth' and Father's 'height'. This turns the work of his fellows into a three-dimensional whole, which is realized in the world beneath him, towards which he is pointing.

The syllable added by Jesus is a suffix, 'S I S', that in nouns of Greek origin denotes action or process. In this case, it adds time to 'G E | N E', the plural of 'Genos', which in ancient Greek means origin, family, or natural kind.[22] Up to this point in Creation, the Word has provided the script, performed by the Trinity, that shapes the passive flesh of the world. It is therefore surprising that, as this process draws to a close, this hierarchical sequence becomes uncertain. The Word now clothes Adam, as if it were a garment that could be inflected by his movements. And, still more dramatically, Adam brings GENESIS to life: his head, held aloft by his body, forms the dot that turns the vertical column beneath him into an 'i', suggesting that he is Jesus, 'the Word made flesh', who completes the work of Creation by articulating it.

This about-turn transports us from the synchrony of language to the diachrony of speakers and, more broadly, from a world of being to one of becoming, where creatures become creators, and effects become causes able to stand apart from *and* influence their source. This brings to mind the objection voiced in *The Marriage of Heaven and Hell* (1790) and Blake's answer to it: 'Some will say, Is not God alone the Prolific? I answer, God only Acts & Is, in existing beings or Men' (16, E40). In the context of the present argument, these lines turn me back to the Word, surprised that I have to this point ignored the body in which the Word comes to life.

Indeed, when I look again at the design it now seems obvious that Heaven is held aloft by Adam, who of course doubles as a figure for the reader, and that 'G E | N E' is held aloft by the broad base of 'S I S' (temporal process). Even the Trinity now seems part of the material world: the light-blue rivulets with which the Father is clothed, the Spirit's rusty-red body, and the Son's blue garments, along with the circle that is holding him aloft, associate them respectively with water, fire, and air – a triumvirate completed when earth is added, represented by Adam.

Even the Word now seems to have been animated from the beginning by temporal/material processes. The body of 'G', for example, beginning from a point near what will be its centre, thickens and then thins as it curves downward, and again thickens and then thins as it curves upward, before tapering again to a point – suggesting both the opening of space from 'nothing' *and* the rhythmic surging (dividing-coupling) of chaos. In both letter 'E's, this freely unfolding form becomes a crescent, the upper and lower halves of which are held in place by a vertical bar. A fleur-de-lis terminates the central horizontal of the first 'E' and a star terminates the central horizontal of the second, which are emblems respectively of royalty and eternal order. The latter is protected by two sharp thorns, one of which seems about to pierce Adam's head (although the same detail also tropes eternal order as the result of a thought-bubble). And although 'N' roughly mirrors the foursquare form of Heaven that it completes, it also adds diagonal and leafy growths, which seem to anticipate the world forming beneath them. Finally, as we have seen, in Adam, the Word (the whole word) becomes flesh. This temporal/material foundation suggests that, if Genesis were articulated differently, creation could take a different form, even though in this design that possibility remains dormant.

Division

In contrast to conventional Christian cosmologies, in Blake's illustrations for Genesis the Fall is the product of obedience rather than disobedience – viz. Adam's attempt to remake himself in the image of the eternal, which proceeds by dividing his mind from the sources of disorder in the body, in the hope of creating a 'spiritual body (a spiritual-natural) distinct from the physical body and entirely subject' to God.[23] As previously mentioned, this aspiration is flagged by the flourish that caps the vertical stroke of 'i', which divides Adam's head and the letter's tittle from the body beneath them; and also by the forces that are dividing the Earth into two. But the same ambition is evident in the design as a whole.

In the *Phenomenology of Spirit*, Hegel describes the opening, 'above the *sensuous* world', of 'a *supersensible* world',[24] which offers a mirror image of the first, with the result that what in 'the first world is sweet, in this inverted in-itself is sour, [and] what in the former is black is, in the other, white'.[25] In the first title-page, the same process is underway. Blake writes in *Jerusalem* that 'Genius' is 'the Holy Ghost in Man; there is no other | God, than that God who is the intellectual fountain of Humanity' (91: 9–10). It seems appropriate, therefore, that in the supersensible world he runs/hovers at the apex of a heavenly triangle; but this position is the mirror image of his status in the lower world, where the gifts of the Spirit, represented by the line of Pentecostal flames, are relegated to the borders of Hell. The elements follow suit: on Earth water falls on the far left of the design, while fire rises on the right, whereas in Heaven water falls on the right and fire rises on the left. Most vividly, the violence and chaos into which Earth is descending reappears in Heaven as balance and peace.

The Holy Spirit's collocation of activity and passivity (running/bridging; impregnating/brooding) was by the Gnostics thought to be proof of his androgyny; but here again, in the design we are considering, this is the mirror image of the divided sexes being produced far below him, on the border between Hell and chaos. These figures form two pairs, one on the left- and the other on the right-hand side of the design, in each of which one member is drawing apart from the other.

Counting from the left, the first looks with hollow eyes and disapproving expression at his companion, with whom he seems once to have been joined at the genitals. With his long, winged penis[26] trailing between his legs, he falls to the left, towards the ocean, while reaching with both hands into the air, in an attempt to grasp the flames above his head. His fall seems in part to be engineered by the heavy, lower body of the first 'S', which is pressing down on the flames above him.

The second figure, the least human of the four, seems female, if the almond-shaped form drawn between her legs, just above the waves, towards which her partner's penis is pointing, represents her vagina. She looks quizzically at her partner, while folding her arms against her chest, in a gesture of disapproval and/or refusal. Her reactions, like her partner's flight, seem related to the serpent that has wound itself around the left side of her body, near the waist, and now places its head and open mouth between them both, immediately in front of her folded arms.

The third figure sits on the ground, facing the viewer. Her lower legs are immersed in the ocean, as she looks across to those on her right, with an expression of interest, perhaps pleasure, on her face. She lifts her right arm into the air, through the line of flames, in order to catch hold of the 'S' above her, while pushing, with her left-hand, against her partner's body. The lower half of this 'S' has become a 'V', the sharp edge of which, guided perhaps by the woman, menaces her partner.

Judging by the expression on his face, he is appalled by her actions. He raises his arms into the air, with the fingers on both of his hands spread wide, in a gesture of despair. With his lower body trapped beneath hers, his upper body falls from her, towards the ocean. For these figures, as for the first and second, the path to Hell/Chaos is opened not by sexual pleasure but by its eclipse, as the sexes are arranged in relations governed by law, power, jealousy, violence, and suffering.

The Garden of Eden

In 'A Vision of The Last Judgment', Blake warns that to 'suppose that before [Adam] <the Creation> All was Solitude & Chaos … is the most pernicious Idea that can enter the Mind' (E563). The first title-page explains why: the belief that we must choose between eternal order and temporal disorder turns the processual, heterogeneous forms of the body, imagination, and time into the unfolding catastrophe of fallen history. The high-point of this process, the moment when the temporal seems momentarily to have been brought into accord with the eternal, is represented by the Garden of Eden, which in the Bible appears in the midst of a world become wasteland, into which after a brief sojourn in Paradise, its inhabitants are returned. This refuge is the subject of Blake's second title-page to Genesis (Figure 1.2).

Given that Genesis has two beginnings, it is odd that it is universally agreed that one of Blake's title-pages must have been intended to replace the other. According to Damon, Blake was dissatisfied with the second and so replaced it with the first.[27] Crosby and Essick argue that if Blake had completed the manuscript, only the second would have been kept.[28] And between these extremes, Butlin describes them as 'alternative title-pages'.[29] But given that neither were actually discarded, the parallels between them make it probable that each is intended to illustrate the other, with the first mapping the acts hidden behind the second, and the second sketching the reality produced by the first – and that this mirrors what Blake wants us to see as the relation between the Bible's 'P' and 'J' narratives.

Although the contours of the first title-page can be traced in the second, its sublime energy has been veiled by beauty, the beauty of the Garden of Eden. This is evoked by the verdant ground on which Adam is standing; the balance of the design as a whole; and by the vegetation that decorates the letters of G E | N E | S I S, particularly the first four, which evokes what Swedenborg would call a spiritual-natural,[30] a sensible world in harmony with the supersensible.[31]

This Garden, like the Creation to which it belongs, was produced by imposing form on chaos. It is therefore not surprising to find those forces likely to prove disruptive have been moved off stage. At the top of the design, only a few ripples are left to remind us of the primordial ocean; and, at the bottom of the design, the waters of chaos lap rather than surge against the Earth/Hell. Elsewhere, the waters have solidified or vanished: the blue waters previously divided by the Father are now painted a heavy black; and the rivulets that cascaded down his body and the streams that tumbled from Heaven to Earth can no longer be seen. Similarly, the rusty-red flames that once clothed the Holy Spirit and that burned on the margins of Heaven and Earth/Hell have also disappeared, apart from a few faint pink smudges. And the female bodies that, in the first title-page, were being divided from male bodies are no longer in sight – or, rather, can be seen only in the contours of a Garden that, as Edmund Burke would argue, is beautiful, feminine, and loved because it submits to Adam/God.[32]

The contours of the Garden of Eden, only just visible in the first title-page, are here sharply outlined. Heaven and Earth are now divided from each other by a thick arch of blue sky. And the former, now in little danger of tumbling to the ground, is held firmly aloft. The trees growing in the left- and right-hand corners of the design hold, respectively, the Son and Father in the air. Further, the design suggests that their heavenly bodies are extensions of the trunks beneath them and that Heaven, the vegetation of which can be seen next to and above them, is the shared crown of both trees.

The contrast between Jesus (Atonement) and the Father (commandment), sketched in the first title-page, is here accentuated because both are now standing upright, with the former holding both arms out wide, in a pose reminiscent of the crucifixion. This contrast, like that between Heaven and Earth, is evidently now inscribed in the nature of things. As Nanavutty remarks, 'emblems of creation, fertility and abundance' are placed amongst the letters 'on the side of Christ', while 'the red roses of martyrdom and the lily of Calvary' can be found in the letters next to Jehovah.[33] Further, growing in space dividing 'G E' from 'N E' are two palms, 'symbols of a Christian salvation and Christian victory achieved through the Crucifixion which unites man with God and God with man in the person of Jesus'.[34]

This sounds like the end of a story, but if so it is a story that ends where it began, in catastrophe, given that Blake describes Atonement as 'Moral Severity, [which] destroys Mercy in its Victim' (*Jerusalem* 35[39]: 25–6, E181). Indeed, it is possible to argue that, at this moment in Creation, the juxtaposition of a heavenly Son (Atonement) and heavenly Father (commandment) frames the dynamic, sketched at the beginning of this section, that turns the mind against the body, Heaven against Earth, and men against women, in the hope of reaching a Garden of Eden beyond the anguish of this world.

Nanavutty is confident that 'Christ stands above the Tree of Life'; 'Jehovah stands above the Tree of the Knowledge of Good and Evil'; and '[t]he uncorrupted Adam bestrides the green earth in simple majesty'.[35] But in this title-page, as in the first, the column/letter hiding Adam's genitals announces that this Creation is the Fall. Further, the flutes that now decorate the body of the 'I' make it look like a classical column. In his later work, Blake links the 'Classics' to those ideologies 'that Desolate Europe with Wars' (E270). The supposedly 'uncorrupted Adam' is therefore here linked with the institution of power, violence, and empire.

Just as problematically for Nanavutty's argument, the 'globular, rose-pink fruit'[36] hanging from the tree on the left, which look to me like apples, and the fruit hanging like 'half-crushed grapes' from the tree on the right,[37] emblems of suffering life, suggest that her identifications should be reversed. Although at first sight perplexing, the collocation of Jesus and the tree of good and evil, and Jehovah and the tree of (suffering) life, amplifies what the design as a whole proposes, namely that there is no supersensible figure able to transport humanity to 'eternal blessedness'.

This last point is, of course, already evident in the form of the trees themselves, which vividly represent the process and product of sublimation, which by drawing on the energies of the 'sensible world' fabricates a '*supersensible*' world. Both trees sink their roots into the dark soil and watery energies below them, which they draw on to build trunks, low-hanging fruit, and finally the supersensible world that, as we have seen, becomes their crown – the supposed origin of their earthly life.

The violence of sublimation is made explicit by the letters on either side of Adam. Both are composed primarily of thin, elongated leaves, which have been gathered, bound together, and then arranged so that each 'S' is formed by four overlapping 'V's. This turns the serpentine form of 'S' into a sequence of spear-heads – the sharpest of which seem intended to keep Heaven and Earth apart from each other, and Adam apart from the tree of life. Ominously, the 'V' at the base of the last 'S' has been plunged into the fruit hanging from the tree of life.

Despite its apparent stability, the Garden of Eden will soon move out of sight, dispatched by the dynamic it helps establish. At the top of the design, the Holy Spirit now looks to his right rather than (as in the earlier title-page) to his left, at the chaos that follows rather than precedes the Creation.

Beneath him, the serpents (or serpentine tendrils) winding around the vertical stroke of the first and second 'E' recall the Father's Law *and* anticipate Adam's and Eve's disobedience. And beneath all of these figures, Adam is about to step forward into the stream of time, which leads to the four creatures, each with a human body and animal head, sitting on the ground at the front of the design, and from there to the present of the reader/viewer.

Reading from left to right, the creatures have the face of a reptile with 'humanoid characteristics', an eagle, a lion, and an ox – features that link them to the four creatures of Ezekiel 1: 10, the four Evangelists, the four creatures of Revelation 4: 7, and, most importantly, Blake's four Zoas.[38] Nanavutty identifies them as, from left to right, the fallen Urthona (imagination), Urizen (reason), Luvah (love), and Tharmas (the senses).[39] The faces of the first and second are marked by cruelty; both wear crowns, symbols of earthly power; and they gaze towards God the father, the source of their authority. The third and fourth look towards the creatures on their right, with expressions of anxiety and surprise on their face. Both raise their arms in an attempt to dissociate themselves from the disaster unfolding around them. These four creatures are the gods who, in concert with the Heaven above them, will weave the web of fallen life.

The Ends of Illustration

The relation between higher and lower powers is illustrated by two diagonals, which gather the levels and elements of the design into a whole. The first joins the Father, Adam, the fallen Urthona and Urizen, and the tree of good and evil. The second links Jesus, Adam, Tharmas and Luvah, and the tree of life. At first sight, these diagonals simply renarrate the story of Creation that Blake's title-pages have been developing, as an interaction between the supersensible (Heaven) and the sensible (Earth/Hell), commandment (the Father) and Atonement (Jesus), that drives the struggle of mind against body, and of order against possible sources of disorder. As such it might recall Paley's claim that in these illustrations 'physical existence is viewed as entirely negative'.

But the diagonals also flag a second narrative, this time of possible change, which like the first is focused on Adam. As we have seen, on the first title-page Adam's role in articulating 'G E | N E | S I S' places him at the centre of the actual *and* the possible. On the second title-page, the vegetation that almost covers 'G E | N E | S I S' suggests that it was last articulated a long time ago. But even here the second narrative is suggested by Adam's position at the centre of both diagonals; by Jesus's step forward, which marks the beginning of the Incarnation; and by the scroll Jesus is handing Adam, which suggests that the Book's beginning and end, hard-and-fast divisions, and commandments and punishments, are not set in stone.

The first narrative culminates in the murder of Abel and the exile of Cain, who, according to the Bible story, carries with him into exile a mark, inscribed on his body by God, which warns that vengeance should be left to the Lord. In the third chapter of Genesis, this mark is one of a long list of distinctions used to define a complex social space, which includes those between God and His subjects, farmers and shepherds, parents and children, the acceptable and the unacceptable, murderers and victims, and so on. Although the last to be introduced, it is arguably the most important because, by distinguishing those outside ('vagabonds', 'fugitives', murderers (Gen. 4: 12–14)) from those inside its spaces, it draws the community into a whole. And, just as importantly, by protecting those it excludes the mark signals the role played by the outcast in constituting the community from which he/she is excluded.

In contrast, the second narrative reaches its conclusion in a mark of forgiveness, left by God on Cain's forehead, which is the subject of the last illustration in the series (Figure 1.3). In this powerful sketch, Cain reaches up to touch God the Father on his right arm, near his shoulder, who leans over to kiss Cain on his forehead, while in the background, in front of a small tent, Adam and Eve kneel together in prayer. As Crosby and Essick note, this constellation of figures establishes 'a typological relationship between the marking of Cain via a kiss on the forehead and the forgiving of [the prodigal] son, which in turn foreshadows Jesus on the cross forgiving his murderers (Luke 23:34)'.[40] But the design is more provocative than this summary allows.

After receiving his inheritance, the Prodigal Son travels 'into a far country', where he wastes 'his substance with riotous living'. Later, when he is penniless and 'a mighty famine [arises] in that land', he returns home, repents, and is accepted once more by his Father (Luke 15: 11–32). In this parable, the Son's repentance is the trigger for the Father's empathy because it enables the latter to recognize himself once more in the former. In contrast, Cain is a murderer rather than libertine, and home-coming must therefore negotiate difference rather than being able to rely on empathy; and this will in turn require the kind of radical-forgiveness (rather than forgiveness-as-response-to-repentance) that is described by Blake in *Jerusalem* as the 'point of mutual forgiveness between Enemies! | Birthplace of the Lamb of God incomprehensible' (7: 66–7, E150). Further, because

Figure 1.3 William Blake, Illustrated Manuscript of Genesis: God the Father marking Cain's forehead (c.1826–7). Pencil on wove paper (29.8 x 20.2 cm). Courtesy of the Huntington Art Collections, San Marino, California.

Cain functions to define the limits of the community from which he/she is excluded, renegotiating the relation between God, Cain, and Adam and Eve implies a home-coming that will change the fabric of the real rather than reaffirming it.

For Geddes and Paine, as we have seen, critique uncovers truth by dismissing fiction. But in Blake's illustrations to Genesis, critique and imagination work hand in hand, with the first revealing that the real is contingent, dependent on a fiction, and could therefore be articulated differently by the imagination. Blake's 'God the Father marking Cain's forehead', we can now say, takes this argument to one of its conclusions. It places Cain in proximity with the two primary causes of his life – God and his parents – in a way that gives each the opportunity to renegotiate their relation with each other.

This is a scene of creation (of re-envisioning) just as powerful as the others, in which God and Cain stand on the same ground, with their relation to each other mediated by affection and intimacy rather than hierarchy and commandment. The first kisses the second, while the second touches the first, with the result that both mark the other's body. Rather than concluding with the imposition of form on matter, creation is in this encounter closely associated with mutuality – mutual care and mutual vulnerability, terms that are conventionally associated with femininity rather than masculinity. And one can surmise that when Cain reaches home this will be followed not by restoration of what once was (a conclusion that, one imagines, even the Bible's Prodigal son will eventually find difficult to swallow), but by a new beginning in which he will have a voice. In the state in which this page was left by Blake, the empty lines that divide the last words of the text ('the | Lord set a mark upon Cains forehead') from the design beneath it neatly evoke this not-yet-circumscribed world and future.

All these marks bring us one last time to the question of illustration, which in Blake's hands expands from explanation (in the service of the restoration of the author's/creator's meaning), to critique, renarration, and re-envisioning. Artist/author and illustrator/reader here stand on the same ground, in the sense that both are involved in drawing the marks, lines, and distinctions that shape everyday life and, in so doing, determine 'the place and the stakes of politics as a form of experience'.[41]

Notes

1 Gilles Deleuze and Félix Guattari, *Anti-Oedipus: Capitalism and Schizophrenia*, trans. Robert Hurley, Mark Seem, and Helen R. Lane (Minneapolis: University of Minnesota Press, 1983), 42.

2 Blake's illustrations to Genesis are reproduced in Mark Crosby and Robert N. Essick, eds, *Genesis: William Blake's Last Illuminated Work* (San Marino,

CA: Huntington Library, Art Collections, and Botanical Gardens, 2012). A digital facsimile is available through the Blake Archive at www.blakearchive.org/
3. Geddes' influence on Blake is discussed in Jerome J. McGann, 'The Idea of an Indeterminate Text: Blake's Bible of Hell and Dr. Alexander Geddes', *Studies in Romanticism* 25 (1986): 303–24.
4. S. Foster Damon, *William Blake: His Philosophy and Symbols* (1924; rpt. London: Dawsons of Pall Mall, 1969), 220.
5. Christopher Rowland, *Blake and the Bible* (New Haven, CT: Yale University Press, 2010), 95.
6. Piloo Nanavutty, 'A Title-Page in Blake's Illustrated Genesis Manuscript', *Journal of the Warburg and Courtauld Institutes* 10 (1947): 114–22: 122.
7. Morton Paley, *The Traveller in the Evening: The Last Works of William Blake* (Oxford: Oxford University Press, 2003), 266.
8. Crosby and Essick, *Genesis,* 38.
9. All Bible quotations will be taken from *Bible: Authorized King James Version*, ed. Robert Carroll and Stephen Prickett (Oxford; New York: Oxford University Press, 1997), and will be cited parenthetically in the text.
10. The formal features of Genesis are neatly summarized in Donald E. Gowan, *From Eden to Babel: A Commentary on the Book of Genesis 1–11* (Grand Rapids, MI: William B. Eerdmans and Edinburgh: Handsel Press, 1988), 14, from whom I am in part drawing. See also Ana M. Acosta, *Reading Genesis in the Long Eighteenth Century: From Milton to Mary Shelley* (Aldershot, Hampshire: Ashgate, 2006), 13–15.
11. Gerhard von Rad, *Old Testament Theology: The Theology of Israel's Historical Traditions*, trans. D. M. G. Stalkes (London: S. C. M. Press, 1975), 141.
12. Ibid.
13. Alexander Geddes, 'Preface to the First Volume', in *The Holy Bible, or the Books Accounted Sacred by Jews and Christians*, trans. Geddes (London, 1792), vol. 1: i–xxiii: xix–xx.
14. Acosta, *Reading Genesis*, 60.
15. Geddes, 'Preface', in *The Holy Bible*, vol. 1: i.
16. Alexander Geddes, *Critical Remarks on the Hebrew Scriptures: Corresponding with a New Translation of the Bible* (London, 1800), vii.
17. Thomas Paine, *The Age of Reason. Part the Second. Being an Investigation of True and Fabulous Theology* (London, 1796), 79.
18. All quotations of Blake's work are drawn from David V. Erdman, ed., *The Complete Poetry and Prose of William Blake*, comm. by Harold Bloom, newly rev. edn (New York: Anchor-Doubleday, 1988) and will be cited parenthetically in the text, giving page numbers, preceded by 'E'; and, in the case of the illuminated poetry, plate and line numbers as well.
19. Although the first title-page is on paper marked 'J Whatman / Turkey Mill / 1821' and the second 'J Whatman / 1826', this doesn't prove that one or other of the designs was created first.

20 Norman Cohn, *Cosmos, Chaos and the World to Come: The Ancient Roots of Apocalyptic Faith*, 2nd edn (New Haven, CT; London: Yale University Press, 2001), 137. See also Alexei M. Sivertsev, *Judaism and Imperial Ideology in Late Antiquity* (Cambridge: Cambridge University Press, 2011), 65–74.

21 John Milton, *Paradise Lost*, ed. Alastair Fowler, 2nd edn (London and New York: Longman, 1998), 60 (Book I: ll. 21–2).

22 John V. A. Fine, *The Ancient Greeks: A Critical History* (Cambridge, MA.: Belknap Press of Harvard University Press, 1983), 36. See also Nigel Wilson, ed., *Encyclopedia of Ancient Greece* (New York and London: Routledge, 2006), 404.

23 Peter Otto, *Blake's Critique of Transcendence: Love, Jealousy, and the Sublime in 'The Four Zoas'* (Oxford: Oxford University Press, 2000), 116.

24 Georg Wilhelm Friedrich Hegel, *Phenomenology of Spirit*, trans. A. V. Miller (Oxford: Oxford University Press, 1977), 87. Hegel describes the supersensible world as 'the first, and therefore imperfect, appearance of Reason' (87–8).

25 Ibid., 97.

26 For discussion of this motif in *The Four Zoas*, see Peter Otto, '"A Pompous High Priest": Urizen's Ancient Phallic Religion in *'The Four Zoas'*, *Blake: An Illustrated Quarterly* 35 (2001), 4–22, and *Blake's Critique of Transcendence*, 120–3, 145.

27 Damon, *William Blake*, 221.

28 Crosby and Essick, *Genesis*, 36.

29 Martin Butlin, *The Paintings and Drawings of William Blake* (New Haven, CT: Yale University Press, 1981), 596. Nanavutty, 'A Title-Page', 122, describes the second title-page as 'the more highly finished and aesthetically pleasing'.

30 Emanuel Swedenborg, *A Treatise Concerning Heaven and Hell, and of the Wonderful Things Therein* (London, 1784), 19 (para. 31).

31 Robert R. Wark, 'Blake's Illuminated Manuscript of Genesis', in *Genesis*, ed. Crosby and Essick, 17–22: 21.

32 Edmund Burke, *A Philosophical Enquiry into the Sublime and Beautiful*, ed. James T. Boulton (New York: Routledge, 2008), 113. Wark, 'Blake's Illuminated Manuscript', 21, describes the scene as 'balanced, benign, and beautiful'.

33 Nanavutty, 'A Title-Page', 116.

34 Ibid., 122.

35 Ibid., 120, 122.

36 Ibid., 120.

37 Ibid.

38 Crosby and Essick, *Genesis*, 40, usefully elaborate the associations I have listed here.

39 Nanavutty, 'A Title-Page', 121–2.

40 Crosby and Essick, *Genesis*, 46.

41 Jacques Rancière, *The Politics of Aesthetics: The Distribution of the Sensible*, trans. Gabriel Rockhill (London & New York: Continuum, 2004).

2 | 'With a Master's Hand and Prophet's Fire': Blake, Gray, and the Bard

SOPHIE THOMAS

Although Blake is best known for his extraordinary accomplishments as an artist and a writer, and particularly as the creator of his own 'illuminated books', a great deal of his time and artistic energy went into producing images for the work of others.[1] Though Blake never used the term 'illustration' or its cognates in print, this labour was primarily of that kind, as we would understand it now (the nuances of this terminology will be addressed below); and while reproductive engraving was his primary source of income, Blake also produced an impressive number of original designs for major literary texts.[2] These include Edward Young's *Night Thoughts* (1797), Thomas Gray's *Poems* (1797–98), John Milton's *Paradise Lost* (1807–8), Robert Blair's *The Grave* (1808), and *The Book of Job* (1821) – and he left unfinished at his death sets of illustrations for Bunyan's *Pilgrim's Progress* and Dante's *Divine Comedy*. Blake's use of images in his own work builds creatively on the conventions of eighteenth-century book illustration, as others have shown, but his work as an illustrator tells us at least as much as his illuminated books do about his view of the relationship between image and text.[3] Fundamentally, pictures are to be seen as independent entities within an integral unit, capable of speaking for themselves, and Blake often used his visual designs as a way of commenting upon and occasionally 'correcting' the written text. Though generally faithful to the source text, his illustrations reveal a fiercely imaginative and individual approach to the work of others, as he makes their work into his own.

At the heart of this chapter is an analysis of Blake's watercolour extra illustrations for Gray's poem 'The Bard', which he produced for Ann Flaxman in 1797. This analysis is situated, first, in relation to the approach of other illustrators to Gray's poem (such as Richard Bentley), and to the popularity of the bard as a subject for artists. The bard figures centrally in the Celtic revival that marks the later eighteenth century, apparent in the historically self-conscious projects that animated antiquarians and affirmed an emergent sense of cultural nationalism. In Gray's poem, the bard is prophetic, visionary, and a force for resistance to subjugation. These qualities were clearly attractive to Blake, for a variety of political as well as aesthetic purposes. However, they also make the bard a challenging figure for illustrators, by illuminating (so to speak) the tension between words and images – and their purchase on questions of visualization and representation – that animated debates about illustration in the Romantic period. To tease this out further, the final part of this chapter approaches the theme of the bard in Blake from a different angle, shifting attention to his exhibition of a painting on the same theme, *The Bard, from Gray*, as part of the public exhibition of work mounted in 1809. For this exhibition, Blake compiled a *Descriptive Catalogue*, where he makes a number of remarks about painting that shed light on illustration as a practice, and on his practice of illustration more specifically. Here we may more fully take the measure of Blake's resistance, spelled out in the *Descriptive Catalogue*, to the critical orthodoxy that pictures (like prophets) should simply mimic the real.

The term 'illustration', as has been noted elsewhere in this volume, was used somewhat more widely at the turn of the nineteenth century than it is today, and the nuances of that use are important for my argument. Literally, of course, the term means to light up or to shed light on – to illumine. It also means to elucidate, explain, or exemplify, as for example in the illustration of a subject or a book *pictorially*, though this sense of illustration was not dominant until the 1820s. Before this, 'illustration' was a much broader term, referring more generally to exemplification and enhancement, or as Martin Meisel puts it, to 'the extension of one medium or mode of discourse by another'.[4] Thus, a text may 'shed light' on an image, as readily as images do for texts – and much illustration in the Romantic period operates precisely in this fashion (as in the case of literary annuals, for example, for which texts were commissioned to accompany high-quality, steel engraved images).[5] Blake's illuminated books so cleverly integrated text and image that the precise agent of illumination, text or image, can be difficult to establish. Either way, the principles of illustration are closely embedded in the very process of giving form to, or representing, ideas – and arguably, illustrations in general, and Blake's in particular, can function as 'openings' in a text that *show*, that create mini-exhibition spaces where the drama of meaning making (and meaning altering) unfolds, in and beyond the temporal space of reading.

I Painting the Bard

Thomas Gray's 'The Bard, A Pindaric Ode' was completed in 1757, after an inspiring encounter with the blind harpist John Parry.[6] Gray included an advertisement with his poem explaining that 'the following Ode is founded on a tradition current in Wales, that Edward the First, when he completed the conquest of that country, ordered all the Bards, that fell into his hands, to be put to death'.[7] Gray offered the following, more extensive, summary in his notebooks:

> The army of Edward I. as they march through a deep valley, are suddenly stopped by the appearance of a venerable figure seated on the summit of an inaccessible rock, who, with a voice more than human, reproaches the King with all the misery and desolation which he had brought on his country; foretells the misfortunes of the Norman race, and with prophetic spirit declares, that all his cruelty shall never extinguish the noble ardour of poetic genius in this island; and that men shall never be wanting to celebrate true virtue and valour in immortal strains, to expose vice and infamous pleasure, and boldly censure tyranny and oppression. His song ended, he precipitates himself from the mountain, and is swallowed up by the river that rolls at its foot.[8]

This is, broadly speaking, the drama Gray's poem enacts: it opens with the voice of the (one remaining) bard effectively cursing the mission of Edward I and his armies as they advance along the slopes of Mount Snowdon in the area of the river Conway. The second stanza offers the unforgettable image of the bard perched high on a crag overhead:

> On a rock, whose haughty brow
> Frowns o'er old Conway's foaming flood,
> Robed in the sable garb of woe,
> With haggard eyes the Poet stood;
> (Loose his beard, and hoary hair
> Stream'd, like a meteor, to the troubled air)
> And with a Master's hand, and Prophet's fire,
> Struck the deep sorrows of his lyre. (15–22)[9]

In stanza III, the poet names Edward's other victims – the bards Cadwallo, Urien, and Modred – who join him in weaving the fabric or 'winding sheet' of Edward's fate, which is presented in the manner of an historical tableau, but of events as yet to come. Much of the poem thus reads like an ekphrasis of an imaginary tapestry, conveyed in an unsettling prophetic register that details the horrors that lie ahead for Edward's line, and foretells the return of Welsh sovereignty, in the form of the house of Tudor – and with it the triumphal reinvigorating of British poetry. At the end of his speech, the bard throws himself headlong off the mountain to his death:

> 'Enough for me: With joy I see
> 'The different doom our Fates assign.
> 'Be thine Despair, and scept'red Care,

> 'To triumph, and to die, are mine.'
> He spoke, and headlong from the mountain's height
> Deep in the roaring tide he plung'd to endless night. (139–44)

The poem is a direct expression of Gray's interest in Welsh and Old Norse poetry, and indeed in Welsh harp music, which he actively researched.[10] Like 'The Triumph of Owen: A Fragment', 'The Bard' celebrates the druidic singers 'as essential pillars of Celtic society'.[11] It thus occupies a central place in the Celtic revival of the later eighteenth century, evident in recuperative antiquarian projects such as Evan Evans's *Specimens of the Poetry of the Ancient Welch Bards* (1764) that served to fuel cultural nationalism and affirm a conscious sense of history. In general, as Ian Balfour notes, 'the British and Druidic figure of the Bard is much like the epic poet, an individual repository of people's histories, legends, and myths', and thus distinct from the biblical prophet whose immediate concern is 'impending crises'.[12] Gray's bard however crosses both categories: he represents a unifying national culture *and* functions as a figure of political resistance, even a spur to revolutionary action, which would have had wider resonance in the later years of the eighteenth century.[13]

This makes the figure of the bard an attractive one to co-opt, and not only for a culture coping with a long history of subjugation. In the wake of the publication of Gray's 'The Bard', and James Macpherson's Ossian poems (1760–65), as Katie Trumpener notes, English culture was gripped by an 'enthusiasm for bardic poetry and for the picturesque landscapes of Wales, Scotland, and Ireland'.[14] It was not difficult to subsume this tradition within reigning aestheticizing agendas, which tended to blunt the edges of its political critique, and overlook its distinctive historical and cultural meaning. Thus, while for the Welsh the figure of the bard represented a whole community and spoke for its historical suffering ('for nationalist antiquaries, the bard [was] a mouthpiece for a whole society, articulating its values, chronicling its history, and mourning the inconsolable tragedy of its collapse'), for the English, the bard was of interest individually 'as an inspired, isolated, and peripatetic figure', and for a notion of poetry that was equally dislocated, 'standing apart from and transcending its particular time and place'.[15]

Given this broad cultural and historical appeal, and its central place in the myth of a new Britain, it is not surprising that both English and Welsh artists frequently took up the figure of the bard, derived principally from Gray's poem, as a subject. Richard Altick states that between 1761 and 1820 there were at least a dozen paintings, numerous drawings, as well as Blake's watercolours.[16] One of the preeminent interpretations of Gray, with

Figure 2.1 Thomas Jones, *The Bard* (1774). Oil on canvas. National Museum Wales / Bridgeman Images.

clear visual debts to Salvator Rosa, is Thomas Jones' *The Bard*, 1774 (see Figure 2.1).

The bard, harp in hand, advances towards the cliff edge, while in the background, the bodies of the dead bards are visible – as are, very much in the distance, Edward and his army. Meanwhile, the inclusion to the left of a structure reminiscent of Stonehenge references the association of the Welsh bards with the ancient druids. The dramatic and windswept landscape is itself a key element, given the extent to which solitary figures such as Gray's bard became associated with particular scenography – a link suggested by the specifics of the poem, and reflecting a broader trend in paintings inspired by the pictorialism of much eighteenth-century poetry, which, as Altick suggests, tended to 'place' characters in a landscape with which they would become closely identified. An earlier painting of Gray's bard by Paul Sandby called *Historical Landskip, Representing the Welch Bard* (1761) simply needed – in addition to its descriptive title – to bear the motto 'But oh! what glorious scenes, etc.' to conjure up the rest.[17] Sandby's bard has been lost, which is unfortunate if William Mason's rapturous praise of the painting is anything to go by: 'Sandby has made such a picture! Such a bard! Such a headlong flood! Such a Snowdon! Such giant oaks! Such desert caves!'[18] Mason declared it unequivocally among the best pictures of the century.

This tendency to express the essence of the narrative through landscape is present in two watercolour paintings by J. M. W. Turner that contain more nuanced references to Gray. In the first, *Caernarvon Castle, North Wales* (1800), the castle built by Edward I in the thirteenth century is just barely visible in the background – while off to the left in the foreground, a diminutive bard sits at his harp, attended by a small group of listeners.[19] In the second, *Looking down a Deep Valley towards Snowdon, with an Army on the March* (1798–1800), we strain to see Edward's army making its way snake-like through the vast landscape, with the peak of Snowdon floating in the distance. That painting, also known as *The Destruction of the Bards by Edward I*, is thought to be an unfinished illustration of Gray's poem, and a darker counterpart or pendant to *Caernarvon Castle*.[20] In both paintings, certainly, the human drama is very much subordinated to the sublimity of the landscape.[21] This is also the case in John Martin's well-known rendition, *The Bard* (1817), which characteristically features human actors almost comically dwarfed by their surroundings.[22]

Other noteworthy treatments of Gray's poem by artists include Benjamin West's *The Bard*, which was exhibited at the Royal Academy in 1809 – the same year as Blake's exhibition. It was evocatively described in *The Examiner*:

> A venerable Bard standing on the brow of a stupendous rock, agonized at the murders of his inspired brethren, and falling country, and imprecating prophetic vengeance on a sanguinary foe, is a subject partaking of the sublime […] The mixed feelings of grief, and an anger which pours curses on an advancing enemy, are powerfully pourtrayed in the Bard's face, turned head, and extended arm. […] Terror, destruction, and death, hover with the Eagles who are waiting for their prey.[23]

In this case, by contrast, the figure of the bard is front and centre, filling the canvas almost entirely. The subject was tackled in a similar manner by Fuseli in designs for Du Roveray's edition of Gray's poems, published in 1800, of which two were exhibited that year at the Royal Academy.[24] In the version engraved to illustrate the text, the figure of the bard also dominates the image (again, with a dramatically turned head, and extended arms), relegating other key elements (Edward's army, the waters of Conway) to the corners. Philippe de Loutherbourg's design, finally, balances these elements more equally, and depicts the bard on the cliff-side in the upper centre of the scene, energetically plucking the strings of his harp (striking 'the deep sorrows of his lyre'). The lines of Gray's poem (15–22), which the image clearly illustrates, are appended below it, creating a free-standing composite.

Blake, Gray, and the Bard   53

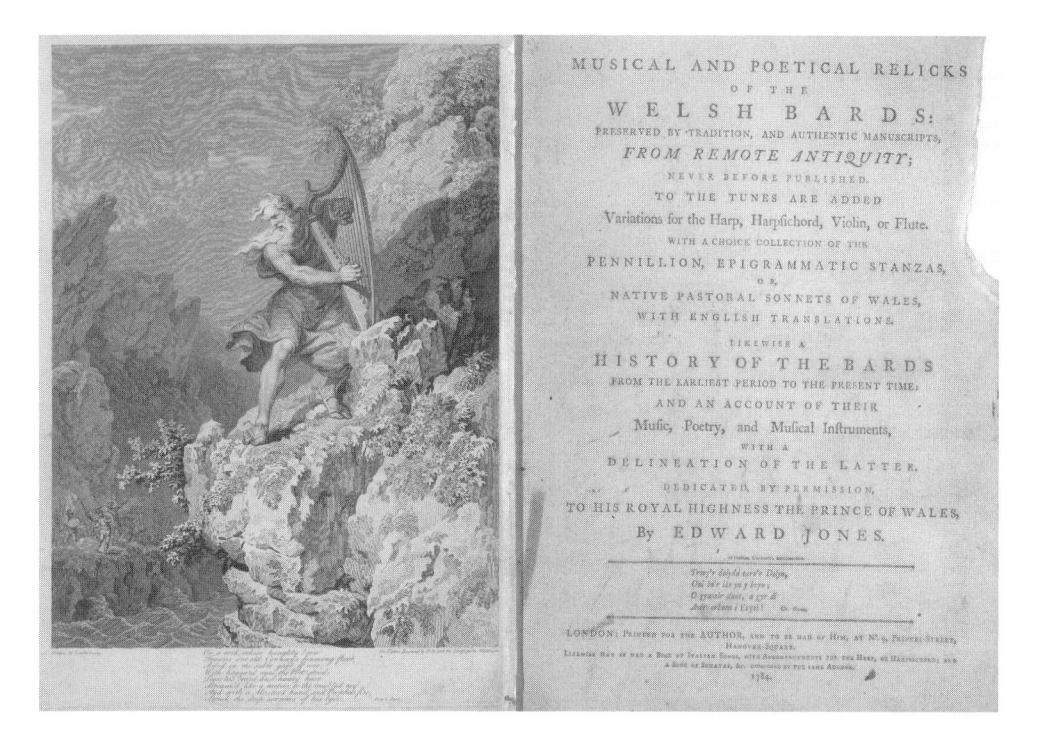

Figure 2.2 Charles Hall and Samuel Middiman, after Phillippe-Jacques de Loutherbourg, frontispiece and title-page from Edward Jones, *Musical and Poetical Relicks of the Welsh Bards* (1784). Engraving and letterpress. Yale Center for British Art, Paul Mellon Collection.

Appropriately, the image was used facing the title-page in Edward Jones's *Musical and Poetical Relicks of the Welsh Bards*, 1784 (see Figure 2.2).

    All of these examples allude more or less explicitly to Gray, thus functioning as extensions or illustrations of his poem. The poem is itself insistently pictorial: its images are composed in an inherently painterly manner (whether it is the figure of the bard poised on his cliff, or the way the bard and Edward face off against each other in the same frame).[25] And as Jean Hagstrum has commented, 'in the "Bard" Gray has achieved unity of pictorial form: he presents in a single scene, the entire action of the poem', effectively distilling the historical narrative into one controlling image.[26] Hagstrum comments specifically on how the poem points back to the European pictorial traditions Gray admired, while Lawrence Lipking extends that argument by emphasizing the extent to which Gray's bard is himself an image maker.[27] Weaving his prophetic tapestry out of visions, it is his function to *see*:

'In yon bright track, that fires the western skies,
'They melt, they vanish from my eyes.
'But oh! What solemn scenes on Snowdon's height
'Descending slow their glitt'ring skirts unroll?
'Visions of glory, spare my aching sight,
'Ye unborn Ages, crowd not on my soul!
'No more our long-lost Arthur we bewail.
'All-hail, ye genuine Kings, Britannia's Issue, hail! (103–10)

With the bard's fatal plunge, the canvas of the poem is effectively 'emptied of its central figure': the poem comes to a sudden apocalyptic end. Yet throughout the poem Gray has put himself in the bard's shoes, seen through his eyes (as he said, 'I felt myself the Bard'), and celebrated unequivocally a visionary mode of perception, 'a primitive power of seeing', that operates under conditions of 'heroic difficulty'.[28] Some of this, paradoxically, would not seem to lend itself easily to pictorial illustration, insofar as the bard has already visualized – and illustrated – what has occurred.

II Illustrating Gray

Although it has been argued that the requirements of book illustration are different to those of painting, perhaps demanding closer adherence to a textual source, it is often the case in the period that the two are closely intertwined (as the examples above of the work of Fuseli and de Loutherbourg, destined for use in books, reveal), and in the case of 'The Bard', there is notable continuity in the choice and arrangement of central motifs. Among the earliest illustrations of Gray's poems were the designs by Richard Bentley, undertaken at the instigation of Horace Walpole, and published by Robert Dodsley in 1753. This book, *Designs by Mr. R. Bentley, for Six Poems by Mr. T. Gray*, which was immediately successful and went through six further editions by 1789, has been hailed as a 'milestone in the history of book illustration'.[29] Loftus Jestin argues, in his study of these illustrations, that rather than offering miscellaneous and 'mechanical' embellishments, Bentley made the volume 'thematically and pictorially coherent', largely by developing its main themes in an integrated way 'not surpassed until William Blake's work in the 1780s'.[30] Gray expressed his satisfaction with this enterprise in verse, in his 'Stanzas to Mr. Bentley', where he praised his capacity to bid 'the pencil answer to the lyre', such that 'each transitory thought / Fixed by his touch[,] a lasting essence take[s]'.[31] This observation is anticipated rather wittily by Bentley in the title-page vignette, which depicts the poet as Apollo at his lyre – and the artist as an eager ape, sitting at a canvas nearby, brush at the ready.

Bentley's work centred on six of Gray's odes. 'The Bard' was not one of them, although Bentley prepared a number of preliminary studies for a volume to be published separately by Walpole's Strawberry Hill Press (along with 'The Progress of Poesy') in 1757. These are not uniformly successful at capturing the dramatic nature of the poem. Certainly, Walpole was enthusiastic about the prospect of these drawings being engraved, and wrote to Bentley: 'Nothing but you, or Salvator Rosa, and Nicolo Poussin, can paint up to the expressive horror and dignity of it … Now the two latter are dead, you must of necessity be Gray's painter'; Gray himself, however, had reservations about their effectiveness and the publication never went forward.[32] In spite of this, in Dodsley's fifth edition of the poems that appeared in 1766, we find a tailpiece supplied by Bentley at the end of 'The Bard', which subsequently appeared in William Sleater's pirated 1768 edition, facing the title-page: this image, which captures the bard mid-leap at the conclusion of the poem, is thought to have informed de Loutherbourg's rendition in the early 1780s.[33]

Regarding other illustrated editions, there were at the other end of the spectrum from Bentley's artist's book a variety of smaller format texts that were rising in popularity, such as the pocket-books of British poems, novels, and classics, published as serials, for example Bell's *Poets of Great Britain* (1777–82), and Cooke's *Cheap and Elegant Pocket Library* (1794–1805). These books, and the reprint industry to which they often belonged, are noteworthy at the very least for the opportunities they created for artists and illustrators, since it became standard practice to include an engraved title-page, frontispiece, and sometimes also portrait of the author. As William St Clair has pointed out, many of the best-known artists of the period (such as Stothard, Fuseli, Opie, Turner, and Westall) came to prominence as painters after being employed to produce designs for such illustrations.[34] A series such as Bell's shaped and legitimated the English literary canon, not least by giving it the visual embellishment it was felt to merit. These pocket-sized texts are also of interest for the use they made of the 'British Bard' as a marketing tool.

A volume of Gray's poems appeared in Bell's edition of *The Poets of Great Britain* in 1782, the 95th volume of 109 – a volume shared with Richard West, and one of the very few in the second half of that series not to have been drawn by Stothard (it included an engraved frontispiece drawn by Biagio Rebecca and engraved by Robert Marcuard).[35] In Cooke's *Pocket Library*, Gray featured in 1795 as the 13th of 136 volumes.[36] Cooke's series was marketed in an innovative way: price, and the desires of the purchaser, dictated the number of illustrations. A key selling point was that each edition would include a 'scenic representation' of a passage in the text (where it would be inserted), and for twice the price, the purchaser could have a portrait of the poet and 'a "Vignette Frontispiece" in each volume that served (like Bell's) as a series half-title page'.[37] This emphasis on illustration was reflected on the elaborate title-pages, which for the first 30 or so volumes read in full: *Cooke's Pocket Edition / of the Original & Complete Works of / Select British Poets, / or Entertaining Poetical Library / containing the Poetic Productions of the most / Esteemed British Bards, / Superbly Embellished*.[38]

The second edition in 1799 has an illustration of 'The Bard' as the central feature of an elaborate title-page.[39] This use of the Bard as an indicative image for Gray is noteworthy, and clearly in step with the general cultural investment in the figure of the bard discussed above. This moment does appear to pass, however, and by 1796 Cooke had dropped the line 'British Bards' from the title-pages.[40] For various reasons the power of the bard as a controlling metaphor had diminished, and so had its purchase on public sentiment. 'Bardic' nationalism, as Katie Trumpener argues, had been caught up in a strong sense of place, that is, in the relationship of landscape to the distant reaches of history (which readily provided subject matter for illustrations in volumes such as Cooke's).[41] Moreover, the bard operated, in Cooke's serial network, 'as a vehicle for bringing together an imagined community', for the term cropped up frequently as a kind of leitmotif in the prefaces, in relation to this or that poet.[42] Those references disappeared along with the 'Esteemed British Bards' of the title-pages, underscoring perhaps an ironic tension between the primitive force of the bardic legends, with their relationship to oral traditions, and a commercial enterprise such as Cooke's, with its tentacles deep into print culture and middle-class reading markets. The cult of the bard, dismissed by Samuel Johnson as 'a deluded retrojecting fantasy', stood increasingly uneasily alongside his professional men of letters thriving in the commercial marketplace (the kind of figures who populate his *Lives of the Poets*, 1779–81).[43]

Yet the figure persists as a symbol of poetic power long after Johnson's critique, and Trumpener's argument that late eighteenth-century nationalism(s) are more dialectical than we tend to appreciate is apposite here. As she points out, 'new losses invoke the old: the modernization process triggers cultural memory both because modernizers and improvers appear determined to suppress and replace it and because new forms of economic oppression are being joined to old forms of political oppression' (23). Certainly, Blake's interest in 'Ancient Britons' such as the druidic bards may be understood in these terms, where politics and culture conjoin. His representation of the bardic as tied up in *giving voice*, evident for example in the introduction to *Songs of Experience* (1794) – 'Hear the voice of the Bard! Who Present, Past, & Future sees' – draws much of its pedagogic imperative from his discomfort with the dissociation of poetry and song inflicted by the 'mechanical' and disembodied nature of print. It would not be too outlandish to suggest that Blake's visual productions work equally hard to shore up the defences of the prophetic imagination, and toward an understanding of 'illustration', broadly understood, as a potentially generative and original practice.

III Blake and the Bard

In the late 1790s, when numerous editions of Gray's poems were published that package the poet and his work along clearly established lines, Blake produced his own illustrations. Although there is no evidence for exactly when Blake first encountered Gray's poems, it is generally held that it was early in his life (likely in the mid-1770s) and that they made a deep impression.[44] 'The Bard', as Geoffrey Keynes remarks, clearly caught Blake's attention, with its combination of 'drama, legend, imagination and prophetic utterance'.[45] He exhibited a watercolour illustration of 'The Bard, from Gray' at the Royal Academy in 1785 (the image is untraced – yet another lost bard).[46] Blake's illustrations to Gray were produced in 1797–98 as a private commission, by the sculptor John Flaxman, as a birthday present for his wife Ann. She records this in a letter that exalts Blake as a '*Nature Poet he* &c one who has sung his wood notes wild – of a strong & singular Imagination – he has treated his Poet most Poetically – Flaxman has employ'd him to Illuminate the works of Gray for my Library.'[47] This figuring of Blake and his undertaking in terms drawn from nature is suggestively echoed by Blake himself in a couplet that appears under his list of designs for Gray's 'Ode on the Spring': 'Around the springs of Gray my wild root weaves / Traveller repose & dream among my leaves.'[48] At the end of the series is a dedicatory poem to Ann that extends the organic metaphor ('A little Flower grew in a lonely Vale') in a fascinating allegory of both Blake's educative purpose and effect in relation to Ann, and his accomplishment in transplanting Gray's verses themselves to 'a Mountains brow' through illustration, where they can better flourish.[49]

Where Bentley's illustrations succeeded in 'perfectly catching Gray's stylish irony', most evident perhaps in poems such as 'Ode on the Death of a Favourite Cat', Blake's proceed along two fronts, 'correcting' Gray's potentially limiting melancholy turn – what Irene Tayler calls 'his pallid caution, [...] his retreat from life' – and also tapping into, exposing perhaps, the power often latent in his poems.[50] In Blake's approach to Gray's later poems in particular ('The Bard', 'The Fatal Sisters', 'The Descent of Odin', and 'The Triumphs of Owen'), which reference legendary themes that foreground drama and violence, Tayler observes that 'the designs less often illustrate half-obscured implications of the language, more often draw on the subject matter itself; and the composition is correspondingly more daring and advanced, with new and exciting uses of angle and perspective and of the allotment of space on the page'.[51] This is clearly the case with Blake's energetic re-imagining of 'The Bard'. The image for the title-page of the poem is evocative if somewhat static: in a visual echo of the design for 'The Voice of the Ancient Bard', first composed for *Songs of Innocence* (1789), a statuesque bard, in flowing, starry robes, stands facing the viewer – holding the enormous harp standing beside *him* as though it were a sign or a lamp-post.[52] Blake's third design, however, which corresponds to the opening of the poem – 'The Bard weaving Edward's fate' (see Figure 2.3) – is vigorous and concentrated.

The vast strings plucked by the bard, here thick ropes dripping with blood, reference the 'warp' of Edward's fate (i.e. the woven tissue of his winding sheet). The image is spare, with a powerful downward movement that is carried forward into the sixth design, in which the trio of slaughtered bards is depicted gripping similarly rope-like harp strings, which in this case also form the cliff-side to which they cling.[53] These are the relevant lines from Gray:

> 'On yonder cliffs, a griesly band,
> 'I see them sit, they linger yet,
> 'Avengers of their native land:
> 'With me in dreadful harmony they join,
> 'And weave with bloody hands the tissue of thy line.' (44–8)

Among the 14 watercolour designs there are others that depict the bard (or bards) directly, such as the second, illustrating the advertisement, in which 'The Slaughtered Bards', arrayed in white (and identified by Keynes as indicative of the present, the past, and the future) are laid out on the ground.[54] The three bards appear again in the tenth and the eleventh designs, in observing and supporting roles in scenes from a future as yet to unfold (the death of Edward's queen, Eleanor; the advent of Elizabeth I), implicitly part of the central vision of the principal narrator-bard. The final

Figure 2.3 William Blake, *The Bard*; Page 2: Advertisement, Object 54 (Butlin 335.54). Yale Center for British Art. Copyright © 2017 William Blake Archive. Used with permission.

design captures his fatal plunge (here, more of a clear-eyed and graceful dive, now that his work is complete) with a lightness of touch. What Blake brings together, across the sequence, are two opposed functions of the prophet, as Frank Vaughan helpfully makes clear.[55] The prophet for Blake is one who clearly sees (and says) what *is*, what forces obtain in the moment, and who can correctly identify where they could lead (this is not the same as being in passive possession of knowledge regarding a pre-determined fate). A prophecy, then, such as that seized upon and expressed by the central bard from Gray's poem, involves both a warning and a depiction: the former perhaps most naturally takes verbal form – the form of a text – and the latter, an image.

No discussion of Blake's illustrations to Gray's poems would be complete without a consideration of his materials and technique, which were similar to his procedures for Edward Young's *Night Thoughts*, an undertaking that he had completed immediately prior to his work on Gray. Blake made use of the same large sheets of Whatman paper, into which he cut vertical rectangular 'windows', where he mounted the pages of the letterpress text of *Poems by Mr. Gray*, taken from an octavo edition published in London by John Murray in 1790. To this end, Blake completely dismantled the book, and then reconstructed it (at the end of the process his sheets were rebound), hence his 'leaves'. Gray's poems, printed on paper thin enough for the text printed on one side to be visible on the other, were carefully glued into these slightly off-centre openings, with the original sequence preserved. Around them, in a literal 'picture-frame', Blake produced his designs – generally indicating with an 'x' the specific lines to which they refer. All of the descriptions I have read use the term 'window' to describe what Blake has created, which naturally implies something one can look through: what he has effected materially thus speaks for the more metaphorical sense in which he creates openings in Gray's poems, or rather opens up Gray's text, to the new vistas that his illustrations can offer. This point is underscored, paradoxically, by the fact that the 'windows' are in fact blocked up with text, and with blocks of text, which are comparatively uninteresting to look at. In fact, these slabs of text, though printed on paper that is somewhat transparent, suggest tombstones, sites of inscription suitable perhaps for an epitaph ('Traveller repose and dream among my leaves'), superimposed upon a landscape of dynamic, coloured, fluid form. One has to look, thus, around the text in more ways than one. And typically, forms appear to exist behind the text boxes, where the design, we are to suppose (but can only imagine), continues.

Blake's watercolour illustrations of Gray were clearly unique objects, not easily reproducible, and intended for private consumption, but they look forward to new techniques in printing that would make it possible to integrate the letterpress and the engraving in the process of production – even though, as Vaughan argues, on the level of scale and interest, the tension between text and image (indeed the explicit lack of integration between the two) makes a deliberate statement not just about Blake's independent approach to Gray, but also about the act of illustration.[56] Certainly, the project as a whole pushes the boundaries of the 'book' in fascinating ways. On the one hand, Gray's *Poems* are a book taken into and reconstituted by another, while Blake's illustrated Gray is an instance of the book unbound in more ways than one, with its elements of extra-illustration and its suggestion of a portable literary gallery.[57]

IV Blake's 1809 Exhibition

In May 1809, Blake mounted an exhibition of his work in the Soho hosiery shop of his brother, in Broad Street, Golden Square.[58] This was a somewhat unusual venture, given the relative novelty of art exhibitions, as Martin Myrone has shown – although he also points out that Blake was among a number of artists setting up their own shows out of dissatisfaction with the status quo at the Royal Academy.[59] Blake's argumentative *Descriptive Catalogue* was also to some extent in step with developments around him: that it begins with 'Conditions of Sale' suggests a relationship with other commercial ventures in the way of exhibition making – and the title, *Descriptive Catalogue*, was being used to accompany various ambitious exhibition programs as well as for sale catalogues.[60] Nevertheless, the exhibition was famously unsuccessful, with few visitors, no paintings sold, and a scathing review in *The Examiner* that dismissed Blake as an 'unfortunate lunatic' and his catalogue as 'the wild ebullitions of a distempered brain'.[61]

The relationship between exhibition and illustration had meanwhile been clearly established – from the example of the literary galleries, to the display at Royal Academy summer exhibitions of paintings that would serve as the basis for illustrative engravings, and to instances of publishers, such as Cooke, who devoted gallery space at the back of his shop to the exhibition of the originals.[62] Blake's exhibition itself serves to illustrate in the broader sense of the term: the work in it exemplifies a set of passionately held principles, and that work of illustration is also extended in the *Descriptive Catalogue* that accompanied the paintings (where text illustrates image). Those principles include reviving the 'grand style in art' by painting in fresco, or watercolour, effectively making a deliberate return to older forms and ideas about image-making that would bring new (old) power back to artistic production in his time (a gesture that would perhaps support Trumpener's claim about 'new losses invoking the old'). Blake wrote: 'Clearness and precision have been the chief objects in painting these Pictures. Clear colours unmuddied by oil, and firm and determinate lineaments unbroken by shadows, which ought to display and not to hide form, as is the practice of the latter Schools of Italy and Flanders.'[63] This is, I'd suggest, another act of opening, a gesture that repeats something of Blake's undertaking in relation to Gray's poems: here, though, the *surround* is the text that both frames Blake's endeavour in mounting the exhibition and focuses attention on the individual works.

Of the 16 pictures on display in Blake's exhibition, the fourth picture was Blake's painting of *The Bard, from Gray*, executed in tempera (with gold – see Figure 2.4).

Blake's description makes details of the scene clear to the viewer:

> King Edward and his Queen Elenor are prostrated, with their horses, at the foot of a rock on which the Bard stands; prostrated by the terrors of his harp on the margin of the river Conway, whose waves bear up a corse of a slaughtered bard at the foot of the rock. The armies of Edward are seen winding among the mountains.[64]

The figures of Mortimer and Gloucester also 'lie spellbound behind their king'. The bards (again, three) are weaving the winding sheet from the strings of their broken harps, seen also in Blake's illustrations to Gray. In his biography of Blake, Peter Ackroyd describes this painting as confident and exuberant: 'with its sweeping contours like long lines of energy emanating from the artist himself, it affords an extraordinary sensation of power, of violence and of exaltation'.[65] The painting also reiterates Blake's revolutionary insistence on 'the moral and social power of the inspired bard', as David Erdman puts it – and it is noteworthy that another painting in the exhibition, *The Ancient Britons*, also featured 'the swan song of a patriotic bard "singing to his harp" in defiance of armed invaders'.[66]

In his catalogue entry, Blake cites lines from Gray ('On a rock, whose haughty brow / Frown'd o'er old Conway's foaming flood', etc.) and comments that 'weaving the winding sheet of Edward's race by means of sounds of spiritual music and its accompanying expressions of articulate speech is a bold, and daring, and most masterly conception, that the public have embraced and approved with avidity'.[67] Later in the entry, Blake defends the visions of the prophets, who exercise their 'imaginative and immortal organs', against his critics: 'A Spirit and a Vision are not, as the modern philosophy supposes, a cloudy vapour or a nothing' but rather 'organized and minutely articulated beyond all that the mortal and perishing nature can produce'.[68] Blake concludes: 'He who does not imagine in stronger and better lineaments, and in stronger and better light than his perishing mortal eye can see does not imagine at all.' This speaks loudly for Blake's practice as an illustrator, and for his efforts to see, and to show, 'in a stronger and better light' than his contemporaries.

Figure 2.4 William Blake, *The Bard, from Gray* (c.1809). Copyright © Tate, London 2018.

In effect, to see so clearly is to illuminate, but to illuminate (or illustrate) in this manner is also to generate. It is in this passage of the *Descriptive Catalogue* that Blake attacks the critical orthodoxy that pictures (like prophets) should simply mimic the real: 'shall Painting be confined to the sordid drudgery of fac-simile representations of merely mortal and perishing substances, and not be as poetry and music are, elevated into its own proper sphere of invention and visionary conception? No, it shall not be so.'[69]

Notes

1 Jean Hagstrum estimates that Blake produced around 1,200 such images. *William Blake: Poet and Painter* (Chicago, IL: University of Chicago Press, 1964), 119.
2 For an excellent account of Blake's long career as a commercial engraver, see Robert N. Essick, *William Blake's Commercial Book Illustrations: A Catalogue and Study of the Plates Engraved by Blake after Designs by Other Artists* (Oxford: Clarendon Press, 1991). In the 1780s, over half of these commissions came through Blake's friendship with Thomas Stothard, while later relationships with Joseph Johnson, William Hayley, Henry Fuseli, and John Flaxman 'directly or indirectly determined most of his commissions as a reproductive engraver until 1820' (7). Essick argues convincingly for the importance of this work for the development of Blake's own composite art, and for the development of the pictorial 'as a medium for symbolic representation interacting with the text but not bound to it' (15).
3 See for example Kay Parkhurst Easson, 'Blake and the Art of the Book', *Blake in his Time*, ed. Robert N. Essick and Donald Pearce (Bloomington, IN; London: Indiana University Press, 1978), 35–52. Easson examines how Blake imaginatively reworks three common features of book illustration (decorative, textual, and full-page) in the eighteenth century, and shows 'points of contact between Blake's commercial career as copy engraver and his vocation as book artist' (36).
4 Martin Meisel, *Realizations: Narrative, Pictorial, and Theatrical Arts in Nineteenth-Century England* (Princeton, NJ: Princeton University Press, 1983), 30.
5 For a more sustained examination of this use of 'illustration', see my essay 'Poetry and Illustration: "Amicable Strife,"' *A Companion to Romantic Poetry*, ed. Charles Mahoney (Malden, MA: Wiley-Blackwell, 2011).
6 Gray had begun the poem as early as 1754, but left it unfinished until his encounter with Parry, who performed in Cambridge in 1757, suggested the way forward. As Gray wrote to Mason in May of that year, 'Mr. Parry has been here, & scratch'd out such ravishing blind Harmony, such tunes of a thousand year old with names enough to choak you, as have set all this learned body a'dancing, & inspired them with due reverence for *Odikle* [*The Bard*], whenever it shall appear.' *The Complete Poems of Thomas Gray*, ed. H. W. Starr and J. R. Hendrickson (Oxford: Oxford University Press, 1966), 208.
7 *The Complete Poems of Thomas Gray*, 18.
8 *The Complete Poems of Thomas Gray*, 208.
9 Gray own notes tell us that 'The image (of the Bard) was taken from a well-known picture of Raphael, representing the Supreme Being in the Vision of

Ezekiel.' Elsewhere, Gray is known to have claimed inspiration from another painting, Parmigianino's 'Moses'. See the discussion in Jean H. Hagstrum, *The Sister Arts: The Tradition of Literary Pictorialism and English Poetry from Dryden to Gray* (Chicago, IL; London: University of Chicago Press, 1958), 311–12. Richard Altick points out a likely textual source in Milton, since it recalls his description of Azazel's banner in *Paradise Lost* (1. 537), which 'Shone like a meteor streaming to the wind'. *Paintings from Books: Art and Literature in Britain, 1760–1900* (Columbus: Ohio State University Press, 1985), 394.

10 Cf. his fragmentary 'The Triumph of Owen', one of a series of fragments that imitated Old Norse poetry. See Sandro Jung, *The Fragmentary Poetic: Eighteenth-Century Uses of an Experimental Mode* (Bethlehem: Lehigh University Press, 2009), 40.

11 Jung, *The Fragmentary Poetic,* 42.

12 Ian Balfour, *The Rhetoric of Romantic Prophecy* (Stanford, CA: Stanford University Press, 2002), 30–31.

13 For a detailed account of Gray's complex influences, and their impact in turn on Blake's deployment of the bard in poems such as *Milton*, see Jason Whittaker, *William Blake and the Myths of Britain* (Houndmills, Basingstoke, Hampshire: Macmillan Press; New York: St. Martin's Press, 1999), 59–113.

14 Katie Trumpener, *Bardic Nationalism: The Romantic Novel and the British Empire* (Princeton, NJ: Princeton University Press, 1997), 6.

15 Trumpener, *Bardic Nationalism,* 6. Peter Lord explores some of the complexities in the evolution and deployment of the image of the bard, by both Welsh and English artists and intellectuals, in the period leading up to the 1820s. See 'The Bard – Celticism and Visual Culture', in *Gwenllian: Essays on Visual Culture* (Llandysul, Dyfed, Wales: Gomer, 1994), 103–28. Lord comments that 'the Bard is an ambiguous image, inconsistent and riddled with self-delusion, an image of all things to all people, and yet an image central to the evolution of the Welsh mind' (112).

16 Altick, *Paintings from Books,* 395.

17 Altick, *Paintings from Books,* 33.

18 See Malcolm Andrews, *The Search for the Picturesque: Landscape Aesthetics and Tourism in Britain, 1760–1800* (Aldershot: Scolar Press, 1989), 128.

19 The painting was first exhibited at the Royal Academy in 1800, and in the catalogue Turner included the following lines of verse, thought to be his own: 'And now on Arvon's haughty tow'rs / The Bard the song of pity pours, / For oft on Mona's distant hills he sighs, / Where jealous of the minstrel band, / The tyrant drench'd with blood the land, / And charm'd with horror, triumph'd in their cries, / The swains of Arvon round him throng, / And join the sorrows of his song.' See the painting and the catalogue entry on the *Tate* website, www.tate.org.uk. Accessed 22 January 2018, www.tate.org.uk/art/artworks/turner-caernarvon-castle-north-wales-d04164

20 See *Tate* website. Accessed 22 January 2018, www.tate.org.uk/art/artworks/turner-the-destruction-of-the-bards-by-edward-i-d04168
21 Yet another painting, *Dolbadern Castle, North Wales* (RA 1800), is part of this conversation. See Eric Shanes, *The Life and Masterworks of J. M. W. Turner* (New York: Parkstone Press, 2008), 86–7.
22 See the *Yale Center for British Art* website, www.britishart.yale.edu. Accessed 22 January 2018. http://interactive.britishart.yale.edu/art-in-focus-wales/185/the-bard
23 Robert Hunt, 'Royal Academy Exhibition', in *The Examiner* (21 May 1809), 331.
24 Altick, *Paintings from Books,* 396. The version published in the text may be consulted on the *Thomas Gray Archive* website, www.thomasgray.org.
25 F. I. McCarthy points this out in '*The Bard* of Thomas Gray: Its Composition and its Use by Painters', *National Library of Wales Journal*, 14: 1 (Summer, 1965): 107.
26 Hagstrum, *The Sister Arts*, 306.
27 Ibid., 307–14. Lawrence Lipking, 'Quick Poetic Eyes: Another Look at Literary Pictorialism', *Articulate Images: The Sister Arts from Hogarth to Tennyson*, ed. Richard Wendorf (Minneapolis: University of Minnesota Press, 1983), 22–23.
28 Ibid., 23.
29 Loftus Jestin, *The Answer to the Lyre: Richard Bentley's Illustrations for Thomas Gray's Poems* (Philadelphia: University of Pennsylvania Press, 1990), 83.
30 Ibid., 85. See p. 87 for an elaboration of the 'contrapuntal' effects created between poet and artist, and how 'the suggestion of extratextual pictorial analogues [Bentley's additions and extensions to the text] undercuts the prettiness of the scenes and helps to make visual Gray's verbal exposure of vanity and self-deception' (87).
31 Ibid., 94–5.
32 McCarthy, '*The Bard* of Thomas Gray', 108. See also Jestin's account of their inadequacy to the poem, *The Answer to the Lyre,* 218–20.
33 Ibid., 101, 220–1.
34 William St Clair, *The Reading Nation in the Romantic Period* (Cambridge: Cambridge University Press, 2004), 134.
35 Thomas F. Bonnell, *The Most Disreputable Trade: Publishing the Classics of English Poetry 1765–1810* (Oxford: Oxford University Press, 2008), 102.
36 Ibid., 234, 242.
37 Ibid., 232.
38 Ibid., 245. For evidence of the attractiveness of the volumes, one might recall here Leigh Hunt's reminiscence of how he had 'doted on their size; … their type, their ornaments, on their wrappers, containing lists of other poets, and on the engravings from Kirk' (238–9).
39 The image may be consulted on the *Thomas Gray Archive* website. Accessed 11 November 2017, www.thomasgray.org/cgi-bin/view.cgi?collection=primary&edition=1799&text=bapo#panel_diglib. The next (and only other) edition of Gray's

poems to foreground 'The Bard' in this way is the 1826 *Poetical Works* printed for John Sharpe.

40 See Bonnell, *The Most Disreputable Trade,* 250–1.
41 Trumpener, *Bardic Nationalism,* 33; Bonnell, 248.
42 Bonnell, *The Most Disreputable Trade,* 249.
43 This is Trumpener's apt phrase in *Bardic Nationalism*, 79; see also Bonnell, *The Most Disreputable Trade,* 250. For more on Johnson's views of Gray's poem, and of his 1774 Welsh tour (in contrast to Gray's response to Wales, and to Parry's music), see J. R. Watson, 'Wordsworth, North Wales and the Celtic Landscape', *English Romanticism and the Celtic World*, ed. Gerard Carruthers and Alan Rawes (Cambridge: Cambridge University Press, 2003), 87–93. It should be pointed out however that in Wales at least, the power of the iconography associated with the 'Druid-Bard' persisted right through the nineteenth and into the twentieth century. See Lord, 114–28.
44 See Irene Tayler's discussion of this point in *Blake's Illustrations to the Poems of Gray* (Princeton, NJ: Princeton University Press, 1971), 14.
45 Introduction to William Blake, Thomas Gray, and Geoffrey Keynes, *William Blake's Water-Colour Designs for the Poems of Thomas Gray* (London: Eyre Methuen Ltd; Paris: Trianon Press, 1972), 1.
46 Ibid., 1–2, for further details.
47 The text of this letter was first made public by Mary Woodworth in *Notes and Queries* (August 1970), 312–13. The typographical oddities are in the original.
48 Blake's illustrations to Gray's *Poems* may be consulted on the *Blake Archive* website, www.blakearchive.org, where they are fully digitized. For this design, see www.blakearchive.org/copy/but335.1?descId=but335.1.wc.02 (accessed 22 January 2018).
49 Jon Saklofske advances a reading of Blake's relationship to Gray that is grounded in the language Blake uses in these significant additions to the text, and argues that Blake's contribution (the weaving in of his 'wild root') works to fundamentally renew, perhaps even re-generate, Gray's inherent enlightenment perspectives, through reflective and expanded perception. 'A Fly in the Ointment: Exploring the Creative Relationship Between William Blake and Thomas Gray', *Word & Image: A Journal of Verbal/Visual Enquiry* 19: 3 (2003): 166–79.
50 Irene Tayler, 'Two Eighteenth-Century Illustrators of Gray', *Fearful Joy; Papers from the Thomas Gray Bicentenary Conference at Carleton University*, ed. James Downey and Ben Jones (Montreal: McGill-Queen's University Press, 1974), 121, 122.
51 Tayler, *Blake's Illustrations to the Poems of Gray*, 94. Tayler's description of the entire sequence, 94–109, is detailed and clear.
52 In copy B of the *Songs of Innocence*, held at the Library of Congress, this earlier image of the bard is Object 13. See the *Blake Archive*, www.blakearchive.org/copy/s-inn.b?descId=s-inn.b.illbk.13 (accessed 22 January 2018).
53 Frank A. Vaughan reads the difference between these first images in terms of a Blakean development, in which the initial depiction of the bard as 'rigid and

vacuous' is meant to convey his mental state, and subsequently, in the next designs, its underlying causes. 'Blake's Illustrations to Gray's "The Bard"', *Colby Quarterly* 17: 4 (December, 1981), 214–8. At issue in the third design and its depiction of the bard are the inherent limitations of violent wrath and its naked expression in the form of vengeance, which for Blake must always be tempered by clear-sighted, honest speech (218–20), and ultimately, for the bards, by patience (237). Vaughan's ideas are further developed in his book-length study, *Again to the Life of Eternity: William Blake's Illustrations to the Poems of Thomas Gray* (Selinsgrove, PA: Susquehanna University Press; London: Associated University Press, 1996). See also Tayler's discussion of this issue in *Blake's Illustrations*, 115–6.

54 Blake, Gray, and Keynes, *William Blake's Water-Colour Designs*, 57.
55 See Vaughan, *Again to the Life of Eternity*, 212–13.
56 Vaughan proposes that Blake's retention of the letterpress, whose effect is pointedly antithetical to his vibrant designs, 'may be seen as an intended assertion of an opposition between the public and mechanical vision of Gray and the private and spontaneous vision of Blake as it expands from the kernel in which it started.' *Again to the Life of Eternity*, 18–19.
57 Luisa Calè argues suggestively that features of Blake's illustrations to Young's *Night Thoughts* can be situated 'at the crossroads between the literary gallery ventures, medieval book illuminations and the visual format of the alternative printing techniques that Blake described in his 1793 prospectus'. 'Blake and the Literary Galleries', *Blake and Conflict*, ed. Sarah Haggarty and Jon Mee (Basingstoke: Palgrave Macmillan, 2009), 199–200. Although there are significant differences between the two projects (of the 537 designs Blake created for *Night Thoughts*, 43 *were* engraved and published), the Gray illustrations share some of these features, at least in terms of format.
58 See the description of this venture in G. E. Bentley, Jr, *The Stranger from Paradise: A Biography of William Blake* (New Haven, CT: Yale University Press, 2001), 325–33.
59 William Blake, *Seen in My Visions: A Descriptive Catalogue of Pictures*, ed. and introduction Martin Myrone (London: Tate Publishing, 2009), 14–18. All references to Blake's *Descriptive Catalogue* are to this volume.
60 Myrone, Introduction, *Seen in My Visions*, 20.
61 Myrone, 31–2. On the public response, which ranged from bafflement to outrage, see also Bentley, *The Stranger from Paradise*, 330–1.
62 St Clair, 134.
63 Blake, 44.
64 Blake, 67.
65 Blake, 289.
66 David V. Erdman, *Blake, Prophet against Empire: A Poet's Interpretation of the History of His Own Times* (Princeton, NJ: Princeton University Press, 1969),

49. On the scope, composition, and loss of Blake's (by all accounts) remarkable *Ancient Britons*, see also Bentley, *The Stranger from Paradise,* 326–7.
67 Blake, *Seen in my Visions*, 65–6.
68 Blake, *Seen in my Visions*, 66–7.
69 Blake, *Seen in my Visions*, 66.

3 | Seeing History: Illustration, Poetic Drama, and the National Past

DUSTIN M. FRAZIER WOOD

Introduction

In 1845, the engraver John Pye reflected that 'the first features of the people's new source of knowledge and pleasure' – that is, illustration – had emerged not in a gallery or a work of creative literature, but in Paul Rapin's *History of England*, published serially in 1732–33 with illustrations by George Vertue. According to Pye, the work 'opened a field for engraving in England' that inspired the ambitious projects of William Hogarth and John Pine.[1] The success of Rapin's *History* also inspired other publishers to issue illustrated histories and historical images to meet the demands of buyer-viewer-readers across an increasingly broad market. By the 1780s it was possible for an artist such as James Northcote to turn for his living from portraiture to 'small historical and fancy subjects from the most popular authors of the day … sure of sale amongst the minor print dealers'.[2] Both Northcote's contemporary and Pye's retrospective observations highlight the multi-disciplinarity of early Romantic illustration production, the importance of format, cost, and distribution of illustrations, and an appreciation for the wider visual culture in which any given illustration circulated and signified, all features of modern illustration studies. However, the division into distinct academic disciplines of what eighteenth-century writers regularly referred to as literature seems to be mirrored in the separation of illustrated histories from illustrated poetry, prose, and drama in illustration studies. Although both types of work have received much needed critical attention, the links between the illustrations in printed histories and those in editions of imaginative literature remain underexplored.[3]

The links between history and literature are important thematically as well as artistically. Historical subjects provided eighteenth-century writers with inspiration for poetry, fiction, and popular drama, which was itself rendered visual in frontispieces to printed scripts, portraits of contemporary dramatic celebrities, and decorative paintings and prints depicting actors such as David Garrick in the guise of any number of historical figures.[4] From the perspective of production, it must also be noted that few artists produced either illustrations or paintings in a single genre or for a single type of publication.⁵ Leigh Dillard and others have argued that any given illustration or set of illustrations should be understood not merely within the confines of the physical book in which it appears but within a 'spectrum of parallel visual responses'.⁶ That spectrum must be broad enough to cross the formal boundaries of eighteenth-century visual media and the generic and disciplinary ones from within which latter-day scholars cast a retrospective gaze on eighteenth-century and Romantic-era visual culture.

This chapter aims to demonstrate the importance of illustrated histories for the development of a more nuanced understanding of the ways in which illustrations engaged in conversation with one another both within and across genres, audiences, and media. I take as my case study a historical figure whose life was illustrated repeatedly in textual, visual, and dramatic modes in the second half of the eighteenth century: Elfrida, a now little-remembered tenth-century queen of Anglo-Saxon England. The evolution of Elfrida's image proceeded through a series of intentional and circumstantial interactions between text, image, and performance. Illustrations of Elfrida appeared in multiple genres (poetry, drama, history, reviews) and media (history paintings, decorative prints, book illustrations), each with its own audiences and its own conventions. The very existence of these contemporary, interwoven illustrations provides an opportunity for testing the nature of Dillard's 'spectrum of parallel visual responses' as well as Christina Ionescu's assertion that illustrations are not 'merely *reflective* of a historical and cultural context … [but] *constitutive* elements of discourse'.⁷ The sections that follow trace the textual and visual illustrations of Elfrida in the period c.1750 to c.1800, revealing the inseparability of these fields where representations of historical figures are concerned. It also reveals the operation of what are commonly considered to be Romantic attitudes toward history and historical figures at work in an Enlightenment tradition of popular literary and artistic medievalism.⁸

Because few figures from medieval history enjoy such an ambivalent reputation, or one so overtly shaped by the biases of posthumous representations, it is necessary to begin with biography. Ælfthryth (964/5-1000/1) in 973 became the first royal consort to be anointed and crowned Queen of England. In the words of a modern biographer, Elfrida (as Ælfthryth is more commonly known) is 'the archetypal wicked stepmother', remembered today largely for her presumed but unproven role in the death of her stepson Edward the Martyr in 978.⁹ This overly simplistic reputation persists despite scholarship that reveals her to have been an intelligent, resourceful, influential, and respected figure who played an active role in the ecclesiastical and secular politics of her day and whose legacy influenced the politics of late Anglo-Saxon and early Anglo-Norman England.[10] If today Elfrida plays a relatively minor role in histories of Anglo-Saxon England, however, in the second half of the eighteenth century she enjoyed a period of prominence as a notorious figure in histories of England, as a character in poetry and drama, and as the subject of history paintings, book illustrations, and decorative prints. Much of this prominence resulted from an imaginative engagement by authors with Elfrida's early life: the story of a beautiful, pious young woman trapped between the conflicting desires of her father, her husband, and her king provided ready material for the sentimental historiography and historical drama that Mark Phillips has identified as having emerged in the second quarter of the eighteenth century.[11] In addition, Elfrida's connection to major, celebrated historical figures such as King Edgar, Edward the Martyr, and Æthelred the Unready allowed her story to be co-opted into an important strain of British patriotic Anglo-Saxonist medievalism.[12] Each illustration of her life – whether textual, visual, or theatrical – operated alongside and in reference to the others, offering sometimes contrasting and sometimes complementary Elfridas, each of which played a part in shaping the composite image that has been passed down to the present day.

Elfrida in History

> *Q.* Had [King Edgar] any children?
> *A.* Yes … by his third wife, (the beautiful *Elfrida*) he had a son, (*Ethelred*) who succeeded *Edward* II. *Edgar* had murder'd *Elfrida*'s husband. […] Elfrida, to expiate her husband's death, (though she had no hand in it) erected, over the place where his blood was spilt, a monastery of nuns, to sing over him.
> […]
> *Q.* In what manner did [King Edward] die?
> *A.* Being one day hunting in a forest … he arrived at last at a country seat, (of his step-mother's *Elfrida*) call'd *Corvesgate*, or *Corf-castle* … This cruel princess, who saw him coming at a distance, order'd one of her servants to kill him; and the better to effect it, she ran out to meet him with a smiling countenance. The King telling her that he was athirst, she commanded some wine to be brought him; but just as he was beginning to drink, this wicked woman gave him two deep wounds in the body with a dagger.[13]

Perhaps no eighteenth-century text so succinctly reveals the conflict at the heart of historical accounts of Elfrida's life as John Lockman's *New History of England by Question and Answer*, from which this extract comes. An abridgement of Rapin's *History of England*, it follows Rapin (and, ultimately,

William of Malmesbury) in presenting an account of Elfrida that is both contradictory and 'affected by common misogynistic stereotypes', praising her as a faithful young wife and condemning her as a villainous older woman.[14] In a brief preface Lockman writes that English history 'affect[s] us in a stronger manner' than does classical history because it contains 'incidents which happen among [our] near relations'.[15] This framing encourages readers not only to sympathize with Elfrida but to understand her in genealogical terms, thus drawing her imaginatively nearer to readers who find themselves not quite so removed from the early medieval past as they might have thought.

Seeking to capitalize on the growing market for historical prints and portraits excited by George Vertue's illustrations for editions of Rapin published by James, John, and Paul Knapton, Thomas Astley commissioned a series of 32 copperplates for Lockman's *New History* that he first printed in 1747.[16] It is in this series that Elfrida makes her first appearance in illustrated form. Tellingly, she is not named in the caption to the image designed by Samuel Wale, which reads 'EDWARD the MARTYR Stabb'd by Order of his Mother in Law', a clear indication that either Astley, who commissioned the illustration, or Wale, who designed it, conceived of Elfrida in instrumental terms. (It is unlikely that Lockman was involved, as he refers to Elfrida as Edward's 'step-mother' as opposed to the colloquial 'mother in law'.[17]) In Wale's image, Elfrida stands looking up at Edward, who appears on horseback in a pose reminiscent of seventeenth-century equestrian portraits. Her outstretched hand suggests welcome and hospitality, reiterated by the cup in Edward's hand and the servant holding an empty salver waiting to receive it from him. Lurking behind the king is another of Elfrida's servants holding a poniard the blade of which, like the assassin's right arm, disappears out of the illustration's simple line frame. All the visual power and the viewer-reader's sympathy belongs to Edward, who remains unaware of the danger presented by his dissembling step-mother.

More significantly, Wale's image focuses the viewer-reader's attention on one episode from Elfrida's life, thereby tipping the balance in favour of a reading of Elfrida as a 'wicked woman'. It also simplifies Lockman's text in at least two ways. First, Lockman writes that Elfrida 'order'd one of her servants to kill [Edward]' but that she herself 'gave him two deep wounds in the body with a dagger', despite Rapin's observation that only the fourteenth-century chronicler Henry Knighton believed Elfrida had murdered Edward herself, in contradistinction to most other historians.[18] Wale's image removes all ambiguity by picturing Elfrida standing by while a man-servant prepares to stab the king. Second, Lockman follows Rapin in calling the legitimacy of Edward's canonization into question, and refers to him throughout as

Figure 3.1 William Sherlock after Samuel Wale, *Edward the Martyr Stabb'd by Order of his Mother in Law*. Engraving for the fifteenth edition of Locksman's *New History of England* (1752). Private collection.

Edward II, a more anti-monastic and perhaps anti-Catholic form than Rapin's 'Edward II, *the martyr*'. Wale again tends away from Lockman, simplifying and amplifying Edward's saintly status in his caption, and in doing so emphasizing the contrast between Edward's royal goodness and Elfrida's immorality. Even if, as seems possible, Wale designed this illustration based on a reading of Rapin's rather than Lockman's text, he offered his viewer-readers neither one author's interpretation nor the other, but a reading of his own. Despite the relatively unsophisticated nature of the illustration published by Astley, Wale's image typifies the complex relationship between text and image even at the non-elite end of the reading and publishing spectrum, serving, in Ionescu's words, to 'invite the reader to view the text in a different light while it draws him in aesthetically'.[19]

Wale's design should also be considered in relation to the other three illustrations that Astley commissioned to represent England's Anglo-Saxon past. These include the battle of Guy of Warwick and the Danish giant Colbrand, the coronation of Alfred the Great by Pope Hadrian II, and King Canute ordering the sea to retire as a remonstrance to sycophantic courtiers. Each was an apocryphal episode that had entered into folklore as a result of its popularity in the ballad tradition (Guy of Warwick) or earlier historians' embroidering of accounts from medieval sources (Alfred and Canute).[20] Even though Lockman relates all three episodes as fact, Rapin does not mention Guy and Colbrand or Alfred's coronation, and presents the story of Canute at the sea-side with the qualifier 'if there be no exaggeration in what Historians say of him'.[21] In the context of the episodic visual narrative Wale creates for Lockman's *New History*, Edward's death and Elfrida's role in it must share the sensational, folkloric qualities of the other three images. Wale's illustrations thus present the viewer-reader not only with an alternative reading of Lockman's text and of the larger historical narrative, but with a second alternative narrative of national history based not on modern scholarly sources but on a series of traditional popular stories imaginatively brought to life in visual form.

Wale's image proved remarkably durable, becoming a stock image for illustrated histories of England until well into the nineteenth century. Wale himself created a more aesthetically sophisticated version of the same basic composition for Thomas Mortimer's *A New History of England*, which carried an engraving by Charles Grignion dedicated to Edward Stanley, Earl of Derby.[22] A retouched version appeared in numerous competing histories published over the next decade, including Temple Sydney's *A New and Complete History of England*, William Augustus Russel's *A New and Authentic History of England*, and George Frederick Raymond's

A New, Universal and Impartial History of England.[23] Wale's composition also served as the obvious inspiration for Edward Edwards' 'Edward the Martyr stabbed by order of his Step Mother ELFRIDA, at Corfe Castle in Dorsetshire', engraved by John Hall and first published by George Kearsley in 1776, later appearing in Edward Barnard's *The New, Impartial and Complete History of England*.[24] Aside from Thomas Mortimer's history, the inscribed plates of which suggest that publication relied heavily on the patronage of the dedicatees, each of these texts seem to have combined subscription and part-sales in order to reach a broad, popular reader-viewership. Sydney, Raymond, and Russel were each published by John Cooke, and Barnard by Alexander Hogg, Cooke's one-time employer. According to Thomas Bonnell, Cooke and Hogg were among the first and most successful purveyors of 'cheap "Paternoster Row numbers", or standard popular works issued in weekly parts', and Hogg's advertisement for Barnard's history puffs the work by declaring it 'not only the most perfect, complete, and impartial, but also the most elegant, cheap and superb Work of the Kind ever published'.[25] In each case, Wale's image would have been available for sixpence along with a section of the respective history. By Antony Griffiths' calculation, at that price these illustrations would have been affordable for a relatively large segment of the population that included skilled artisans as well as the middling sort and upper classes.[26] Each of the decorative printed frames surrounding these images contains a formulaic line indicating which history it was meant to accompany, usually displayed prominently at the top of the folio or quarto sheet, a common practice that enabled the illustrations to stand independently of their texts as a form of marketing that could double as a decorative object. Appearing in so many iterations of the same image firmly linked Elfrida to Edward's murder while simultaneously providing the potential for her to appear decoupled from any text, the illustration and its brief caption providing a hint from which new viewer-readers could construct their own imaginative versions of her story.

William Mason's *Elfrida* and Dramatic Illustration

Illustrations of Elfrida did not, however, remain solely focused on her presumed role in the death of Edward the Martyr or remain confined to histories of England. In 1752, John and Paul Knapton published William Mason's *Elfrida, A Dramatic Poem*, which dramatized Elfrida's relationship with her first husband, Athelwold, who according to tradition had been sent by King Edgar to discover if she was as beautiful as she was rumoured to be.[27] Instead of telling Edgar the truth, Athelwold had married Elfrida himself in secret and hidden her away in his castle, only to be found out later by Edgar who killed Athelwold and married Elfrida himself. Historians differed on Elfrida's role in this sequence of events, some accusing her of revealing herself to Edgar in order to become queen and others absolving her of all blame. Mason presented his title character as a sympathetic and praiseworthy figure whose wifely devotion outshone all of her other traits. Mason probably began work on the poem sometime in 1750, shortly after the publication of his 'Musæus' (1747) and 'Ode to Music' (1749). According to Thomas Gray, a close friend for whom Mason would later become biographer and literary executor, *Elfrida* 'is (unfortunately) in the manner of the ancient drama, with choruses, which I am, to my shame, the occasion of'.[28] In a letter to Horace Walpole, Gray reveals that Mason had begun the work as a poem but had intended to 'change it to a play fit for the stage', but that Gray had dissuaded him from doing so because he thought 'the lyric parts … the best of it'.[29] The resulting dramatic poem became a minor sensation, running to six editions by 1759.[30] A critic for the *Monthly Review* offered hyperbolic praise, writing that 'we dare almost venture to predict, that the author of *Elfrida* may one day be esteemed the first tragic writer of the present age, which this nation hath produced'.[31]

Although the same *Monthly Review* critic noted that '*Elfrida* was not intended for the stage', Mason seems to have intended it for performance all along. An undated entry in Mason's commonplace book labelled 'Elfrida' includes extracts relating to Elfrida from the list of English dramatists and their works appended to Thomas Whincop's *Scanderbeg*, and from Gerard Langbaine's *An Account of the English Dramatick Poets*.[32] Mason notes four works: Aaron Hill's *Elfrid, or the Fair Inconstant* 'acted with some success 1707' and *Athelwold* 'an alteration of the former' (Whincop), Rymer's *Edgar or the English Monarch* 'acted 1678 with no success', and Edward Ravenscroft's *King Edgar & Alphreda a Tragycomedy* of 1677 (Langbaine). He might also have used Langbaine's entry for Ravenscroft as a kind of reading list, as it contains the assertion that 'the Story of [Elfrida and Edgar] be sufficiently Famous, not only in Novels both *French* and *Italian*: but in almost all the Historians of those Times', followed by a list of historians stretching from William of Malmesbury to Petruccio Ubaldino, whose *Le vite delle Donne illustri del regno d'Inghilterra, & del regno di Scotia* Mason also noted.[33] Tellingly, Mason's *Elfrida* confines itself to the same episodes as the earlier plays, focusing on her marriage to Athelwold, King Edgar's discovery of Athelwold's deceit, and Athelwold's death.

In Mason's hands, Elfrida's story becomes one of virtue in distress, a departure from the historical account found in Rapin that the *Monthly Review* critic was quick to point out and to downplay. 'Our author has departed in only this one material circumstance; that, whereas the *historian* supposes *Elfrida* to have concurred in the catastrophe of her husband, the *poet* makes her a perfect pattern of conjugal tenderness and fidelity.'[34] Elfrida maintains her devotion to Athelwold, rejecting Edgar's advances and resisting her father's attempts to force her to marry the king. When Edgar kills Athelwold, Elfrida calls on her father, Orgar, to help her seek justice:

> ELFRIDA
> Inhospitably butcher'd;
> The Tyrant's savage self – Stand you thus cool?
> Where is the Saxon spirit, where the fire
> Of Offa's race? – O foolishness of grief!
> Alas, I had forgot; had Edgar spare'd him,
> That sword, to which my madness call'd for vengeance,
> Ere long was meant to do the bloody deed,
> And make the murder parricide. Have I
> No friend to do me right?[35]

Mason's references to Offa, the eighth-century King of Mercia, and to the 'Saxon spirit' of heroism and justice that stands opposed to the savagery of the 'Tyrant' Edgar reveal at least a passing familiarity with Anglo-Saxon history and tap into a strain of political Anglo-Saxonism apparent in Rapin's *History* and already familiar to the reading public from works such as James Thomson and David Mallet's *Alfred: A Masque*, the original vehicle for 'Rule, Britannia'.[36] Such narratives tended to contrast paternalistic, law-abiding kings such as Alfred with barbaric Danes or Normans, 'tyrants' who sought to replace English rule of law with foreign absolutism. In *Elfrida*, Edgar's behaviour renders him an un-Saxon or un-English tyrant rather than a good king – an act of historical revisionism that draws on medieval chroniclers' accounts of Edgar's lecherousness in order to cast Elfrida and Athelwold in a more positive light.[37] Elfrida's invocation of the Saxon spirit highlights her status as the only principal character who behaves correctly and virtuously.

If there are few traces of Malmesbury's conniving Elfrida or of the wicked stepmother familiar from Wale's illustrations, Mason's characterization replaces the misogyny of medieval chroniclers with the misogyny of Georgian conduct manuals. After Athelwold's death Orgar leaves to try and convince Edgar to marry Elfrida despite her grief; Elfrida vows to enter a nunnery as the ever-present chorus of British virgins sing an ode to constancy, piety, and virtue. The only roles available to Elfrida are those of daughter, wife, nun, or object of desire; she must withdraw from the world rather than challenge or compete with the men who surround her. Exhibiting neither political acumen nor independent agency, Mason's Elfrida is a character to be admired and pitied. As such, she stands in contrast to the earlier dramatic works that Mason discovered in Whincop's list. Aaron Hill's *Elfrid: or the Fair Inconstant*, performed in London just two decades before the publication of Mason's *Elfrida*, presented its title character as power-hungry and scheming. 'Were this King gone! or wou'd he never go! / I know not which of those to wish with Joy, / My Vertue points me one, one my Desire', she soliloquizes, before choosing Edgar for the power it will bring her and as retaliation for the now-repentant Athelwold's earlier duplicity.[38] Abandoning historical verisimilitude for tragic effect, Hill concludes the play with the deaths of both Elfrida and Athelwold, leaving Edgar to lament the loss of his friend, though not of his would-be lover. Hill's play flopped at Drury Lane in 1710, and neither its 1723 revival nor its later reworking under the name of *Athelwold*, in which the deaths are more spectacular and the dialogue more stilted than in the original, met with greater success.[39] Yet Mason's revision captured the public imagination. In the words of John Draper, *Elfrida* epitomized 'the true "she-tragedy" of the period, pathetic without ethos, tearful usually without cause: its subject was immaculate virtue in dire straits; and its method, Sentimentalism'.[40]

Despite a 'want of incidents, and of the usual variety of characters', *Elfrida* premiered at Covent Garden in 1772 in an unauthorized adaptation by one of the theatre's patentees, George Colman, with music by Thomas Arne.[41] Colman's original cast included Robert Bensley as Edgar, William 'Gentleman' Smith as Athelwold, Matthew Clarke as Orgar, and, most importantly, Elizabeth Hartley as Elfrida. The *Monthly Review* remarked that it was received 'with a much warmer, more general, and more lasting approbation than … even the most sanguine admirers of the poem could have expected'.[42] Although the reviewer suggested that Colman's success lay in overcoming the stiltedness of the poem's original neoclassical form, the *Critical Review* remarked that 'a classical spectator must receive pleasure … while the native beauty of the poem … commands the approbation of the whole audience' and the *London Chronicle* offered unmitigated praise.[43] Performances continued throughout the autumn and winter of the 1772–73 season, becoming so notable that Maria Macklin reported to her father in February 1773 that '*Elfrida* alone drew houses'.[44] In addition to a quarto edition of the choruses from the play, Robert Horsfield published a seventh and eighth edition of Mason's poem in December 1772 to meet renewed demand. Colman's edited text of *Elfrida* was performed in 1772, 1773,

1774, 1775 and 1777; and a new edition by Mason himself was performed (albeit with considerably shorter runs) in 1779, 1781, 1783, 1785 and 1792. Three performances, on 2 December 1772, 8 December 1773, and 14 April 1785, were staged by royal command and George III and Queen Charlotte attended at least the first of them.[45]

The popularity of Mason's *Elfrida* in both its poetic and its dramatic form almost certainly explains the appearance during the last forty years of the eighteenth century of a series of history paintings that depict the first half of Elfrida's life story. The earliest of these paintings was Andrea Casali's now lost 'An historical picture of K. Edgar, Elfrida and Athelwold', displayed at the Society of Artists' exhibition in 1761 (a painting to which I will return). A decade later, Angelica Kauffman's 'The interview of King Edgar with Elfrida, after her marriage to Athelwold' appeared in the Royal Academy's summer exhibition. Kauffman situates Elfrida on a step above Edgar and Athelwold, thus emphasizing the power of her beauty over them. The effect is not lost on Edgar, who looks at her with an expression suggesting lust or awe, or on Athelwold, whose pained or panicked expression foreshadows the imminent loss of his wife to his king. Elfrida's appearance from behind a curtain being pulled back by a servant, like the rather flat background and Renaissance costumes, suggests a tableau or stage production rather than an attempt at an accurate representation of a tenth-century historical event. A contemporary reviewer remarked that it was among 'the best of her pictures in the present exhibition' despite the reviewer's distaste for pre-Conquest history and romances.[46] The painting was eventually purchased by John and Theresa Parker for Saltram House in 1775, though not before being reproduced by the fine art printmaker William Wynne Ryland in 1772, a print that was retouched and reissued by Ryland's wife Mary in 1786.[47]

William Hamilton's 'King Edgar's First Interview with Elfrida' (1774) borrows Kauffman's arrangement but exchanges the interior setting for one in front of a castle gate, heightening the medievalism of the scene while also suggesting a parallel with the by-now traditional illustrations of Elfrida and Edward in front of Corfe Castle. In 1778 the Society of Artists exhibited another work by Casali entitled 'Ethelwold introducing King Edgar to his Wife Elfrida'. Labelled in the catalogue as 'a sketch', it might have been a preparatory study for his 1761 oil painting exhibited at a time when Elfrida's story enjoyed particular currency.[48] In a rare explicit reference to the artist's source, the catalogue entry concludes with the words 'See Rapin, Vol. 1. (8vo Edition) Page 406'.[49] Such a note suggests not only that Casali's earlier oil painting was likely to have been based on Rapin's

Figure 3.2 William Wynne Ryland after Angelica Kauffman, *The Interview of King Edgar with Elfrida, after her Marriage to Athelwold* (1786). Engraving. Trustees of the British Museum.

History of England, but that such a clarification had become necessary after six seasons during which *Elfrida* had been a regular and celebrated feature of the Covent Garden repertoire.

Indeed, numerous paintings explicitly illustrated Mason's poem in its dramatic incarnation. In 1774 the miniaturist James Nixon showed a portrait of 'Elizabeth Hartley in the character of Elfrida' at the Royal Academy's summer exhibition, a piece singled out for praise by a reviewer for *The Public Advertiser*.[50] William Dickinson's mezzotint of Nixon's miniature, published in February 1779, presents a half-length depiction of a pensive Hartley with a suggestively low neckline in front of a gothic building half hidden in dense foliage, powerfully evoking Mason's description of Athelwold's castle in Harewood Forest and perhaps providing a glimpse of the production's set. The following two decades saw the appearance of numerous images from the play, including James Birchall's 'Orgar and Elfrida' (1784) and Jean François Rigaud's 'Penitence, as described in Mason's Elfrida' (1791). Each of these works offers a decidedly theatrical image that suggests not only that it was actors rather than artists who truly illustrated Elfrida and the other

Figure 3.3 William Dickinson after James Nixon, *Mrs. Hartley in the Character of Elfrida* (1779). Mezzotint. © Trustees of the British Museum.

characters in the contemporary historical visual imagination, but also that history could be perceived and understood according to dramatic visual conventions.

When *Elfrida* appeared in volume 34 of the third series of *Bell's British Theatre* in 1796, it was prefaced by both a full-length portrait of Hartley as Elfrida by James Roberts and a vignette by Thomas Stothard that depicts

Figures 3.4a & 4b Frontispieces for Bell's British Theatre edition of *Elfrida* (1796). William Leney after James Roberts, 'Mrs Hartley as Elfrida'; and James Heath after Thomas Stothard, untitled scene depicting Elfrida, Athelwold, and the chorus of British virgins. Private collection.

Elfrida in Athelwold's arms with three members of the chorus of British virgins beside them.[51] Both images are set against a woodland backdrop reminiscent of Nixon's portrait, and Stothard depicts Athelwold in a costume that closely resembles the one in Kauffman's oil painting and Ryland's print. If the theatrical portraits commissioned by Bell and created by James Roberts for his editions were indeed taken 'from the life' as he claimed, the consistency of this late portrait print with earlier oil paintings and prints suggests that *Elfrida* as performed by Hartley, Smith, Bensley, and Clarke had directly informed these characters' illustrations in other media.[52]

There is evidence to suggest that Hartley's portrayal of Elfrida came to stand proxy for the historical Elfrida in the visual imagination. In December 1772, Richard Hurd, Bishop of Worcester, wrote to William Mason to report that Lord Mansfield had taken the French ambassador to see *Elfrida* at Covent Garden and returned a satisfactory report. In Hurd's words, 'the success ... may be owing very much to the Music, & especially to the *person* of Elfrida. But enough of this.'[53] Horace Walpole explicitly conflated the two in a letter to Mason the following February, writing that 'Your Elfrida, Mrs Hartley, I am told, is the most perfect beauty that was ever seen.'[54] An anonymous reviewer for *The Covent-Garden Magazine* wrote that Hartley was 'as to person, extremely well calculated for the part; [Elfrida] being represented as a very fine woman with uncommon attractions'.[55] Each of these reviews contains obvious sexual overtones, whether in the form of Hurd's emphasis or the anonymous *Covent-Garden Magazine* writer's references to Hartley's physical attractiveness and to the questionable virginity of the actresses playing the chorus of British virgins.[56] Hartley might even have played Elfrida in a manner not entirely in keeping with Mason's characterization. In July 1772 the actor John Moody wrote to George Garrick (younger brother of David) that the red-haired, freckled Hartley 'talks lusciously, and has a slovenly good-nature about her that renders her prodigiously vulgar' with 'a superficial glare about her' that Moody knew would please audiences.[57] Such descriptions, like her involvement in the Vauxhall Affray and later elopement with William Smith, make it clear that Hartley's public persona was a highly and perhaps an intentionally sexualized one, and one that must have seemed at odds with the virtuous, pious character of Elfrida.[58] References like the ones mentioned here suggest that at least some members of the audience saw the irony in Hartley's being cast as Elfrida and her continuation in the role until her retirement at the end of the 1779–80 season. Nevertheless, according to Leslie and Taylor, 'the crowd flocked to see Mrs. Hartley kneel in *Elfrida*', and in doing so helped to raise Hartley and Elfrida to greater notoriety.[59]

Competing Images

Although illustrations of the young Elfrida (whether or not based on Mason's text) and illustrations of Elfrida and Edward usually appeared in separate contexts over the course of several decades, they did at times appear in close physical and temporal proximity. In 1761, Andrea Casali exhibited both 'An historical picture of K. Edgar, Elfrida and Athelwold' and 'An historical picture of Edward the Martyr' at the exhibition of the Free Society of Artists.[60] Like the Society of Artists from which it had seceded, the Free Society existed to promote English art and to support the development of a native English school of history painting, a mission that would later be taken up by the Royal Academy of Arts and by entrepreneurs such as Thomas Macklin, Richard Bowyer, William Boydell, and Henry Fuseli.[61] Casali's image of Edward the Martyr, which won the Society's 100-guinea premium, shares much in common with Wale's earlier design; the engraved print of it issued by John Boydell in 1773 depicts a more decorative, Italianate, and gothic version of Wale's image rather than a reconceived composition. Even the caption, 'Edward the Martyr stabbed by the Order of Elfrida at Corfe Castle' suggests a traditional reading of the episode. Unfortunately, although both paintings were eventually purchased by Alderman William Beckford and displayed at Fonthill until 1801, Casali's imagining of Edgar, Elfrida, and Athelwold is untraced and in the absence of an engraving nothing definitive can be said of its depiction of the characters or the episode.[62] However, given that no earlier eighteenth-century illustration of this episode is known to exist, the two likeliest explanations for Casali's decision to depict the two are either his familiarity with the historical account or his knowledge of Mason's poem. His only addition to Wale's image suggests that Casali did know his history: instead of Elfrida appearing alone or accompanied by maids and servants, in 'Edward the Martyr' the young Æthelred appears at Elfrida's left. This inclusion makes Casali's illustration significantly more political than Wale's and restores a degree of Elfrida's agency by reminding the viewer that, according to some historians, she had orchestrated Edward's murder in order to ensure Æthelred's coronation and a consequential increase in her own authority.[63] Although Casali depicts Æthelred as a child instead of the young man he would have been, his decision to emphasize the political aspects of Elfrida's story adds weight to Constance McPhee's claim that Casali probably intended the paintings to tell a story of Elfrida as 'quite literally a *femme fatale* to her first husband … and stepson'.[64] At the same time, Casali cannot have failed to be aware of the familiarity of Elfrida's early life that resulted from the success of Mason's poem. It is highly likely that Casali understood the tension that would result from presenting two episodes from Elfrida's story so open to different and perhaps contradictory interpretations.

An alternative pair of images of these two scenes appears in Temple Sydney's *New and Complete History of England*, published shortly after *Elfrida*'s dramatic premier and the surge of renewed interest in Mason's poem. In addition to a more technically accomplished version of his earlier illustration of Edward the Martyr, Samuel Wale also designed 'King Edgar's first Interview with Queen Elfrida', a curious image in which Elfrida appears to offer Edgar a cushioned chair on a raised dais while Athelwold enters through an open door, looking at Edgar with a scowl. Reprinted at

Figures 3.5a & 5b Rennoldson after Samuel Wale, *King Edgar's First Interview with Queen Elfrida*; and Charles Grignion after Samuel Wale, *King Edward the Martyr treacherously Assassinated at the Gate of Corfe Castle by order of his Step-Mother Elfrida*. From Temple Sydney's *A New and Complete History of England* (1773). By permission of the Spalding Gentleman's Society.

least once, in Raymond's *New, Universal and Impartial History*, Wale's image offers an obvious alternative to Mason's poetic drama. As in his illustration for Lockman's *History*, the character of Wale's Elfrida is revealed by her offering of her husband's 'throne' to the king, a gesture that the keen student of history would have been expected to recognize as an indication that Elfrida seduced Edgar in order to secure political power for herself. These two illustrations make a visual claim for the 'correctness' of the historical text over the poetic or the dramatic one, for a reading of Elfrida as an exemplar of wicked rather than virtuous behaviour. As visual artworks that their publisher sought to use to induce viewer-readers to purchase one of numerous competing histories of England, however, the illustrations entered the market as competitors with the illustrations of Elfrida's story offered by Mason and the company at Covent Garden, and by artists like

Kauffman and Stothard. What John Cooke offered subscribers to Sydney's *History* was a textual and visual alternative to the sentimental version of Elfrida, which he must have assumed would draw the public eye and custom to his own product.

Such works suggest that Mason's poem and its stage productions competed with historical accounts as the accepted version of Elfrida's story in the popular imagination and that audiences confronted with these characters were as likely to think of a poetic or dramatic Elfrida as one who more closely matched the descriptions found in a published history. In their images of the tenth-century queen, her husbands and her children, eighteenth-century artists and publishers revealed the blurred line between history writing and creative writing, both of which were understood to comprise literature in much the same way that literary and mythological subjects were included alongside historical ones in the broad category of history paintings. The lack of distinction between these genres becomes clearest in the literary galleries of the 1790s, which shared not only what numerous scholars have identified as a common civic humanist agenda and public/private, political/commercial agenda, but also a common desire to promote history painting as a broad, inclusive genre, a fact easily obscured by their arrangement around single works or authors.[65] As Calè points out, the history paintings that filled the literary galleries 'participated in the invention of a cultural tradition and canon'.[66] So too did less prestigious series such as John Bell's *British Theatre*, which contemporaries understood (or were encouraged to understand) in similar terms.

In 1796, for example, Bell's edition of *Elfrida* competed with Robert Smirke's 'The Treachery of Elfrida' on display in Bowyer's Historic Gallery, which breaks with the traditional composition established by Wale by depicting Elfrida handing the cup of wine to Edward, 'thereby emphasizing the part she has played in the planning of the murder'.[67] Members of the reading, exhibition-going and print-buying publics were thus presented with two apparently contradictory illustrations of the story and character of a single historical figure. On the one hand, Mason's sentimental textual illustration of Elfrida sat alongside James Roberts' theatrical portrait of the celebrity beauty Elizabeth Hartley and Thomas Stothard's vignette of a scene from the play rendered in a 'romantic vein' common to Bell's editions.[68] On the other, Smirke's painting offered a highly critical representation of Elfrida that was purportedly based on Hume's *History of England*, the most popular eighteenth-century history of England and a work that provided 'the most important set of images of English history available at the close of the eighteenth century'.[69] An article printed in *The Times* in 1790

Figure 3.6 William Bromley after Robert Smirke, *The Treachery of Elfrida*, engraving for Robert Bowyer's edition of David Hume's *History of England* (1806). By permission of the Spalding Gentlemen's Society.

attributed the 'present spirited plans of Boydell and Macklin' to the success of Bell's Shakespeare and British Poets, and encouraged all three publishers to 'go hand in hand to the Temple of Fame' as a reward for encouraging public patronage of the arts in Britain.[70] Although they offered far different illustrations of her, both Bowyer and Bell placed Elfrida firmly in the canon of English (hi)story – at least temporarily.

Conclusion

Mason's *Elfrida* – like images of Elfrida's early life – quickly fell out of favour after 1800, and scenes of the death of Edward the Martyr based on the compositions of Wale and Smirke once again came to represent Elfrida and her character for viewer-readers of new national histories. Yet the competing illustrations of Elfrida's life and story reveal the powerful effects of cross-fertilization that influenced literary and historical works that sought to define English stories in visual terms. In the case of Elfrida, and almost certainly in the case of other historical figures whose lives were illustrated in the theatres, galleries, and printshops, the result is a kind of synaesthesia, a conflation of history, creative writing, and visual art in which the historical figure, the written narrative, the personalities of actors, and the painted or printed illustration each informed the ways in which reader-viewers encountered, understood, and imagined the other.

Notes

1 John Pye, *Patronage of British Art, an Historical Sketch* (London: Longman, Brown, Green, and Longmans, 1845), 53–4.
2 James Northcote, 'James Northcote's Autobiography', BL MS Add. 47792, 14; quoted in Isabelle Baudino, 'Works of Historical Fancy? Samuel Wale's illustrations for Thomas Mortimer's "New History of England"', paper presented at Fancy-Fantaisie-Capriccio, Toulouse, 31 December 2017, 2, https://hal.archives-ouvertes.fr/hal-01663098.
3 For literary illustration, see the works cited here and in the Introduction to this volume. For historical illustration, see, e.g., Francis Haskell, *History and Its Images: Art and the Interpretation of the Past* (New Haven, CT: Yale, 1993), 279–303; Rosemary Mitchell, *Picturing the Past: English History in Text and Image 1830–1870* (Oxford: Oxford, 2000), 20–55; Martin Myrone and Lucy Peltz, eds, *Picturing the Past: Aspects of Antiquarian Culture and Practice 1700–1850* (Aldershot: Ashgate, 1999).
4 J. F. Kerslake, ed., *Catalogue of Theatrical Portraits in London Public Collections* (London: Society for Theatre Research, 1961); Kalman A. Burnim and Philip H. Highfill Jr, *John Bell, Patron of British Theatrical Portraiture: A Catalog of the Theatrical Portraits in his Editions of Bell's Shakespeare and Bell's British Theatre*

(Carbondale: Southern Illinois University Press, 1998); Desmond Shawe-Taylor, *Dramatic Art: Theatrical Paintings from the Garrick Club* (London: Dulwich Picture Gallery, 1997).

5 Hans Hammelmann, *Book Illustrators in Eighteenth-Century England*, ed. by T. S. R. Boase (New Haven, CT: Yale, 1975).

6 Leigh G. Dillard, 'Drawing Outside the Book: Parallel Illustration and the Creation of a Visual Culture', in Christina Ionescu, ed., *Book Illustration in the Long Eighteenth Century* (Newcastle, 2011), 195–242 (195–6).

7 Christina Ionescu, 'Introduction' to *Book Illustration in the Long Eighteenth Century: Reconfiguring the Visual Periphery of the Text* (Newcastle: Cambridge Scholars, 2011), 43.

8 For a concise overview of common perceptions of the relationship between Romanticism, history and medievalism, see the introductions to Rosemary Mitchell, *Picturing the Past* and Clare A. Simmons, *Popular Medievalism in Romantic-Era Britain* (New York: Palgrave MacMillan, 2011).

9 Elizabeth Norton, *Elfrida: The First Crowned Queen of England* (Stroud: Amberley, 2013), 6.

10 Pauline Stafford, 'The Portrayal of Royal Women in England, Mid-Tenth to Mid-Twelfth Centuries', in Janet Parsons, ed., *Medieval Queenship* (Stroud: Sutton, 1993), 143–67; 'The King's Wife in Wessex', *Past and Present* 91 (1981): 3–27.

11 Mark Salber Phillips, *On Historical Distance* (New Haven, CT: Yale, 2013), 61–96; *Society and Sentiment: Genres of Historical Writing in Britain, 1740–1820* (Princeton, NJ: Princeton, 2000).

12 See, *inter alia*, John D. Niles, *The Idea of Anglo-Saxon England 1066–1901: Remembering, Forgetting, Deciphering and Renewing the Past* (Oxford: Blackwell, 2015), 147–219; Joanne Parker, *'England's Darling': The Victorian Cult of Alfred the Great* (Manchester: MUP, 2007), 46–81; Simon Keynes, 'The Cult of King Alfred', *Anglo-Saxon England* 28 (1999): 292–318.

13 John Lockman, *A New History of England, by Question and Answer*, 8th edn (London: T. Astley, 1752), 34, 37.

14 Stafford, 'The Portrayal of Royal Women in England', 157–8.

15 Lockman, 'Preface', in *A New History of England*.

16 George Vertue, *The Heads of the Kings of England, Proper for Mr. Rapin's History* (London: James, John and Paul Knapton, 1736); Paul Rapin, *The History of England*, trans. Nicholas Tindal, 2nd edn, 2 vols (London: James, John and Paul Knapton, 1732); Louise Lippincott, *Selling Art in Georgian London: The Rise of Arthur Pond* (New Haven, CT: Yale, 1983), 149–53.

17 Lockman, *A New History of England*, 37.

18 Rapin, *The History of England* (1732), I: 111n1.

19 Ionescu, *Book Illustration in the Long Eighteenth Century*, 35.

20 Alison Wiggins and Rosalind Field, eds, *Guy of Warwick: Icon and Ancestor* (Rochester: D. S. Brewer, 2007); see also above, note 4.

21 Rapin, *The History of England* (1732), I: 126.
22 Thomas Mortimer, *A New History of England, from the Earliest Accounts of Britain, to the Ratification of the Peace of Versailles, 1763*, 3 vols (London: J. Wilson and J. Fell, 1764).
23 Temple Sydney, *A New and Complete History of England* (London: J. Cooke, 1773); William Augustus Russel, *A New and Authentic History of England* (London: J. Cooke, 1777); George Frederick Raymond, *A New, Universal and Impartial History of England* (London: J. Cooke, 1785).
24 Edward Barnard, *The New, Comprehensive and Complete History of England* (London: Alexander Hogg, 1783). At least one subsequent edition was published, c.1790/1, almost certainly as a result of the popularity of the engravings rather than the text.
25 Thomas Bonnell, 'Cooke, John (1730/31–1810)', *Oxford Dictionary of National Biography* (*ODNB*); Advertisement, 'Barnard's New and Complete History of England' (1790), BL HS.74/1987(12).
26 Antony Griffiths, *The Print Before Photography: An Introduction to European Printmaking 1550–1820* (London: British Museum, 2016), 368.
27 William Mason, *Elfrida: A Dramatic Poem, Modelled on the Ancient Greek Tragedy* (London: John and Paul Knapton, 1752).
28 Thomas Gray to Horace Walpole, 20 February 1751. Paget Toynbee and Leonard Whibley, eds, *Correspondence of Thomas Gray*, corrections and additions by H. W. Starr, 2nd edn, 3 vols (Oxford: Clarendon, 1971), I: 343.
29 Ibid.
30 With his father James and brother Paul, John Knapton had earlier published Rapin's *History of England*, and by mid-century had established himself as a publisher of high-quality editions of literary and historical works. D. Nichol, 'J. J. and P. Knapton', in James K. Bracken and Joel Silver, eds, *The British Literary Book Trade, 1700–1820*, vol. 154, *Dictionary of Literary Biography* (London: Gale, 1995), 170–5.
31 *Monthly Review* 6 (1752), 387.
32 William Mason, commonplace book, mid-18th century. York Minster Archive, MS Add 25, fol. 49r; M. Whincop, ed., *Scanderbeg: Or, Love and Liberty … To which are added A LIST of all the DRAMATIC AUTHORS, with some Account of their Lives; and of all the DRAMATIC PIECES ever published in the English Language, to the Year 1747* (London: W. Reeve, 1747), 248.
33 Gerard Langbaine, *An Account of the English Dramatic Poets* (Oxford: George West and Henry Clements, 1691), 420.
34 *Monthly Review* 6 (1752), 387.
35 Mason, *Elfrida*, 73.
36 Michael Burden, *Garrick, Arne and the Masque of Alfred: A Case Study in National, Theatrical, and Musical Politics* (Lampeter: Edwin Mellen, 1994), 44–97; Oliver J. W. Cox, 'Frederick, Prince of Wales, and the First Performance of "Rule, Britannia!"', *The Historical Journal* 56 (2013): 931–54.

37 William of Malmesbury, *Gesta Regum Anglorum,* ed. and trans by R. A. B. Mynors, R. M. Thomson and M. Winterbottom (Oxford: Clarendon Press, 1998), 257; Rapin, *The History of England,* 109; Lockman, *A New History of England,* 35.
38 Aaron Hill, *Elfrid: or the Fair Inconstant* (London: Bernard Lintott, 1710), 21.
39 *The Dramatic Works of Aaron Hill*, 2 vols (London, 1760), I: ix–xv and 345–6.
40 John Draper, *William Mason: A Study in Eighteenth-Century Culture* (New York: New York University, 1924), 177.
41 David Erskine Baker, Isaac Reed and Stephen Jones, *Biographia Dramatica; or, a Companion to the Playhouse*, 3 vols (London: Longman, Hurst, Rees, Orme and Brown, 1812), I: 496.
42 'Chorus of the Dramatic Poem of Elfrida. As Performed at the Theatre-Royal in Covent-Garden', *Monthly Review* 47 (1772): 486.
43 Ibid.; 'Chorus of the Dramatic Poem of *Elfrida*. As performed at Covent-Garden', *Critical Review* 35 (1773): 71; 'An Account of Elfrida', *London Chronicle*, 21–24 November 1772.
44 Quoted in George Winchester Stone, Jr, ed., *The London Stage 1660–1800: Part 4: 1747–1776* (Carbondale: Southern Illinois University, 1962), 1654.
45 Stone, 1676, 1768; Charles Beecher Hogan, ed., *The London Stage 1660–1800: Part 5: 1776–1800*, 3 vols (Carbondale: Southern Illinois University, 1968), 787.
46 R. Baker, *Observations on the Pictures Now in Exhibition at the Royal Academy, Spring Gardens, and Mr. Christie's* (London: John Bell, 1771), 18.
47 Wendy Wassyng Roworth, 'Kauffman and the Art of Painting in England', in *Angelica Kauffman: A Continental Artist in Georgian England* (London: Reaktion, 1992), 11–95 (61–2).
48 Royal Academy of Arts, *The Exhibition of the Royal Academy* (London: W. Griffin, 1774), 13.
49 Algernon Graves, *The Society of Artists of Great Britain 1760–1791, The Free Society of Artists 1761–1783; A Complete Dictionary of Contributors and their Work from the Foundation of the Societies to 1791* (London: George Bell, 1907), 52.
50 *The Public Advertiser*, undated cutting (1774). Royal Academy of Arts, 'Royal Academy Critiques &c. Vol. I, 1769–1793', fol. 47.
51 John Bell, ed., *Bell's British Theatre* 34 (London: John Bell, 1797).
52 Burnim and Highfill, *John Bell, Patron of British Theatrical Portraiture,* 21.
53 Richard Hurd to William Mason, 24 December 1772, in Leonard Whibley, ed., *The Correspondence of Richard Hurd & William Mason, and Letters of Richard Hurd to Thomas Gray. With Introduction and Notes by Ernest Harold Pearce* (Cambridge: Cambridge University Press, 1932), 80. Emphasis Hurd's.
54 Horace Walpole to William Mason, 1 February 1773, in W. S. Lewis, Grover Cronin Jr and Charles H. Bennett, eds, *Horace Walpole's Correspondence with William Mason*, The Yale Edition of Horace Walpole's Correspondence, vols. 28–29 (New Haven, CT: Yale, 1955), I: 61.
55 'Theatrical Intelligence', *The Covent-Garden Magazine* (November 1772): 187.
56 Ibid.

57 John Moody to George Garrick, 26 July 1772 in *The Private Correspondence of David Garrick with the Most Celebrated Persons of His Time*, 2nd edn, 2 vols (London: Henry Colburn, 1835), I: 476.
58 *The Vauxhall Affray; or, the Macaronies Defeated* (London: J. Williams, 1773).
59 C. R. Leslie and T. Taylor, *Life and Times of Sir Joshua Reynolds*, 2 vols (London: 1865), II: 42n1. Leslie and Taylor agree with Moody's earlier observation that Hartley would please only for a while, and suggest that her retirement occurred not at the height of her popularity, as her *ODNB* entry suggests, but as a result of declining favour. See C. Conroy, 'Hartley, [*née* White] Elizabeth', *ODNB*.
60 Graves, *The Society of Artists,* 52; Free Society of Artists, *Catalogue* (London, 1761), nos 15 and 20.
61 Matthew Hargraves, *'Candidates for Fame': The Society of Artists of Great Britain 1760–1791* (New Haven, CT: Yale, 2005), 15–19; Graves, 305.
62 'Edward the Martyr' survives at Burton Constable Hall, Yorkshire.
63 Rapin, *The History of England,* 110–11.
64 Constance Curran McPhee, 'The Exemplary Past? British History Subjects in London Exhibitions, 1760–1810', unpublished PhD dissertation (University of Pennsylvania, 1995), 30.
65 John Barrell, *The Political Theory of Painting from Reynolds to Hazlitt: The Body of the Public* (New Haven, CT: Yale, 1995), 309; David Solkin, *Painting for Money: The Visual Arts and the Public Sphere in Eighteenth-Century England* (New Haven, CT: Yale, 1992), 19–23; Cynthia Roman, 'Pictures for Private Purses: Robert Bowyer's Historic Gallery and Illustrated Edition of David Hume's *History of England*', unpublished PhD dissertation (Brown University, 1997), 108; Luisa Calè, *Fuseli's Milton Gallery: 'Turning Readers into Spectators'* (Oxford: Clarendon, 2006), 18–20.
66 Calè, *Fuseli's Milton Gallery,* 29.
67 Ronald Hutton, 'Robert Bowyer and the Historic Gallery: A Study of the Creation of a Magnificent Work of Art', unpublished PhD dissertation, 4 vols (University of Chicago, 1992), IV: 446. Hutton provides a useful overview of some of the earlier images that informed Smirke's painting on pages 444–7.
68 Burnim and Highfill, *John Bell, Patron of British Theatrical Portraiture,* 22.
69 Mitchell, *Picturing the Past,* 34–5.
70 'The Competition of Bell, Boydell, and Macklin', *The Times* 1751 (13 December 1790): 3.

4 | 'Fuseli's Poetic Eye': Prints and Impressions in Fuseli and Erasmus Darwin

MARTIN PRIESTMAN

> Let us then suppose the mind to be, as we say, white paper, void of all characters, without any ideas: – How comes it to be furnished? … The impressions … made on our sense by outward objects that are extrinsical to the mind; and its own operations about those impressions, … are, I conceive, the original of all knowledge.
> (John Locke, *An Essay Concerning Human Understanding*, 1690)[1]

> The words expressive of [the] ideas belonging to vision make up the principal part of poetic language. That is, the Poet writes principally to the eye, the Prose-writer uses more abstracted terms.
> (Erasmus Darwin, *The Botanic Garden, Part Two: The Loves of the Plants*, 1791)[2]

> *Fuseli's* poetic eye;
> Whose daring tints, with SHAKESPEAR'S happiest grace,
> Gave to the airy phantom form and place.
> (Ibid.)[3]

> Philosophical Ideas made intuitive, or Sentiment personified, suit, in my opinion, Small Canvasses eminently.
> (Henry Fuseli, Letter to William Roscoe, 22 October 1791)[4]

According to the eighteenth century's most influential theorist of the mind, John Locke, all our ideas are based on sense-perceptions by way of the 'impressions' which external objects imprint on the *tabula rasa* or 'white paper' of the mind. Towards the end of the century this theory remained fundamental for the scientist-poet Erasmus Darwin, who insisted on the special role of poetry in reproducing the immediacy of visual impressions, leaving the job of 'abstracting' ideas from them to prose. This division of labour is clearly reproduced in Darwin's three long scientific poems – the two parts of his most popular work, *The Botanic Garden* (1791), and the later *The Temple of Nature, or The Origin of Society* (1803) – where the explanatory notes virtually equal the verse in length and weight. Darwin's stress on the importance of visual impressions as the foundation of ideas made it logical for him to seek to include carefully conceived illustrations in his work, densely freighted with meanings to be unpacked elsewhere in his texts, or more directly in the mind of the reader/viewer. The illustrator with whom he worked most closely was Henry Fuseli, whose 'poetic eye' he praised for its ability to give specific form to the 'airy phantoms' of his scientific thoughts and imaginings. For Fuseli too, this match with Darwin fitted his sense that personifications and 'Philosophical Ideas made intuitive' worked best in 'Small Canvasses' – a phrase which can be taken to include the folio pages of his Darwin designs.[5]

The way in which 'philosophical' or scientific ideas can be conveyed 'intuitively' – through an immediate impact on the feelings – is well exemplified through Fuseli's most celebrated work, *The Nightmare*, or at least through Darwin's reading of it. Though a fair-sized painting rather than a 'small canvas', it was Darwin's encounter with this picture that established the *rapport* between the two which then developed into a highly fruitful partnership.

Mental Impressions: *The Nightmare*

Widely reproduced in our day as in his, Henry Fuseli's *The Nightmare* is by far his best-known work.[6] Its combination of eroticism, darkness, and the supernatural evokes strong immediate associations with our ideas of the Gothic and Romantic, but its puzzling combination of unexplained elements then seems to demand a more detailed scrutiny. Picked out in luminous white from the surrounding darkness, the central figure is a sleeping woman stretched out on her back, the disordered position of her downward-hanging head and left arm suggesting that her sleep is severely troubled. Above her on the left, a horse's head protruding through her bedcurtains with glowing eyes suggests a literal reading of the word 'nightmare', but there is less of an obvious explanation for the ugly, dun-coloured male figure seated firmly on the woman's midriff and frowning challengingly out at the spectator.

While this challenging look seems to defy easy explanations, some light can be thrown on this figure with a glance at the etymology of 'nightmare', which has links to the Scandinavian word *mara*, meaning a spirit that brings harm to sleepers by riding on their sleeping bodies. The fact that in some versions *mara*s also treat horses in the same way may account for the haunted appearance of the horse on the left of the picture, though this creature also offers viewers a sop to standard English misreadings of 'nightmare'.[7] Leaving the definitional specifics aside, a central mystery still surrounds the male figure: is it primarily an incubus, embodying the woman's erotic dreams of something forbidden or unacceptable, or does it represent something whose presence *causes* her sleep to be disturbed in a more directly physiological way?

First sketched in March 1781 and exhibited in 1782, Fuseli's painting made such an impression that it was soon widely circulated in print form, and from 1783 one set of these prints was accompanied by four lines of verse which directly address some of the above mysteries:

> So on his NIGHTMARE through the evening fog
> Flits the squab Fiend o'er fen, and lake, and bog;
> Seeks some love-wilder'd Maid with sleep oppress'd,
> Alights, and grinning sits upon her breast.[8]

This reading allows the Nightmare itself to be the horse, but focuses attention on the 'Fiend' who now adopts the sleeping Maid as his new steed. Her specifically 'love-wilder'd' state suggests that he is in some way an erotic incubus, but in the words 'oppress'd' and 'sits' there is a further hint that the Fiend in some way *is* the oppression by sleep that causes her bad dreams.

The author of these words was Erasmus Darwin, the Midlands-based doctor, scientific thinker and as-yet unpublished poet who had met Fuseli on a rare visit to London in March–April 1781, around the time of the first sketch of *The Nightmare* and before its first exhibition in 1782.[9] The rest of this chapter is devoted to the complex interactions which arose from this meeting, interactions which normally feature Fuseli as the illustrator of Darwin's poems but begin with the boot on the other foot, with Darwin's four anonymous lines apparently coming from nowhere to illuminate the meaning of Fuseli's image.

The lines come from the first of Darwin's three major long poems, *The Loves of the Plants*, largely completed by 1783 but not published until 1789 due to his considerable reservations about publishing it at all. It was in fact Fuseli – a writer as well as artist – who helped to overcome these reservations by successfully recommending the poem to his own publisher, Joseph Johnson: a three-way relationship which then held firm throughout Darwin's poetic career.[10]

The four lines come from a much longer account of Fuseli's picture, which ties it arrestingly to some of the physiological theories about the unconscious which Darwin explores in *The Loves of the Plants*. So confident does this passage seem about Fuseli's intentions that it is conceivable that Darwin had discussed these theories with him before *The Nightmare* was painted, rather than simply reading them into it afterwards. Be that as it may, Darwin's account is fully alert to numerous details in the painting which might seem merely puzzling to the normal viewer.

> So on his NIGHTMARE through the evening fog
> Flits the squab Fiend o'er fen, and lake, and bog;
> Seeks some love-wilder'd Maid with sleep oppress'd,
> Alights, and grinning sits upon her breast.
> – Such as of late amid the murky sky
> Was mark'd by *Fuseli's* poetic eye;
> Whose daring tints, with SHAKESPEAR'S happiest grace,
> Gave to the airy phantom form and place. –
> Back o'er her pillow sinks her blushing head,
> Her snow-white limbs hang helpless from the bed;
> While with quick sighs, and suffocative breath,
> Her interrupted heart-pulse swims in death.
> …
> In vain she wills to run, fly, swim, walk, creep;
> The WILL presides not in the bower of SLEEP.
> – On her fair bosom sits the Demon-Ape
> Erect, and balances his bloated shape;
> Rolls in their marble orbs his Gorgon-eyes,
> And drinks with leathern ears her tender cries.[11]

As the introductory 'So' suggests, the whole description is in fact an epic simile for something else; in this case for the trance-state induced in the Ancient Greek Delphic Oracle by infusions of laurel-leaves – these latter typifying the very tenuous links on which the curious structure of *The Loves of the Plants* depends, between specific plants and bravura extended passages on a wide range of other matters. As far as Fuseli's painting is concerned, this indirect connection with the Delphic Oracle adds a level of high importance to the dreamer's experiences, suggesting that her deranged visions may on some level tell us things we need to know about ourselves.

In the rest of the passage, Darwin accurately balances the bloodless paleness of most of the dreamer's body with the facial 'blushing' which may equally denote the concentration of all her bodily functions within her brain, and the more specifically sexual content of her 'love-wilder'd' dreams. In the closing description of the seated 'Fiend' or 'Demon-Ape', the word 'Erect' may also have an erotic connotation but more importantly brings out, with the word 'balances', the way this small but heavy creature brings his whole 'bloated' weight to bear down on the sleeper's chest with 'suffocative', immobilizing force. At the same time his petrifying 'Gorgon eyes' and unhearing 'leathern ears' denote not only the uncaringness of the outside world to the dreamer's sufferings but also the suspension of her own normal powers of sight and hearing, so that – rather than being the external night-visitor first described – the Fiend or *mara* is revealed as being a projection of the dreamer's own physical immobilization, whereby her 'WILL presides not in the bower of SLEEP'.

These implications are clearly brought out by Darwin's footnote to the above line, which explains that:

> Sleep consists in the abolition of all voluntary power, both over our muscular motions and our ideas; [but] our nerves of sense are not torpid or inert during sleep[:] many of our muscular motions, and many of our ideas, continue to be excited into action ... and we experience variety of passions. [T]hey are only precluded from the perception of external objects; ... thus the eye-lids are closed in sleep, and I suppose the tympanum of the ear is not stretched, because they are deprived of the voluntary exertions of the muscles appropriated to these purposes.[12]

Thus for the doctorly Darwin, Fuseli's painting ultimately becomes a case study in the physiological analysis of dreaming, as a kind of mismatch between our still-active feelings and our normal powers of expressing or anchoring them in relation to the outside world.

Nonetheless, the visual statement of these essentially abstract physiological ideas has been the special achievement of

> *Fuseli's* poetic eye;
> Whose daring tints, with SHAKESPEAR'S happiest grace,
> Gave to the airy phantom form and place. (3.56–8, p. 97)

The reference to Shakespeare chimes in neatly with the fact that some of Fuseli's best-known works apart from *The Nightmare* depicted Shakespearean scenes, partly through his contributions to Boydell's Shakespeare Gallery;[13] but there is a more specific reference to Theseus' speech in *A Midsummer Night's Dream*, whereby

> as imagination bodies forth
> The forms of things unknown, the poet's pen
> Turns them to shapes and gives to airy nothing
> A local habitation and a name.[14]

It is Fuseli's special ability to give visualizable 'form and place' to the 'airy nothings' of abstract, sometimes scientific, speculations that make his eye 'poetic' in Darwin's sense – and became the reason why Darwin increasingly turned to Fuseli to convey the often-abstruse science of his

Figure 4.1 Henry Fuseli, *The Nightmare*: portrait version. Opposite p. 126 of Erasmus Darwin, *The Botanic Garden, Part Two: The Loves of the Plants*, 5th edition (1799). With permission of the British Library.

long 'philosophical' poems, in images which were immediately arresting but nonetheless repaid detailed complex analysis of the kind Darwin here devotes to *The Nightmare*.

By the time Darwin paid this tribute, *Loves* itself was chiefly in need of the detailed plant-drawings that would be provided by Frederick Nodder and other botanical artists, so no illustrations by Fuseli feature in its first edition of 1789 or its revised 1791 edition as the second part of *The Botanic Garden*. However, a later edition (1799) does incorporate an engraving of *The Nightmare*, based on a later version in 'portrait' format better suited to inclusion in a book than the original 'landscape' one.[15] Compressing the three main figures into a tighter composition with sleeper's head, fiend and horse forming a diagonal from bottom left to top right, Fuseli has changed his original plump, ugly *mara* into something whose long, pointed ears are more clearly 'fiend'-like as well as 'leathern', and whose malicious leer down at his victim comes closer to the 'grinning' attributed to him in Darwin's account than the original version's forbidding scowl. This chain of shifting significations from painting to text to repainting and then to textually incorporated print usefully exemplifies the circularity between image and text contained within the broad idea of 'illustration' at this period.

Impressions of Nature: *The Economy of Vegetation*

The Loves of the Plants, essentially a playful introduction to the Linnaean system of botanical classification, was always planned as only the second part of a longer work called *The Botanic Garden*. The first part, *The Economy of Vegetation*, was initially designed – as its unassuming title implies – as a comparatively brief account of the larger context into which botany fitted, but gradually expanded into an immensely ambitious exploration of the physics and chemistry of more or less the whole ecosphere, from exploding suns to volcanoes, from deserts to icecaps, and from the early science of the ancients to the scientific-industrial achievements of Darwin's own friends James Watt, Josiah Wedgwood and Joseph Priestley.

To cover this vast territory, Darwin divided his poem's four cantos up between the activities of the traditional 'four elements' of fire, earth, water, and air, allotting to each element a different kind of spirit: salamanders (or fire-nymphs) for fire, gnomes for earth, nymphs for water and sylphs for air. Derived from the sixteenth-century alchemist Paracelsus and other 'Rosicrucian' sources, these spirits are nominally anchored around the central figure of Flora, the Goddess of Botany, who approvingly describes the activities of each elemental group in turn before a final section at last gives some evidence of how their various activities do indeed assist the processes of 'vegetation'.

This highly fanciful situation, which needs to be constantly borne in mind for the poem to make much sense, is the subject of Fuseli's first commissioned illustration for Darwin, *Flora attired by the Elements*.[16] Mainly constructed to explain *The Economy of Vegetation*, it is commandingly placed as the Frontispiece to the whole *Botanic Garden* including *Loves of the Plants*, with whose separate Frontispiece by another artist (Emma Crewe), also featuring Flora, it sets up a range of echoes.[17]

In an oval frame topped with flowers, *Flora attired by the Elements* presents the relationship between botanical goddess and elemental spirits with instantaneous visual clarity. With flowers in her hair and around her neck, the large seated figure of Flora is surrounded and adoringly gazed at by the smaller or less fully-visible figures of the four elements in a roughly diamond-shaped arrangement, with Fire and Air above, Water on a level with her, and Earth below. A fifth figure – presumably a more subservient 'gnome' – emerges from the ground and hands a new plant to the Earth-figure, who is herself handing a basket of plants up to Flora.

Each element is immediately identifiable: Earth by the lowly, plant-offering position just described; Air by the large butterfly incorporated into her hat; Water by the fountain-base she sits by, from which her wavily-outlined garment seems to flow; and Fire by a flaming headdress whose wings clearly embody the principle that heat rises. These upward-tending wings, and Fire's prominent place at the top-centre of the composition, also prepare us for the leading role the fiery salamanders will play in the opening Canto, being responsible for the primal cosmic explosion from which earth is described as emerging, and for the sun as the primal source of the earth's heat in general.

Another aspect of Fire's leading role in the composition is the large oval mirror she holds up to Flora, allowing her to admire the results of her elemental 'attiring' – as represented particularly by the butterfly-hatted Air-sylph's adjustment of the flowers in her hair. Flora's reflection in this mirror is invisible to us but her rapt gaze into it – echoing but ignoring the elements' rapt gazes at her – strikingly converts what might have been a static tableau to a much more dynamic balancing of attention-flows. And since the mirror's oval shape echoes that of the oval frame through which we are viewing the whole composition, the viewer is invited to put her/himself in the position of Flora, keen to penetrate further into the botanical mysteries to be revealed in the forthcoming poem (or poems, if we take the mirror to

Figure 4.2 Henry Fuseli, *Flora Attired by the Elements*: Frontispiece to Erasmus Darwin, *The Botanic Garden* (1791). From author's copy.

beckon us also to the Linnaean teachings of *The Loves of the Plants*). Since Darwin's text makes many appeals to a specifically female readership,[18] such readers may also be invited to view their own reflections in the poem's mirror, as naturally partaking of the beauties of flowers and their goddess.

Apart from its Frontispiece *The Economy of Vegetation* contains a range of illustrations of diverse subjects whose precise objective details matter more than any 'poetic-eyed' rendition of their inner significance. Hence the geological structure of the earth, Wedgwood's abolitionist medallions and the designs on the Roman 'Portland Vase' are drawn by artists other than Fuseli, ready to have their details explicated by extensive factual notes. Fuseli's one contribution apart from the Frontispiece is, however, truly dramatic.

Dominating the foreground, an enormous dog-headed man wearing only a loincloth stands with his back to us and his arms raised in prayer to a star shining at the top-centre of the picture. Between his legs some high hills can be seen, between two of which a waterfall feeds a river which flows towards us between the giant figure's widely planted feet at the bottom of the picture. Above the waterfall and visible beneath the dog-man's hanging loincloth, an aged, winged and bearded figure seems to fly towards us, pouring rainwater from his beard and outspread arms while his hands release flashing bolts of lightning. Somewhere near the dog-man's gigantic feet a pair of pyramids identify the scene as being set in Egypt, and hence the river surging towards us, replenished by the distant rainfall, as the Nile.

This stupendous image illustrates the following passage from the poem, which is not in itself particularly striking:

> Sailing in air, when dark *Monsoon* inshrouds
> His tropic mountains in a night of clouds;
> Or drawn by whirlwinds from the Line returns,
> And showers o'er Afric all his thousand urns;
> High o'er his head the beams of *Sirius* glow,
> And, Dog of Nile, *Anubis* barks below.[19]

Keyed to these few lines, a footnote explains African summer monsoons at great scientific length, followed by a much briefer reference to the comparative-mythographer Abbé Pluche's comment that:

> as Sirius, or the dog-star, rose at the time of the commencement of the flood its rising was watched by the astronomers, and notice given of the approach of inundation by hanging the figure of Anubis, which was that of a man with a dog's head, upon all their temples.
> (Darwin, *Economy of Vegetation*, note to 3.129)

From this – rather than from the one or two very cryptic verse lines on the subject – it seems to emerge that Fuseli's elaborate montage of images is based on the Egyptian priest-astronomers' repeated perception that the

104   MARTIN PRIESTMAN

Figure 4.3 Henry Fuseli, *Fertilization of Egypt*, engraved by William Blake. Opposite p. 127 of Erasmus Darwin, *The Botanic Garden, Part One: The Economy of Vegetation* (1791). From author's copy.

beneficial flooding of the River Nile coincided with the appearance of the 'dog-star' Sirius as a kind of watchdog, an idea which they externalized in the figure of the canine-headed god Anubis. The water-showering old man personifies the rainy African monsoons, while the gigantic dog-headed figure worshipping the dog-star both *is* the god Anubis, and the Egyptian priests' deliberate construction of this figure out of the astronomical facts they have observed.

Fertilization of Egypt thus encapsulates some fairly complex geography, science, and comparative mythology in a single, immediately striking image, with all its key elements – star, dog-head, African Monsoon, and flooding Egyptian Nile – arranged along a single vertical line from top to bottom. But despite this visual immediacy, the fact that the connection between all these elements can only be rationally explained by reading all the way through Darwin's scientific note to the mention of Anubis at the end, is very much part of Darwin's declared scheme for *The Botanic Garden*, which is:

> To inlist Imagination under the banner of Science; and to lead her votaries from the looser analogies, which dress out the imagery of poetry, to the stricter ones which form the ratiocination of philosophy.[20]

In this case, given the obscurity of the relevant verse lines, the work of 'loose analogy' has been handed over from poetry to draftsmanship, in a dramatic demonstration of the harnessing of 'Fuseli's poetic eye' to Darwin's scientific ends.

However, *Fertilization of Egypt* opens up further vistas if we notice the tiny lettering beneath the image itself, which reads on the left 'H. Fuseli, RA, *inv*' and on the right 'W. Blake, *sc*', with '*inv*' meaning '*invenit*' or 'invented' and '*sc*' meaning '*sculpsit*' or engraved. Fuseli's role as inventor or conceiver of the design may in fact have been quite embryonic, as is suggested by a very rudimentary sketch showing the key elements listed above – star, dog-man, and vaguely discernible winged figure beneath the latter's loin-cloth – but with barely any further detail. At the bottom of this sketch the words 'Sketched by Fuseli for Blake to engrave from' have been written, probably by William Blake's nineteenth-century disciple Frederick Tatham. Despite some disputes these words seem accurate enough, suggesting that a great deal of the final picture's detail is purely the work of Joseph Johnson's engraver, William Blake.[21]

This is particularly interesting regarding the distant, winged rain-making figure. With no discernible face, beard or dripping garments, and outspread arms vigorously raised some degrees above the horizontal, Fuseli's rudimentary figure seems full of youthful energy when contrasted to the frowning, heavily bearded old personage, with arms at a firm 180 degrees, who floods all beneath him in Blake's finished print. The energy of the Fuseli figure's raised arms is endorsed by his yet more upward-tending wings (for which Fuseli has sketched two differently angled versions); Blake includes these wings but again at a nearly horizontal level, virtually parallel to the arms. While still identifiable as Darwin's Monsoon in the context of this plate, the ideas of aged power evoked by Blake's reworking of Fuseli's few lines suggest a more firmly established being connected with torrential rain and lightning, such as the Roman Jupiter Pluvius or the pre-Olympian sky-god Uranus of classical mythology.[22]

Bearing this association in mind, I would argue that this figure from the 1791 *Botanic Garden* strikingly anticipates the depiction of the aged, tyrannical Urizen in Blake's prophetic books, *Visions of the Daughters of Albion*, *America* (both 1793), and *The First Book of Urizen* (1794). In all of these Urizen not only has the flowing beard of Blake's Monsoon-figure, but a range of variations on his widespread arms and/or wings. In possibly his first appearance, the title-page of *Visions* shows Urizen (partly conflated with the rapist Bromion) pursuing the heroine Oothoon across a wild sea, his enormous horizontal wings echoing those of Monsoon while his arms draw perverse attention to his clearly distorted mental state by hugging his body tightly – an unnatural position which seems to be reversed in *Visions*' final, more positive image of the liberated Oothoon flying towards us with arms freely outspread.[23] Otherwise, Urizen/Bromion strikingly resembles Monsoon in flying towards us with a miserable, frowning face through massed rain-clouds, and pouring rain from his outspread wings which are also licked by flames suggesting, if not exactly copying, the lightning wielded by Monsoon.

In Plate 10 of *America*, Urizen loses his wings but spreads his arms in the same space-commanding horizontal over the clouds which continue to be his favoured element.[24] Now giving the old tyrant the leading role, *The First Book of Urizen* works a series of changes on the spread-armed *motif*: we see him ambidexterously writing his books of 'stony law' with a hand stretched out on each side of his body on the title-page (Plate 1), spreading one of these books out in Plate 4, spreading his arms to save himself from drowning in Plate 11, and in the final plate (26), struggling to keep them still spread wide when tied down by the 'Net of Religion' which he himself has woven.[25]

Linking Blake's Urizen to his earlier filling-out of Fuseli's Monsoon suggests a possible dimension to the aged tyrant beyond those normally considered. I have suggested elsewhere that sometimes Blake's mythical names seem to reverse classical names, or parts of them – Los for 'Sol' or sun, Orc for Cronus or time, and Urizen for Uranus, the primal sky-and-weather-god.[26] Another often-suggested source for Urizen's name is 'horizon', implying the limits arbitrarily set to perceptions which should be infinite;[27] but I would suggest this punning association is given a powerful boost if we consider the insistent horizontality – claiming as much as possible of the space below – of the outspread arms and/or wings of the being who begins as a rain-personification, then transforms into the god of various kinds of bad weather, and only then comes to embody the idea of mental horizons, in a logical extension from this characteristic physical gesture.

But if we return to *The Fertilization of Egypt* without such Blakean spectacles, perhaps another reading of the bearded weather-bearer springs more directly to mind. He looks more simply like traditional depictions of the Christian God, and since the whole plate represents the birth of one aspect of religion – the Egyptian worship of Anubis for astronomical reasons – perhaps the bearded figure suggests the birth of another, ultimately from the same kind of source. According to the radical French revolutionary Constantin-François Volney's atheistic work *The Ruins, or a Survey of the Revolutions of Empires*, all Western and Middle-Eastern religions derived from similar astronomical observations by the Egyptian magi, including (via Moses) Judaism and thence Christianity.[28] Darwin's note on the Monsoon cites a different, earlier work by Volney, but it is very possible that he mischievously suggested this passage for illustration because as a radical near-atheist himself he would be aware, like Fuseli, that Joseph Johnson was about to publish *Ruins* in its first English translation as *The Botanic Garden* went to press. Given that as Johnson's regular engraver the religiously unorthodox Blake would also be well aware of this, it is possible that *Fertilization of Egypt* is at least a hint from all three men that the established Christian religion, with its aged power-wielding deity, was in fact born between the legs of Egyptian astronomy.

Another version of the weather-god can be found in a plate designed by Fuseli and engraved by Blake, which did not appear in *The Economy of Vegetation* until the 1795 edition.[29] Called *Tornado*, this depicts an angry, lightning-wielding Zeus-like figure battling with a black-winged serpent which emerges from the sea and twists round him, in such a way that the god's body and the serpent's head and wings seem inextricable. Similarly serpent-entwined figures are frequent in Blake,[30] and the battle between god and sea-serpent also closely echoes Fuseli's major oil painting *Thor Battering the Midgard Serpent*, for which he received his entry-diploma for the Royal Academy.[31] Somewhat as stormy air and swirling water become entwined together, so do some of the persistent preoccupations of both Blake and Fuseli in the formation of *Tornado*.

With the partial exception of *Tornado*, the three plates considered so far all focus on the act of perception.[32] Rather than presenting us with scenes or figures designed to be looked at as passively aesthetic objects, they focus on central figures who are themselves doing the looking, in ways which largely define the meanings of their respective engravings. While *The Nightmare*'s sleeper may seem an exception to this, her closed, straining eyelids are very much the picture's ultimate focus, viewed upside-down and with difficulty though they are. The *mara*-fiend's enigmatic glare, directed straight at us, may get our attention more immediately, but the challenge it really embodies is that of guessing what is going on in the sleeper's mind, and what visions are being projected onto those closed, upside-down eyelids. Darwin's poem offers a range of answers:

> – Then shrieks of captured towns, and widows' tears,
> Pale lovers stretch'd upon their blood-stain'd biers,
> The headlong precipice that thwarts her flight,
> The trackless desert, the cold starless night,
> And stern-eye'd Murder with his knife behind,
> In dread succession agonize her mind.[33]

But as viewers of Fuseli's picture there is no real need to tell us this: our attention is already focused on imagining the kinds of thing she is hearing through her ears made 'leathern' to the outside world, and seeing with those firmly-closed eyes.

As already discussed, *Flora attired by the Elements* is constructed round a series of gazes, finally pulling us into an identification with Flora's rapt gaze into the mirror, in which both she and we hope to find the mysteries of botany revealed. On the other hand, like *The Nightmare*, *The Fertilization of Egypt* is focused on an act of seeing we do not actually see: the dog-man's worshipful observation of the star that will alert the Egyptians to the imminent flooding of the Nile on which their prosperity depends. It is only by similarly observing and worshipping him when he makes his visible appearance as multiple depictions of Anubis, hung by the wise priest-astronomers on 'all their temples', that the Egyptians can take advantage of those astronomers' initial 'seeing' of the connection between flood and dog-star.

Cross-impressions: *The Temple of Nature*

Perception, or the registering of sense-impressions, remains a key theme in Fuseli's most programmatically planned work for Darwin. The latter's last poem, *The Temple of Nature, or The Origin of Society* (1803), has only four illustrations, one for each canto and all by Fuseli. In striking anticipation of his grandson Charles's theories, Darwin's poem describes the evolutionary growth of organic life from primal microbes to more advanced species, and is hence awash with close descriptions of plants and animals. Given that his art centres almost entirely on the human form, Fuseli makes no attempt to enter this non-human world, conveying his meanings by firmly anthropomorphic means and externalizing natural and mental processes through allegorical myths and personifications. In various ways, all four of his plates for *Temple* show the contents of at least one consciousness being impressed or imprinted on another.

The Frontispiece, *The Temple of Nature*, is keyed to a passage from Canto One, where the Priestess/hierophant Urania is conducting the poet's 'Muse' and other 'votaries' round the eponymous allegorical temple where all the mysteries of Nature are about to be revealed. She has finally reached the central area where she 'in part unshrouds' the silently standing figure of the Goddess Nature herself, in response to the Muse's plea:

> PRIESTESS OF NATURE! while with pious awe
> Thy votary bends, the mystic veil withdraw;
> Charm after charm, succession bright, display,
> And give the GODDESS to adoring day![34]

The goddess herself is described thus:

> SHRIN'D in the midst majestic *Nature* stands,
> Extends o'er earth and sea her hundred hands;
> Tower upon tower her beamy forehead crests,
> And births unnumber'd milk her hundred breasts.
>   (1.129–32)

Fuseli's Frontispiece reduces this monstrous being to more manageable proportions, with no visible hands or babies at her breasts, of which however the visibility of three – rather than the specified hundred – is sufficiently disconcerting. But the dynamic power of Fuseli's design depends on an interplay of different ways of looking: from the goddess's inscrutable blankness to the rapt attention of the kneeling Poetic Muse in the foreground and the more chattering attention of the crowd of other votaries just visible on the left. Welding all these elements together, the Priestess Urania divides her physical attention between pointing at the goddess's strange central breast and looking over her shoulder at the votaries to whom she is ostensibly directing her teaching, while the angle of her body in fact projects her message more forcibly towards us and the kneeling Poetic Muse, who has her back to us but whose total receptivity to both lecture and goddess is shown by her gesturing arms and tensely upright posture.

110 MARTIN PRIESTMAN

Figure 4.4 Frontispiece to Erasmus Darwin, *The Temple of Nature* (1803). With permission of the British Library.

With this instantly graspable composition, Fuseli extracts the central situation from what many readers have found a bafflingly elaborate handling of the poem's opening temple-allegory, which Darwin stretches to a forbidding 222 lines before the scientific instruction actually begins. The key element in both poem and picture is instruction *about* Nature, delivered *to* the votaries and Poetic Muse (i.e. the reader via Darwin), *by* the Priestess who will actually speak most of the rest of the poem. Hence we as viewers 'enter' the picture, as it were, from behind the Poetic Muse whose perspective we share, have our attention arrested by the well-lit, busily instructing Priestess, and then find it redirected by her pointing finger to the darkened, part-veiled goddess, on whom it comes to rest as the ultimate goal of our inquiry.[35]

The scientific part of the poem's first canto – which Urania is here about to launch into in response to the Muse's questions – concerns the evolutionary 'Production of Life', whose starring cast of microbes, plants, birds, and mammals offers no natural subjects for the relentlessly human-centred Fuseli. The same might be said of Canto Two, 'Reproduction of Life', with its focus on the shift from parthenogenic or non-sexual earlier life-forms to the eventual intervention of sexual reproduction – which Darwin called Nature's '*chef d'oeuvre*' – across most of the plant and animal kingdoms. There is, however, a moment when Darwin shifts the latter event to a human level by way of a strikingly blasphemous re-reading of the Eden myth. In this reading, the story of Adam's self-fulfilling dream of a 'new sex' in the shape of Eve actually 'originated with the magi or philosophers of Egypt, with whom Moses [the supposed author of *Genesis*] was educated', and allegorized the leap from asexual to sexual reproduction, as still observable in aphids, and as well understood from the Egyptian magi's 'profound inquiries into the original state of animal existence':[36]

> The potent wish in the productive hour
> Calls to its aid Imagination's power,
> O'er embryon throngs with mystic charm presides,
> And sex from sex the nascent world divides.
> …
> Unmarried Aphides prolific prove
> For nine successions uninform'd of love;
> New sexes next with softer passions spring,
> Breathe the fond vow, and woo with quivering wing.
>   So erst in Paradise creation's LORD,
> As the first leaves of holy writ record,
> From Adam's rib, who press'd the flowery grove,
> And dreamt delighted of untasted love,
> To cheer and charm his solitary mind,
> Form'd a new sex, the MOTHER OF MANKIND.[37]

Attempting none of the biological back-story implied by Darwin's 'So' (135), Fuseli's design, *The Creation of Eve*, simply depicts what it says. Adam

Figure 4.5 Henry Fuseli, *The Creation of Eve*. Opposite p. 55 of Erasmus Darwin, *The Temple of Nature* (1803). With permission of the British Library.

lies sleeping on his back on some rocks, with his left arm curled behind his head and his right hand pointing to his lower ribcage. Dominating the picture, Eve floats up vertically from his prostrate body, on which she could almost be standing if there were any signs of her weight pressing on him. With her long tresses floating free, she raises her arms in what seems like worship towards the light which streams down from a gap in the clouds above.

As usual, this picture can be read in terms of the play of perceptions. Eve's rapt gaze upwards to the light breaking the clouds suggests more than one kind of dawning: not only her awakening consciousness but the opening up of a new and better future for the whole of 'organic life' through the possibility of sexual reproduction she represents. And, as with *The Nightmare*, Adam's closed eyes enhance, rather than obstruct, our focus on what he might be perceiving. The hand pointing to his ribs suggests his awareness that something has happened – or should happen – in that region but, more importantly, the whole apparition of Eve has a liminal status between the physical reality it seems to be and the dream-scene still playing behind Adam's eyelids, at least until he 'wakes, and finds it truth', in Keats's words.[38]

For readers of the famous rendition of this scene in Milton's *Paradise Lost*, the contrast between the dozing Adam and Eve straining up towards the light may suggest a further possibility: that despite her nominal blameworthiness as the cause of the Fall, the restless curiosity of Milton's Eve makes her by far the most mentally 'alive' of the primal couple, from her first self-narrated moment of consciousness onwards.[39] Imputing this Miltonic reference to Fuseli is by no means irrelevant since he adapted this plate directly from one of the paintings exhibited in his ambitious though ultimately unprofitable 'Milton Gallery' in Pall Mall (1799–1800), based specifically on *Paradise Lost*'s account of this scene. In this *Temple of Nature* version, the beam of light substitutes for a hazily defined supernatural being whose presence in the painting was objected to by some viewers as either blasphemously representing God or, just as blasphemously, not doing so. One of these objectors being *Temple*'s Unitarian publisher Joseph Johnson, Fuseli here replaces this figure by a light-beam representing a more general deistic 'enlightenment' far more appropriate to Darwin's intended progressive message.[40]

While from Darwin's evolutionary perspective the mind develops on a continuum which certainly includes animals, the main focus of his psychological third canto, 'Progress of the Mind', does at last shift to human beings. Given that *Temple*'s subtitle is 'The Origin of Society', Darwin is particularly concerned with the natural causes of the social impulse which often overcomes the more belligerently self-centred tendencies described in earlier cantos. In a key allegorical passage he connects this social impulse to the 'Sentimental Love' represented by Eros, who is supposedly distinguished from the Sexual Love strongly identified with Cupid in the previous canto:[41]

> Now on swift wheels descending like a star
> Alights young *Eros* from his radiant car;
> On angel-wings attendant Graces move,
> And hail the God of *Sentimental Love*.
> …
> Warm as the sun-beam, pure as driven snows,
> The enamour'd god for young Dione glows;
> …
> Drinks with mute ecstacy the transient glow,
> Which warms and tints her bosom's rising snow.
> With holy kisses wanders o'er her charms,
> And clasps the Beauty in Platonic arms;
> …
> O'er female hearts with chaste seduction reigns,
> And binds *Society* in silken chains.[42]

As the oxymoron 'chaste seduction' suggests, the separation of sentimental from sexual love is not particularly easy, at least for the erotically minded Darwin, and much might seem to depend on the precise identity of the 'Dione' who is the object of Eros's affections. In Canto 1, Dione is Darwin's usual name for Venus, who is generally thought of as the mother of Cupid; according to some other sources such as Robert Graves she is actually Venus/Aphrodite's mother, which would make her Cupid/Eros's grandmother.[43] By insisting on the difference between the sexual Cupid and the 'older' Eros normally thought of as simply his Greek version, Darwin arguably avoids evoking a directly incestuous relationship with Dione: nonetheless, his choice of such normally sexualized deities as Eros and Venus/Dione raises questions about the 'platonic' nature of even the purest social love.

Eros and Dione, Fuseli's riddling illustration of this passage, wrestles directly with these complexities.[44] It gives the immediate impression of being about sexual love, but then repeatedly denies this in its details. Clearly based on a much-copied statue of the amorous winged couple Cupid and Psyche, then in Florence's Medici Collection,[45] it expands Eros's wings to angelic proportions, displacing Cupid's arrows and boyishly mischievous form to the bottom left of the picture along with a phallic dolphin, and Psyche's traditional butterfly wings – about which Darwin has much to say elsewhere[46] – to an actual butterfly on the bottom right.

Fuseli reinforces the 'Platonic' nature of the couple's affection by making Dione taller than Eros, crossing her legs and dressing her almost fully, apart from her exposed breasts. However, though both she and Eros are now gazing directly into each other's eyes, these relative positions would make it very easy for Eros's eyes to follow the direction indicated by Darwin, over 'her bosom's rising snow' and other 'charms' (3. 193–4). This emphasis on her – possibly maternal, if she is in fact Venus – bosom as an object of love ties this whole passage on Sentimental Love in to an immediately preceding account of the origin of our sense of beauty when, as a baby, each of us:

> Eyes with mute rapture every waving line,
> Prints with adoring kiss the Paphian shrine,
> And learns erelong, the perfect form confess'd,
> IDEAL BEAUTY from [the] Mother's breast.[47]

Darwin returns again to this issue after the Eros and Dione episode, suggesting the strong link he wishes to make between society's silken chains and the sense of 'ideal beauty' imprinted (as William Hogarth suggests) through universal memories of the maternal breast.[48] In this post-Freudian age the separation Darwin asserts between the sexual Cupid and the platonic, breast-admiring Eros may seem questionable, and Fuseli's plate greatly magnifies these questions by noting down all the alternative sexual possibilities surrounding the mutually adoring gazes between this deity and his taller, breast-baring companion.

Less anchored to its canto's main arguments than the preceding three, *Temple*'s fourth and last plate, *The Power of Fancy in Dreams*, seems much more geared to Fuseli's interests than Darwin's.[49] The lines it illustrates –

> So holy transports in the cloister's shade
> Play round thy toilet, visionary maid!
> Charm'd o'er thy bed celestial voices sing,
> And Seraphs hover on enamour'd wing.[50]

– seem rather foisted into the forth canto's discussion 'Of Good and Evil' in order to give Fuseli his head, and may refer specifically to his painting of *Queen Katherine's Dream* – illustrating a scene from Shakespeare's *Henry VIII* – which was exhibited at the Royal Academy in 1781.[51] Transposing some of this painting's elements from landscape to portrait shape, Fuseli removes its Shakespearean specifics to turn the dying, vision-blessed Katherine into a more generic and somewhat comically eroticized nun, the leading 'Spirit of peace' in her vision into a power-gesturing embodiment of Fancy, and her alert attendant into a woman dozing over a book, wearing the kind of elaborate head-and-neckware which often carries strong fetishistic overtones in Fuseli's private sketches.[52]

Yet what appears a somewhat serio-comic jumble of echoes from a range of other works arguably fuses them together into a new narrative commenting on the circulation of ideas – from the textual to the visually imagined to the ultimately truthful and back again – which has been central to the whole Fuseli-Darwin project. A woman drowsing over a book dreams of (herself as?) a nun awakening to a vision of a floating female figure (her own Fancy/Imagination?) pointing upwards to the Holy Spirit in the dim form of a dove hovering over her head: a ladder of perceptions and self-perceptions which will doubtless re-inform her reading when she wakes. From the factual words on the page, through intensely imagined human/metaphorical figures, to some greater meaning and back to the text again, has throughout their partnership been the route by which Fuseli's images have exponentially raised the game of Darwin's declared poetic intention, 'to inlist Imagination under the banner of Science'.[53]

Notes

1 John Locke, *An Essay Concerning Human Understanding* (London: Dent Everyman, 1947), Book 2, 1. 2 and 24, pp. 26, 33.
2 Erasmus Darwin, *The Botanic Garden, Part Two: The Loves of the Plants* (London: J. Johnson, 1791). Interlude 1, p. 48.
3 Ibid., 3. 56–8, p. 97.
4 Henry Fuseli, Letter to William Roscoe, 22 October 1791, quoted in Martin Myrone, *Henry Fuseli* (London: Tate Gallery Publishing, 2001), 43.
5 These were all designed at this scale except for *The Temple of Nature*'s *The Creation of Eve*, whose pre-existence as a larger painting in Fuseli's Milton Gallery is discussed below. The portrait-shaped version of *Nightmare* was only belatedly included in the 5th edition of *The Botanic Garden* (1799), as a reminder of this picture's pre-existence elsewhere. *The Power of Fancy in Dreams* (in *Temple*) owes debts to several paintings and is hence a new design (see below).
6 So well known in its original landscape form that we have not included it here: copies can be easily viewed on Google Images and elsewhere.
7 Christopher Frayling suggests that the horse may have been added to Fuseli's original design on Erasmus Darwin's advice. C. Frayling, 'Fuseli's *The Nightmare*: Somewhere between the Sublime and the Ridiculous', in Martin Myrone, Christopher Frayling, and Marina Warner, *Gothic Nightmares: Fuseli, Blake and the Romantic Imagination* (London: Tate Publishing, 2006), 9–40, 15.
8 As engraved by Thomas Burke in 1783, this version of the picture can be seen in Myrone, Frayling, and Warner, *Gothic Nightmares*, 49.
9 See Desmond King-Hele, *Erasmus Darwin: A Life of Unequalled Achievement* (London: de la Mare, 1999), 172–3. For the dating of Fuseli's sketch see John

Knowles, *The Life and Writings of Henry Fuseli*, 3 vols (London: H. Colburn and R. Bentley, 1831), vol. 1: 64.
10 See King-Hele, *Erasmus Darwin: A Life*, pp. 201–2.
11 Erasmus Darwin, *The Botanic Garden, Part Two: The Loves of the Plants* (1791), 3.51–4, 63–8, pp. 97–9.
12 Darwin, *The Loves of the Plants* (1791), note to 3.74, p. 98.
13 See Myrone, *Henry Fuseli*, 56–60.
14 William Shakespeare, *A Midsummer Night's Dream*, V, i.
15 Henry Fuseli, *Nightmare*, opposite p. 126 of Erasmus Darwin, *The Botanic Garden, Part Two: The Loves of the Plants*, 5th ed. (1799). See Figure 4.1.
16 Fuseli, *Flora attired by the Elements*. Frontispiece to Darwin's *The Botanic Garden* (London: J. Johnson, 1791).
17 Emma Crewe's *Loves of the Plants* frontispiece is called *Flora at Play with Cupid*, and brings out that poem's playful eroticism by giving Cupid's bow and arrows to a mischievous-looking Flora, and her gardening implements to him.
18 See particularly the 'Proem' to *Loves of the Plants*, vii–ix.
19 Darwin, *Economy of Vegetation*, 3.129–34, pp. 126–7.
20 Darwin, *The Botanic Garden*, 'Apology', v.
21 See Essick, Robert N. and Rosamund A. Paice, 'Newly Uncovered Blake Drawings in the British Museum', *Blake: An Illustrated Quarterly*, 37: 3 (Winter 2003/2004): 84–100, 88–9.
22 Monsoon specifically resembles an image of Jupiter Pluvius in Bernard de Montfaucon's *L'antiquité expliqué* (Paris 1719), which Darwin also consulted on other occasions: see Gert Schiff, *Johann Heinrich Füssli, 1741-1825: Text und Oeuvrekatalog*, 2 vols (Zurich: Verlag Berichthaus, 1973), vol. 1: 533.
23 William Blake, *Visions of the Daughters of Albion* (London, 1793), Plates 1 and 11; in *William Blake: The Complete Illuminated Books*, introduced by David Bindman (London: Thames & Hudson, 2000), 142, 152.
24 William Blake, *America* (London, 1793), Plate 10; *Complete Illuminated Books*, 163.
25 William Blake, *The First Book of Urizen* (London, 1794), Plates 1, 4, 11, 26; *Complete Illuminated Books*, 203, 206, 213, 228.
26 Martin Priestman, *Romantic Atheism: Poetry and Freethought, 1780-1830* (Cambridge University Press, 1999), 102–4, 110–11.
27 See, e. g., David V. Erdman, *Blake: Prophet Against Empire*, revised edition (New York: Anchor, 1969), 179.
28 Constantin-François Volney, *The Ruins, or a Survey of the Revolutions of Empires*. Trans. Anon. (London: J. Johnson, 1795), Chapter 22, 'Origin and Genealogy of Religious Ideas', 218–96.
29 *Tornado*, from the 'Air' canto of *The Economy of Vegetation*, in *The Botanic Garden* (London: J. Johnson, 1795), keyed to lines 4.71–8.
30 For example, *The First Book of Urizen* Plate 4, p. 207 in *Complete Illuminated Books*.
31 Fuseli, *Thor Battering the Midgard Serpent*, in Myrone, *Henry Fuseli*, 51.

32 Even in *Tornado*, the matching glares of the angry god and the serpent partly embedded in his head catch immediate attention.
33 Darwin, *The Loves of the Plants*, 3.63–8, pp. 97–8.
34 *The Temple of Nature*, 1.167–70.
35 Schiff finds classical sources for the goddess and priestess, and one for the Muse with her back to us in Raphael's painting *Fire in the Borgo*, where a similarly foregrounded woman likewise focuses our gaze on what is going on beyond her. Schiff, *Johann Heinrich Füssli*, vol. 1: 579.
36 Darwin, *The Temple of Nature*, Additional Notes 10, p. 42.
37 *The Temple of Nature*, 2. 117–20, 131–40, pp. 53, 55.
38 John Keats, Letter to Benjamin Bailey, 22 November 1817.
39 John Milton, *Paradise Lost* (1674) 4.449–91.
40 See Luisa Calè, *Fuseli's Milton Gallery* (Oxford University Press, 2006), 146–7.
41 Darwin, *Temple*, note to 3.178, p. 98; see also 2.221–50.
42 *Temple of Nature* 3. 176–80, 187–8, 193–6, 205–6, pp. 98–100.
43 See Robert Graves, *The Greek Myths*, 2 vols (Harmondsworth: Penguin, 1955), vol. 1: 49–50.
44 Copies of this and the other illustrations to *The Temple of Nature* can be found in *The Temple of Nature by Erasmus Darwin*, ed. Martin Priestman, Romantic Circles, 2006 at: www.rc.umd.edu/editions/darwin_temple/engravings.html
45 This statue of the winged couple from the second century CE appears on the far left of Joseph Zoffany's painting *The Tribuna of the Uffizi* (1772–8). Fuseli also copies elements of a similar but unwinged statue in Rome's Capitoline Museum: see Schiff, *Johann Heinrich Füssli*, vol. 1, p. 580. As Schiff points out, Fuseli had earlier sketched a lesbian version of this Roman statue, as *Two Women Kissing Each Other* (1795–1800), vol. 2: 337.
46 See *Temple*, note to 2.223, p. 60.
47 *Temple of Nature*, 3.173–6.
48 See *Temple*, note to 3.207, pp. 100–2, relating this idea to William Hogarth's *The Analysis of Beauty* (1753).
49 See note 44.
50 *The Temple of Nature* 4.201–4.
51 Darwin may have seen this painting on a rare visit to London in 1781. Schiff connects it to the plate being discussed (*Johann Heinrich Füssli*, vol. 1, 337) and it is reproduced in Myrone, Frayling, and Warner, *Gothic Nightmares*, p. 153.
52 For the power-gesture see Anne and Titania in *Garrick as Gloucester Waiting for Lady Anne* and *Titania and Bottom* in Myrone, *Henry Fuseli*, 15 and 59. For Fuseli's hair-and-neck fetishism see ibid., 71–5.
53 Darwin, *The Botanic Garden*, 'Apology', v.

5 | Henry Fuseli's Accommodations: 'Attempting the Domestic' in the Illustrations to Cowper

SUSAN MATTHEWS

The adjectives 'small' and 'domestic' are not commonly applied to Henry Fuseli's work. But the eight illustrations engraved from small paintings by Fuseli for Joseph Johnson's 1806 edition of Cowper's *Poems in Two Volumes* fit both these labels. In 1986, John Barrell identified two voices in Fuseli's academic lectures: one which announces the public role of the artist and a second which is inescapably complicit in the commercialized privacy he attacks. Barrell thinks that 'as Fuseli got older […] his belief in the value of compromise […] becomes increasingly clear'.[1] But since 1986, most accounts have focused on Fuseli as a painter of the sublime, an artistic persona that Rosie Dias sees as 'carefully cultivated'.[2] While Fuseli's public pronouncements construct this persona, his letters reveal an artist taken up with small works for engravers and publishers in a world where vast paintings can disappoint and sublime galleries fail. Fuseli's growing willingness to accept an art of compromise may derive not just from the necessity to work for the booksellers after the failure of the literary galleries but from a more extensive accommodation to the new circumstances of art consumption in the first decade of the nineteenth century.

According to Martin Myrone, 'Blake inverted the heroic model of art perpetuated by Fuseli, taking it down in scale'.[3] Fuseli's Homer paintings for the publisher Francis Isaac Du Roveray's *Iliad* (1805) and *Odyssey* (1806) started out as 'kit-cat size' but were shrunk by a factor of eight at the hands of the engravers. While Fuseli's work for Du Roveray struggles with the task of miniaturizing the epic, his paintings for Cowper's *Poems in Two Volumes* offer instead a dark version of domesticity revealing the cultural process by which 'the ambition, activity, and spirit of public life is shrunk to the minute detail of domestic arrangements'.[4] This chapter will trace a double narrative of this shrinking: from the 1790s project of the Gallery of the Miltonic Sublime to the illustrations for Du Roveray, and from the Grand Gallery of the Louvre (visited in 1802) to Fuseli's Cowper images. In doing so it will ask what happens when we replace small work within a larger cultural narrative and what happens to 'the minute detail of domestic arrangements' when it enters Fuseli's imagined world.

The Failure of the Gallery

There is no doubt that Fuseli valued size. He thought of himself as a painter of the sublime and large canvases were considered necessary to sublime effects.[5] In 1787 James Northcote reported that Fuseli wanted a larger canvas for his 'darling subject of Macbeth and because nine feet of canvas was not enough for him Boydell has allow'd him six inches more than any other person'.[6] At work on paintings for his Gallery of the Miltonic Sublime in 1791, Fuseli repeatedly notes sizes, writing to William Roscoe that '*Satan Sin and Death* would not Suffer me to think of any thing mortal or immortal till I had flung them into picturesque Existence on a Miniature-Canvas of thirteen feet by ten'.[7] After his encounter with the Sistine Chapel in Rome in the 1770s, Fuseli dreamed of a sublime gallery (devoted at this stage to Shakespeare): 'He saw in imagination a long and shadowy succession of pictures. He figured to himself a magnificent temple, and filled it as the illustrious artists of Italy did the Sistine with pictures from his favourite poet.'[8] Looking forward to the opening of the Milton Gallery, William Seward foresaw the moment when

> Painting, on fearless pinions borne, ascends
> The stars exalted region, and, set free
> From every feculence of this vile earth,
> Bursts through the flaming barriers of this world.[9]

But Fuseli couldn't exhibit his work in the 'stars exalted region' and in 1796 he complained that even 'the Largest room in London will not perhaps be capacious enough to hold what I have finished, advanced or begun'.[10] The problem facing any artist with epic ambitions was that oversize canvasses could only be produced, exhibited and stored in large rooms.

The Sistine chapel offered not just scale but permanence and a settled order. However large, the exhibition spaces of London (Spring Gardens, Somerset House, the Boydell gallery, Macklin's Poet's Gallery, the Gallery of the Miltonic Sublime, the Lyceum) proved impermanent, whether subject to an annual rehang and reselection, or forced to close through lack of visitors and commercial failure. When Fuseli finally found a space in the building vacated by the Royal Academy in Pall Mall, the installation he had spent almost a decade creating was short-lived. Almost as soon as the gallery opened on 20 May 1799 he was worried about attendance. Success seemed impossible without fashionable, and specifically female, approval. On 5 June William Shepherd wrote to Roscoe to try to drum up support: 'Could you by writing to your female *cognoscenti*, viz. Dames

Berry, &c &c give him a lift?'¹¹ In 1798, Mary Berry had spent over half an hour at the Lyceum looking at one painting from the Orleans collection, though she recognized that the location was not ideal 'not near any of the great haberdashers for the women, nor Bond St. or St. James's St. for the men'.¹² An endorsement from Mary and Agnes Berry, friends of Horace Walpole, would have meant fashionable approval of the kind Fuseli desperately needed. He had the support of his fellow academicians: when the gallery reopened in 1800, the Royal Academy held a dinner with tickets priced at 15 shillings and two weeks later, William Godwin dined at the Milton Gallery with painters, sculptors, engravers and print sellers.¹³ But the support of the male art establishment could not save the gallery and it closed again four months later.

Fuseli's explanation is revealing: 'All who go, praise', he wrote, 'but Milton Can not stand the Competition of *Seringapatam* and the posies of portraits and Knickknacks of Sommerset-house'. The rival exhibitions, it seems, appealed to taste coded as feminine: 'posies', 'Knickknacks' and national sentiment. The exhibition at the Lyceum of *The Storming of Seringapatam*, a semi-circular painting that 19-year-old Robert Ker Porter had completed in six weeks, met a wartime demand for topical images of British military heroism, providing, as Mary Favret points out, a daily re-enactment of a British victory.¹⁴ The accompanying *Descriptive Sketch* emphasized that 'THE PAINTING is executed upon a large scale, comprehending 2,550 square feet of canvas, and contains several hundred figures as large as life, with near Twenty Portraits of British Officers.'¹⁵ There is no record that the Berry sisters visited Fuseli's gallery, but Mary Berry noted in her journal on Saturday 5 October 1799 that the only good news came from India 'where those who really know say that the death of Tippoo Sahib [at Seringapatam] for the present entirely secures our possessions, and frustrates all the designs of the French, even if they ever reach India'.¹⁶ The ironic sublimity of Fuseli's Satan may not have catered to an appetite for patriotic art amongst women who, according to Linda Colley, 'were more prominently represented among the ranks of conventional patriots in [the wars against Revolutionary and Napoleonic France] than in any of Britain's previous wars'.¹⁷

Fuseli's disappointment is evident in his letters: 'my exhibition must be broke up', he tells Roscoe, 'and the Question now remains what am I to do?' In language both tender and self-mocking he imagines his vast paintings as vulnerable to damage and destruction: 'The greater part of my exhibition', he writes in August 1800, 'the rejected Family of a silly Father, are now again rolled up, Or packed together against the Walls of my Study to be Seasoned for dust, the worm, and oblivion'.¹⁸ The paintings are both his 'bantlings' and the 'Enormous Miltonic Lumberstock.' In 1791, Fuseli had described a painting which he had sent to the engraver Sharpe as 'now at Nurse'.[19] His paintings are now monstrous babies outgrowing his home and in 1803 force him to 'take a Step which I had Long meditated and Long delayed, to take a house of Larger dimensions in order to Save from utter ruin the Mass of my Milton Pictures'. The move from Queen Anne Street to 'a commodious house' in Berners Street (just to the west of Newman Street, the 'artists'' street discussed in Chapter 10) allowed him to accommodate the engraver Moses Haughton.[20] Fuseli's lost Lycidas painting (no. XXVII in the Milton Gallery) survives in a 29 by 24 cm stipple engraving completed in 1803 by Moses Haughton. It shrinks further in 1832 to a 9 by 9 cm woodcut vignette accompanying the entry for Milton in Arthur Malkin's 1832 *Gallery of Portraits* for the Society for the Diffusion of Useful Knowledge. The same year, 1832, it appears as a 7 x 7.7 cm woodcut in Knight's *Penny Magazine*.[21] One of these images was copied in 1833 in a tiny watercolour by Charlotte Brontë.[22] The engraver reduced history paintings to a size that would fit within a bourgeois home, whether as a framed furniture print on a wall, within a portfolio or in the pages of a book ranged on a library shelf as a form of domestic exhibition.[23]

Elegant Epic

Writing to George Cumberland in 1800, William Blake remarked 'that London in so few years from a City of meer Necessaries or at l[e]ast a commerce of the lowest order of luxuries should have become a City of Elegance in some degree & that its once stupid inhabitants should enter into an Emulation of Grecian manners'. The change had occurred because there were 'as many Booksellers as there are Butchers & as many Printshops as of any other trade'.[24] Whereas a painter's history would see the literary galleries as a first step on the road, in 1824, to a national gallery, an engraver's history might give priority to the bookseller, reminding us that it was Joseph Johnson's commission for Fuseli 'to paint thirty pictures, which were to be put into the hands of the ablest engravers of the time' that led to the Milton Gallery.[25] Booksellers financed Fuseli as he worked on his gallery: 'I do what I Can to earn Something by work that does not for any Length of time interfere with Milton', he wrote in 1797, noting that he had 'just finished four Small pictures for Heaths Shakspeare at 60 Guineas'.[26] Fuseli's work for the booksellers continued after the literary galleries had closed: in all, more than 300 subjects were engraved after his designs.[27] So far, most scholarly attention has been directed to the relatively modest octavo editions published by Du Roveray between 1798 and 1806 for which Fuseli produced 30 designs.[28] But this work is not usually considered a significant part of Fuseli's oeuvre: it seems to Myrone that with the failure of the literary galleries 'the most intensively productive period of his life was over' and that it would be 'difficult to claim any great innovation in his art from this period'.[29] Writing on Fuseli's prints and illustrations, however, David Weinglass sees the first decade of the nineteenth century as 'one of Fuseli's most productive periods'.[30]

Du Roveray's editions offered modest luxury, elegance on a small scale with works both designed and engraved by the leading artists of the English school. Fuseli joined Du Roveray's team for the second volume, *The Rape of the Lock* (dated 1798 but published the following year). The prospectus announced 'A NEW AND ELEGANT EDITION' and explained:

> Whilst so many inferior productions of our literature have been published with all the decorations of fine printing and elegant engravings, to many it will doubtless appear strange that equal honours should not have not been bestowed on that most attractive and excellent of all comi-heroick poems, the RAPE OF THE LOCK.[31]

Illustration is not presented here as a form of interpretation (a reading of the text) but as confirmation of literary status. The plates provided by Du Roveray are adornment and decoration, words which this culture takes seriously: Blake's marginal comment on his copy of *The Works of Sir Joshua Reynolds* announces that 'Necessaries Accomodations & Ornaments are the whole of Life' (637E). Du Roveray's point is that the literary merit of Pope's poem deserves decoration: 'since decorations of the most expensive kind have been lavished on other works of equal celebrity, no apology will, it is presumed, be thought necessary for the present edition of one so well adapted to display the progress made by this Country in the Arts of Painting and Engraving.'[32] His promise that the pictures were to be 'engraved by the First Artists' reveals the status accorded to engravers: the promotion of English engravers had been one of Boydell's achievements. But Du Roveray's promise of 'elegant engravings' also gestured towards aesthetic values associated with the French.[33] Richard Altick points out that the visual language of English illustration was, at this period, still strongly marked by a 'French elegance of line' derived from Hubert François Gravelot who had illustrated around a hundred books during his time in England from 1732 to 1745.[34] Elegance was also associated with the painters who worked for Du Roveray, especially Richard Westall whose illustrations Hazlitt described as 'the elegant antithesis to the style of Hogarth, where, instead of that originality of character which excludes a nice attention to general forms, we have all that beauty of form which excludes the possibility of character'.[35] If originality and character stand for Englishness, elegance is potentially foreign.

In his work for Du Roveray, Fuseli seems to have done his best to resist an aesthetic of adornment, keen to assert his identity as painter and genius. Whereas Stothard's plates for Du Roveray's *The Rape of the Lock* are signed, 'Thos Stothard R.A. del^t' (drawn or designed), his proudly announced 'H. Fuseli, R.A. pinx^t' (painted). Whereas Stothard offered Du Roveray a choice of medium (india ink at two guineas or colour at three), Fuseli not only demanded a larger format but asked and got 30 guineas. Du Roveray's first approach to Fuseli in March 1798 skated around the embarrassingly small nature of the commission: 'I beg the favor of your informing me whether you would do a Drawing for me, in water colours, 4 inches by 3 upright […] If you objected to make so small a drawing I should be obliged to you to mention the size that would be agreeable to you.'[36] Over a month's negotiation, Fuseli increased the size to 24 inches upright, and having agreed the larger fee, upped the size again for no added cost.[37] Engraved by Thomas Holloway, Cadell and Davies viewed the design as 'a very admirable Proof of what may be done on a small Scale, from a Picture of Mr. Fuseli's'.[38] In Du Roveray's edition of Pope's Homer, almost all the images derived from paintings: they are 'Painted by H^y. Fuseli R.A' or 'Painted by T. Stothard R.A.' When Joseph Johnson reissued the Homer illustrations in 1810 to accompany Cowper's Homer after a warehouse fire had destroyed the copies of Pope's translation for which they had been intended, he emphasized that these were the work of leading painters: 'ILLUSTRATIONS | OF THE| ILIAD AND ODYSSEY OF HOMER | FIFTY ENGRAVINGS OF | FUSELI, HOWARD, SMIRKE, STOTHARD, WESTALL, &C. &C.| ROYAL ACADEMICIANS'.[39] This was to be an epic collection on a small scale and the challenge for the artist and the engraver was to adapt epic to these new constraints.

Fuseli, however, affected to despise the work of the engraver.[40] Commenting in 1802 on Bromley's proof of *Satan Calling up his Legions* he complained that 'It is too much of one depth; *all* the Shadows want more work, more finish; the feet, the hands, the knees of Satan want more precision; more making out.'[41] Isaac Taylor, who engraved four of Fuseli's Homer designs, blamed this experience for his 'habitual error' of 'too much colour', explaining that 'So many of Fuseli's fall to my lot' and 'no man can Show much less obtain a light style from Copying pictures So much loaded with Colour'.[42] By 'loaded with colour' Taylor seems to indicate the intense shadows of Fuseli's work, what Dias calls 'an apparently infinite shroud of darkness', which function as a means of suggesting infinite depth even where the length and breadth of the image were limited.[43] But as Dias also notes, Fuseli's paintings 'acquired an altogether new dimension as they were given redefinition by line engravings'.[44] The skill of the engraver translated the infinite gloom of the sublime into elegant forms that allowed the viewer to read 'minute detail'.

'Immense, but': The Sublime Gallery in Paris

Before Fuseli began work on the Homer paintings in November 1802, however, he was to experience another encounter with the sublime gallery – one that I will argue helps to shift his view of the meaning of scale in the smaller paintings on which he worked on his return. In 1802, the short-lived peace of Amiens allowed painters, illustrators, engravers, and tourists to cross the channel for the first time since the outbreak of war with France. For many, this visit crystalized thoughts on the rival identities of the British and the French school and, exploiting his French background, Du Roveray briefly toyed with the idea of using French engravers for his edition of Pope's *Works* (1804).[45] Most, however, went to see the Grand Gallery of the Louvre that now contained art looted from across Europe by Bonaparte's victorious army. In one vast gallery the greatest paintings in the world were now gathered together. Attempting to retain this experience, the painter Joseph Farington used a version of the art of memory, carefully locating the works in their position on the wall. On one visit he noted the

> outlines of the arrangement of the pictures on the right hand side of the Gallery, and began to do the same on the left side. This appeared to me to be a good mode of reviving in my Mind the different works which I thought a representation of their respective situations would much contribute to do.[46]

On that visit he bumped into Maria Cosway who was 'Colouring a print from the picture by Titian of the Supper at Emaus'. Cosway had come to France specifically to copy paintings for '*publication of the Gallery*', an 'immense work' that would allow the purchaser to 'form a museum within his own Apartments on the plan of the Louvre'.[47] J. M. W. Turner was there and he filled a sketchbook (128 x 114 mm) with illustrations of paintings together with written descriptions.[48] Mary Berry, who had given Fuseli's Milton Gallery a miss, was in Paris with the sculptor Anne Damer, eager to compare the best that France could offer to London's exhibition scene.[49] She described how you 'first enter a large square room about twice the size of the exhibition room in Somerset House, lined with all the finest Italian pictures, very well placed as to light'. But the Grand Gallery outclassed any in the world:

> Out of this room you enter a gallery – *such* a gallery! But *such* a gallery!!! as the world never before saw, both as to size and furniture! So long that the perspective ends almost in a point, and so furnished that at every step, tho' one feels one must go on, yet one's attention is arrested by all the finest pictures that one has seen before in every other country, besides a thousand new ones.[50]

Fuseli went to Paris intending to research a 'critical account of the principal pictures and statues which then adorned the Louvre'.[51] But his reaction was unexpected. He wrote to William Roscoe that: 'The Coup d'oeil of the Louvre-gallery is Certainly immense, but when You have recovered from the first Shock, when examination takes place of Surprise it appears Little Superiour to a huge auction Room.'[52] Farington complained in his diary that 'It is not in the promiscuous arrangement of an Auction room that the mind will go farther than to admire the admirable skill of the Artist, and the beautiful effects of his Art' (V,1832). In London, auction rooms (which opened for two or three days before a sale) functioned as a replacement for a public gallery in a city that as yet offered no permanent public display of art.[53]

The Grand Gallery claimed permanence but was haunted, for visitors, by the memory of locations from which the paintings had been taken. The French, Fuseli wrote, 'have plundered but not Stript the Seats of Art – all the buildings, all the Frescoes of Rome, Bologna, Mantua, Parma, &c. remain where they were'.[54] Parisian culture was inhospitable to the appreciation of great art precisely because of the loss of a sense of the sacred present in the churches for which these masterpieces had been painted. As Fuseli explained, 'That *recueillement* [composure] of Mind, that Solemn twilight, that "magnum Loci Silentium" ["great silence of the place"] for which each great Master painted his work, are not here'.[55] Weinglass thinks that the phrase 'magnum Loci Silentium' may derive from Virgil. But another possible source exists in the Abbé Barruel's *Histoire du Clergé pendant la Révolution Francoise*, published in London in French in 1793 and in English translation the following year. There, Barruel associates 'un profond silence' and 'recueillement' with the sacrament of mass:

> Des habitans de *Viens* en Provence entendoient la messe de leur ancien pasteur dans la chapelle du château; le saint sacrement étoit exposé, & tout ce bon peuple dans un profond silence, dans un parfait recueillement, se livroit aux sentimens de la piété la plus édifiante.[56]

In the words of the 1794 translation 'At Viens in Provence a congregation of the faithful were devoutly assisting at the Mass of the old curate; the blessed sacrament was exposed, and in silence and profound recollection these pious souls were pouring out their souls to God.'[57] In this translation, 'recueillement' is rendered not as Weinglass's 'composure' but as 'recollection', a moment of recovered memory. Farington, as usual, echoes Fuseli with the comment: 'The most capital works were intended to strengthen religious impressions and in the Sanctuaries for which they were designed they were contemplated with awe & respect as representations that elevated the mind to a state proper for performing its most solemn duties.'[58] Mary Berry found it difficult to appreciate individual paintings for more prosaic reasons: 'it would be very long before I should sufficiently get the better of the astonishment to be able to fix my mind quietly to one picture or one set of pictures.'[59] Despite the size of the gallery, Farington describes it being 'so crowded, it being a *public day*, that it appeared to smoke with dust'.[60] The Grand Gallery of the Louvre may have challenged the assumption that vast paintings are best appreciated in sublime galleries.

Taste in the Bed Chamber

The house of Madame Recamier, another compulsory stop for the tourist, was, however, universally praised. Miss Berry's party 'were resolved not to leave Paris without seeing what is called the most elegant house in it, fitted up in the new style'.[61] Elegant, an etymologically French word used by Blake to describe a city of booksellers and by Du Roveray to market *The Rape of the Lock*, is here applied to the height of Parisian interior decoration. Miss Berry records the decoration and furniture of the house in extraordinary detail and at greater length than can be quoted here: 'There are no large rooms, nor a great many of them; but it is certainly fitted up with all the *recherche* and expense possible in what is now called *le goût antique*.'[62] She is especially struck by Madame Recamier's bed which 'is reckoned the most beautiful in Paris – it, too, is of mahogany enriched with ormolu and bronze, and raised upon two steps of the same wood'.[63] Fuseli visited 'the House of Madame Recamier, the ultimate Standard of Parisian Taste' with Robert Smirke, the architect son of the artist and illustrator of the same name. While Smirke 'not only measured but' drew the bedchamber 'with a Taste which improves it', Fuseli was fascinated by the secrets of the bed: 'As Harriot Loves Latin as well as Italian I will gratify You both with the Inscription on the Pedestal of a Small marble figure of Silence at the head of the Bed: "Tutatur Amores et Somnos, Conscia Lecti." ["She who knows the pleasures of the bed, protects lovers and those who are asleep."]'[64] It is as if the room makes Fuseli's painted world of dreams and sexual fantasies come true. The painter of *The Nightmare* (1781) returned frequently, almost obsessively, to the subject of the woman's bedchamber, in sketches and in paintings. But Fuseli's private fantasy was shared by his culture and drew on a long history. To Farington, Madame Recamier's bedchamber seemed 'more like the design of a painter for a reposing place for Venus than as intended or proper for Mortal use'.[65] Whereas the Grand Gallery seemed to disappoint visitors – too many pictures, too many people, or too much dust – Madame Recamier's bedroom turned interior space satisfyingly into art.

It was not just a contrast between public and private space but a matter of class. The Royal Academy had always excluded the lower orders through an entry fee and a ban on servants in livery, but when the Louvre opened to the public in 1793 as the *Muséum Français* the revolutionary museum was a statement of the 'communal ownership' of art and there was no charge or restriction on entry.[66] Madame Recamier's house represented the taste of a post-revolutionary moneyed elite; her husband, a banker, was one of Napoleon Bonaparte's chief backers. When a description of her house appeared in the 1803 *Monthly Review* as part of 'A Rough Sketch of Modern Paris' it was prefaced by an account of the three classes that made up post-revolutionary Parisian society: '1st, *l'ancienne noblesse*, or old nobility; 2ndly, the governmental class, or constituted authorities; and, 3dly', the class represented by Madame Recamier, '*les parvenus, ou nouveaux riches*, upstarts, or new gentry'.[67] Farington denied that the house was simply a display of wealth: 'The rich and costly appearance of the furniture is only a second consideration', he wrote, 'It is the taste & the elegance which most delights the eye.' The words 'taste' and 'elegance' turn capital into cultural capital. Nor does this scheme represent, for Farington, the tarnished sphere of fashion: 'The whole is so ideal, that is so little similar to any fashion which prevails, that it certainly has the same effect on the mind that looking at a beautiful design in painting would have.' There is no dividing line here between the work of the 'artist' and the interior designer just as, for Du Roveray, the word 'artist' could also be used of the engraver. This was the

Figure 5.1 Robert Smirke, *Elevation of one wall of Madame Recamier's bedroom, Hotel Recamier, Paris* (1802).

period in which Stothard might create a design for a piece of silverware before adapting the design to use for a painting.⁶⁸ Not so much had changed since Gravelot, the prolific French engraver of illustrations had also been employed 'to design for cabinet-makers, upholsterers, &c.'⁶⁹ The modest luxury of the illustrated book in the early nineteenth century appealed to a post-revolutionary consumer taste.

The antique style, however, carried more troubling associations in the hands of Jacques-Louis David. His unfinished *Portrait of Juliette Recamier*, painted in 1800, was still in the painter's studio in the Louvre where David's family also had rooms. Visiting the studio one day with Fuseli, Farington noticed 'Stool chairs made after antique patterns, which might serve the painter to imitate in Classical compositions.'⁷⁰ David's classicism was tainted for English visitors by his active role in the Terror and a perceived inability to evoke sympathy in his paintings: 'When he looked at David', Fuseli said, 'he could never divest his mind of the atrocities of the French Revolution'.[71] Fuseli describes France in a letter to Roscoe as the 'Land of blood', an association that may have been strengthened by the death of his lifelong friend Johann Caspar Lavater in January 1801 as a consequence of a bayonet wound inflicted in 1799 by Bonaparte's invading army.[72] Whereas the antique style as interpreted in interior decoration was received with delight, in David's painting it still carried dark memories of revolutionary excess.

Fuseli returned from Paris in October 1802 and settled down to 'a quantity of diminutive work'. He wrote to Du Roveray with his selection of Homer subjects in December and was able to report a year later: 'I have just cleared my room of the Last pictures of a Series I painted for a New Edition of Pope's Homer, Kitcat Size alas, where his Heroes and Heroines are convulsed or slain by puny pangs &c in puny battles.'[73] Fuseli's Homer illustrations try to insist on the grandeur of their subjects, creating an impression of massive scale by moving the figures close to the frame and by folding the human form as if it is too large to fit within the picture space: in 'Blinded Polyphemus Checks the Sheep as they leave the Cave' for the *Odyssey* (177 x 106 mm,1806), the giant crouches in front of the cave opening while the leg of a human being, hidden from the monster who has eaten his companions, sticks out beneath the sheep.[74] Terror is still present in this image. Richard Westall, by contrast, conjures an antique world that recalls Madame Recamier's elegant home: the frontispiece to the *Iliad* Volume II shows Paris reclining on a couch, enmeshed in Helen's glance. Such images forget the associations of the antique with the 'Land of blood' and offer instead what Blake calls 'an Emulation of Grecian manners' and Miss Berry '*le gout antique*'.

Home as Spectacle

Neither the bedchamber of Madame Recamier, nor the classicism of Westall's Homer illustrations are exactly domestic, offering instead a fantasy or spectacle of taste unaffordable to most purchasers of the Du Roveray volumes. Open to visitors on select terms, the Recamier house showcased a new form of advanced taste, putting into practice the ideas of Napoleon's architects Charles Percier and Pierre-François-Léonard Fontaine who in turn inspired London's taste maker, Thomas Hope, a banker who like the Recamiers would go on to fund Napoleon's empire.[75] In May 1802, just back from a trip to Paris, Hope opened his newly completed neoclassical

Figure 5.2 Richard Westall, *Paris Reclining on a Couch Looking up at Helen*. Etching and engraving James Heath, published F I Du Roveray (1805). Image size 123 x 88 mm © Trustees of the British Museum.

mansion in Duchess Street (one minute's walk from Fuseli's St Anne Street house) to over 1,000 guests including the Prince of Wales: his mission was to reform taste and spread the principles of interior decoration, a phrase he introduced into English in his 1807 volume *Household Furniture and Interior Decoration*. Mary Berry had noted that there were 'no large rooms, nor a great many of them' in the Recamier house; likewise the Duchess Street house did not have especially large rooms and could not provide a home for vast canvases: as Sébastian Allard points out, 'enormous history paintings […] could no longer be accommodated in the modern home, in which comfort was the main aim'.[76] Exquisite taste was displayed instead in displays of sculpture, classical vases, paintings by Westall, and sculpture by Flaxman (as well as a strikingly beautiful wife). Thomas Hope's 1807 volume helped 'the lover of elegant refinement to find at home those objects of superior design and execution, which formerly he could only obtain from abroad'.[77] Whereas elegance had previously been coded as French, Thomas Hope's style made neoclassical interior decoration an expression of national pride.

Fuseli's illustrations to Cowper reimagine a 25-year-old text in terms of up to the minute Regency elegance. Joseph Johnson had published the first illustrated edition of Cowper's 1782 *Poems* in 1799 (dated 1798) with ten illustrations by Thomas Stothard which are sensitive both to Cowper's celebration of domesticity and to the religious seriousness of the work.[78] Stothard's pictures spell innocence in a scene of the 'Cottager who weaves at her own door' or the boy who sits 'linking cherrystones'. We see Cowper walking with the 'tim'rous hare' in the background. But Fuseli's illustrations show a world stratified by class lines, reimagined as a series of elegant interiors and sublime landscapes, transporting the reader into an imaginative world which has more in common with his vision of, say Wieland's *Oberon* published by Cadell and Davies in 1806 than with Cowper's hares, country walks, and winter fireside. Offered in two octavo formats, one with generous margins, with eight illustrations translated by the top engravers (Raimbach, Bromley, Rhodes, Neagle, and Warren) and printed by Thomas Bensley (responsible not only for the Du Roveray volumes but Hope's *Household Furniture and Interior Decoration*), this was an edition that would grace any home. To Benjamin Robert Haydon, writing in 1838, Fuseli was simply the wrong choice of artist: '[w]hen Fuzeli attempted the domestic, as in the illustrations to Cowper, his total want of nature stares one in the face, like the eyes of his own ghosts.'[79] It is surprising that Haydon deems the Cowper illustrations worthy of inclusion in his survey of the British school.

The Task is also a poem about furniture, telling how 'a generation more refined/Improv'd the simple plan, made three legs four,/Gave them a twisted form vermicular,/And o'er the seat with plenteous wadding stuff'd/Induced a splendid cover green and blue'. The frontispiece to the first volume shows Cowper on a sofa that would almost do in Hope's household (Figure 2.3).

Figure 5.3 Henry Fuseli, frontispiece to the first volume of Joseph Johnson's edition of *Poems of William Cowper* (1806). Engraved by Abraham Raimbach. Untitled proof version © Trustees of the British Museum.

Falling asleep, the poet has dropped his copy of the *Iliad* (open at the Greek word 'MHNIN' or Wrath).

This is a variation of Westall's frontispiece to volume II of Du Roveray's *Iliad* (Figure 5.2) and *The Task* thus becomes the dream of a poet who has fallen asleep reading Du Roveray's edition. *The Task* displays the domestication of epic, the poem that sings 'Domestic happiness', as the 'only bliss/ Of Paradise that has survived the fall!' As Cowper sleeps, his muse leans down to crown him with laurels, watched by a cheeky boy whom Weinglass identifies as Phantasy.[80] The engraver, Raimbach, was paid 25 guineas for each of the plates, a sizable amount of money. It is curious then that an alternative version of the frontispiece was engraved in which the muse is bare-breasted rather than modestly garbed, and a bare-headed (rather than turbaned) Cowper rises up from an antique-style couch closely resembling that on which Madame Recamier lies in David's painting.[81] This unused version makes explicit both the eroticism which is veiled in the published version and the classical trappings of the scene.

Fuseli's illustrations for Cowper disproportionately focus on the negative (as we might expect from a painter who displays a 'single-minded sense of pessimism' in his Milton paintings).[82] This pessimism is evident in Fuseli's two designs for Cowper's moral satire, 'The Progress of Error', a work which excoriates the moral corruption of a society in which 'Man, thus endued with an elective voice,/ Must be supplied with objects of his choice'. Fuseli's version of *Virtue Reclaiming Youth from the Arms of Vice* closely echoes Stothard's but provides a subversive twist: in Stothard's version, Virtue, arrayed in a white gown, places a kindly hand on the young man's shoulder as she guides him towards the light.[83] By contrast, Fuseli's young man is slumped in the lap of Pleasure, awed by the sternly classical figure of a dark-haired Virtue who warns perhaps of the slide of classical style into luxury. Fuseli's second illustration, *A Dressing Room*, shows a society committed to consumer luxury in a scene which channels *'le gout antique'*. The elegant women are in a room with no visible window, facing only a mirror on an antique-style dressing table. The figures are elongated in a way that exaggerates the body types of fashion illustration and the drapes and dressing table form a kind of altar. Reviewing Cowper's translation of Homer, Fuseli had noted that in Cowper's version of the 'toilet of Juno' there is 'no idle étalage of ornaments ready laid out, of boxes, capsules, and cosmetic; the ringlets rise under her fingers, the pendants wave in her ears, the zone embraces her breast'.[84] Whereas Cowper's Homer escapes the clutter of a commercial society, the minute detail of the engraving shows both the clutter of the dressing table and the mirror image which the woman reaches out to touch. Cowper contrasts 'folly' and 'innocence', but Fuseli's figure of 'innocence' appears weak and hesitant.

The bourgeois interiors of the Cowper illustrations are claustrophobic, cut off from the world outside. The pose of the mother in *A Mother with her Family in the Country* recalls in its elegant informality one of Joshua

Figure 5.4 Henry Fuseli, *A Dressing Room*. Engraving by Rhodes, published by Joseph Johnson (1807) © Trustees of the British Museum.

Reynolds's images of mothers with children.[85] Yet the daughter entertains the baby with a butterfly she has caught, while the son points to the garden outside: even in this image there is a hint of entrapment. Stothard's illustration of the fireside in 'The Winter Evening' shows the man of the house between two women reading the newspaper, comfortable in the knowledge that 'The sound of war/ Has lost its terrors ere it reaches me'. Fuseli's image for *The Task* IV, 30–33 shows instead a fashionable group which Leigh Hunt described as 'a preposterous conspiracy of huge men and women, all bent on showing their thews and postures, with dresses as fantastical as their minds'.[86] Hunt is disturbed by the way the clothes cling to bodies, creating the appearance of nakedness. But a reader in 1807 would have recognized that they are sporting fashion 'à l'Antique'. The men wear their hair short and curled *à la Titus*, their tight trousers (pantaloons) of stretchable, knitted fabrics reveal their bodies as if they were antique sculpture. Despite this, their bodies appear soft and feminized. The women's neoclassical dresses of draped muslin represent the kind of advanced taste described by Thomas Baxter in his *Illustration of the Egyptian, Grecian and Roman Costume* (1810), a volume dedicated to Fuseli. But despite the sharply gendered clothing, a woman holds the newspaper and dominates the group. This scene represents the everyday domesticity of the middle classes as a series of rituals which release the subversive worlds of dream and vision into the material world. The low viewpoint, which places the viewer in the position of a child or lapdog looking up at the assembled company, turns them into giants: we see the feet and chins of this mostly seated gathering. But the tea urn looms above the head of the woman at the front as if it were a monumental piece of sculpture while the disproportionately large mantelpiece makes the people seem tiny. This is precisely the dislocation of scale that Cowper describes 'From many a mirror, in which he of Gath,/ Goliath, might have seen his giant bulk/Whole.' But whereas Cowper's poetry can look into the fire and see 'strange visages, express'd/ In the red cinders' and hear 'the roar of the great Babel' in the newspaper, Fuseli is complicit in the scene he represents, caricatures and produces.

Two of the illustrations demonstrate Fuseli's ability to miniaturize the sublime, suggesting the scale of the gallery within the limits of an octavo book. In *Kate* (with the caption '-------Kate is crazed'.) a woman excluded from polite society takes up three-quarters of the picture space: seated on a rock she towers over the landscape. The horizon, marked by stormy waves is half-way up her leg and rain and winds lash her cloak. And Fuseli creates a figure of real power in his image of *The Negro Reveng'd*, illustrating Cowper's *The Negro's Complaint*. The change of title may be significant for this image appeared four months after the Abolition of the Slave Trade Act, introduced to parliament in January 1807, entered the statute books on 25th March. In Cowper's lines, God's anger speaks through 'Wild tornadoes/ Strewing yonder sea with wrecks'. Taken out of context, placed beneath Fuseli's image, these lines suggest that the negro is casting thunder and lightning at the shipwreck. This is not complaint but revenge for the negro is the God

Figure 5.5 Henry Fuseli, *The Newspaper in the Country* (1807). Engraved Neagle, untitled proof version © Trustees of the British Museum.

who revenges his people. Both *Kate* and *The Negro Reveng'd* are pictured on the edge of a stormy sea, like modern day prophets, chastising the nation.

Conclusion

Fuseli's illustrations to Cowper represent a new location for art at the opening of the nineteenth centiury – no longer the crowded scene of the literary galleries, the democratic space of the revolutionary museum or the sublime gallery packed with the loot of a conquering army, but instead the tasteful homes of a bourgeois elite. The strangeness of the images may derive from the fact that they are neither exactly satire nor celebration: Fuseli's imagination is drawn to the elegance of the bedchamber, it revels in the secrets of the boudoir and the jealousies of the fireside while it resents the power of feminine taste and the need to serve the private fantasies of the rich. It is significant that the dressing room in Fuseli's second illustration to 'The Progress of Error' is not mentioned in Cowper's text: the scene Fuseli illustrates is bred in his own imagination.

The critique of the new scene of art, implicit in the letters and the Cowper illustrations, becomes explicit in Fuseli's final lecture. In this lecture, Fuseli shows no regret for 'public and private exhibitions' which 'tread on each other's heels' as 'panorama opens on panorama, and the splendour of galleries dazzles the wearied eye'.[87] He rejects Bonaparte's gallery because public art cannot be 'an ostentatious display of ancient and modern treasures of genius, accumulated by the hand of conquest or of rapine'.[88] Recognizing that revolution has not cleansed France's public culture of art, he calls (like Thomas Hope) for a revolution of taste. What is required for the arts to thrive is indeed 'a total revolution', the creation of an 'inward sense' which embeds the aesthetic sense within a whole society for '[w]hatever is commodious, amene, or useful, depends in a great measure on the Arts: dress, furniture, and habitation owe to their breath what they can boast of grace, propriety, or shape: they teach Elegance to finish what Necessity invented, and make us enamoured of our wants'.[89] The language echoes Thomas Hope's plan for 'the association of all the elegancies of antique forms and ornaments, with all the requisites of modern customs and habits'.[90] Yet Fuseli also believes that art depends on a shared sense of the sacred and his trip to Paris showed that 'He who has no visible object of worship is indifferent about modes, and rites, and places'. The art produced within the temple of taste can only be a narcissistic image of bourgeois comforts. The 'Arts of France' Fuseli warns, 'should they disdain to become the minions and handmaids of fashion, may soon find that the only public occupation left for them will be a representation of themselves, deploring their new-acquired advantages'.[91] In the windowless *Dressing Room* Innocence and Folly view their own image in the mirror. The *Newspaper in the Country* shows an elite unmoved by the struggles recorded in the newspaper. Fuseli's imagination revels in the modes and rites of bourgeois elegance but the domestic interior cannot fully replace the sacred space of art. As Haydon realized, the domestic interiors of the illustrations to Cowper are haunted by 'the eyes of [Fuseli's] own ghosts', whether the ghosts of revolutionary violence or of those who exist at the margin of the nation: the mad woman and the freed slave.

Notes

1. John Barrell, *The Political Theory of Painting from Reynolds to Hazlitt: 'The Body of the Public'* (New Haven, CT; London: Yale University Press, 1986), 261.
2. Rosie Dias, *Exhibiting Englishness: John Boydell's Shakespeare Gallery and the Formation of a National Aesthetic* (New Haven, CT; London: Yale University Press, 2013), 166.
3. Martin Myrone, *Bodybuilding: Reforming Masculinities in British Art 1750–1810* (New Haven, CT; London: Yale University Press, 2005), 306.
4. John Knowles, *The Life and Writings of Henry Fuseli*, 3 vols (London: Henry Colburn and Richard Bentley, 1831), III: 48. Hereafter Knowles.
5. William L. Pressly, *The Artist as Original Genius: Shakespeare's 'fine Frenzy' in Late Eighteenth-Century British Art* (University of Delaware Press, 2007), 106.
6. David H. Weinglass, ed., *The Collected English Letters of Henry Fuseli* (London, Kraus International, 1982), 39. Hereafter, *Letters*, 39.
7. *Letters*, 74.
8. [C. R. Smith], 'Pictorial Illustrations of Shakespeare', *Quarterly Review* 142 (1876): 457–79, 460–1.
9. William Seward, *Supplement to the anecdotes of some distinguished persons, chiefly of the present and two preceding centuries* (London: Cadell Jun. and Davies, 1797), 265.
10. *Letters*, 154.
11. *Letters*, 199.
12. Quoted in Francis Haskell, *The Ephemeral Museum: Old Master Paintings and the Rise of the Art Exhibition* (London and New Haven, CT: Yale University Press, 2000), 27.
13. *The Life and Writings of Henry Fuseli*, by and ed. John Knowles, 3 vols, London: Colburn and Bentley, 1831, I, 230 (hereafter, Knowles); http://godwindiary.bodleian.ox.ac.uk/diary/1800-05-17.html
14. Mary A. Favret, *War at a Distance: Romanticism and the Making of Modern Wartime* (Princeton, NJ; Oxford: Princeton University Press, 2010), 218–19.
15. *The Descriptive sketch of the Storming of Seringapatam* (Edinburgh, n.d. [1800?]).
16. Theresa Lewis, ed., *Extracts from the Journals and Correspondence of Miss Berry from the Year 1783 to 1852*, 3 vols (London: Longmans, Green and Co., 1866), II: 99–100.
17. Linda Colley, *Britons: Forging the Nation 17807–1837* (London: Pimlico, 1992), 254.
18. *Letters*, 217–18.

19 *Letters*, 74.
20 Knowles, 1: 284.
21 D. H. Weinglass, *Prints and Engraved Illustrations by and after Henry Fuseli* (Aldershot: Scolar Press, 1994), 222–4.
22 Watercolour on paper. 4 March 1833. The Brontë Society. Brontë Parsonage Museum. Haworth.
23 On houses as mnemonic systems see Paul Connerton, *How Modernity Forgets* (Cambridge: Cambridge University Press, 2009), 99.
24 To George Cumberland, 2 July 1800, E706.
25 Knowles, 1: 171–2.
26 *Letters*, 175.
27 Weinglass, *Prints and Engraved Illustrations*, xiv.
28 'F. I. Du Roveray, Illustrated Book Publisher 1798–1806 [Series of four parts]', comprising D. H. Weinglass, 'The Life of a Huguenot Publisher and Connoisseur in London' and three sections by G. E. Bentley Jr: 'The Amateur and the Trade', 'Du Roveray's Artists and Engravers and the Engravers' Strike' and 'A Bibliography of his Publications', *Bulletin of the Bibliographical Society of Australia and New Zealand*, 12: 1–4 (1988, issued May 1990).
29 Martin Myrone, *Henry Fuseli* (London, Tate Gallery, 2001), 65.
30 Weinglass, *Prints and Engraved Illustrations*, xxii.
31 Ibid., 190-1.
32 Ibid., 190.
33 Dias, *Exhibiting Englishness*, 217.
34 Richard D. Altick, *Paintings from Books: Art and Literature in Britain, 1760–1900* (Columbus: Ohio State University Press, 1985), 39.
35 Quoted in Altick, *Paintings from Books* 39–40.
36 *Letters*, 180.
37 Bentley, 'Du Roveray's Artists', 108.
38 Weinglass, *Prints and Engraved Illustrations*, 188.
39 Ibid., 271.
40 Ibid., xxiii.
41 *Letters*, 253.
42 *Letters*, 353.
43 Dias, *Exhibiting Englishness*, 160.
44 Ibid.,166.
45 Bentley, 'Du Roveray's Artists', 100.
46 Kenneth Garlick and Angus Macintyre, eds. *The Diary of Joseph Farington, Vol V*. (New Haven, CT; London: Yale University Press, 1979), 1901.
47 Ibid., 1909; Haskell, *The Ephemeral Museum*, 44; Percy Noble, *Anne Seymour Damer: A Woman of Art and Fashion, 1748–1828* (K. Paul, Trench, Trübner & Company, Limited, 1908), 180.
48 J. M. W. Turner, *Studies in the Louvre Sketchbook*, 1802. Tate Britain.
49 Noble, *Anne Seymour Damer,* 174–85.

50 *Journals*, II: 133–4.
51 Knowles, 1: 254.
52 *Letters*, 256–7.
53 Richard Altick, *The Shows of London* (Cambridge, MA and London: Belknap, Harvard University Press, 1978), 101.
54 *Letters*, 257.
55 Ibid.
56 Abbé Augustin Barruel, *Histoire du Clergé pendant la Révolution Francoise; Ouvrage dédié à la Nation Angloise* (London: Debrett, 1793), 262.
57 *The History of the Clergy during the French Revolution, a work dedicated to the English Nation* (London: Debrett, 1794), 101.
58 Farington, V: 1832–3.
59 *Journals*, II: 177.
60 Farington, V: 1863.
61 *Journals*, II: 191.
62 Ibid.
63 Ibid.
64 *Letters*, 255.
65 Farington, V: 1886.
66 Holger Hoock, *The King's Artists, The Royal Academy of Arts and the Politics of British Culture 1760–1840* (Oxford: Clarendon Press, 2003), 206; Andrew McClelland, *Inventing the Louvre: Art, Politics, and the Origins of the Modern Museum in Eighteenth-Century Paris* (Cambridge: Cambridge University Press, 1994), 9; Christopher Rovee, *Imagining the Gallery: The Social Body of British Romanticism* (Stanford, CA: Stanford University Press, 2006), 4–5.
67 *The Monthly Review, or Literary Journal*, XL (January to April, 1803), 380.
68 Shelley M. Bennett, *Thomas Stothard, The Mechanisms of Art Patronage in England circa 1800* (Columbia: University of Missouri Press, 1988), 51.
69 Pye, *Patronage of British Art*, 56.
70 Farington, V: 1861.
71 Knowles, 1: 258.
72 Knowles, 1: 253; *Letters*, 256.
73 'Kitcat Size' (named after the portraits that Sir Godfrey Kneller painted of the members of the Kitcat dining club) was also used for Hogarth's *Marriage A-la-Mode* series and Joseph Highmore's paintings illustrating *Pamela*. 'See Jacob Simon, 'The Account Book of James Northcote', *Walpole Society*, vol. 58, 1996, note 66, 33; *Letters*, 257; 290.
74 Engraved I. G. Walker (Schiff 1252) after a painting (91 x 71 cm, Schiff 1194).
75 David Watkin and Philip Hewat-Jaboor, eds, *Thomas Hope, Regency Designer* (New Haven, CT; London, Yale University Press, 2008).
76 See 'Between the Novel and History: French Portraiture towards 1835', *Citizens and Kings:Portraits in the Age of Revolution 1760–1830* (London: Royal Academy of Arts, 2007), 37–8.

77 Thomas Hope, *Household Furniture and Interior Decoration Executed from Designs by Thomas Hope* (London: Longman, Hurst, Rees and Orme, 1807), 6.
78 Altick, *Painting from Books*, 412; Vince Newey, 'Cowper's Woodman Illustrated', in Joan Kee and Emanuele Lugli, eds, *Art History*, April 2015 (38: 2): 246–403.
79 B. R. Haydon, *Painting* (Edinburgh: Adam and Charles Black, 1838), 214.
80 Weinglass, *Prints and Engraved Illustrations*, 314. Weinglass sees the Muse as summoning Cowper to his 'Task' but it seems equally possible that Cowper's dream is generating the poem.
81 Schiff, 1973 1337; Weinglass, *Prints and Engraved Illustrations* 1994 267A.
82 Myrone, *Henry Fuseli*, 62.
83 Painting Schiff 1230, 91:71 cm; engraving Schiff 1330, 126:86 mm.
84 Quoted in Knowles, 1: 88.
85 Schiff, 1973 1332, Weinglass *Prints and Engraved Illustrations*, 1994 270.
86 Quoted in Weinglass, *Prints and Engraved Illustrations*, 318. On Leigh Hunt and domesticity see Rodney Stenning Edgecombe, *Leigh Hunt and the Poetry of Fancy* (London and Toronto: Associated University Press, 1994), 34.
87 Knowles, III: 47, 49–50.
88 Knowles, III: 51.
89 Knowles, III: 42.
90 Hope, *Household Furniture*, 7.
91 Knowles, III: 51.

6 | Reading the Romantic Vignette: Stothard Illustrates Bloomfield, Byron, and Crabbe for *The Royal Engagement Pocket Atlas*

SANDRO JUNG

Focusing on the engraved illustrations of three numbers of Thomas Baker's little-known annual diary-cum-almanac, *The Royal Engagement Pocket Atlas* (1779–1826), this chapter will establish the publication's significance for a historical understanding of the Romantic canon. It will pay attention to Thomas Stothard's illustrative-interpretive work in the format of the vignette, a small-scale engraved design or ornament of varied shape (ranging, in the case of Baker's publication, from rectangular, oval, and octagonal), and measuring approximately 4.2 x 2.5 centimetres. Over a period of more than 30 years, from 1781 to 1826, Stothard annually supplied sets of 24 (and, from 1820, 12) vignettes illustrating different literary texts for Baker's *Pocket Atlas*.[1] He was one of the most prolific book illustrators of the late eighteenth and early nineteenth centuries, embellishing editions of hundreds of literary texts with his engraved designs. In addition to the editions Stothard illustrated (and in which he visually, closely represented, and made sense of, particular scenes or moments from the chosen work), he catered to elite consumers' desire for print collecting, producing, for instance, furniture prints – in monochrome and coloured variants – of Bunyan's *Pilgrim's Progress* and many other 'classic' texts. While these prints have survived in portfolios and other collections, his work for *The Royal Engagement Pocket Atlas*, a publication issued at the end of each year for use in the following, but frequently disposed of thereafter, has largely disappeared from the print cultural archive of the period. Its recovery will not only contribute to an understanding of how the miniature galleries of his vignettes rendered interpretive narratives of visualized textual moments, but the distinct form of vignette illustration, unlike the illustration accompanying an edition of the printed text, takes priority in the reading process and enables first and foremost a visual experience of the text rather than one where the illustration serves as an interpretive complement to the typographic text of a literary edition.

Each of the engraved, ruled diary pages – two per month – featured at its head a vignette by Stothard. These vignettes, which were engraved by William Angus and included only minimal textual captions, illustrated the works of authors ranging from Chaucer's *Canterbury Tales* and Spenser's *The Faerie Queene* to Samuel Rogers's *Italy* and six of Sir Walter Scott's novels. In the course of its long life, the pocket diary hosted an archive of more than 640 illustrations (including frontispieces) of 26 different texts, some of which were illustrated in more than one number, which comprised such dead moderns as Matthew Prior and Thomas Parnell, but also widely recognized living authors, including William Cowper, William Hayley, James Hurdis, Anna Seward, and Thomas Campbell. In addition, Baker selected Alain René Le Sage's *Gil Blas* and François Fénelon's *Les Aventures de Télémaque* for illustration, as well as the works of English novelists, including Samuel Richardson's *Clarissa* and Oliver Goldsmith's *Vicar of Wakefield*. The canon that Baker presented to his readers in miniature represented a multi-generic and transnational one. Cumulatively, the numbers of the pocket diary from the late 1790s to 1826 created an institutionalized Romantic canon, which, due to the ephemeral nature of the publication, has not been recovered, even though it offers a rare opportunity of studying large-scale literary-critical mediation, via illustration, at work.

The Vignette

Even though Hilary Thompson terms 'the wood-engraved vignette' 'that form of illustration which became so popular with Romantic artists',[2] the vignette, albeit realized in the copper-engraved medium, had been used in Britain well before the Romantics, and its uses by Stothard were affected by developments in continental European book illustration.[3] Well before the mid-century, the interpretive vignette – a vignette engaging with the work it accompanied through an act of textual visualization, rather than purely an ornament without text-specific reference – was deployed in such works as illustrated editions of John Gay's *Fables*. Beyond Britain, it featured centrally in editions of the works of the Swiss poet, bookseller, painter, and engraver, Salomon Gessner. In the 1760s and 1770s Gessner developed the vignette in ways that Stothard would adopt for his designs. Whereas William Kent's vignettes for the 1727 edition of *Fables* had used the rectangle to contain the illustration, Gessner's vignettes varied in shape, ranging from unframed vignettes to those contained within frames and serving as head pieces. The transnational popularity of Gessner's Rococo vignettes across Switzerland, the German-speaking territorial states, and France was responsible for their reprinting and simplification and – in the process – their becoming formulaic, codified, and constituting a model of book illustration.[4] Stothard's own practice was clearly influenced by continental developments relating to the vignette, and the popularity of *The Royal Engagement Pocket Atlas* in Germany, as well as reviewers' commendations of the high quality of Stothard's work for the diary,[5] testify to consumers' identification of these vignettes as being part of a tradition of book illustration that Gessner had helped to establish in the German-speaking lands.

Stothard's contemporary, Thomas Bewick, thus was not the first to use the interpretive vignette for the illustration of literary texts. In fact, Bewick derived inspiration from the numerous illustrated editions of *Fables*, including the Newcastle edition of *Select Fables* issued by Thomas Saint in 1776. In addition to his 'magnetic depiction of the familiar',[6] Bewick developed a formal repertoire – with a specific focus on the vignette's centre as interpretive nexus, rather than its periphery and framing edge. It is this centralizing of visual meaning which Stothard assimilated in his own vignette practice, at least initially, when he designed oval vignettes which he subsequently reshaped into octagonal and rectangular vignette illustrations. Even his non-oval vignettes, however, retain their internal focus, and they usually encompass a temporally restricted and highly concentrated moment which relates a story or sentiment. Although the oval vignette is not contained in an outlined frame, it is the regularity of the shape which, in itself, infers a frame, a fact Thomas and John Bewick frequently exploited by doubling framing devices in the manner of surrounding an oval frame by a rectangle or decoration.[7]

In formal terms, but not in the medium used, Stothard's vignettes resemble Bewick's, although the latter's early work is not offered in the form of extensive sequences such as those produced for the *Pocket Atlas*. Bewick's vignettes are also less interpretive in that they focus less on the specific rendering of iconographic scenes, action, and interpersonal relationships, although they frequently capture mood.[8] While Stothard, especially in his early oval vignette designs, is formally aligned with Bewick's practice, surviving wash-drawings of his designs demonstrate that he devised his vignettes as miniaturized, tonal paintings, rather than the line-defined wood engravings by Bewick.[9]

Baker's realization of the vignette in the copper-engraved medium is a hybrid: it combines the formal outline of oval wood-engraved vignettes with the high execution standard and the feminization of subject popularized by Gessner. Like Stothard's, the aesthetic of Gessner's interpretive vignettes was defined by minimal framing ornamentation and an emphasis on the figural within the rectangular vignette shape. Gessner, furthermore, reduced the significance of background and centralized the figure of the putto, his actor

> DER
> TOD ABELS.
> VIERTER GESANG.
>
> Noch sank der nächtliche Thau, noch schwiegen die schlummernden Vögel, und die Stirnen der Berge, und die schwebenden Morgen-Nebel waren noch nicht vergoldet, da gieng Kain schon aus seiner Hütte durch die Dämmrung melancholisch daher. Mehala hatte in den nächtlichen Stunden, unbewufst, dafs er sie behorcht, über ihn geweint und mit gerungenen Händen für ihn

Figure 6.1 S. Gessner, Vignette 4, *Der Tod Abels* (Zurich: Gessner, 1758). Reproduced from a copy in the author's collection.

of choice, as a placeholder for adult figures such as the biblical Cain and Abel and the Thomsonian pair of lovers, Damon and Musidora[10] (Figure 6.1). The feminization, via the representational medium of the putto, of the murderer Cain or of the lover Damon spying on the denuding Musidora mediate by toning down the phenomena of fratricide or physical, erotic desire. Translated into the representational embodiment of putto figures, figures of violence and erotic love are decontextualized from their adult identities as murderers or voyeurs and are thus discernible to those only with knowledge of the text-image dynamic at work and how the vignettes render the texts.

Stothard's vignettes for the *Pocket Atlas* were conceived as series and had to be read sequentially, much in the narrative method that Gessner used to underpin his smaller sequences. In devising ambitious series of vignettes, Stothard was furthermore indebted to the German vignette books of the mid-eighteenth century. Like one of the more impressive vignette books, Christian Lorenz Hirschfeld's *Das Landleben* (1768), which boasted 24, unframed vignettes of varying sizes, Stothard would equally furnish 24 vignettes for the *Pocket Atlas* until 1808. However, the vignettes in Hirschfeld's work neither follow a uniform format, nor do they offer the interpretive complexity of Gessner or Stothard's vignettes. These vignettes are examples of German Rococo vignettes that feature putto compositions, yet they convey mood and sentiment rather than advance the concrete interpretive readings of literary texts that Gessner's series of vignettes for such works as the different editions of *Der Tod Abels* or *Idyllen* convey. While the representational style of Stothard's figures is no longer informed by the figure aesthetic of the Rococo, the structure of the vignette, as well as its functioning as part of a larger narrative sequence, aligns it with Gessner, at a time when Gessner's influence as a visual artist of book illustrations was not generally felt in Britain. Unlike Bewick, who strove for naturalism in his vignettes, Stothard adopted a mode of representation akin to Gessner's putto designs. Yet even Stothard's feminized representational style, sacrificing the accuracy of portraiture in favour of youthful, childlike characters, which underpins his entire illustration oeuvre, is significantly more realistic than Gessner's.[11] The annually recurring format of Stothard's vignette and its association with providing visual realizations of canonic or popular modern literature promoted an understanding of the very form of the vignette of the *Pocket Atlas* as a medium of the tasteful engagement with literary celebrity.

The Choice of Works to be Illustrated and the Canon

While book illustration, especially as part of the popular series of the poets of Great Britain produced by John Bell and Charles Cooke, was thriving in Britain in the 1770s and 1790s, these booksellers' multi-volume series, for reasons of copyright, did not include the works of living authors.[12] Bell and Cooke's collections represented a backward-looking canon, a body of works that were included in their series ostensibly on the basis of their relevance for a history of poetry. And that is exactly what these collections constituted: histories of the supposed rise of poetry up to the death, in 1764, of the eighteenth-century satirist, Charles Churchill. The canon that Bell and Cooke, as well as others, created with their series was based on the use of out-of-copyright works that were available for unregulated reprinting. It constituted an economic canon, facilitated by the possibility to repackage and reissue material that was no longer subject to license. Booksellers did not select the constituent components of their canon on (primarily) aesthetic grounds. According to William St Clair, '[i]n this canonising process, literary historians, critics, and editors had played only a small part. The old canon of poetry owed its birth and its long life more to the vagaries of the intellectual property regime, than to carefully considered judgements'.[13] The agents of print, the booksellers, designers, and engravers contributing to the production of illustrated editions of literary texts, shaped the selection, arrangement, and presentation of material, thereby trying to affect the buying and reading public in particular ways.

From the mid-1770s book illustrations became central to the formation of the canon, for they helped to shape meaning and were centrally employed by Bell and Cooke not only to embellish, but also to create a marketable identity for, their volumes. At the same time, they served as media which, through their representational make-up, evoked particular styles and uniformity that generated both brand identity and a canon. Paratextual devices such as notes and, above all, illustrations that adhered to a specific series-defined format underscored the connections between individual volumes of a series and the canon they generated.[14] Furthermore, illustrations were an area of book production where innovation in terms of product design was possible.[15] Different designs in multifarious styles made possible differentiation among different booksellers' publications in a marketplace for illustrated works which, especially in the 1790s, was becoming increasingly competitive. Copper-engraved illustrations were costly and considered an investment, but they were also associated with a specific cultural status reserved to elite print objects. In Scottish, as opposed to English, editions of poetry, illustrations frequently conveyed nationalist-patriotic concerns which were reinforced by ideologically pertinent paratexts.[16] The Scottish Morison firm of Perth issued a series of volumes entitled *The Scotish Poets* from the mid-1780s, including an edition of the works of Robert Fergusson, who had died as recently as 1774. It was to take at least another 22 years, however, until the poetical works of two living poets, Charlotte Smith and John Sargeant, the first to be featured in a series, were included in the eclectic series of 'Elegant Pocket Editions' of poetry, 'adorned with new plates', which the London booksellers Thomas Cadell and William Davies issued from 1796.[17] Stothard illustrated all the works in the series and thereby helped to shape the reputation of the texts, which were frequently read through the lens of his visual interpretations.

In selecting poetical works for inclusion in *The Royal Engagement Pocket Atlas*, Baker's approach differed markedly from Bell and Cooke's and, especially after 1800, heavily leant towards the illustration of living poets' works. Where the 'old canon' was formed with hindsight, Baker's new, Romantic canon was largely synchronic, capitalizing on the popularity individual texts by living authors enjoyed at the time Stothard translated them into the visual medium. His vignette series offered a snapshot of then widely read and mediated texts. Stothard transposed the texts from an environment that had been dominated by the bibliographical codes and conventions of typography found in editions of literary texts to a new textual condition in which only a fraction of the text was provided (in the form of the poetry caption underneath the vignette), and then in subservient position, while the visual rendering of the text absorbed the reader's attention. Each of Stothard's vignettes was keyed to a line or half-line of the text illustrated. Frequently, the title of the illustrated texts, as well as line references, were given. This practice of excerpting copyrighted text on a very small scale, combined with the user-defined space of the diary as primarily concerned with the business of knowledge organization as opposed to a space for a detailed readerly engagement with belles lettres, avoided confrontations with booksellers holding the copyright of texts that Stothard illustrated. At the same time, the numbers of the pocket diary collectively constituted a canon that included modern authors. In other words, it is Stothard's work for *The Royal Engagement Pocket Atlas* which reflected literary fashions (which would have been supported by review journals), while also offering a statement regarding the cultural currency of texts illustrated.

Baker's decision to include specific authors nowadays recognized as central to Romanticism testifies to the significance of popular print culture for the formation of taste of which his diary, as well as its early competitors, *The Polite Repository* and *Le Souvenir, or, Pocket Remembrancer*, were a part. The in-between status that the illustrated pocket book occupied in relation to editions of literary texts, on the one hand, and ego documents such as non-illustrated diaries and almanacs, on the other, facilitated the varied consumption and preservation of the publication for different reasons throughout its social life: those preserving the volumes or illustrations because of the aesthetic appeal of the vignettes, and those retaining the pocket diary as records of past activities and life experience, engaged in different ways with the publication but ensured its survival in the archive.

Nevertheless, the ephemeral nature of the diary, which was frequently disposed of at the year's end, and the resulting poor survival rates of copies, are responsible for the fact that the vignettes in each of the diaries have not been studied in light of the formation of the Romantic canon. However, the three case studies introduced in this chapter, including sets of vignettes illustrating Robert Bloomfield's *The Farmer's Boy*, George Crabbe's poems, and Lord Byron's works, will demonstrate not only the ways in which Stothard carefully interpreted and made present moments, episodes, and situations from these poems, but also how these illustrations functioned in their own time as indices of cultural production, taste, and fashion. Stothard's vignette series are meaningful artistic interventions in the realm of popular print culture that were produced in response to the formation of authorial and textual reputations and are therefore central to an understanding of a late eighteenth-century visual artist's remediation of current texts and the significance of these vignettes for a study of the reception history of the works of Bloomfield, Byron, and Crabbe.

Robert Bloomfield

Stothard illustrated Robert Bloomfield's long poem, *The Farmer's Boy: A Rural Poem*, for Baker's annual for the year 1802. Remarkably for a first work, the first edition of the poem was embellished by nine wood-engraved vignettes, including one on the title-page, that were engraved by John Anderson, pupil of Thomas Bewick; it went through three editions in 1800 alone, and within two years sold more than 25,000 copies.[18] Apart from the large frontispiece (added to the second edition of 1800) depicting a shepherd figure playing the flute, each of the four seasons-defined parts of the poem is accompanied by two vignettes: a larger vignette engraved in landscape format and another, smaller one functioning as a headpiece at the start of each season. With the exception of the frontispiece, the vignettes are reminiscent of a range of illustrations that accompanied editions of James Thomson's *The Seasons*, some even copying designs that had been produced for editions of Thomson's work.[19] Within two years of the printing of Anderson's vignettes, Charlton Nesbit furnished Vernor and Hood, Bloomfield's publishers, with a set of new designs that were subsequently engraved in wood, and in due course replaced by full-page copper-engraved plates.[20] While at the start of 1802, a new edition of the poem, 'Elegantly printed by [Thomas] Bensley', comprising 'eleven plates, beautifully cut in wood, by Nesbit, from the Designs of J. Thurston',[21] was available, in 1804, booksellers advertised different editions (such as a 'foolscap octavo', 'with Nine Wood-Cuts', at 4s. in boards, and another 'with Four Copper Plates', at 5s.).[22] So, from the start, Bloomfield's poem was regarded as a work worth illustrating but also as capable of feeding a varied printed visual culture.

Baker's decision to commission Stothard to illustrate *The Farmer's Boy* for his pocket atlas occurred within one and a half years of the poem's original publication on 1 March 1800, the pocket atlas being advertised as printed and ready for sale in early December the following year. This decision was likely motivated by the sensational success of the poem, an advertisement noting in October 1800 that *The Farmer's Boy* 'has excited the admiration of the literary world, in a degree beyond all precedent'.[23] H. J. Jackson holds that the visualizability of the poem contributed significantly to its success.[24] In response to the poem's rapidly growing reputation, Baker also deviated from the set phrasing related to the illustrations and the listing of their subjects that he usually used in his advertisements for the pocket atlas. For the 1802 number of the publication, he noted that it visualized 'the simple rural incidents of that pleasing and popular poem', *The Farmer's Boy*.[25]

The publication of Bloomfield's poem was celebrated as a veritable media event. Within a year of the poem's publication, tribute verse to Bloomfield addressed him as the 'Gentle Poet of the rural lyre'.[26] Excerpts from his work were printed in a range of periodicals and anthologies. They also featured in the pages of non-illustrated pocket diaries, including *Gedge's Town and Country Ladies Own Memorandum Book* and *Clarke's Fashionable Ladies Memorandum Book*, both for the year 1801. Baker advertised that year's *Royal Engagement Pocket Atlas*, stating that it was embellished with 'beautiful Vignettes … descriptive of the most interesting Scenes in Bloomfield's Farmer's Boy'.[27] Bloomfield was aware that Baker's volume included what he terms Stothard's 'beautiful engravings from Giles', delightedly telling his brother, George, about the illustrations in a letter of 30 November 1801.[28]

Stothard's 24 vignettes differ fundamentally, in both their formal uniformity and their close reworking and visualizing of the text, from the engravings Anderson produced, and Stothard's visual narrative strongly reflects his earlier illustrations for two numbers of the *Pocket Atlas* for which he furnished sets of visual interpretations of iconographical moments from *The Seasons*. His vignettes depict an unproblematic and romanticized vision of rural life, a version of the farmer's world for the middle and upper classes

Figure 6.2a Thomas Stothard, Vignette for January ('Round Euston's water'd Vale'), *Royal Engagement Pocket Atlas for the Year MDCCCII*. Reproduced from a copy in the author's collection.

Figure 6.2b Thomas Stothard, Vignette for January ('A little Farm his generous Master till'd'), *Royal Engagement Pocket Atlas for the Year MDCCCII*. Reproduced from a copy in the author's collection.

'celebrating', according to Peter Cochran, 'a rural life which few of them knew anything of, and about which they could afford to be complacent'.[29] The two vignettes for January, keyed to lines from the poem – 'Round Euston's water'd Vale' ('Spring', 38) and 'A little Farm his Master till'd' ('Spring', 47) – portray in the foreground the pastoral life enjoyed by the sheep, the shepherd conspicuously absent. By contrast, the background – and notwithstanding its position at the centre of the vignette – only partially admits a view of the country seat owned by Augustus Henry Fitzroy, 3rd Duke of Grafton, the labourer-turned-shoemaker's patron (Figures 6.2a. and 6.2b.). The lake between the sheep and the building fulfils a threshold function, but even this man-made structure blends into the setting and the trees by which it is partially encased. Unlike the illustrators for the first ten editions of Bloomfield's poem, who highlighted the pastoral-georgic aspects of life depicted by the poet's alter ego, Giles, Stothard borrows from the artistic practice of Humphry Repton, who furnished William Peacock's *Polite Repository* with topographical designs representing his own landscape gardening commissions.[30] The Duke's estate offers Giles the opportunity for introspection and for communion with the landscape, for 'The fields were his study, nature his book' ('Spring', 32). It is in the solitary setting of sublime nature that Giles feels at ease:

> Where woods and groves in solemn grandeur rise,
> Where the kite brooding unmolested flies;
> The woodcock and the painted pheasant race,
> And skulking foxes destin'd for the chace;
> There Giles, untaught and unrepining, stray'd,
> Thro' every copse, and grove, and winding glade;
> ('Spring', 39–44)

It is however not only in his wanderings that Giles can be happy. The vignette illustrating the farm scene exudes harmony, and Bloomfield's text paints a vision of plenty and benevolence, which culminates in the ideal of 'Unceasing industry' resulting in personal happiness. The master's consideration of those in his care aims entirely at securing the farm's future through continuous application, which in turn provides security for his labourers: 'Unceasing industry he kept in view; / And never lack'd a job for Giles to do' ('Spring', 55–56).

While the vignettes for the January diary pages had introduced man only from a distance, those for February offer deep-focus depictions of farm labourers ploughing and others milking cows (Figures 6.3a. and 6.3b.). While the theme of work is central to the vignettes, the quotations from *The Farmer's Boy* that define the vignettes state that these georgic activities induce the ploughman to wear a 'smiling brow', whilst the milkmaid is supported by a 'friendly tripod', a stool, on which she will be able to rest. A female figure churning butter in the verso vignette for March smilingly confronts the reader, reducing, as the February designs do, the harshness of labour to a representation of industry that will lead, for those involved, to everyone's happiness. The man feeding the fowl punctuates a scene that is dominated by chickens, turkeys, and geese, as well as a dog (in its kennel) interestedly looking on.

The vignettes for January to March illustrate scenes from 'Spring', the first part of *The Farmer's Boy*, those for April to June visualize iconographic

Figure 6.3a Thomas Stothard, Vignette for February ('With smiling brow the Plowman cleaves his way'), *Royal Engagement Pocket Atlas for the Year MDCCCII*. Reproduced from a copy in the author's collection.

Figure 6.3b Thomas Stothard, Vignette for February ('A friendly tripod forms their humble seat'), *Royal Engagement Pocket Atlas for the Year MDCCCII*. Reproduced from a copy in the author's collection.

moments from 'Summer'. Visual renderings of acts of labour and leisure contrast, and vignettes depicting scenes of mirth and celebration, especially on the occasion of harvest, counter the georgic emphasis on exhausting physical exertion. While a balance, in terms of the number of vignettes allotted to each season, had been observed with regard to 'Spring' and 'Summer', this is not the case for the remaining two seasons, for the designs for 'Winter' occupy the heads of the diary pages for September to December.

In addition to introducing rural man in relation to the environment, Stothard's vignettes reveal his ability to design a range of indigenous animals. His designs introduce the urban user of the pocket atlas to the wildlife that

Figure 6.4a Thomas Stothard, Vignette for July ('With bristles rais'd the sudden noise they hear'), *Royal Engagement Pocket Atlas for the Year MDCCCII*. Reproduced from a copy in the author's collection.

Figure 6.4b Thomas Stothard, Vignette for July ('assembling Neighbours meet'), *Royal Engagement Pocket Atlas for the Year MDCCCII*. Reproduced from a copy in the author's collection.

Bloomfield would have encountered in his day-to-day life as farm labourer in Suffolk. While previous illustrations, especially for *The Seasons*, had introduced animals such as oxen pulling the plough, these animals had always been introduced within the framework of georgic, agricultural labour. Stothard's illustrations of *The Farmer's Boy*, however, portray a different vision of animal life: one that removes the animals from the farming context of hard, physical labour and that introduces them as free agents into a pastoral as opposed to a georgic landscape. This, then, is a further development in Stothard's visual practice, in that he foregrounds visualizations of animals which, before 1800, he had largely used as the subjects of the decorative vignettes at the heads of the additional memorandum pages following the actual diary section of Baker's annual.[31] He thus moves them from the periphery to the centre, and in the process transforms them from ornament to meaningful interpretive paratext (Figures 6.4a. and 6.4b.). The verso vignette for July introduces the entertaining tale of pigs thirsty and eager to refresh themselves by drinking from a 'rush-green pool' ('Autumn', 22), invading the realm of the 'wild duck' ('Autumn', 23), the latter starting and, in doing so, startling the pigs:

> With bristles rais'd the sudden noise they hear,
> And ludicrously wild, and wing'd with fear,
> The herd decamp with more than swinish speed,
> And snorting dash through sedge, and rush, and reed:
> ('Autumn', 29–32)

The vignettes for December, while both featuring animals, represent them in different contexts, the verso offering a hunting scene in which a pack of hounds pursue a nimble fox, while the huntsmen on horseback are trying to keep up. Compared to other graphic depictions of hunting scenes (such as the designs for *The Royal Engagement Pocket Atlas* for 1804, illustrating William Somervile's *The Chace*), Stothard's is sanitized and sentimentalized. It is unlikely that Stothard's hounds are set on destroying the fox, and Bloomfield's text does not inform the reader of the outcome of the hunt but moves directly to a (mock-)elegy for a dog, 'Poor faithful Trouncer' ('Autumn', 305): 'And though high deeds, and fair exalted praise, / In mem'ry liv'd, and flow'd in rustic lays, / Short was the strain of monumental woe: / "Foxes rejoice! Here buried lies your foe"' ('Autumn', 331–4). Facing this hunting scene, the recto vignette for December turns to the farm yard where Giles is carrying hay, while the cows, without his being aware, help themselves to the food:

> Deep-plunging Cows their rustling feast enjoy
> And snatch sweet mouthfuls from the passing boy
> Who moves unseen beneath his trailing load
> Fills the tall racks, and leaves a scatter'd road.
> ('Winter', 53–6)

Stothard conveys through the cows' and pigs' attitude and expression their exploiting a moment in which the farm hand is not paying attention to them, offering a tongue-in-cheek statement on the harmonious working together of man and animals. The animals are opportunist but also, in Bloomfield's anthropomorphic descriptions of them, know Giles's benevolent character. 'Bloomfield treats his subjects empathetically, focusing on Giles's feelings about the seasons, the land, and his work, but also considering the feelings of farm animals'.[32] Above all, Stothard's visualizations of the poet's characters – both human and animal – convey a positive, light-hearted and often humorous version of farm life that, in the representational mode of the vignette, reduces its hardships and, via the miniature format, invites readerly familiarity. Bloomfield's view of the Suffolk countryside is one in which the different realms of man and animals, labour and leisure, as well as community and solitary contemplation, are inextricably and seamlessly interconnected. But the scenes that Stothard depicts are so small that readers need to study the vignettes attentively, not only to grasp the complexity of the composition realized on the printed diary page but also to relate the small engraved text underneath the vignettes to the images. This close observation necessitated the readers' physical proximity to the vignettes, and magnifying glasses were retailed by a number of pocket book sellers to enhance the perception of the vignettes and to accommodate the detailed examination of Stothard's miniature paintings.

In one respect, Bloomfield's subject does break with tradition, however. The singling out of lower-class individuals for illustration – unlike the stylized pastoral vignettes for *The Royal Engagement Pocket Atlas* numbers rendering *The Seasons* – had not previously occurred in Stothard's sets of designs for Baker. Bloomfield, too, would remain the only labouring-class author whose works were illustrated. This is surprising to a degree, since Robert Burns's works were illustrated increasingly after 1801,[33] not only in Scotland but in England as well. Despite the novelty of *The Farmer's Boy*, it was – in both criticism and the poem's illustrations – closely aligned with *The Seasons*, whereas with Burns this would not have been possible. Bloomfield's poem was the first best-selling work by a contemporary poet that Baker selected for illustration. After 1801, Stothard largely moved away from furnishing designs for works whose authors were dead and that had been assigned the cultural status of literary classics worth enshrining in a canon of multi-volume editions of the British poets. Between 1800 and 1812, he illustrated Le Sage's *Gil Blas* (1800), Cowper's *Task* (1801), Bloomfield's *Farmer's Boy* (1802), Gisborne's *Walks in a Forest* (1803), Somervile's *Chace* (1804), Goldsmith's *The Vicar of Wakefield* (1805), John Moore's *Edward* (1806), Scott's *The Lay of the Last Minstrel* (1807), Samuel Rogers's *Pleasures of Memory* (1808), Scott's *Marmion* (1809), Hurdis's *Poems* (1811), and Scott's *Lady of the Lake* (1812).[34]

Eight out of the 12 texts illustrated were authored by living or recently deceased authors, whereas the oldest of the remainder (*Gil Blas*) dated to 1715. None of the works Stothard illustrated for Baker had been illustrated as diversely (including the copper plates that Vernor and Hood commissioned in late 1801 and bound in a range of different editions thereafter) within such a short period of time as *The Farmer's Boy*. The extensive visual response to the poem is undoubtedly due to the work's 'unusually strong visual appeal'.[35] According to Jackson, the 'illustrations that accompanied it from the start catered to genteel interests in art and the picturesque', and this is certainly the case once Stothard's miniaturized gallery of vignettes is assembled in the diary section of the pocket atlas.[36]

George Crabbe

George Crabbe's poems were selected for illustration in the 1810 number of *The Royal Engagement Pocket Atlas*, which opened with a frontispiece depicting a scene subscribed 'Marriages', a concrete rendering of a textual moment illustrating part of the poet's recent work, *The Parish Register* (1807), which contrasts with the allegorical frontispieces that had accompanied earlier numbers of the *Pocket Atlas*, including the one comprising Stothard's vignettes of *The Farmer's Boy*. By the time Stothard designed vignettes rendering *The Village* and *The Parish Register*, Crabbe's reputation as a poet capable of depicting social realism in poetry was well established. By his earliest critics he was repeatedly compared to Oliver Goldsmith, whose poem 'The Deserted Village' dealt with similar social problems but in less realistic detail. Stothard had illustrated Goldsmith's work for the 1799 number of the pocket atlas, and his later vignettes depicting episodes from Crabbe's poems contrast strikingly with his earlier identification of the idyllic in Goldsmith's poem. In James Montgomery's view, Crabbe's achievement in *The Village* consisted in his revaluation of Arcadian pastoral, for 'Crabbe had nothing to do but to look at home, in his own parishes (the one near a smuggling creek on the sea-coast, and the other among the flats of Leicestershire) to become the most original poet that ever sang of village life and manners'.[37] Furthermore, Stothard's task to make present in visual form two poems that in terms of their composition were 20 years apart posed the problem of having to bridge their ideational difference. Only those readers attentive to the poetry keyed to the 24 vignettes would identify that the designs illustrated two works, as opposed to the title the advertisement of the pocket atlas announced, for it was noted that the 'Engravings are taken from the deservedly popular work, Crabb[e]'s Poems'.[38] The very reference to 'Poems' promotes the idea of unity and coherence of poems whose diachronic distance from one another is erased through the material arrangement of these works on the printed pages of the volume. Stothard's visual rendering of the two works illustrated – *The Village* and *The Parish Register* – in a way that erased their difference and that promoted them as realist productions demonstrates how, through the medium of the vignette series, the artist was able to reinscribe Crabbe's productions. At the cost of an accurate interpretation of the different works, he embedded them within a visual matrix viewers would have associated with the predominant, recent representational mode used by the poet.

Stothard's series of vignettes casts the designs into a sequence of impressionistic snapshots of the life of country folk, as well as the manners and living conditions that the illustrator sought to capture. He thus levels the differing comparative interpretations of *The Village* and *The Parish Register* that had been advanced shortly after the publication of *Poems*, for in 1808, a reader found that 'An unrivalled vividness, and a certain painful truth of painting, characterise'[39] *The Village*. By contrast, in the same year, *The Parish Register* was commended for its 'chaste and natural description of rural life'.[40] According to a reviewer for the *Annual Review*, 'it is on the whole less gloomy, less poetical … and [possesses] more depth of thought' than *The Village*.[41] Its 'pictures' – episodes and short tales that Crabbe grouped under the headings of 'Baptisms', 'Marriages', and 'Burials' – distinguish it from the naturalistic critique of social ills in the earlier poem. Whereas in *The Village*, Crabbe 'colours darkly',[42] in *The Parish Register* he provides a greater spectrum of human agents, offering 'pictures' of which 'some are pathetic, some humourous [sic], [but] all show[ing] a lively conception and extensive knowledge of character'.[43]

Reflecting contemporaneous responses to the text, the vignettes representing concerns from *The Village* focus on issues of decline, the lack of charity and poverty (Figure 6.5a). While Crabbe critiqued the unequal distribution of wealth and the perversion of man's social and moral nature, he illustrated the extremes of poverty by highlighting the transformation of those used to a hard life as fishermen, who – through the influence of 'Rapine and Wrong and Fear' (*The Village*, 1: 111) – have turned into inhuman agents of destruction, wreckers, benefitting from the misfortune of others.[44] This 'bold, artful, surly, savage race' (*The Village*, 1: 112), according to the poet,

> Wait on the shore and, as the waves run high,
> On the tossed vessel bend their eager eye,
> Which to their coast directs its vent'rous way,
> Theirs, or the ocean's, miserable prey.
> (*The Village*, 1: 115–18)

Figure 6.5a Thomas Stothard, Vignette for February ('the Ocean's miserable prey'), *Royal Engagement Pocket Atlas for the Year MDCCCXXV*. Reproduced from a copy in the author's collection.

Figure 6.5b Thomas Stothard, Vignette for June ('Where loitering stray a little tribe'), *Royal Engagement Pocket Atlas for the Year MDCCCXXV*. Reproduced from a copy in the author's collection.

It is their actual, eager anticipation of shipwreck that Stothard depicts in his vignette. Arms raised and excited, these pirate-smugglers are prepared to do what it takes to take possession of the ship's cargo – even at the cost of human lives.

The Village is not only a poem that laments the changes society and rural communities have undergone, but its speaker is also keen to memorialize those whom the changing community spirit is unlikely to remember. This focus on remembering and memorialization is introduced in two different ways: a man reflecting on his own life and realizing that it is coming to an end, whereas another vignette represents a funeral scene, where only the children, once the service is completed, loiter to remember their departed friend (Figure 6.5b). Children are endowed with the ability to keep memories of the dead alive. Equally, they are capable of experiencing 'gleams of transient mirth and hours of sweet repose' in what Crabbe otherwise defines as 'a life of pain' (*The Village*, II, 4, 2).

Lord Byron

While the domestic culture of farming, village life, and the rural poor had been central to Stothard's illustrations for the numbers of the pocket atlas that illustrated Bloomfield, Crabbe, and Hurdis's *Village Curate*, after 1819, the artist repeatedly visualizes texts set in exotic locales and engaging with non-English culture. Between 1813 and 1815, Baker included vignettes illustrating, in 1813, Campbell's *Gertrude of Wyoming* and, in 1815, Scott's *Bridal of Triermain*. The number of the pocket atlas for 1814, the subject of which A. C. Coxhead does not list in his study of Stothard's work, illustrated *Childe Harold's Pilgrimage*, the first two cantos having been published in 1812.[45] This number remains untraced, but the increasing popularity of Byron motivated Baker, after 1816, to commission a set of designs that extended Stothard's illustrations of Cantos I and II of *Childe Harold*. An actual copy of the number for 1818, like the earlier number illustrating Byron's poem, has not been traced, but the British Museum Print Room holds a number of proof sheets as part of Robert Balmanno's collection of Stothard material (including the ones featuring Stothard's second set of illustrations of Byron's poems), which make possible the charting of subjects included in the 1818 volume.[46]

The 1818 issue of *The Royal Engagement Pocket Atlas* differs from all remaining numbers of the title in the rationale for the selection of texts to be illustrated.[47] While not all annual numbers illustrated a single literary text (even though many did), for the 1818 number Stothard illustrated scenes from seven of Lord Byron's texts, ranging from short productions such as 'The Dream', 'Darkness', 'The Prisoner of Chillon', and 'Churchill's Grave' to *Childe Harold's Pilgrimage*, *The Siege of Corinth*, and *Parisina*. In doing so, Stothard presented to the readers of *The Royal Engagement Pocket Atlas* a wide-ranging visual index to works which were widely read and which underpinned Lord Byron's reputation as one of the most eminent poets of his day. The number not only served as an indicator of Byron's status in the cultural economy of best-selling literature, but it moreover advertised these poems as part of a recent development in Romantic poetry, at the same time possibly promoting the sale of new editions of Byron's work. Stothard constructed an anthology which relied on readers' extensive visual and cultural literacy to understand his iconotextual interpretations of Byron's works. His visualizations of moments from Byron's poetry encompassed poems that had been published between 1812 and 1816. These illustrative epitexts to which are keyed unusually unspecific one-line quotations from the poems illustrated tied in with Stothard's other illustrative work rendering Byron's poetry in visual form, especially his illustrations for *Twelve Plates, Illustrative of the Poems of Lord Byron*, which were published in 1815 (and which included visualizations of *The Bride of Abydos*, *Childe Harold*, *The Corsair*, and *Lara*, among others). Whereas *Twelve Plates* was conceived as an elite subscription venture (in octavo format) aimed at collectors, the miniaturized vignettes for the *Pocket Atlas* offered a visual tour-de-force of often anthologized material. The captions that in other numbers of Baker's annual provide specific quotations from lines of the texts selected for illustration offer only minimal information, specifically the titles of the shorter poems and the number of the canto from the longer poems, some lines of which would have provided the specific reference for illustration. By not furnishing line numbers, as most vignettes in other numbers of the pocket diary do, Stothard most likely relied on readers' familiarity with the visualized texts which, if sufficient, would not require specific cues and referencing. In the manner of late eighteenth-century literary picture galleries, Stothard's vignette illustrations are part of a trend to assemble miniaturized picture books not only of one text but of what was conceived to be Byron's representative output at the time. Stothard's creating a visual anthology also consolidated the growing corpus of Byron's compositions by gathering them together in the format – albeit mediated by engraved images – of the poet's collected works, ahead of John Murray's issuing such a collection.

The 24 vignettes that Stothard supplied for the 1818 number of Baker's annual comprised four illustrations of scenes from 'The Dream' (for the September–October diary pages), seven vignettes illustrations of *Childe Harold* (February, April, May, June, and the verso page of the diary page for July), one illustration of *The Siege of Corinth* (recto page of July), two illustrations of *Parisina* (August), two illustrations of 'Darkness' (November), one illustration of 'The Prisoner of Chillon' (December verso), and one illustration of 'Churchill's Grave' (December recto). The frontispiece offered a visual rendering of the lines: 'He gazed, he saw, he knew the face, / It was Francesca by his side' (*The Siege of Corinth*, XX, 10, 12), even though this cue to the frontispiece omits an entire line, 'Of beauty, and the

Figure 6.6 Thomas Stothard, Frontispiece (The Siege of Corinth), *Royal Engagement Pocket Atlas for the Year MDCCCXVIII.*

form of grace', contracting the quotation for the sake of visual concentration, as well as eliminating the references to abstractions such as 'beauty' and 'grace' (Figure 6.6). Unlike the vignettes, Stothard's frontispiece invokes the iconographical conventions of theatrical painting, depicting the astonishment on the part of Alp at unexpectedly encountering the 'maid who might have been his bride'. The movement of his hands – his right hand raised to his head to express his shock at beholding Francesca, his left turned towards her, while she is holding on to his arm – is indicative of the psychological-emotional drama that Stothard seeks to convey. Altogether the various vignettes, as well as the dramatic frontispiece, gave readers access, through the visual medium, to the imaginative oriental realm that Byron had constructed since 1812.

The four vignettes for the November and December diary pages illustrate Byron's shorter poems and portray the gloom, melancholy, and despondency that characterize the three poems illustrated. Users of the diary examining these illustrations can infer the contemplative character of the vignettes and will identify human beings implanted into scenes of incarceration, a cemetery with its associations of loss and memorialisation, and the hopelessness and apocalyptic vision of 'Darkness'. Those with detailed textual knowledge of these poems will be able to discern a significant shift in terms of mood from the vignettes representing scenes from Byron's

Figure 6.7a Thomas Stothard, Vignette for November ('Darkness'), *Royal Engagement Pocket Atlas for the Year MDCCCXVIII*.

Figure 6.7b Thomas Stothard, Vignette for November ('Darkness'), *Royal Engagement Pocket Atlas for the Year MDCCCXVIII*.

long poems to the shorter production. The text that dominates Stothard's miniaturized gallery of vignettes is Byron's *Childe Harold*, specifically the cantos that had been published post-1812. Stothard's bringing together of all the texts included represents an effort to demonstrate both the range and modal differences among Byron's poems.

The first vignette for November captures two figures on their knees and watching a fire, which to them represents hope as well as the medium to define identity (Figure 6.7a). Stothard transforms Byron's 'Darkness' into a depiction of a social scene in which two figures confront one another, even though they do not engage with one another but look intently into

Figure 6.7c Thomas Stothard, Vignette for November ('The Prisoner of Chillon'), *Royal Engagement Pocket Atlas for the Year MDCCCXVIII*.

the fire. Stothard contracts two textual moments from the poem, the one depicting that 'all hearts / Were chill'd into a selfish prayer for light: / And they did live by watchfires' ('Darkness', 8–10), and the other the burning of homes, which facilitates one last moment of recognition in which 'men were gathered round their blazing homes / To look once more into each other's face' ('Darkness', 15–16). The kneeling position, associatively linked to acts of prayer, is not depicted as such but as a last attempt to retain proximity to the light of the fire and, consequently, its power to ensure survival. Man, in this scene, has already been degraded, but there is still an anthropocentric focus in the vignette, whereas the second vignette illustrating 'Darkness' centralizes two dogs and a vulture which are devouring a dead person (Figure 6.7b). Emblematic of the power of darkness, these predators benefit from the disappearance of light and establish a pre-Promethean world of chaos that erases not only old enmities but that is also likely to wipe out decadent humanity altogether. Iconographically, these predatory animals are reminiscent of the monstrous, dragon-like figures of evil that Stothard illustrated for earlier numbers of the pocket atlas, especially his set of illustrations of the *Faerie Queene*.[48]

While the destruction of man was central to Stothard's second visual interpretation of lines from 'Darkness', the subject is revisited in his vignette of the three brothers incarcerated as a punishment for their father's faith, suffering 'For the God their foes denied' (24) (Figure 6.7c). The image depicts the speaker's statement that 'Three were in a dungeon cast, / Of whom this wreck is left the last' ('The Prisoner of Chillon', 25–26). Even though three figures are visible, it is the central figure who survives as a 'wreck' as well as testimony of the persecution and suffering that his five siblings and himself, as well as their father, had experienced. For his vignettes illustrating Byron's poems, Stothard, for the first time since undertaking the illustration of the numbers of *The Royal Engagement Pocket Atlas* in the early 1780s, shifted from the sentimental impulse that had been dominant in his vignettes series to the depiction of the morbid and gloomy. The emphasis on introspection is nowhere more prominent than in his visual renderings of Byron's work.

Conclusion

The decision, on Thomas Baker's part, to commission illustrations of works by Bloomfield, Crabbe, and Byron for *The Royal Engagement Pocket Atlas* was motivated by the bookseller's awareness of these poets' well-known public status. Both Bloomfield and Byron were celebrities, whereas with Crabbe Baker capitalized on his established reputation as the author of *The Village*, now brought to readers' attention again through the publication of *The Parish Register*. The meteoric rise to fame that Byron experienced, his growing reputation as a poet, as well as his prolific and critically acclaimed output, induced Baker to commission Stothard to produce a second set of designs illustrating the poet's productions for the 1818 number of the pocket diary. Having his works illustrated twice for the publication made them comparable, in terms of textual status, to the two instances – Milton's 'L'Allegro' and 'Il Penseroso' and Thomson's *The Seasons* – when the same texts had been rendered in two different sets of vignettes for the *Pocket Atlas*.[49]

Baker's annual incorporated two different notions of the canon, the first an established one based on the well-known reputation of a writer whose works were no longer protected by copyright and could therefore be reprinted freely. The second notion of the canon was not based on 'classic' qualities characterizing texts that had stood the test of time. Rather, it was a canon of the present and based on literary celebrity, where contemporary reviewers offered stamps of approval, which facilitated success on a scale not possible at a time when reviewing was not professionalized in the way it came to be at the start of the nineteenth century. Illustrations consolidated reviewers' assessments of value and added to both the symbolic and material capital of editions of celebrity authors' texts. The canon of moderns that Stothard illustrated from 1801 onwards brought together three fundamentally different celebrities, Bloomfield, Byron, and Sir Walter

Scott, and it is no coincidence that their works were illustrated widely for the next 50 years, even though Bloomfield's decline in popularity occurred early in the Victorian period.[50]

Stothard's sets of vignettes contributed to generating a visual archive which, on occasion, was removed from the environment of the print publication in which it originally appeared in order to be transferred to an album, which was prized as a collectible. That Stothard's vignettes were collectibles is evidenced by the sale of collections of proof sheets of these illustrations, as well as the sale of the original vignette designs, at times in coloured versions, to collectors. The miniature format of these vignettes required detailed attention from their viewers: this need for close study to grasp the meaning of the ways in which these vignettes made sense of the texts visualized, as well as of the cumulative meaning of the series as a whole, encouraged readings that were significantly more participatory than readings of single book illustrations that were neither conceived as a series nor included in an edition of a literary text. Removed as these vignettes were from the full texts of the works they illustrated, readers had to infer these works or, in the absence of textual knowledge, construct their own textual narratives. While retelling visually prominent elements from a range of literary works, the vignette series by Stothard also encouraged readers' (re-) imaginings of these texts' meanings.

Notes

1 The research for this article was made possible through the award of a Paul Mellon Centre research grant. I am grateful to the staff of the British Museum Print Room for their assistance. For an account of Baker's pocket diary, see Sandro Jung, 'Thomas Stothard's Illustrations for *The Royal Engagement Pocket Atlas*, 1779–1826', *The Library*, 12: 1 (2011): 3–22; Sandro Jung, 'Illustrated Pocket Diaries and the Commodification of Culture', *Eighteenth-Century Life*, 37: 3 (2013): 53–84, as well as Sandro Jung, 'Thomas Stothard, Milton and the Illustrative Vignette: The Houghton Library Designs for *The Royal Engagement Pocket Atlas*', *Yearbook of English Studies*, 45 (2015): 137–58. Also: Nancy Finlay, 'Parnell's "The Hermit": Illustrations by Stothard', *The Scriblerian and the Kit-Cats*, 18 (1985): 1–5, as well as Nancy Finlay, 'Thomas Stothard's Illustrations of Thomson's *Seasons* for the *Royal Engagement Pocket Atlas*', *The Princeton University Library Chronicle*, 42 (1981): 165–77.

2 Hilary Thompson, 'Narrative Closure in the Vignettes of Thomas and John Bewick', *Word & Image*, 10: 4 (1994): 395.

3 See Sandro Jung, *Kleine artige Kupfer: Buchillustration im 18. Jahrhundert*, Wolfenbütteler Heft 36 (Wiesbaden: Harrassowitz, 2018): 5–16.
4 Gessner's *Der Tod Abels* was originally published in Zurich by Gessner himself in 1758 and then featured five exquisitely executed vignettes signed by Gessner. These same vignettes were reprinted and simplified by the Leipzig publisher, Johann Georg Löwe in 1760, 1762, and 1767, each time further revising the vignettes, which entails significant loss of complexity and tonality. Gessner's *Daphnis* (1756), which featured four rectangular vignettes, was equally, transnationally popular.
5 See Joachim von Schwarzkopf, *Über Staats- und Adress-Calender. Ein Beitrag zur Staatenkunde* (Berlin: Heinrich August Rottmann, 1792), 170; *Allgemeiner Litteratur-Anzeiger*, 161 (14 October 1799): 1593, and *Morgenblatt für gebildete Leser*, 12 (1818): 33.
6 Nigel Tattersfield, *Thomas Bewick: The Complete Illustrative Work*, 3 vols (London: The British Library, The Bibliographical Society, Oak Knoll Press, 2011), 1: 94.
7 Thompson, 'Narrative Closure', 396.
8 There were exceptions, however: The vignettes Bewick produced for Thomas Saint's 1783 edition of Richardson's *Pamela* do in fact render different scenes from the novel in more complex ways than he usually does in his vignette designs. He retells the heroine's trials and tribulations in six woodcuts and appears to take inspiration from subjects that had already been introduced in the illustrated sixth edition that Richardson had published in 1742. See Tattersfield, *Thomas Bewick*, 2: 331.
9 The Graphic Arts Department at Princeton University Library holds the set of wash-drawings Stothard designed for the issue of *The Royal Engagement Pocket Atlas* illustrating Thomas Parnell's 'The Hermit'.
10 He illustrated Cain and Abel as part of two vignette sequences he contributed to editions of *Der Tod Abels*. The vignette representing putto versions of Damon and Musidora featured on the title-page of the 1760 Zurich edition of Thomson's *Sommer*.
11 Stana Nenadic notes the 'striking feminization of … images' in the late eighteenth century, implying that this feminized image material catered to a new taste and a new group of consumers, including women. See Stana Nenadic, 'Print Collecting and Popular Culture in Eighteenth-Century Scotland', *History* 82: 266 (1997): 208.
12 Thomas Bonnell, *The Most Disreputable Trade: Publishing the Classics of English Poetry, 1765–1810* (Oxford: Oxford University Press, 2008), 97–133.
13 William St Clair, *The Reading Nation in the Romantic Period* (Cambridge: Cambridge University Press, 2004), 128.
14 Bonnell, *The Most Disreputable Trade*, 98. See also, Margaret J. M. Ezell, *Social Authorship and the Advent of Print* (Baltimore: Johns Hopkins University Press, 2003), 131–6.
15 See James Raven, *The Business of Books: Booksellers and the English Book Trade* (New Haven, CT: Yale University Press, 2007), 269–70.

16 See Sandro Jung, 'Thomson, Macpherson, Ramsay, and the Making and Marketing of Illustrated Scottish Literary Editions in the 1790s', *Papers of the Bibliographical Society of America*, 109: 1 (2015): 5–61.
17 *Oracle and Public Advertiser*, 13 November 1797.
18 According to St Clair, *The Reading Nation in the Romantic Period*, more than 100,000 copies sold between 1800 and 1826 (582).
19 Sandro Jung, *James Thomson's 'The Seasons', Print Culture, and Visual Interpretation, 1730–1842* (Bethlehem, PA: Lehigh University Press, 2015), 214–5. Some of the illustrations of *The Farmer's Boy*, specifically Anderson's head vignettes for 'Summer' and 'Winter', were reused in American editions of *The Seasons*. See *The Seasons: Containing Spring, Summer, Autumn, Winter by James Thomson* (New York: E. Duyckinck, 1813).
20 See Bruce Graver, 'Illustrating *The Farmer's Boy*', *Robert Bloomfield: Lyric, Class, and the Romantic Canon*, ed. Simon White, John Goodridge and Bridget Keegan (Lewisburg, PA: Bucknell University Press, 2006), 49–69. B. C. Bloomfield, 'The Publication of *The Farmer's Boy* by Robert Bloomfield', *The Library*, 15: 2 (1993): 75–94, esp. 88–90.
21 *Salisbury and Winchester Journal*, 8 February 1802.
22 *Gloucester Journal*, 29 October 1804.
23 *Ipswich Journal*, 25 October 1800.
24 H. J. Jackson, *Those Who Write for Immortality: Romantic Reputations and the Dream of Lasting Fame* (New Haven, CT: Yale University Press, 2014), 207–8.
25 *Salisbury and Winchester Journal*, 23 November 1801.
26 'To Robert Bloomfield, Author of the Farmer's Boy', *Staffordshire Advertiser*, 14 February 1802.
27 *Morning Post*, 16 December 1801.
28 www.rc.umd.edu/editions/bloomfield_letters/HTML/letterEEd.25.70.html (accessed 12 July 2015).
29 Peter Cochran, 'Introduction', *'The Farmer's Boy' by Robert Bloomfield: A Parallel Text Edition*, ed. Peter Cochran (Newcastle: Cambridge Scholars Press, 2014), 13. All quotations from Bloomfield's poem are from this edition.
30 See Nigel Temple, 'Humphry Repton, Illustrator, and William Peacock's "Polite Repository," 1790–1811', *Garden History*, 16: 2 (1988): 161–73.
31 A prominent example is Stothard's set of vignettes illustrating Goldsmith's 'The Deserted Village', which were published in the 1799 number of *The Royal Engagement Pocket Atlas*.
32 Jackson, *Those Who Write for Immortality*, 207.
33 See Sandro Jung, *The Publishing and Marketing of Illustrated Literature in Scotland, 1760–1825* (Bethlehem, PA: Lehigh University Press, 2017), 112–16 and 140–6.
34 The dates given in the parentheses indicate the year of illustration in the *Royal Engagement Pocket Atlas*.
35 Jackson, *Those Who Write for Immortality*, 207.

36 Ibid.
37 *George Crabbe: The Critical Heritage*, ed. Arthur Pollard (London: Routledge, 1972), 74.
38 *Hampshire Chronicle*, 1 January 1810.
39 *Annual Review*, 6 (1808), 514.
40 *Gentleman's Magazine*, 78 (1808), 59.
41 *Annual Review*, 514.
42 *Critical Heritage*, 68.
43 *Annual Review*, 514.
44 George Crabbe, *The Complete Poetical Works*, ed. Norma Dalrymple-Champneys, 3 vols (Oxford: Clarendon Press, 1988). All quotations from Crabbe's *The Village* are from the first volume of this edition.
45 A. C. Coxhead, *Thomas Stothard, RA.: An Illustrated Monograph* (London: A. H. Bullen, 1906), 53.
46 The Houghton Library, Harvard University, has a volume of Stothard's original sets of wash-drawings for five numbers of Baker's *Pocket Atlas* (Houghton Library shelfmark: f MS Typ 791).
47 The texts illustrated were mentioned in a German review of Baker's title. See *Morgenblatt für gebildete Leser*, 12 (January 1818), 33.
48 *The Royal Engagement Pocket Atlas* for 1795 featured Stothard's set of vignettes illustrating Spenser's *Faerie Queene*.
49 On the 1788 and 1826 numbers illustrating Milton's poems, see Jung, 'Thomas Stothard, Milton and the Illustrative Vignette', 145–54. On the 1793 and 1797 numbers illustrating *The Seasons*, see Jung, *James Thomson's 'The Seasons', Print Culture, and Visual Interpretation*, 158–63.
50 Unlike Byron, Coleridge and Wordsworth's works were not illustrated shortly after their appearance. See G. E. Bentley, Jr., 'Coleridge, Stothard, and the First Illustration of "Christabel"', *Studies in Romanticism,* 20: 1 (1981), 111–16.

7 | Intimate Distance: Thomas Stothard's and J. M. W. Turner's Illustrations of Samuel Rogers's *Italy*

MAUREEN MCCUE

Introduction

On 14 August 1830, *The Edinburgh Literary Journal* published a review of the forthcoming, newly revised and now illustrated edition of Samuel Rogers's *Italy*.[1] Like most post-Waterloo articles on Italy, the reviewer praises Italy as the 'especial home of the arts'. Whilst mourning the historical destruction caused by the 'fierce Arab and the rude Goth', the reviewer assures his readers that in Italy the 'mind of man' can still catch inspiration from those 'exuberant charms of nature' unique to the peninsula. The reviewer describes Italy as being somehow out of time: the traveller in Italy walks beside and breathes the same air as Virgil, Petrarch, Raphael, Tasso, and Alfieri, 'expecting to see their forms crossing us at every turn'. Italy's siren's call becomes too strong and the reviewer urges his readers to escape the wet British weather and depart 'this instant for Italy, if not in the body, at least in the spirit'. Whether in Italy or in front of their own home fires, imaginative travellers will move through Italy's sunny clime 'conversing with the mighty spirits who still sway the moods of men'. They will, of course, require a personal cicerone or two, and

> What better guides can we ask for such a journey, than those whom we have selected? There is Rogers, the patriarch of our age's poetry – amiable, accomplished, tasteful, and not deficient in power. There is Stothard, the Rogers of painting. There is Turner, daring and original, over whose faults no one could exult with a senseless triumph, unless incapable of feeling his power. […] In gallant company we set out for the land of song and painting, and invite all who love the sunny sparkle of its waters, to make one of our party.[2]

In many ways this review acts as an advertisement for this newly illustrated edition of Rogers's *Italy*. While earlier editions of *Italy* had been unpopular and had remained unsold, this edition, illustrated primarily by Thomas Stothard (1755–1834) and J. M. W. Turner (1775–1851), would prove to become an indispensable part of every fashionable reader's library throughout the nineteenth century.[3] While scholars and even some of

Rogers's contemporaries have argued that it was the illustrations themselves that saved the text, *The Edinburgh Literary Journal*'s review suggests that perhaps there was a more symbiotic relationship between text and image than has previously been recognized. By treating this 'gallant company' as equals, the reviewer eschews traditional debates surrounding the sister arts and suggests that their contributions must be experienced collectively. Furthermore, reading this text was also determined by the ways Italy itself was rendered in the text and the ways in which this reinforced its place in the British imagination. The 'land of song and painting' is as much between the leaves of the text, as it might be in the reader-viewer's imagination or on Italy's shores. Blending together poetry and images, illustrated editions of *Italy* materially manifest all that the Italian peninsula had come to mean in the British imagination. The reviewer opens his invitation to all those readers with an imaginatively fuelled love of Italy, yet circumscribes this democratizing impulse through his definitions of Rogers, Stothard, and Turner. Turner's original but flawed genius is tempered by established patricians, Rogers, and Stothard. Fashionable readers can therefore be reassured that their own standing and taste will be reinforced as they journey through the pages of *Italy*.

'Aided by thy verse and Turner's pencil'

The review article replicates *Italy*'s narrator's journey through the Italian peninsula, focusing particularly on the verbal and visual vignettes which compose the sections on Venice, Florence, and Rome. The reviewer is careful to balance his attention between Rogers, Turner, and Stothard, moving, like a camera lens, between various written and illustrated scenes. This sense of movement and framing is important. Not only does it reflect the inherent movement in the Giro d'Italia (as does Rogers's poem), but it also reproduces a central quality of *Italy*, which is the fluid narration between personal musings; the retelling and/or translation of tales, local legends or passages from literature; picturesque and sublime perspectives; and studious observations of the local inhabitants. Though such narratives, whether rendered visually, verbally or both, may be retellings of the past, they are often conveyed to the reader-viewer in the present moment through the very act of reading. Indeed, as we shall see, the narrator often relates a historical fact into the present moment or integrates a passage from literature without signalling to the reader that he is doing so. Such techniques, when coupled with the illustrations, conflate the past and the present; reality and the imagination; and the perspectives of the reader and the narrator, lending a sense of internal movement within each visual-verbal vignette, and encouraging the reader to modulate his or her imaginative distance to the subject at hand. The reviewer from *The Edinburgh Literary Journal* captures something of this movement and structure between scenes as he asks his readers to share various perspectives:

> let us stand with the painter […] and view the city of palaces. […] [L]et us enter the walls of the Medici Palace.[…] Let us escape from the city walls […]. Let us seek the Campagna […]. And here [at Galileo's Villa] we stop to pay homage to the genius of Turner, which has so poetically handled this subject […]. Onward! This is Rome![4]

While his job is certainly to review and even advertise this new and improved edition of *Italy*, the reviewer may offer a new perspective on how we might read illustrations produced during the 1820s and 1830s. While his movement replicates the journey Rogers takes his audience on, it simultaneously recreates (or anticipates) the ways in which Rogers's and the reviewer's shared audience will engage with *Italy*. The review, while conscious of the increasingly worn Sister Arts debates, wants to accommodate both the visual and verbal aspects of *Italy*:

> Aided by thy [Rogers'] verse and Turner's pencil, we gaze on the placid beauty of the lake of Geneva, and advance past the wilder scenery which surrounds Tell's Chapel and St Maurice, up to the topmost summit of the Great St Bernard. And here we are somewhat at a loss to determine which had succeeded best – the painter, in bodying forth to us the wild and frozen crags, the massive convent walls, the dead dark lake – or the poet, in animating this stern outward show, by his homely but hearty picture of the inhabitants and their occupations. One thing is in favour of the latter, it is easier to transplant his verse into our pages, than Turner's designs.[5]

Although unable to transfer Turner's or Stothard's actual designs onto his own page, the reviewer describes the illustrations to his readers while including key passages of Rogers's poetry as well. Without a clearly dominant art form, the review must stay more or less balanced between text and image. This review suggests that contemporary readers may have valued the verbal text as much as the visual texts, and that Stothard was as valuable as Turner, a point overlooked by much scholarship. The varying perspectives achieved by reading Rogers, Stothard and Turner together create for the reader an intimate distance with both the material text and the Italian peninsula.

History of Rogers's *Italy*

Despite a rather rocky start, *Italy* broke new ground both culturally and materially. Rogers published the first part of his poem anonymously in 1822 and then again, with his name, in 1824. Working again with John Murray, Rogers then brought out the second part in 1828. When these iterations of the text failed, Rogers bought back all remaining copies and destroyed them.[6] In response to a growing appetite for illustrated gift-books and annuals, Rogers brought out an illustrated edition in 1830, though he would continue to add to the text until 1834.[7] As noted above, the bulk of the illustrations were done by Turner and Stothard, though Samuel Prout also contributed a few designs. As J. R. Hale has demonstrated, Rogers was deeply involved in the design process and spent a great deal of time and money perfecting *Italy*.[8] This illustrated edition was highly praised and the text remained sought after throughout the nineteenth century. The text and illustrations were available in several different formats, and even illustrators of other Italianate publications were encouraged to buy India Proofs of the vignettes.[9] The 1830 edition's illustrations, for example, were inset into the text, while the larger 1838 edition included full-sized plates. A fashionable gift item, the text would continue to evolve throughout the nineteenth century to suit a variety of tastes and budgets.[10]

With the considerable funds Rogers devoted to making *Italy* saleable, it is no surprise that he called on Thomas Stothard's expertise.[11] Indeed, Stothard's career perfectly reflects the state of the arts in Britain at the turn of the nineteenth century. By exhibiting history paintings consistently at the Royal Academy from 1778, Stothard was able to build a reputation as a serious artist and as an essential member of the RA establishment, as signaled by his appointment as the RA's librarian from 1812. However, Stothard also regularly produced illustrations for a wide variety of books and magazines, as well as designs for Wedgwood, furniture makers and various printed ephemera such as pocket-books and shop-cards.[12] Despite the RA's bias against engraving as a form of mechanical reproduction, these activities were not mutually exclusive. Between 1778 and 1786, as M. G. Sullivan notes, Stothard 'produced forty-two illustrations for John Bell's *Poets of Great Britain*, 244 illustrations for John Harrison's *Novelist's Magazine*, 90 illustrations for G. Robinson's *Ladies' Magazine*, and numerous other smaller commissions. Stothard showed some of his original designs for these publications at Royal Academy exhibitions between 1780 and 1782 and in 1785'.[13] Significantly, Sullivan lumps all of this activity under the term 'book illustration'. Although not accurate (the *Ladies' Magazine* is just that, a magazine), this gloss reflects the changing marketplace, the trajectory of Stothard's career and the textual spaces which illustrations negotiated throughout the long nineteenth century. The market for visual and print cultures at the turn of the century was often jumbled, multifarious and moveable; books, magazines, annuals, merchandized exhibition spaces, extra illustrations and prints were formed, combined and consumed in a variety of ways. While the Royal Academy would try to separate history painting from its engraved counterparts, market tastes dictated another reality, one which Stothard used to his advantage and which would shape what we now think of as book illustration.[14]

Throughout his career, whether in oil or in print, Stothard tended to focus on those subjects which would typically form the basis for history painting, i.e. subjects taken from literature, classical myths and the Bible. This emphasis on painting and illustrating historical subjects was a key factor to his ongoing success. Praised for historical accuracy in his illustrations for Chaucer's *Canterbury Tales*, audiences trusted Stothard's taste and simple designs.[15] Furthermore, fashionable patrons commissioned Stothard to design furniture for their residences, thereby acknowledging the justness of his taste. To own or consume something designed by Stothard – whether painting, shop-card, chair or engraving – therefore conferred the same fashionable elegance to the consumer.

A similar sort of established elegance was also acquired through the consumption of Samuel Rogers's poetry. Rogers and Stothard worked together on several projects, including illustrations for Rogers's *Pleasures of Memory* (from 1793) and designs for Rogers's home in St James' Place. Stothard's work also appeared as headings for *The Royal Engagement Pocket Atlas* and were 'illustrated' by snippets of Rogers's poems. For nineteenth-century middle-class consumers, both Rogers and Stothard represented unquestionable elegance and authoritative taste based on deep antiquarian knowledge. Furthermore, Stothard's well-honed understanding of the factors which were necessary to create a successful art commodity, as well as his 'pliable and submissive attitude', cemented his reputation with both booksellers and consumers. It is also worth pointing out that Rogers requested that some of Stothard's figures be integrated into at least two of Turner's pictures, a fact often overlooked by Turner scholars.[16] The close working relationship between Rogers, Stothard, Turner and various engravers is manifested in the text's implicit dialogue between pictures and words. Image and text rely on each other, representing a growth point in the creation of illustrated books.

This close relationship has resulted in what we might characterize as a 'proto-cinematic' text, particularly because this relationship between these graphic texts creates a sense of movement for the reader-viewer. This movement is not limited to what is happening in the text or between the leaves of the text, but also the individual reader-viewer's physical eye and inner eye. In her book *Moving Pictures*, Anne Hollander suggests that cinema is the 'the newest form of illustration' and identifies some key qualities of what she calls 'proto-cinematic art', including illustrations.[17] In particular, she explores cinema's inheritance from the Northern European painting tradition, claiming that unlike art from the classical tradition (Italian Renaissance and Baroque paintings) which places the artist and his skills at the forefront of the work's meaning, Northern European work tends to highlight 'optical experience rather than formal ideas'. Rather than offer a comprehensive image, proto-cinematic art requires the eye's movement between parts in order to comprehend the whole. Importantly then, proto-cinematic art is characterized by its psychological and 'emotional effects' on the viewer, creating what is essentially a private experience:

> One feature of such [proto-cinematic] art has been that it enters public awareness privately, affecting persons one at a time. [...] So do reproductions, and so always did illustrations. In contrast to great frescoes in churches or great exhibitions in museums, or to performances on stages, to which people must go in public groups in order to know they are seeing art, reproduced art and illustrative art have been offered in books and journals and single sheets for private consumption. Each one of their thousands of copies aims at one viewer at a time. In magazines and newspapers, television and movies, images strike each of us personally and without preparation, affecting us almost without acknowledgement, perhaps all the more strongly for that.[18]

Although this is perhaps a limited reading of how illustrations might be consumed or used – particularly with regards to their social function in Romantic-period Britain – nonetheless, Hollander's emphasis on the individual viewer's optical experience is useful here. In the case of Rogers's *Italy* and through the relationship between the illustrations and poetry, the Italian peninsula is rendered by the reader-viewer's eye into a series of scenes, framed by a shared cultural heritage. Illustration and text determine the reader-viewer's proximity to or distance from the sites, history and culture of Italy. The reader-viewer's movement through the text mimics the narrator's movement through the peninsula, rendering both spaces as imaginative galleries without fixed boundaries. Each space within Italy and *Italy* is dynamic, has its own story and will be rendered in ways which seem to correspond to the city or landscape's inherent temperament. By examining the ways in which two different spaces – Venice and Florence – are rendered in *Italy*, we will gain a greater insight into the many uses for illustrations in the first half of the nineteenth century.

Venice

The first stop in Italy proper is Venice, but unlike many nineteenth-century accounts which describe the city rising from the waves as a way into the city itself, Rogers approaches Venice three times before allowing readers to fully arrive at their destination. Even as Turner's opening vignette (Figure 7.1) places the reader-viewer in the moment of arriving on the shores of Venice, the poet simultaneously places and dis-places Venice before the reader's imaginative eye. He writes,

> There is a glorious City in the Sea.
> The Sea is in the broad, the narrow streets,
> Ebbing and flowing; and the salt sea-weed
> Clings to the marble of her palaces.
> No track of men, no footsteps to and fro,
> Lead to her gates. The path lies o'er the Sea,
> Invisible; and from the land we went
> As to a floating City – steering in,
> And gliding up her streets as in a dream. (45)

When placed next to Turner's illustration, the reader intuitively wants to read the opening lines of the 'Venice' section as Rogers describing Turner's illustration. But as she reads on, the actual distance from Venice becomes apparent. Even as the speaker moves towards Venice and imagines 'gliding up her streets as in a dream', still the 'path lies o'er the Sea' and the speaker has yet to arrive.

This disconnect between Turner's opening view and Rogers's anticipatory image of Venice enhances the sense of movement within and between these visual and verbal scenes. This is strengthened by the speaker's own restless eye and musings. Venice was familiar to any nineteenth-century would-be traveller's imagination. While anticipating viewing Venice for the first time, the speaker's focus shifts and he begins to lament that he cannot describe modern Italians as well as the poet George Crabbe. Without 'thy pencil Crabbe', the Italian character proves too 'cameleon-like; and mocks / The eye of the observer' (47). The speaker's mind, eye and imagination move rapidly between historical knowledge; well-known, though at this point

Figure 7.1 J. M. W. Turner, *Venice* (1838), reproduced from a copy in the author's collection.

imagined or, from Rogers's perspective, remembered, views of Venice; literary associations; and observations, all of which occur in quick succession. This rapid movement between time and space strengthens the relationship between the speaker and the reader, as the reader is called to imagine these various components. The eye's attention is once again interrupted as 'a voice aloft proclaims "Venezia!"/ And, as called forth, she comes' (47); in this moment both the speaker's attention and the city are 'called forth' as the traveller finally sees Venice for the first time. Taken from one of Rogers's journal entries, this moment mimics the endless stream of impressions that a traveller might experience on a journey. Furthermore, in replicating the physical approach to the city, this moment emphasizes the ways in which the movement of the eye anticipates and parallels the physical movement of a person through space or across distances. As the speaker moves closer to Venice, the reader's eye frames Venice in multiple ways, with varying degrees of proximity to the city. Importantly, this sense of movement is supported and enhanced by both the order and nature of the illustrations, as well as the poetic description of moving through Venice's waterways and history.

The voice which announces 'Venezia!' draws both the traveller and the reader's attention back to the journey. Though they have yet to arrive, Venice is now on the horizon. But while the description is, as it were, approaching Turner's opening illustration, the verbal and visual moments do not quite reproduce the same perspectives, as Venice remains at a distance from the traveller. Though in tune, the poetic description and the illustration are out of sync. This is a key element of the success of Rogers's *Italy*; the bulk of the illustrations do not always depict one specific, identifiable moment, but rather tend to convey a more general sense of an ongoing or unfolding encounter with Italy. It also reflects Rogers's writing style itself, which often resists naming sites or directly acknowledging literary passages from which he borrows. After this second invocation of Venice, the speaker meditates on the history of Venice, relating the legend of how the Romans settled in Venice in order to escape Attilla the Hun. Finally, however, Venice

> Rose, like an exhalation from the deep,
> A vast Metropolis, with glistering spires,
> With theatres, basilicas adorned;
> A scene of light and glory, a dominion,
> That has endured the longest among men. (48)

The approach to Venice is rendered three times in the poetry, which encourages the reader to move between the poetry and the illustrations, returning to various vignettes as the poem unfolds, in order to situate himself within the physical landscape of both the book and Italy.

Like the other sections of *Italy*, Venice is divided into several subsections, not all of which are illustrated. However, the poetic subsections and the sequence of vignettes tend to bring readers into an ever-closer proximity to Venice, its inhabitants, its history and its culture. The vignettes dealing with Venice and Venetian subjects include engravings after works by Turner, Titian and Stothard. Importantly, Turner and Stothard's works share similar framing devices, such as softened edges, which invite the reader in, while Titian's work – with its exact lines, perspectives and sharp framing – requires that the reader-viewer maintains a respectful distance to the artist, the engraving and the city in his mind's eye. When combined together and in conjunction with Rogers's work, these framing devices negotiate the reader's relationship with Italy. Throughout the text, Rogers often describes a historical event or a passage from literature as happening before his very eyes, and this is paralleled in the way the reader's eye encounters the vignettes. The moment depicted is always present before the reader's eye, regardless if it is an historical or a contemporary event. Indeed, historical and contemporary moments are often conflated in both the poetry and the vignettes. As in the poetic description, Stothard's 'Tournament in St Mark's Place', for instance, shows a medieval-style jousting tournament as happening before the reader's very eyes. In *Italy* (and Italy), the past is always unfolding before the viewer, a feeling reinforced by Rogers's choice to include both Titian's depiction of a doge's funeral procession in St Mark's Square and Stothard's view of St Mark's. When taken together and in order, the illustrations create a sort of proto-cinematic storyboard for the viewer's encounter with Venice, moving ever deeper into the city. As already noted, Turner's 'Venice' evokes the moment of arriving in Venice, though the traveller has yet to touch down upon the shore. The next vignette is David Allen's engraving of *Palazzo San Marco* and the doge's funeral procession supposedly by Titian. Although Rogers's and Turner's texts have now situated the reader-viewer within Venice, Titian's view maintains a more formal engagement with the city. With its clearly defined boundaries, Titian's work emphasizes the *palazzo*'s architecture and maintains a slightly raised perspective; the eye takes in the whole scene, but in order to do so, a certain distance must be maintained. In addition to the main vignettes which are interleaved between the verbal text, there are several small illustrations of particularly Venetian characters, including a Doge in his robes and Scaramouch from *Commedia dell'Arte*, sprinkled throughout the 'Venice' section. While such illustrations may pique the reader-viewer's interest, a certain distance is maintained as these figures are regarded as merely Venetian curiosities or markers of an encounter with the other. However, the next vignette which situates the reader in direct relationship with the city is Stothard's 'Brides of Venice'. As we shall see, this vignette invites reader-viewers to fully immerse themselves and participate in all that Venice has to offer, an invitation extended by the section's last two vignettes, Stothard's 'Tournament' and the tourist attraction of a Venetian leader's tomb. As the speaker explores Venice, the vignettes create and reinforce various perspectives on the city. The visual and verbal texts guide the reader-viewer towards ever increasing intimacy with the city, ensuring that she moves from a mere observer to a participant.

The first two illustrations included in the 'Venice' section showcase the architecture and, in Turner's case, the atmosphere of the city. However, Stothard's 'Brides of Venice' is the first illustration to emphasize the city's human element and its traditions. A footnote explains that the story being related happened on the eve of the Purification of the Virgin (i.e. the eve of Candlemas Day) in 944. Before this, the tradition had been that marriages between the great families of Venice took place on this day. But on this day in 944, as the nuptials were being read, a corsair named Barbaro and his six brothers stormed the church and kidnapped the brides. Rogers's poem tracks the commotion caused by this act as the whole city is called to action:

> In an hour
> Half VENICE was afloat. But long before,
> Frantic with grief and scorning all controul [sic],
> The Youths were gone in a light brigantine,
> Lying at anchor near the Arsenal;
> Each having sworn, and by the holy rood,
> To slay or to be slain. (69)

At this point, Rogers's text blends history with a chivalric tale of ruthless corsairs, dedicated, active townsfolk and, of course, virtuous maidens and their loyal, successful champions. After the maidens are rescued, celebrations of thanksgiving ensue. With the help of Stothard's illustration, Rogers transforms the historical event into a pageant happening before the viewer:

> And through the city, in a stately barge
> Of gold, were borne with songs and symphonies
> Twelve ladies young and noble. Clad they were
> In bridal white with bridal ornaments,
> Each in her glittering veil; and on the deck
> As on a burnished throne, they glided by;
> No window or balcony but adorned
> With handing of rich texture, not a rook
> But covered with beholders, and the air
> Vocal with joy. Onward they went, their oars
> Moving in concert with harmony,
> Through the Rialto to the Ducal Palace,
> And at a banquet, served with honour there,
> Sat representing, in the eyes of all,
> Eyes not unwet, I ween, with grateful tears,
> Their lovely ancestors, the Brides of VENICE. (71)

The origin of the tale – the event in 944 – marks the beginning of an important Venetian tradition, but in the final line the brides who had been kidnapped by the corsairs morph into their present-day descendants who are re-enacting the celebrations of thanksgiving. Rogers's sleight of hand is echoed in and supported by Stothard's illustration, which places the boat carrying the brides at the foreground of the engraving. As we have seen, the first two illustrated encounters with Venice place the city at a distance from the viewer, allowing the viewer to survey the city and its inhabitants. Turner's recreates one's arrival to the city and while the engraving of Titian's painting brings reader-viewers to *Palazzo San Marco*, its emphasis on the architecture, the formal procession and even the formal boundaries of the engraving itself, maintains the viewer's formal distance. The reader-viewer observes this event but does not necessarily participate. Taken together, the move from Turner's 'Venice' through Titian's to Stothard's illustration of the brides, anticipates the sweeping motion characteristic of film, panning from one scene to the next, and from a wide shot to a more intimate close-up. The distance which marks Titian's work is shattered by Stothard's vignette, as the brides approach the reader-viewer and nearly sail out of the frame (Figure 7.2). The brides and their boat are in the foreground and fill more than half of the vignette, while the perspective suggests that perhaps the reader is witnessing the nautical procession from the *Ponte di Rialto* as it sails to the Doge's Palace. There is energy and movement in the crowd, while the brides seem to be heading straight towards the reader. Soon, Stothard's illustration seems to suggest, the brides will pass under the bridge and away from view. Just as the brides in Rogers's text slipped from the past into the present moment, so too does the reader slip from distanced observer into the role of active participant in these festivities.

The montage created in the verbal text between key moments in Venice's long history is reinforced in both the verbal text's relationship with the illustrations and in the illustrations' relationship to each other. The illustrations condense the city into an increasingly knowable space. As the verbal text ranges through various spaces in Venice – including the canals, in a gondola, and in several squares, palaces and rooms – the reader-viewer participates in the unfolding of the city and gains a deeper understanding of Venice. Taken as a whole, *Italy* might be likened to a proto-cinematic painting, which, according to Hollander, relies on a sustained

> drama of imminent disclosure and incipient revelation. The story is not explained to an audience but revealed to a participant. The scene of expectation is uneasy: what is going to happen? Not in the plot, but simply before our eyes. […] Paintings that convey this feeling tend not to repay a minute, satisfying study of many details. They seem to demand glancing at, glancing away, and then glancing back, as if the eye had missed something it might yet apprehend the next instant. They bear watching. Details

Figure 7.2 Thomas Stothard, *Brides of Venice* (1838), reproduced from a copy in the author's collection.

> may indeed abound, but no study yields an obvious relationship among them, only the strong sense of imminent meaning for us.[19]

The whole of the Italian peninsula has been rendered into this singular work, which nonetheless has a plethora of moving parts. The subsections of *Italy*, bracketed as they often are by illustrations, find a parallel in proto-cinematic paintings in that they offer spaces of 'drama' and 'revelation', whereby the reader-viewer is encouraged to move forward and backward between sections. While the verbal text is rich with historic details, these details are lightened by both the illustrations and variations in poetic techniques and voice. Rogers often interrupts his own voice in the narrative, either by translating other literary or musical works directly into his own text without prior warning, or, as we shall see in the 'Florence' section, by leaving out important information about the origin of his material. In 'The Gondola' subsection of 'Venice', for example, the reader is jarred as Rogers's respectable, antiquarian speaker is suddenly replaced by a new 'I' seducing his lover. It only becomes clear that this is not actually Italy's narrator, when Rogers's own voice returns to explain that these lines have come from the lay of a love-sick Venetian and an accompanying footnote makes it clear that this section is largely a translation of *La Biondina in Gondoletta*. Written in 1788 by Anton Maria Lamberti (1757–1832), *La Biondina* was a popular Venetian air which may have been familiar to much of Rogers's audience. However, this drastic change in voice disrupts, if only momentarily, the narrative's structure and adds to that quality of Italy being 'revealed to a participant'. Together, the visual and verbal texts, framed by the different perspectives of Rogers, Turner and Stothard, present a complex narrative of Italy, which the reader-viewer must traverse in order to make meaning out of these various moving parts and become deeply knowledgeable about Italy.

Florence

One of the next major stops on the tour is Florence. The 'Florence' section includes the city itself, as well as Fiesole, Pisa (or rather the rivalry between Pisa and Florence), Galileo's home in Arcetri and the wider *campagna* around Florence and along the Arno. From the opening lines and in virtually all the corresponding illustrations, history's presence is felt. While, as we have seen, the past was certainly a key element in the framing of the Venice section, Florence's past functions in a more complex way. The city's past is not just made up of historical figures or events, but also literature and art. As an art collector and Italophile, Rogers presents Florence's past as composed of several interlocking puzzle pieces, and historical political figures or events must contend not only with authors and painters, but with the very texts and paintings themselves. Celebrating Florence as the home of the Renaissance, Rogers writes,

> Of all the fairest Cities of the Earth
> None is so fair as FLORENCE. 'Tis a gem
> Of purest ray; and what a light broke forth,
> When it emerged from darkness! 'Tis the Past
> Contending with the Present; and in turn
> Each has the mastery. (96)

Florence's past, whether historical or literary, is felt, experienced and recited in the present moment. Indeed, for Rogers, all of these elements must come together in order to get to the truth or essence of Florence.

Rogers, however, is not always forthcoming in the information he offers readers in order to help them locate themselves within the cityscape. Sometimes (and more frequently in later editions) he will offer a footnote which names the site or figure he is describing, or he may embed clues within the text by, for example, describing one site before naming another, associated site. Rogers seems to assume that his readers have a good working knowledge of Florence and its most distinguished citizens, particularly Dante, or that they will be reading *Italy* in conjunction with a guidebook. In the space of a few pages, for example, the speaker moves from contemplating 'this chapel', which, through its connection to the *Sasso di Dante* readers might come to realise is *Il Basilica di Santa Maria del Fiore* (i.e. *il Duomo*), before inviting the readers to 'Enter the Baptistery'. We are then taken to the chapel of *San Lorenzo*, which is only named as the 'Chamber of the Dead', before going to visit the Venus de' Medici (which the footnote specifies is in the Uffizi's *Tribuna*). As the speaker guides readers through key sites in Florence, he invokes sections of Dante's *Divina Commedia* as if *Purgatorio*'s various levels depicted real life, before also mentioning Filippo Strozzi (who, after a description of his character and deeds, is finally named in a footnote)[96–9]. Rogers's elisions may reflect the central importance of Dante to Romantic-period readers, as well as the popularity of Florence itself; Rogers may safely assume his readers' familiarity with these topics. But it may also suggest that, like his more dynamic Romantic counterparts, Rogers is placing himself within a shared literary tradition by claiming a certain inheritance from Dante. Dante's *Divina Commedia* makes Florence, its citizens and its history, literary. As in Shelley's *The Mask of Anarchy*, the shades of the Florentine leaders Dante's pilgrim meets in *Purgatorio* are simultaneously taken from real life and rendered into politico-poetical allegories. Rogers oscillates between, for example, invoking Dante as a poet and as a man, and then in another section, translating sections or scenes from *Divina Commedia*. Sometimes the origin of these translations is acknowledged or highlighted, but at other times they are completely subsumed into his own writing. Rogers's treatment of this city and its surrounding countryside emphasizes that stone, artistic and literary innovation, and a rich history are the essential components of Florence's architecture.

Although not unusual for this period, this claim to a shared Anglo-Italian literary history is a central theme throughout *Italy* and is a key avenue through which the reader-viewer may relate to Italy. Rogers builds his vision of Florence through its literary and artistic associations. This vision, which would come to inform the long nineteenth-century's understanding of Italian culture, includes a wide range of figures, text and interests, particularly from the medieval period. When the speaker ventures to the *Campagna* for his morning stroll through Fiesole, he recounts the story of Cimabue meeting Giotto; Galileo's accomplishments and Milton's visit to the scientist; mentions Machiavelli; and also integrates scenes from Boccaccio's *Decameron*. Rogers invokes the literary content of Boccaccio's text, places Boccaccio within a wider literary canon and relates some of the history of the plague, while Stothard's 'A Rural Entertainment' captures the essence of both Rogers's treatment of Boccaccio and the tone of Boccaccio's work itself (which Stothard had illustrated in 1825).

While Rogers's text and the illustrations help the reader-viewer navigate those physical spaces unique to Venice, in the Florence section both texts and illustrations construct a cultural inheritance shared between Britain and Italy. Medieval art, literature and social institutions are blended with the present moment in order to create this shared culture; and the illustrations go a long way to making this cultural space accessible. Turner's illustrations for this section are atmospheric, while Stothard's develop or supplement the reader-viewer's understanding of his or her literary inheritance. More so than his work for the Venice section, Turner's illustrations for Florence instruct the would-be traveller in how she might approach the city and engage with this shared cultural inheritance. The first illustration, 'Florence' (Figure 7.3), offers a picturesque view of the city taken from Fiesole. This approach to the city was a popular vista and similar views were included as a frontispiece to *The Improvisatrice* (1824). In the context of *Italy* itself, however, it is important to note that it encapsulates both the city's most important architecture and also the campagna (both from where the viewer is situated and the whole perimeter of Florence). The figures in the foreground – present-day monks – also foreshadow the intrigues of medieval Florence and the Medici court more particularly, which will form a core component of Rogers's poetic treatment of the city. Although such figures were not Turner's strong suit – indeed, Stothard contributed several figures for Turner's *Italy* illustrations – these figures do help to establish the ways in which Florence's medieval and Renaissance past continued to shape Rogers's contemporary moment. Another of Turner's illustrations shows Galileo's villa in Arcetri at night with a waxing moon and his scientific instruments in the off-centre foreground (Figure 7.4). This is not the only night scene included in *Italy*; others include 'Rome' (with St Peter's

Figure 7.3 J. M. W. Turner, *Florence* (1838), reproduced from a copy in the author's collection.

Bascillica), and two different 'Villas'. These illustrations are recognizably by Turner as they all communicate an ephemeral atmosphere through the use of light and shade. However, these later illustrations all feature full moons, which in themselves become almost as important as the thing they depict. The viewer's distance from the eye's object is thus highlighted. 'Galileo's Villa', on the other hand, encapsulates a much softer, quieter atmosphere, which is also mirrored by the verbal text. Both texts ask the reader-viewer to meditate on the villa's wider cultural significance.

As a Cicerone-type figure, Rogers's speaker takes his readers on a walking tour of the countryside around Florence. When he comes upon Arcetri, he celebrates it for its associations with Galileo and Milton:

> Nearer we hail
> Thy sunny slope, ARCETRI, sound of Old
> For its green wine; dearer to me, to most,

Figure 7.4 J. M. W. Turner, *Galileo's Villa* (1838), reproduced from a copy in the author's collection.

> As dwelt on by that great Astronomer,
> […] Sacred be
> His villa (justly was it called The Gem!)
> Sacred the lawn, where many a cypress threw
> Its length of shadow, while he watched the stars!
> Sacred the vineyard, where, while yet his sight
> Glimmered, at blush of morn he dressed his vines,
> Chanting aloud in gaiety of heart
> Some verse of ARIOSTO! There, unseen,
> In manly beauty MILTON stood before him,
> Gazing with reverent awe – MILTON, his guest,

> Just then come forth, all life and enterprize;
> […] Little then
> Did GALILEO think whom he received;
> That in his hand he held the hand of one
> Who could requite him – who would spread his name
> O'er lands and seas – great as himself, nay greater;
> MILTON as little that in him he saw,
> As in a glass, what he himself should be,
> Destined so soon to fall on evil days
> And evil tongues – so soon, alas, to live
> In darkness, and with dangers compassed round,
> And solitude. (107–8)

Rogers evokes *Il Gioiello* in a Wordsworthian cadence as he imagines the astronomer tending his vines and gazing at the stars. Both the illustration and Rogers's text place the reader-viewer at the scene and the eye is able to wander from the poem's indication of Galileo's lawn, cypress trees, vineyards and the sky, to the corresponding elements in the engraving. Without figures there is a certain ambiguity of time in the engraving, which is itself akin to the experience of literary tourism. Turner has included Galileo's instruments in his work, suggesting an absent presence. Has Galileo just walked back into his villa, or is this how the villa is now presented to contemporary tourist-pilgrims? In the poem, Rogers evokes the past, but maintains the present's distance to the past. While Rogers does not blur these time lines, Turner's illustration allows reader-viewers to inhabit the past and the present simultaneously. There is also the suggestion of the future as well, as this site will now be recognizable should the fireside traveller join the growing crowd of literary tourists.

Rogers is certainly not the only Romantic-period poet-traveller to Italy to follow in Milton's footsteps. Such connections between Italian and British writers, thinkers and poets promoted the British interest in Italy by suggesting a shared heritage. Such associations were especially rich in Tuscany and could register a number of political as well as cultural alliances. While, for example, the Byron-Shelley circle would claim such an inheritance in order to create a new hybrid identity, later writers might celebrate such an alliance to argue in support of the *Risorgimento*. Illustrations such as Turner's 'Galileo's Villa' support the individual reader's ability to create such connections with Italian figures, while other illustrations, such as Stothard's 'Buondelmonte' enriched the reader-viewer's knowledge of Italian literature. In a slightly later passage, Rogers imagines Milton reclined on the banks of the Arno, reciting poetry. This bucolic scene is interrupted as the narrator begins to think of the other historical associations with this spot, asking 'Where is the ground that did not drink warm blood/ The echo that had learnt not to articulate/ The cry of murder?' (111). He begins to imagine a fateful day which would come to shape Florence's entire history:

> Fatal was the day
> To FLORENCE, when ('twas in a narrow street
> North of that temple, where the truly great
> Sleep, not unhonoured, not unvisited;
> That temple sacred to the Holy Cross –
> There is the house – that house of the Donati,
> Towerless, and left long since, but to the last
> Braving assault – all rugged, all embossed
> Below, and still distinguished by the rings
> Of brass, that held in war and festival-time
> Their family-standards) fatal was the day
> To Florence, when at morn, at the ninth hour,
> A noble Dame in weeds of widowhood,
> Weeds by so many to be worn so soon,
> Stood at her door; and, like a sorceress, flung,
> Her dazzling spell. Subtle she was, and rich,
> Rich in a hidden pearl of heavenly light,
> Her daughter's beauty; and too well she knew
> Its virtue! Patiently she stood and watched;
> Nor stood alone – but spoke not – In her breast
> Her purpose lay; and, as a Youth passed by,
> Clad for the nuptial rite, she smiled and said,
> Lifting a corner of the maiden's veil,
> 'This had I treasured up in secret for thee.
> This hast thou lost!' He gazed and was undone!
> Forgetting – not forgot – he broke the bond,
> And paid the penalty, losing his life
> At the bridge-foot; and hence a world of woe!
> Vengeance for vengeance crying, blood for blood;
> No intermission! Law, that slumbers not,
> And, like the Angel with the flaming sword,
> Sits overall, at once chastising, healing,
> Himself the Avenger, went; and every street
> Ran red with mutual slaughter. (pp. 111–3)

In this long section Rogers recounts the story of Buondelmonte de' Buondelmonti, a central figure at the heart of Florence's deadly Guelph-Ghibelline rivalry. In 1215, as part of a peace agreement, Buondelmonte

Figure 7.5 Thomas Stothard, *Buondelmonte* (1838), reproduced from a copy in the author's collection.

had been engaged to a woman from the Amidei family but abandoned her to marry a woman from the Donati family. On the morning of his wedding day, as he was crossing Ponte Vecchio, the Guelph Buondelmonte was ambushed by Oddo Arrighi, the uncle of the Amidei woman, and his Ghibelline gang, an event which came to symbolize the start of the Guelph-Ghibbelline war.[20]

Buondelmonte is only named in Stothard's illustration (Figure 7.5). In this way, Stothard's illustration works in a similar way as other paratextual indicators such as footnotes. By naming Buondelmonte, the title of the illustration fills in the gaps of the narrative, even as it captures the fateful moment the veil is lifted. Although chroniclers in the thirteenth and fourteenth centuries presented Buondelmonte's decision to marry the Donati over the Amidei woman in several different ways, the inclusion of this story in *Italy* sets Rogers up as a serious Italianist. In later editions of *Italy*, his footnotes will demonstrate that he was familiar with both Giovanni Villani's chronicle and Dante's accounts in the *Inferno* (canto 28) and *Paradiso* (canto 16) of Buondelmonte.[21] Both the illustration and the poem freeze this moment even as they indicate that what happens next will have drastic consequences. The horse skitters to a stop as the veil is lifted, but the events of the next moment seem inevitable through the tense muscles of both horse and rider. Rogers repeatedly names this day as 'fatal' to Florence, spends much of the passage indicating where this moment takes place, hints at what the story entails and who the key actors may be (although Buondelmonte remains 'a Youth', the Donati family is named), before fast-forwarding to the ensuing slaughter. For those readers without Rogers's deep knowledge, it is necessary to have both the tale and the illustration in order to understand the event. Rogers is also creating a subtle lineage with these earlier Florentine writers. As N. P. J Gordon has indicated, Buondelmonte's story and the ensuing rivalry shaped both the civic and physical boundaries of Florence itself.[22] By locating this event with precision in his text and in relation to various other landmarks in the city, Rogers is extending this tradition and translating it for a British audience. Stothard's illustration supports this endeavour by asking the reader to situate herself in relation to the fateful moment. Florence's story is now part of British literature.

Conclusion

In both the Venice and Florence sections, Rogers, Turner, and Stothard pull together a web of literary, social, cultural and historical associations for the reader-viewer. The visual and verbal texts negotiate the individual's knowledge of and proximity to Italy's most important sites. This will continue through the rest of the text as the complexities of Rome and its *compagna* are explored and rendered in a range of verbal and visual vignettes. Some of the most touching vignettes are those whose human elements intrigue the reader-viewer and invite her to emotionally engage in the scene before her. Scenes such as Rogers's description of a nun taking the veil and Stothard's accompanying vignette 'The Nun' allow the reader-viewer to encounter unfamiliar scenes and assess them emotionally. Turner's landscapes offer the opportunity to see Italy, if only in the mind's eye, and therefore to take part both in the growing tourism industry and the fashion for stunning material texts. The *Edinburgh Literary Journal* closed its review with the following remarks:

> we conclude this rambling article by remarking, in more sober prose, that the forthcoming new edition of Rogers's 'Italy,' illustrated by fifty-six engravings, so exquisite as those which we have been alluding, will be one of the most delightful books imaginable.[23]

When the individual elements are taken together, Rogers, Turner and Stothard's *Italy* gives us insight not only into how Italy was understood by nineteenth-century British travellers and readers, but also into the complex aesthetic values and literary associations such readers were hungry for.[24] The gap between the verbal description and the illustrated vignette provides an important space for the reader-viewer's imagination. The visual illustrations' resistance to rendering the verbal text in precise, frozen moments, allows for the eye's movement that is so essential to establishing the proto-cinematic quality of the text. It also encourages the reader-viewer to become an active participant in both the visual and verbal texts. Such a text suggests that the growth of illustrated texts in early to mid-nineteenth-century Britain reflects the needs of a more sophisticated audience than has previously been acknowledged. Over the course of several years, Rogers, Stothard and Turner laboured to create a work distinct enough to break through an already crowded marketplace. Working with steel engravings, particularly when text and image appeared on the same page, was time-consuming and costly, with several proofs taking over two years to complete.[25] Through its associations with Rogers and Stothard, *Italy* opened the door to taste for its middle-class audience, but this respectability was also instrumental in bringing Turner to an audience beyond the walls of the Royal Academy's annual exhibition. By creating a multi-generic, illustrated book, Rogers was not just recouping his original loss, but offering his audience a new experience that they were now ready to undertake, with 'one of the most delightful books imaginable'.

Notes

1 'Literary Criticism [*Fifty-Six Engravings Illustrative of Italy. A Poem*. By Samuel Rogers, Esq. London. Jennings and Chaplin. 1830. (*Unpublished.*) *Pompeiana, or Observations of the Topography, Edifices and Ornaments of Pompeii*. By Sir William Gell, F. R. S., &c. New Series. Parts 1, 2, 3. London. Jennings and Chaplin. 1830.]', in *The Edinburgh Literary Journal; or, Weekly Register of Criticism and Belles Lettres*, 92 (14 August 1830): 101–4.
2 Ibid., 101.

3 All citations refer to the 1838 edition of Rogers's *Italy*.
4 *Edinburgh Literary Journal*, 102.
5 Ibid.
6 See *The Italian Journals of Samuel Rogers*, ed. by J. R. Hale (London: Faber and Faber, 1956), 110.
7 See Maureen McCue, *British Romanticism and the Reception of Italian Old Master Art, 1793–1840* (Farnham, Surrey: Ashgate, 2014), 127–59.
8 J. R. Hale, 'Samuel Rogers the Perfectionist', *The Huntington Library Quarterly*, 25: 1 (1961): 61–7. See also *The Italian Journals of Samuel Rogers*, 111.
9 *The London Literary Gazette and Journal of Belle Lettres, Arts, Sciences, &c.*, 'BOOKS PUBLISHED THIS DAY: Rogers's *Italy*', No. 713 (September 18, 1830), 616.
10 *The London Literary* advertised the 1830 edition for £1,1s in boards, or £2,2s in boards, with proofs before letters. Amateurs and illustrators in particular were encouraged to buy portfolios of the prints themselves, which they could do so for as little as £2, 12s, 6 d, or as much as £4, 4s for 'India Proofs, before the letters' (Ibid.).
11 The initial print run for the illustrated edition was ten thousand copies and cost Rogers £7,335, £2,016 of which was for embellishments (Shelley M. Bennett, *Thomas Stothard: The Mechanisms of Art Patronage in England circa 1800* (Columbia: University of Missouri Press, 1988), 26).
12 M. G. Sullivan, 'Stothard, Thomas (1755–1834)', *Oxford Dictionary of National Biography* (Oxford University Press, 2004); online edn, September 2012, www.oxforddnb.com/view/article/26603 (accessed 22 November 2017); and Bennett, *Thomas Stothard*, 52–61. See also the relevant sections of Sandro Jung's and Mary Shannon's chapters in this book.
13 Ibid.
14 See, for example, David H. Solkin's *Painting for Money: The Visual Arts and the Public Sphere in Eighteenth-Century England* (New Haven, CT: Yale University Press, 1993); and Gillian D'Arcy Wood, *The Shock of the Real: Romanticism and Visual Culture, 1760–1860* (New York: Palgrave, 2001).
15 See Bennett, *Thomas Stothard*, 45; and Dennis M. Read, *R. H. Cromek: Engraver, Editor and Entrepreneur* (Farnham, Surrey: Ashgate, 2011), 45–86.
16 Bennett, *Thomas Stothard*, esp. 22–35; and Hale, *The Italian Journals of Samuel Rogers*, 111. For more on Turner's involvement in illustrating *Italy*, see Adele M. Holcomb, 'Turner and Rogers's *Italy* Revisted', *Studies in Romanticism*, 27: 1 (1988): 63–95; Holcomb, 'A Neglected Classical Phase of Turner's Art: His Vignettes to Rogers's *Italy*', *Journal of the Warburg and Courtauld Institutes* 32 (1969): 405–10; and David Blayney Brown, ed., *J. M. W. Turner: Sketchbooks, Drawings and Watercolours* (Tate Research Publication, December 2012), www.tate.org.uk/art/research-publications/jmw-turner/project-overview-r1109225 (accessed 9 May 2018).

17 Anne Hollander, *Moving Pictures* (Cambridge, MA: Harvard University Press, 1991) (originally published 1986), 9.
18 Ibid., 5.
19 Ibid., 29.
20 See N. P. J. Gordon, 'The Murder of Buondelmonte: contesting place in early fourteenth-century Florentine chronicles', in *Renaissance Studies* 20: 4 (2006): 459–77 (459).
21 See for example the 1848 edition published by Edward Moxon (338).
22 Gordon, 'The Murder of Buondelmonte', 459.
23 *Edinburgh Literary Journal*, 104.
24 McCue, *British Romanticism*, 127–59.
25 Bennett, *Thomas Stothard*, 27.

PART II

The Business of Illustration

8 | Illustration, Terror, and Female Agency: Thomas Macklin's Poets Gallery in a Revolutionary Decade

IAN HAYWOOD

The flourishing of literary galleries in the 1790s is one of the most conspicuous and innovative cultural manifestations of the 'explosion' of illustration in the late eighteenth century.[1] Indeed, Richard Altick goes so far as to call these unique institutions a 'half-way house' on the road to the creation of the public art gallery.[2] But while considerable critical attention has been given to Boydell's Shakespeare and Fuseli's Milton Galleries, Thomas Macklin's Poets' Gallery has remained in the background: the first book-length study of Macklin's career only appeared in 2016, and there is very little detailed work on the exhibited works and ancillary print culture.[3] The aim of this chapter is to begin to rectify that neglect on three inter-related fronts: bibliographical, historicist, and hermeneutic. To begin with, I propose a new bibliographical methodology which focuses on the literary gallery as a serial mode of print illustration: in other words, as a way of transferring the aesthetic grandeur and impact of painting onto the printed page where it interacted with a textual envelope to produce what Stuart Sillars calls a 'whole new reading experience'. In Genettian terms, the image was transformed from an external epitext into an internal peritext.[4] This approach has two benefits: it enables comparison with similar and competing publishing initiatives such as the cheap, serialized, illustrated editions of literary classics; and it encourages close reading of the *mise en page*. Second, I consider how the historical context of the revolution debate and the Jacobin terror in the 1790s may have given a radical tinge to the textual construction of Macklin's gallery in the press publicity upon which it relied so heavily. Third, I extend this historicist approach to the illustrations themselves in order to elicit intriguing new readings: through one case study, I show that the combination of text and image can be interpreted in variously subversive ways, including a conspicuous and controversial role for heroic female agency. By way of conclusion, I reinsert illustration into the visual communication circuit of the literary gallery in order to reconsider the homologous relationship between the edited page and the curated exhibition.

The Serial Mode of Production

As numerous critics have observed, the primary cultural aim of the expansion of illustration in the late eighteenth century was the re-canonization of classic, mainly 'old canon' British literature through visualization: in Morris Eaves' words, to 'tie the fortunes of British images to the prestige of British words'.[5] This change was facilitated by a number of large-scale publishing and exhibition projects beginning with John Bell's British Poets series and peaking with the literary galleries. The epic ambition of these ventures (nothing less than to elevate British art into a national, public institution),[6] required a serial mode of production. Practically, it was simply not possible to do everything in one go, but serial publication also had a commercial motive, recruiting a loyal consumer base for a branded product that combined high quality with a patriotic purpose. Seriality operated in three ways that corresponded to the three major cultural forms in use: the series (books), the season (paintings, literary galleries), and the 'number' (the merchandised, reproductive prints). One of the vital areas of research into Romantic illustration is to analyse how these three products or cycles meshed together. If we believe the claims in the publicity of the publishers and entrepreneurs behind these projects (supported by reviews and literary tributes), the system worked seamlessly: the illustration revolution simultaneously elevated art and literature by audaciously investing mechanical reproduction with the aura of great art. The named artists and engravers guaranteed quality, whether operating at the level of the miniaturized, virtual gallery of the illustrated edition, or in the exhibition hall of the literary gallery, a real place with real paintings that rivalled the more prestigious Royal Academy.[7] The crucial difference between established venues of display and the literary gallery was that the exhibited works in the latter were phenomenologically and aesthetically in an unstable state, constantly transmuting or remediating into the serialized, reproductive prints that were the precondition of their existence. In Christopher Kent Rovee's words (referring to the Shakespeare Gallery), 'No painting existed in its own, original splendour, but only and always in tension with its reproductions.'[8] In this respect, the literary galleries were a kind of paratextual sublime: on the one hand they were a tightly conceived and capital-intensive commercial endeavour with an apparently clear, linear set of products and cultural goals; on the other hand, their evolving, sprawling, open temporal nature, their peculiarly contingent combination of exhibition and serial reproduction, and their immersion in print culture across more than a decade of (in this case) revolutionary time, made them highly porous to contextual influence or even contamination. This is particularly apparent in the fourth number of Macklin's gallery which appeared in 1794 at the height of the Terror.

The 'Steward of Public Munificence'

A brief overview of Macklin's project is required if we are to understand and appreciate the complexities of its print products. The Poets Gallery was first announced in January 1787, and though this was just after a similar notice for Boydell's Shakespeare Gallery, Macklin's was the first gallery to open on 15 April 1788, one year earlier than his competitor. The original plan was ambitious: according to the prospectus, the project would be 'illustrative of the most celebrated British poets', and 63 poets ranging from Chaucer to Barbauld were named.[9] The word 'illustrative' here means 'representative' rather than visualized, and shows how illustration at this time had not acquired its modern meaning.[10] The job of the impressive array of commissioned artists was to 'illustrate' (meaning to exemplify, instantiate, adorn and showcase) this selection of Britain's finest poets. The advertised list of 'Masters' is a veritable who's who of British painting at the time, including Joshua Reynolds, Thomas Gainsborough, Henry Fuseli, Philip de Loutherbourg, John Opie, Thomas Stothard, Maria Cosway, Angelica Kaufmann, Benjamin West, and Francis Wheatley. Some of these artists were already employed by John Bell, but Macklin (followed by Boydell) expanded and consolidated their role as illustrators. Macklin also employed Britain's leading (and most expensive) engraver, Francesco Bartolozzi. The project had two main elements: an annual exhibition of the paintings and the sale of the reproductive prints. The latter was to take the form of 25 large folio-sized numbers (18 inches by 14 inches)[11] issued twice per year for over a decade: each number would contain four pictures with textual excerpts, making a grand total of 100 images which could be collected, framed, bound together or displayed in the domestic space.[12] The former required an exhibition space for the new 'Gallery of British Poets'. The first venue was at Temple Bar, a site very close to Macklin's bookshop at 39 Fleet Street. It is telling that he renamed his shop the 'Poets Gallery' and used the premise (like John Bell's 'British Library') to display and sell paintings.[13] The chiasmus of the names of his two venues is indicative of the reciprocal and fluid relationship between painting and print publication.[14] Admission to the gallery was the standard middle-class shilling which included a catalogue. In total, there were eight annual exhibitions between 1788 and 1796.

Competition between Macklin and his rivals was fierce. For the third and fourth exhibitions, Macklin moved to the 'nucleus' of the literary galleries, Pall Mall: this was the location of both the Shakespeare Gallery and Henry Bowyer's Historic Gallery (and, in 1799, Fuseli's Milton Gallery).[15] By this point, he had expanded into two parallel ventures: an illustrated Bible (for which de Loutherbourg supplied the designs) and a Shakespeare series illustrated by Henry Bunbury which was clearly aimed at rivalling or exploiting the Boydell market.[16]

As Sophie Thomas has noted, Macklin's aim was to 'explicitly showcase' British poets and to excel his rivals in promoting British art.[17] He lost no opportunity to puff this mission in the gallery literature.[18] One exhibition catalogue hailed him as 'the steward of public munificence' and in another he claimed that 'my Prints illustrative of the Poets have been honoured with the approbation of the best judges'.[19] Both contemporary and current critical opinion suggests that these rather hyperbolic claims were not in fact too wide of the mark,[20] but if the ambitious cultural objective of the literary gallery met with considerable success, the same cannot be said of its commercial prosperity.[21] Like Boydell, Macklin grossly underestimated the production costs and delays of his endeavour. Unlike Bell's pocket-sized editions, Macklin's large folio prints were expensive: though it cost only a shilling per visit to see the paintings, the numbers cost three guineas to subscribers and four guineas to non-subscribers. Proofs (early impressions) cost as much as eight guineas in hand-coloured versions. Despite financial incentives such as paying only half the price up front and making individual prints even more expensive (one guinea uncoloured or two guineas coloured), the production schedule faltered. Thirty-five paintings by 18 artists were exhibited, and only 24 were engraved (16 by Bartolozzi), facilitating six numbers between 1788 and 1799. Only 19 of the 63 poets in the original proposal were included. In order to recoup some of the losses, the gallery was eventually sold by auction, the same fate that met Boydell's Shakespeare.

Macklin's gallery floundered on the rocks of poor business acumen. The situation was not helped by the depleted overseas market for prints during the war against revolutionary France, a situation which led some loyalists to accuse the literary galleries of a self-interested opposition to the war: John Reeves, for example, declaimed that the 'present righteous and glorious war' prevented the Boydells from selling 'prints and engravings, worth 30 or 40,000 l. sterling'.[22] It is also the case that the high price of the prints may have actually made it easier for the galleries to espouse a Jacobin-inflected, democratic rhetoric of bringing art to the people, as there was no chance of this message reaching a mass public and thus stirring up trouble. But accepting these caveats, it is still feasible to conclude that the highly charged ideological atmosphere of the 1790s intensified and deepened the subversive potential of the literary galleries. Rosie Dias argues that the galleries were 'suffused with an air of liberty and patriotism, operating through a system of artistic meritocracy and acknowledging the patronage and interest of the public, they allowed the political concerns of the 1790s to operate discursively within the art world'.[23] In the next section, I consider how Macklin's gallery 'operated discursively' as a textual construct of the press during a decade when the 'political concerns of the 1790s' became decisively more antagonistic to 'liberty' and the 'interest of the public'.

Puffery and Politics

Like his rivals, Macklin relied heavily on adverts and notices in the press to market both his shop (open all year round) and the exhibition (open annually for the season). This was not a new technique: 50 years earlier, William Hogarth had pioneered the use of carefully controlled press releases in order to maximize public interest in his paintings and engraved prints. But the format of advertising in late eighteenth-century newspapers to some degree undermined or vitiated such control by placing all adverts together on a single (usually the front) page. How these cluttered pages were read and utilized is still an open question,[24] but it is possible to hypothesize that some semiotic cross-pollination between the congested items may have occurred. Though there was no conscious editorial choreography at work, the eye forged links and associations as it moved around the page. In 1794, adverts for Macklin's projects were never very far away from the ongoing narrative of the war with revolutionary France. It is worth a reminder that this was the year in which Pitt's Tory government intensified its attack on the reform movement: leaders of the London Corresponding Society were arrested in May and tried for treason in November.

On 10 May 1794, the same month as the arrests of the radicals, the *Morning Chronicle* announced that the fourth number of the Poets Gallery was to be published on 24 May, along with the 28th instalment of the illustrated Bible and the fourth issue of the Bunbury Shakespeare. Among other things, this advert shows just how extensively the late Georgian consumer was locked into a 'reprint industry'[25] of illustration in which publishers like Macklin issued multiple, overlapping series at different cyclical velocities. But the more important point is that the advert appeared directly underneath another advert for an exhibition at the Pall Mall Historic Gallery of de Loutherbourg's royally commissioned painting of the Duke of York's siege of Valenciennes. The spatial intimacy of the two adverts operates both ideologically and metonymically. The juxtaposition shows that art was beginning to be mobilized for anti-Jacobin, loyal purposes, and it also virtualizes the geographical congestion and commercial competitiveness of the Pall Mall illustration hub which was now being sucked into the war effort (the de Loutherbourg advert makes clear that the point of the exhibition is to garner subscribers to the engraved print).

In the *Morning Post* on 28 June, an advert declared that the release date for the fourth number had been changed to 3 July. This delay enabled the textual construction of Macklin's gallery to rub up against further doses of jingoistic, anti-Jacobin cultural activity which surrounded it on the page, in this case a spectacular naumachia of Admiral Howe's recent naval victory staged at Astley's amphitheatre. This was the increasingly politicized context in which the fourth number was to appear, and in which the democratic credentials of the literary galleries could be both showcased and tested. There is no extant evidence that the four illustrations in the fourth number (which the advert identified) were chosen as a radical statement, nor that reader-viewers perceived them in this way, but it is not a requirement of historicist interpretation to find empirical verification, and (as in most cultural criticism) ideological agency can be inferred through the close reading of the artefact's content, form and contexts. There is no disputing the fact that, by mid-1794, British culture was being polarized into loyal and disloyal camps. For popular publishers, the line between commercial and political motivations was becoming blurred, as any attempt to enlighten the people could be viewed with suspicion by the authorities. The high stakes are exemplified by adverts which appeared in the *Oracle* on 25 October 1794. Adjacent to an advert for the latest instalment of Macklin's Bible, there is an advert for John Bell's serialized account of the imminent treason trials. Bell may well have been cashing in on the sensationalism of the trials, but the series bolstered his democratic affiliations and placed political reportage alongside the cheap illustrated editions of poetry which were his metier.

The fourth number of the Poets Gallery was ideologically overdetermined. It appeared at a particularly tense time, when British culture had become more politicized, divided and explosive than at any time since the 1640s. It is also important to remember that the fifth number did not appear until 1796, so the fourth number remained the 'live' representation of the gallery in print culture across the most politically contested years of the decade. Adverts in the press in 1795 show Macklin in close proximity to the forces of radical resistance. In the *Morning Chronicle* on 21 October 1795, Macklin appeared beneath an advert for the radical orator John Thelwall's lectures, and in the *Morning Post* on 5 December 1795, he shares a column with the Whig Friends of the People and Robert Bage's Jacobin novel *Hermsprong*. It now remains to be seen to what extent these radical reverberations affected the meanings of the illustrations that made up the fourth number.

Illustration, Terror, and Female Agency

The fourth number, which finally appeared in July 1794, contained four illustrations. In the order in which they appear in the British Library copy, these are: *The School Mistress*, painted by Francis Wheatley and engraved by J. Cole, based on a poem of the same name by William Shenstone, first published 20 March 1794; *The Antient English Wake*, painted by William Hamilton and engraved by J. Chapman, based on a poem of the same name by Edward Jerningham, first published 10 May 1794; *The Cottagers*, painted by Joshua Reynolds and engraved by Francesco Bartolozzi, based on James Thomson's 'Autumn' from his poem *The Seasons*, first published 16 February 1794; and *Mercy Stopping the Rage of War*, painted by William Artaud and engraved by Bartolozzi, based on William Collins' 'Ode to Mercy', first published 16 February 1794 (Figures 8.1.–8.4.). As will become apparent later, this running order may be significant as it places the most overtly political illustration at the end of the 'narrative' of the collection, but a different order would not have undermined the essential point of the following analysis, which is to regard each illustration as an allegory of the revolution debate. This approach might seem counter-intuitive or far-fetched at first glance, as the first three illustrations seem to be anodyne or idealized scenes of English pastoral life in both the past and present. If these scenes do have an ideological function, it is tempting to see them as reassuring, sentimental and nostalgic depictions of English national character, the antithesis of the troubled landscapes of the Romantic poets and the violent iconoclasm of Gillray. This could also explain the prominent position of women, who are the central figures in all the pictures: stereotypically, such prominent, unvictimized women would signify the conservative, domestic values of family life, humility, harmony, peace and order, a curative balm deployed by counter-revolutionary feminists such as Hannah More. But while the following discussion does not deny this interpretation,

206   IAN HAYWOOD

Figure 8.1 Francis Wheatley, *The School Mistress* by William Shenstone. Engraved by J. Cole. Published 20 March 1794. © The Trustees of the British Museum.

it proposes that alternative, more charged readings are possible once we bring the context of the Terror to bear on the illustrations, and once we give both image and text the 'interpretive freedom' that Sillars sees as a distinctive feature of the literary galleries.[26]

For the purchaser of the fourth number (who may, of course, have already seen all the paintings in Pall Mall), the first illustration, *The School Mistress*, may indeed have seemed remote from political and social conflict. The scene shows a middle-aged woman teaching reading to a group of nine young children; the setting is the interior of an unassuming and, we assume, rural cottage (Figure 8.1).[27] The cottage has only one window but this is sufficient to shed light (and enlightenment) on the grateful and generally well-behaved children (significantly, it is a boy who is reluctant to join in and who may just have been chastised). The immediate appeal of the picture derives from its humble subjects, its Dutch realism and the satisfying, self-affirming narrative of its layout: given that the children are learning to read, the excerpted stanza at the bottom of the

Figure 8.2 William Hamilton, *The Antient English Wake* by Edward Jerningham. Engraved by J. Chapman. Published 10 May 1794. © The Trustees of the British Museum.

print provides a teleology for the educative process on view. But these sentimental and comic touches fail to insulate the print from the raging controversy about popular literacy that consumed Britain at this time. The government equated mass education with subversion: once the lower orders could read, it was very difficult to control what they read. This was demonstrated spectacularly when the second, cheap edition of Thomas Paine's *Rights of Man* began to circulate in the lower echelons of the social hierarchy, even in the humble 'cot'. Alarmed by Paine's popularity, the Evangelical Hannah More hit back with her *Cheap Repository Tracts* series and her own educational programmes for the working classes, including Sunday Schools. Although it is not possible to see what the children in *The School Mistress* are reading (one girl waiting in the queue has embroidered the alphabet, so we assume the other books are primers and certainly not the toxic folk and ballad literature so feared by More), opening the image up to the revolution debate assigns the school mistress's role a strong

Figure 8.3 Joshua Reynolds, *The Cottagers*, based on James Thomson's 'Autumn' from *The Seasons*. Engraved by Francesco Bartolozzi. Published 16 February 1794. By kind permission of the Yale Centre for British Art.

ideological charge and places her on the front line of a major controversy as a gate-keeper of social and political stability. It is no coincidence that William Blake chose a similar female tutelary figure for the frontispiece of *Songs of Innocence*, first published in 1789 and reprinted with *Experience* in 1794. From this perspective, the naughty boy on the far

Figure 8.4 William Artaud, *Mercy Stopping the Rage of War*, based on William Collins, 'Ode to Mercy'. Engraved by Francesco Bartolozzi. Published 16 February 1794. © The Trustees of the British Museum.

right of the scene assumes a darker tinge as a symbol of resistance and non-conformism.

The school mistress's symbolic role of keeping the invasive forces of Jacobinism at bay becomes more fraught when the text is brought into play.[28] A feature of the Macklin Gallery was the mobile and malleable nature of the text. Unlike the Shakespeare and Fuseli galleries, it was never the intention of the Poets Gallery to produce an illustrated book. The project was always conceived as the image working in conjunction with a partial or excerpted text. The basic model for this type of illustration was the literary painting with an inscription and the literary frontispiece, where a small amount of text appeared beneath the image, but in the literary gallery this format was scaled up to monumental proportions. Taken together, the illustrations were meant to comprise a museum or anthology of the highlights of British poetry. This implies that the excerpts were carefully chosen before the paintings were commissioned. Macklin claimed in the prospectus that the 'letter press' contained 'the most interesting subjects' in 'a complete section, an entire subject', though this is rather vague, and none of the images carried a key to the chosen moments or episodes. Moreover, Macklin fails to point out that the 'letter press' appeared in several places: on the same print as the image, in the catalogue, and on the facing page of the numbers. The quantity of text in these different publications varied. In the case of *The School Mistress*, the text below the image is the second Spenserian stanza of the poem split into two symmetrical parts, but the catalogue and facing page of the number also contain stanzas VI and XVI. This implies a process of selection (particularly as the stanzas are not continuous) and also gives the reader more text to engage with. Rather than seeing these variations as editorial sloppiness, it is more profitable to view the shifting, fragmented text as an experiment in audience participation, inviting the reader-viewer to fill in gaps, make new connections with the image (with or without an acquaintance with the original text) and produce their own interpretations.

All three stanzas of Shenstone's poem reinforce the power of the school mistress, but with some intriguing divergences. Stanza II stresses the importance of discipline, but stanza VI pushes this to an unpleasant extreme: the teacher's 'sceptre' is tantamount to a weapon of terror, evoking 'anxious fear', 'dark distrust', 'sad repentance', 'stedfast hate', sharp affliction', 'fury uncontrolled', and 'chastisement unkind', a litany of abuses and woes that provides a violent undertow for the emollient image. Stanza XVI sharpens the critique of power with overtly political analogies: the schoolmistress's chair is compared to the coronation throne, and her power to confer 'rank' or favour on her pupils is 'the source of children's and of courtier's pride'. But that is not the end of the story. Readers who were familiar with, or went away to acquire or re-read the original poem, would know that in the subsequent stanza XVII the mistress is described as having the power to 'thwart the proud' and 'the submiss to raise', and in stanza XXXI there are scathing references to the 'proud ambition' and 'pompous dome' of the court. The declared aim of the poem in the first stanza also has a democratic thrust: echoing phrases from Thomas Gray's canonical poem *Elegy in a Country Churchyard*, it seeks to praise the 'modest worth' of 'dull obscurity'. What the text adds to the image therefore is an unstable discourse of power in which the figure of the mistress veers between tyranny and liberation, the two discursive poles of the revolution debate.

The second illustration in the fourth number was a scene from Edward Jerningham's 1786 poem *The Antient English Wake* (Figure 8.2).[29] Unlike *The School Mistress* or Reynolds' *The Cottagers*, this was a scene from a narrative poem, so it is necessary to outline the overall plot to appreciate the choice of episode. The poem is set in the thirteenth century and the principal character is the Earl of Chester, a once great warrior but now retired and 'tortured' by the memory of his daughter Agatha who disappeared after her fiancé died. Years later during one of the annual wakes she reappears incognito in the garb of a pilgrim before throwing herself on his mercy: it is this reunion scene which is depicted (Figure 8.2). The excerpted text gives a portion of her reconciliation speech in which she explains that her fiancé on his deathbed asked her to place his heart in a small casket and donate this to a crusader. Obeying the spirit, not the letter of his instructions, she kept the casket herself and became a disguised female warrior. Having served her religion and country in this muscular way, she then resorted to more domestic issues and decided to heal the rift with her 'Unspous'd, undaughter'd' father. Hence a potentially damaging rupture in merry England's feudal system is healed and once again, as in the *School Mistress*, female agency is at the centre of social cohesion. If we read the print as political allegory, we could initially deduce a reassuringly conservative message: that in the absence of male leadership strong women will step into the breach and (in Coleridge's words from 'France: An Ode') 'repel an impious foe' by preserving the nation's social and moral bonds. The image of a saintly woman (her pilgrim's hat resembles a halo) fighting a 'pagan' enemy abroad and dedicating herself to restoring the nation's morale at home (as personified by the Earl) could be seen as a loyalist antidote to more threatening, Jacobin 'fatal women' such as Southey's Joan of Arc, destroyer of English armies.[30]

However, other prominent aspects of the scene not highlighted by the textual excerpt are quite capable of bearing more radical interpretations (or giving a more radical tinge to the female agency), in particular the depiction of the village wake that occupies the visual background. At first glance, this resembles a glowing image of the mythic knowable community seen in *Songs of Innocence*, but this idealized version of the rural past had already been jacobinized by the mid-1790s. The English custom of dancing round the maypole was regarded as a precursor to the Jacobin planting of the liberty tree.[31] Furthermore, the visual bifurcation of the illustration implies that the Earl in his cave-like or womb-like tent is cut off from his people (the full text of the poem makes clear that the Earl is demoralized and is only going through the motions). Hence Agatha is strategically poised on the threshold between the classes: although her trajectory is towards the elite, her histrionic gesture points out towards the illuminated people and implies that the Earl's destiny – and, if we include the harpist, the future of English culture – lies there. Her dead lover's casket – a 'wonder-working charm' – hovers almost directly over the maypole, an ambiguous symbol of an inspirational but absent, male aristocratic authority which is temporarily usurped by a powerful woman. Finally, it is worth adding that the last line of the poem – 'The curfew tolls the hamlet train to rest', another allusion to Gray's *Elegy* – is also open to radical analysis as the 'curfew' was regarded as a tool of the Norman yoke.[32] Indeed, 'merrie England', medievalism and folk culture were all in the process of being radicalized into what Marilyn Butler calls a 'cult of native Englishness'.[33] Against the background of the treason trials and the Two Acts, Agatha now appears like a desperate *deus ex machina*, anxious to prevent a rupture between the rulers and the ruled.

After this troubling and tense tableau, the reader-viewer may have been relieved to turn to the third illustration, Joshua Reynolds' *The Cottagers* (Figure 8.3). This print is a good example of the aesthetic ambition and massive financial investment of the Poets Gallery: Joshua Reynolds was rewarded with the princely sum of £300 for depicting Macklin's wife and daughter as peasants.[34] At first sight this scene seems quite impervious to a subversive reading. We see an idealization of female rural labour in which poverty (signified by the bare feet) barely registers on the countenances, bodies and garb of the three women. The emphasis, as indicated by the excerpt from Thomson's 'Autumn', is on 'unsully'd beauty' and 'unambitious toil'.[35] Determined to keep up with prevailing taste, Macklin commissioned three illustrations of *The Seasons* for the Poets Gallery, the other two being Gainsborough's *Lavinia* (first published on 5 January 1790, and included in number 2) and Opie's *Damon and Musidora* (first published on 12 March 1796, included in number 5). Given the fact that *The Seasons* was the most illustrated of all eighteenth-century 'old canon' poems (and second overall only to *Paradise Lost*),[36] its inclusion in the Poets Gallery was an understandable response to market demand. Unlike the other two designs which depicted the most popular interpolated episodes from the poem (and in which women appeared in stereotypical eroticized roles as victims or passive objects of beauty), *The Cottagers* shows a generic, non-specific representation of autumnal work. This was in line with a growing Romantic trend to illustrate the poem more naturalistically, and as Sandro Jung has shown, several editions of *The Seasons* also published in 1794 included numerous scenes of rural labour including harvesting and nutting.[37] Despite this allegiance to cultural fashion, the image has been judged rather harshly as a vanity project which kowtowed to the celebrities of the art establishment: Fuseli regarded it as 'insipid', T. S. R. Boase styled it 'a stilted piece of mock rusticity' and for Altick it was a 'fake-rustic conversation piece'.[38] Perhaps that was partly the case, but another way to unsettle the effete, bucolic tranquillity of the print is to expose it to the revolution debate.

To begin with, take the most striking feature of the print: the absence of men. This cannot be explained entirely by the sexual division of labour (men at work, women in the home) as the women are engaged in, if not over-tasked by, precisely the kind of productive labour that would also be done by men, notably spinning and harvesting (hence the image is often referred to as *The Gleaners*). Perhaps the logic of personification at work in the composition is that 'plain innocence' and 'unambitious toil', like 'unsully'd beauty', are stereotypically feminine characteristics. But there is another, more chilling reading of the scene. In the context of the Terror, a different explanation for the men's absence is that they are away at war. This is not a fanciful speculation: in the late eighteenth century, the pastoral motif of a cluster of women and children outside the cottage door usually signified the imminent return of the absent male. As John Barrell has shown, in the hands of Gainsborough the motif acquired a 'darker side', revealing the end of moral economy and the oppression of wage labour, but by 1794 the cottage threshold had also been appropriated for potent anti-war iconography, notably in William Hodges' twinned scenes *The Effects of Peace, The Consequences of War* (1794); the following year James Gillray popularized this trope further with his caricature *The Blessings of Peace, The Curses of War* (1795).[39] These works use the technique of a dyptich in which the cottage is seen 'before' and 'after' the devastating effects of war on the crippled soldier-husband or the blasted landscape. Hence the reader-viewer wonders for how long the smiles on Reynolds's women's faces will remain. A further subversive message appears when we take into account that the lines from 'Autumn' immediately preceding the excerpt praise the simple virtues of an independent, patriarchal peasant life by lambasting luxury:

> Oh, knew he but his happiness, of men
> The happiest he! who far from public rage,
> Deep in the vale, with a choice few retired,
> Drinks the pure pleasures of the Rural Life.
> What though the dome be wanting, whose proud gate,
> Each morning, vomits out the sneaking crowd
> Of flatterers false, and in their turn abused?
> Vile intercourse! …
> What though he knows not those fantastic joys
> That still amuse the wanton, still deceive;
> A face of pleasure, but a heart of pain;
> Their hollow moments undelighted all?
> Sure peace is his; a solid life, estranged
> To disappointment, and fallacious hope.[40]

This civic humanist critique of decadent court culture was popular in the earlier eighteenth century where it blended with a much older tradition of pastoral retreat, but by the 1790s the promise of 'Sure peace' was more like a 'fallacious hope'. The all-female image casts the text in an ironic light and highlights the devastating intervention of history and 'public rage' into the rural community. The absent, contented hero is a conspicuous casualty of the transposition of the poem from the age of Walpole to the age of Terror. Presented with faces of pleasure, we wonder about the hearts of pain.

No such restraint is needed for the fourth and final illustration, William Artaud's *The Triumph of Mercy* (Figure 8.4), as both the image and excerpted text are explicitly and emphatically anti-war. If the political relevance of the print needed to be any clearer, the title on the accompanying page was changed to the highly topical *Mercy Stopping the Rage of War*. If we read the 1794 number as a 'narrative continuum',[41] the illustration can be regarded as the dramatic exposure of the military and ideological conflict that destabilized the previous three images. The print functions as a closing statement for the number and exerts authority in its bold allegorical form (alluding to Rubens' 1629 painting *Peace and War*) and its depiction of daring female intervention into the masculine sphere. The choice of Collins' 'Ode to Mercy' as the source text suggests conscious design and shows how illustration could be used to re-politicize 'old canon' literature by transposing it into the revolutionary decade of the 1790s.[42] Published in 1747 alongside his odes to Peace and Liberty, the poem was both a thinly veiled protest against the War of the Austrian Succession (1740–7) and a plea for clemency for the Jacobite rebel leaders of the '45.[43] There are clear parallels with the war against France and the persecution of radicals in the 1790s, but as in 1746 the allegorical language acted as a discursive shield: war is a 'fiend of nature' rather than the symbol of Pitt's Tory government. The shift from naturalism (*The School Mistress*, *The Cottagers*) and history painting (*The Old English Wake*) to allegory enabled a climactic vision of the national interest without descending into controversial or dangerous particularities. It also elevated the motif of female agency to sublime proportions. The peace-maker Mercy, a 'bride' of Valour, combines the exemplary virtues of her textual female companions: the conciliatory dedication of Agatha, the moral mission of the school mistress and the unsullied beauty of Reynolds' virtuous cottagers. The inter-visual allusion to Romantic depictions of Milton's allegory of 'Satan, Sin and Death' adds to this elevation of female assertiveness.[44] The textual excerpt presents Mercy as a quasi-republican warrior:

> Thy tender melting eyes they own,
> O Maid, for all thy love to Britain shown,
> Where Justice bars her iron tower.

> To thee we build a roseate bower;
> Thou, thou shalt rule our queen, and share a throne.[45]

Although the 'tender melting eyes' evoke a conventional, emotional femininity, the whole illustration is a remarkable assertion of the political rights of women, or at the very least an impressive vision of female activism at a moment of national crisis. It would be 25 years before an equivalent female intervention occurred in the shape of Percy Shelley's personification of Hope in *The Mask of Anarchy* (1819) – sadly, unillustrated and unpublished.

Conclusion

This chapter has focused on the serialized numbers of the Poets Gallery rather than the original displayed paintings as it was in the numbers that the definitive aesthetic and ideological work of illustration took place, joining the images to textual excerpts which were 'illustrated' in the older sense of illuminated, showcased and adorned. It is certainly possible to argue that some of the subversive historicist interpretations advanced here could have applied to the exhibitions, all of which except for the first took place after the French Revolution broke out in 1789. The fourth exhibition in 1791, for example, displayed for the first time *The School Mistress*, *The Old English Wake* and Francis Wheatley's *The Deserted Village*, a provocative group of paintings in the context of the revolution debate. However, the contention of this chapter is that it was chiefly in the numbers that intriguing clusters of illustrations formed into proto-narratives which challenged the prevailing reactionary political climate of the 1790s in both direct and indirect ways, and that this process is best exemplified by the fourth number which appeared at the height of the Terror. This is not to ignore the fact that most paintings were on display each year, so changing patterns of reader-viewer response to the prints could have been recycled back into the experience of spectatorship, which in turn influenced the reaction to the illustrations. There are no extant reviews of the fourth number, so we can only speculate what effect *Mercy Stopping the Rage of War* might have had on the political opinions and actions of its purchasers.[46] What is indisputable is that the image mobilized the resources of Romantic illustration to create a powerful anti-war statement. At the height of the Terror in 1794, the canny editor summoned up a powerful new national symbol of beauty confronting the violent sublime, an icon to rival Britannia.[47] Despite the high cost of the engraved prints, this was a striking and possibly unrivalled way for Macklin to emblematize his aim of democratizing art and literature through the medium of illustration.

Notes

1 The word 'explosion' comes from William St Clair, *The Reading Nation in the Romantic Period* (Cambridge: Cambridge University Press, 2004), 134–5.
2 Richard D. Altick, *The Shows of London* (New Haven, CT; London: Harvard University Press, 1978), 109.
3 G. E. Bentley Jr, *Thomas Macklin (1752–1800), Picture-Publisher and Patron: Creator of the Macklin Bible (1791–1800)* (Lampeter: Edwin Mellen Press, 2016); Sean Higgins, 'Thomas Macklin's Poets' Gallery: Consuming the Sister Arts in Late Eighteenth-Century London' (unpublished PhD, London: Courtauld, 2002); Luisa Calè, *Fuseli's Milton Gallery: Turning Readers into Spectators* (Oxford: Clarendon Press, 2007), 27–8, 70–78.
4 Stuart Sillars, *Painting Shakespeare: The Artist as Critic 1720–1820* (Cambridge: Cambridge University Press, 2006), 288; Gerard Genette, *Paratexts: Thresholds of Interpretation* (Cambridge: Cambridge University Press, 1997), Chapters 13–14.
5 Morris Eaves, 'The Sister Arts in British Romanticism', in Stuart Curran, ed., *The Cambridge Companion to British Romanticism* Second Edition (Cambridge: Cambridge University Press, 2010), 229–61, 248. Eaves echoes a line from William Hayley's verse *Essay on Painting* (London: J. Dodsley, 1781): 'Bid English Pencils honour English Worth' (l. 436). I have taken the idea of re-canonization from Calè, who states that adding a famous artist's name to a well-known text was an act of 'double canonization' (*Fuseli's Milton Gallery*, 74). See also: Thomas Frank Bonnell, *The Most Disreputable Trade: Publishing the Classics of English Poetry 1765–1810* (Oxford: Oxford University Press, 2008), *passim*; Timothy Clayton, *The English Print 1688–1802* (New Haven, CT; London: Yale University Press, 1997), Chapter 6.
6 For an analysis of the relation between the literary galleries and the rise of an 'English school' of art, see Rosie Dias, *Exhibiting Englishness: John Boydell's Shakespeare Gallery and the Formation of a National Aesthetic* (New Haven, CT; London: Yale University Press, 2013), *passim* but in particular Chapter 2 and 72–9.
7 Martin Postle points out that, although the Royal Academy with over 500 paintings was vastly larger than the literary galleries, the latter were becoming attractive for many artists and viewers as they were regarded as more 'modern' and in tune with the drive towards an 'English' school (Martin Postle, *Reynolds: The Subject Pictures* (Cambridge: Cambridge University Press, 1995, 238–9). For the vexed relationship of the Royal Academy to commercial printmaking, see Sarah Hyde, 'Printmakers and the Royal Academy Exhibitions, 1780–1836', in David H. Solkin, ed., *Art on the Line: The Royal Academy Exhibitions at Somerset House 1780–1836* (New Haven, CT; London: Yale University Press, 2001), 217–28.

8 Christopher Kent Rovee, *Imagining the Gallery: The Social Body of English Romanticism* (Stanford, CA: Stanford University Press, 2006), 80; see also Chapter 2 *passim*. Ann Hawkins argues that the Shakespeare Gallery offered 'an experience of Shakespeare in fragments' as its various print products became 'distinct moments in a complicated cycle of Shakespearian representation and consumption in the Romantic era' (Anne Hawkins, 'Reconstructing the Shakespeare Boydell Gallery', in Joseph M. Ortiz, ed., *Shakespeare and the Culture of Romanticism* (Aldershot: Ashgate, 2013), 207–30, 210). Frederick Burwick points out that the Shakespeare Gallery produced a 'seemingly endless recess of images' ('The Romantic Reception of the Boydell Shakespeare Gallery: Lamb, Coleridge, and Hazlitt', in Walter Pape and Frederick Burwick, eds, *The Boydell Shakespeare Gallery* (Bottrop, Essen: Verlag Peter Pomp, 1996), 156). Sillars notes that critics of the Shakespeare Gallery have tended to ignore the reproductive engravings, despite this aspect of the gallery having 'repercussions on the structures and devices used to transmit meaning and the ideological assumptions they enfold' (*Painting Shakespeare*, 256). More generally, Andrew Piper asks: 'how can the romantic engagement with the reproducible illustration be read as part of a larger engagement with the problem of reproducibility itself that was gradually shaping the romantic bibliocosmos?' (*Dreaming in Books: The Making of the Bibliographic Imagination in the Romantic Period* (Chicago, IL; London: University of Chicago Press, 2009), 187).

9 *Poet's Gallery: A Catalogue of the Second Exhibition of Pictures, Painted for Mr. Macklin, by the Artists of Britain, Illustrative of the British Poets* (London [n.p.], 1789).

10 See the Introduction to this volume, 1–6.

11 This converts to 46 x 36 cm.

12 The La Ronde Museum, Devon, has a set of 16 self-framed prints from the Poets Gallery, including three of the illustrations analysed below.

13 An advert in the *World* (29 March 1790) announced that Macklin's shop would be showing and selling 'a valuable collection of pictures' including Titian's *Sleeping Venus* and Caracci's *Cupid and Clytie*.

14 For W. J. T. Mitchell, the Romantic period saw the last great struggle between text and image: see *Iconology: Image, Text, Ideology* (Chicago, IL; London: University of Chicago Press, 1987), 42–3.

15 Dias calls Pall Mall the 'artistic nucleus of the capital' (*Exhibiting Englishness*, 24).

16 See *Poetic Description of Choice and Valuable Prints, Published by Mr Macklin at the Poets Gallery, Fleet Street* (London: T. Benson, 1794).

17 Sophie Thomas, 'Poetry and Illustration: "Amicable Strife"', in Charles Mahoney, ed., *A Companion to Romantic Poetry* (Oxford: Blackwell, 2011), 354–73, 360.

18 Higgins notes that the 'pervasive and repetitious hyperbole' of Macklin's publicity was in line with that of his competitors ('Thomas Macklin's Poets' Gallery', 5).

19 See the catalogues of the third (1790) and fifth Exhibitions (1792).

20 The *Oracle* on 13 June 1789 declared: 'in the advancement of the arts an epoch is formed, and the name of Macklin eminent as their promoter ... Is it to royal patronage that we owe such men? Certainly not ... The spirit of the people is English patronage'. The *Times* on 13 December 1790 printed a glowing endorsement of Bell, Macklin and Boydell, concluding 'let them therefore go hand in hand to the Temple of Fame, to enjoy in triumph and comfort the lasting rewards of their meritorious pursuits'. See also glowing adverts for Macklin in the *Morning Post*, 11 April 1788 ('a standing monument of the English School') and 6 May 1789 ('his Repository of beautiful Paintings'), and the *Morning Chronicle*, 3 March 1792 (a 'Graphic Treasury'). See also Dias, *Exhibiting Englishness*, 54.

21 Altick calls the Poets Gallery a 'moderate success' (*Paintings from Books: Art and Literature in Britain 1760–1900* (Columbus: Ohio State University Press, 1985), 52).

22 J[ohn] Reeves, *The Grounds of Alderman Wilkes' and Boydell's Proposed Petitions for Peace, Examined and Refuted* (London: Walter Downess, 1795), 5. I am grateful to Susan Matthews for this reference.

23 Rosie Dias, '"A World of Pictures": Pall Mall and the Topography of Display', in Miles Ogborn and Charles W. J. Withers, eds, *Georgian Geographies: Essays on Space, Place and Landscape in the Eighteenth Century* (Manchester: Manchester University Press, 2004), 92–113, 93.

24 According to Daniel Stuart, editor of the *Morning Post* in the 1790s, the use of the cluttered page of adverts reflected the diversity of the readership: 'Advertisements act and react. They attract readers, promote circulation, and circulation attracts advertisements' (cited in Frank Presbrey, *The History and Development of Advertising* (New York: Doubleday, 1929), 80). Jeremy Black notes that 'the effectiveness of eighteenth-century advertisements is a question that cannot be answered ... the advertisers presumably thought that they would obtain a return for their investment' (*The English Press in the Eighteenth Century* (1987; London: Routledge Revivals, 2011), 41).

25 Thomas, 'Poetry and Illustration', 357.

26 Sillars, *Painting Shakespeare*, 288–9.

27 Earlier examples of similar anodyne scenes could include Jean-Baptiste Marie-Pierre, *The Schoolmistress* (1741).

28 Shenstone's poem was first published in 1737, revised in 1742 and again in 1748 for inclusion in *A Collection of Poems in Three Volumes by Several Hands* (London: Robert Dodsley), 1: 247–61.

29 See Edward Jerningham, 'The Ancient English Wake: A Poem', in *Poems by Mr Jerningham* 2 vols (London: J. Robson, 1786), 2: 1–22 (lead poem). Jerningham also wrote a laudatory poem on the Shakespeare Gallery.

30 See Adriana Craciun, *Fatal Women of Romanticism* (Cambridge: Cambridge University Press, 2003).

31 For the jacobinization of the maypole ceremony, see Essaka Joshua, *The Romantics and the May Day Tradition* (London: Routledge, 2016), 67.

32 See E. P. Thompson, *The Making of the English Working Class* (London: Penguin, 1977), 94–5.

33 Marilyn Butler, *Mapping Mythologies: Countercurrents in Eighteenth-Century Poetry and Cultural History* (Cambridge: Cambridge University Press, 2015), 135; see also 136–49, and Marilyn Butler, *Romantics, Rebels and Reactionaries: English Literature and Its Background 1760–1830* (Oxford: Oxford University Press, 1981), 149.

34 Edmund Malone, *The Works of Sir Joshua Reynolds* 3 vols (London: T. Cadell and W. Davies, 1801), 3: lxviii. This figure was still less than the £500 Macklin paid for Reynolds's *Holy Family*, one of the paintings for the Bible series. Bartolozzi was also paid handsomely for engraving *the Cottagers*, making it the most expensive of all the prints in the Poets Gallery. The Detroit Institute of Arts has both the original painting (dated as 1788) and a coloured version of the illustration. Assuming the date for the painting is correct, this means that the image was retrofitted for the Gallery.

35 See James Thomson, *The Seasons. Embellished with Fourteen Plates* (London: John Stockdale, 1794), 196.

36 Altick, *Paintings from Books*, 390–4; Sandro Jung, 'Packaging, Design and Colour: From Fine-Printed to Small-Format Editions of Thomson's *The Seasons*, 1793–1802', in Sandro Jung, ed., *British Literature and Culture* (London: Derek S. Brewer, 2013), 97–124, particularly 97–8.

37 Sandro Jung, *James Thomson's 'The Seasons': Print Culture, and Visual Interpretation 1730–1842* (Bethlehem: Lehigh University Press, 2015), 79–98, 138–42.

38 Postle, *Reynolds*, 370; T. S. R. Boase, 'Macklin and Bowyer', *Journal of the Warburg and Courtauld Institutes*, 26. 1–2 (1963): 148–77, 151; Altick, *Paintings from Books*, 303.

39 John Barrell, *The Dark Side of the Landscape: The Rural Poor in English Painting, 1730–1840* (Cambridge: Cambridge University Press, 1983); see also Barrell's 'Spectacles for Republicans', in Ann Bermingham, ed., *Sensation and Sensibility: Viewing Gainsborough's 'Cottage Door'* (New Haven, CT; London: Yale University Press, 2005), 43–73, particularly 62–70; Holger Hoock, *The King's Artists: The Royal Academy of Arts and the Politics of British Culture 1760–1860* (Oxford: Oxford University Press, 2003), 191–2; Philip Shaw, *Suffering and Sentiment in Romantic Military Art* (Aldershot: Ashgate, 2013), 107–16.

40 Thomson, *The Seasons*, 195.

41 If Calè is correct to state that reader-viewers at literary galleries would try to 'link together the episodes' into a 'narrative continuum', there is no reason to doubt that the same process applied to the numbers. See Luisa Calè, 'Blake and Literary Galleries', in Sarah Haggarty and Jon Mee, eds, *Blake and Conflict*

(Houndmills: Palgrave Macmillan, 2009), 185–209, 190. According to exhibition catalogues, *The Antient English Wake*, *The Schoolmistress* and *The Triumph of Mercy* were hung close to each other (numbered 1, 4 and 5) but not grouped as a distinct subset.

42 See William Collins, *Odes on Several Descriptive and Allegoric Subjects* (London: A. Millar, 1747), 20–21.

43 See Dustin Griffin, *Patriotism and Poetry in Eighteenth-Century Britain* (Cambridge, Cambridge University Press, 2002), 137–40.

44 See Ian Haywood, *Romanticism and Caricature* (Cambridge: Cambridge University Press, 2013), Chapter 1.

45 Collins, *Odes on Several Descriptive and Allegoric Subjects*, 21.

46 Sillars notes that literary gallery prints were 'placed on a reading table' where 'they would become the subject of social and critical debate' (*Painting Shakespeare*, 295), though we have no records of such debates for the Poets Gallery.

47 A fruitful line of further enquiry would be to investigate female agency across both Macklin's and other literary galleries.

9 | Maria Cosway's *Hours*: Cosmopolitan and Classical Visual Culture in Thomas Macklin's Poets Gallery

LUISA CALÈ

'Invention in Painting does not imply the invention of the subject; for that is commonly supplied by the Poet or Historian', argued Sir Joshua Reynolds in 1771. What 'strikes upon the publick sympathy' is classical or Biblical: although 'no subject can be of universal … concern', Reynolds recommended 'the great events of Greek and Roman fable and history', and the Bible, which will be 'known in those countries where our art is in request'.[1] The literary galleries reached for an alternative, British literary canon. Proposals headed 'The British Poets', published by Thomas Macklin on 1 January 1787, announced the publication of 'a Series of Prints Illustrative of the Most Celebrated British Poets', from Chaucer to Smith, engraved from 'One Hundred Pictures of the Most Interesting Subjects from the Poets of *Great Britain*'. The list of painters was headed by Sir Joshua Reynolds, the President of the Royal Academy and ended with Benjamin West, 'Historical Painter to his Majesty'. Macklin's British Poets was designed to be 'Published in Numbers, each Number containing Four Prints; with Letter-Press, explanatory of the Subject, extracted from the Writings of the Respective Poets'.[2] If the poets of Great Britain provided the subjects, how would they be translated on canvas? What kinds of invention and what kinds of art did the alliance of poetry and painting offer Britain?

The literary gallery model raised the expectation for an art that would match the Old Masters and compare with the Vatican. Newspaper advertisements announced the publication of the first number and the opening of 'the Exhibition of such Pictures as have been painted for the above Work, at the Poets Gallery, late the Mitre Tavern, Fleet-street'.[3] Associated with Samuel Johnson and the publishing industry, this address suggested the role of commercial enterprise, print, and exhibitions in the circulation of painting. The Mitre's 'Assembly Room' accommodated around 800 people and became a popular venue for the Society for Free Debate from September 1785 to February 1788. Macklin's advertisements in April, therefore, associated the Poets Gallery with a culture of conversation and public debate.[4] Advertisements made bold comparisons to heighten the printseller's national contribution to the field of art: 'this collection of paintings will be as lasting a monument of the powers of the pencil in England, as the Vatican is at Rome, and the names of Reynolds, Peters, Gainsborough, Stothard, Cosway, and Opie, will be held in as high estimation by foreigners as Raphael, Titian, Guido, Corregio, or any ancient master whatever'.[5] Macklin's endeavour to build 'a Monument to the English School' adapted the Horatian claim that writing can build a memorial more lasting than bronze. To compare the Mitre Tavern to the Vatican meant to fashion a counter-narrative about the role of painting in the public sphere of the 1780s.[6]

The chance to compare the Poets Gallery to the Vatican and modern painters to Old Masters depended on the circulation of reproductive prints in the age of mechanical reproduction. Collections of prints constituted museums without walls that had the potential to include the whole field of art.[7] They brought together into a paper repository works dotted on the Grand Tour or closed up in aristocratic cabinets, but they also preserved the visual world of lost collections. After the Old Master paintings of Houghton Hall were sold to Empress Catherine of Russia in 1779, John Boydell's gallery of engravings performed a national function in preserving the collection on paper.[8] Print culture produced a cosmopolitan comparative visual culture due to its transnational circulation across borders. Macklin's proposal emphasizes the 'influence the Fine Arts have on the Taste and Manners, and the Commerce of a Country', arguing for the benefits of reproductive engraving in turning unique artworks into sources of applied design, mechanical reproduction, and trade: 'they excite Genius and employ Industry at home, they extend Commerce and Credit abroad, and ultimately decide the Balance of Profit in favour of the Country in which they are most cherished'.[9] Incongruous though it might seem, the comparison of Fleet Street with the Vatican and of modern painters with the Old Masters calls attention to the role of print in the transnational circulation of art, suggesting how it could be harnessed to national ends.

The national rhetoric shaping the literary gallery phenomenon in promotional publications and press coverage draws out the tension between the British and cosmopolitan coordinates of the field of art. 'Exhibiting Englishness' was key to the literary galleries' role in 'the Formation of a National Aesthetic', as Rosie Dias argues.[10] English literature provides the national element in the first number of Macklin's British Poets, but the first artists chosen to illustrate them stand out for their cosmopolitan artistic identities and careers: the Swiss Johann Heinrich Füssli, who renamed himself Henry Fuseli to sound both English and Italian, was commissioned two illustrations, while the German Angelica Kauffman and the Anglo-Italian Maria Cosway one each; three out of four were engraved by the Italian Francesco Bartolozzi. As foreign artists attracted to Britain by its emerging institutions, commissions, and exhibition culture, they exemplify a transnational field of art. The choice to illustrate British Poets would consolidate their place in the English School; indeed, in 1799 Fuseli became professor of painting at the Royal Academy.[11] However, in 1788 they articulated the transnational possibilities of British art before the Revolution. In this chapter I will focus on the first number of Macklin's British Poets, using Maria Cosway's *The Hours* to examine the cosmopolitan traditions and trajectories it articulates as an engagement between image and text. First, I will compare the exhibition and the serial publication to tease out the tension between painting and poetry, cosmopolitanism and Englishness, setting Cosway's painting against Thomas Gainsborough's *Lavinia*. I will then proceed to reconstruct Cosway's cosmopolitan development as a painter, turning to her corpus of literary paintings and their dialogue with classical visual culture and the Old Masters. Finally, I will explore how the painting is repurposed by Macklin, focusing on two acts of mediation: Francesco Bartolozzi's engraving, and the 'poetic illustration' provided by Thomas Gray's 'Ode on the Spring'.

A visit to the Poets' Gallery entailed an intermedial practice of viewing and reading. The 'poetical descriptive catalogue' included in the one shilling admittance fee lists each exhibit by poet and painter, adding a title and a short excerpt indicating the scene or point in time illustrated. Longer extracts, where possible the poems in their entirety, faced the engravings in the numbers of the British Poets, which often included reference to a page number, and highlighted the point in time specifically represented in italics for ease of reference. From the third number, published in 1791, excerpts are also inscribed in the captions of the prints. Both Fuseli and Macklin compared the dissemination of engravings to the invention of printing. Engraving did for painting what print did for manuscript; in turn, the visual culture of prints produced new channels of circulation for literature.[12] *Poetic Descriptions of Choice and Valuable Prints*, the title of Macklin's 1794 catalogue, captures this dynamic of reciprocal 'illustration'.

The double attribution of a literary subject to a poet and a painter encouraged ekphrastic exercises. Reading the Catalogue from left to right meant seeing the name of the poet, followed by that of the painter, with the excerpt in the middle. This typographical layout bears out Henry Fuseli's claim that 'the excellence of pictures or of language consists in raising clear, complete, and circumstantial images, and turning readers into spectators'.[13]

Fuseli's statement adapts to pictures Joseph Warton's Aristotelian claim about rhetoric's power to bring images to the eyes of the reader.[14] The Poets Gallery shows how a literary quotation works as a common ground, where poet and painter can be measured against each other. This intermedial play of text and image invited readers to associate alternative painters to their favourite texts, or alternative literary inventions to paintings on display.

Employing the most prominent modern painters offered a new contemporaneity to a canon of earlier poets, showing how painting can test and transform literary genres. The first exhibition catalogue, issued in April 1788, gives pride of place to Thomas Gainsborough's *Lavinia*, listed as an illustration from James Thomson's *The Seasons* (1730).[15] The painting is discussed in detail by Fuseli in the *Analytical Review* two years later:

> The lamented name of Gainsborough occupies the first place, with one of the last perhaps, but surely one of the most beautiful products of his pencil. This is a faithful transcript of the forms and hues of nature, and the forms and hues of nature never leave the mind indifferent. … but is this the sympathy that would seize our breast at the sight of such an infant as Lavinia? – the figure before us is the offspring and immediate heir of poverty; the stumpy shortness of her form, the raggedness of her garb and air take nothing indeed from her innocence, but never can allow her to be mistaken for the 'lovely young Lavinia that once had friends, and on whose birth fortune deceitful smiled.' – in framing this child, the artist, we affirm, never dreamt she was to be transformed into the heroine of Thomson's Autumn.[16]

Fuseli rejects Macklin's identification of the character from Thomson's *Seasons* with Gainsborough's rustic subject. He tries to read the painting and the text as two stages of the character's development, but such a plot of improvement proves unconvincing too. Thomson's *Seasons* was one of the most illustrated poems of the eighteenth century, so its choice as a subject for the Poets Gallery could respond to commercial demands.[17] On the other hand, Gainsborough's art becomes the vehicle of a revaluation of Thomson's poetry. As Hazlitt later argued, painting invited the critic 'to read poetry with the eye of a connoisseur': 'an admirer of Teniers or Hobbima might think little of the pastoral sketches of Pope or Goldsmith; even Thomson describes not so much the naked object as what he sees in his mind's eye, surrounded and glowing with the mild, bland, genial vapours of his brain'.[18] Read through a realist visual canon of rustic subjects, the literary pastoral of earlier eighteenth-century poets comes across as abstract and their power of invention divorced from experience and actuality. Exposing Thomson's pen to Gainsborough's brush meant articulating a generational gap and an alternative politics of sympathy.

Seeing literature at the Poets Gallery encouraged exercises in retrospective attribution. While Macklin's plan announced paintings 'Illustrative of the British Poets', and suggested that they were commissioned for the purpose, as Fuseli pointed out, 'It appears that some of the pictures were not painted for the collection, or ever could be intended to illustrate any of the poets which the gallery professes to celebrate.'[19] Gainsborough's *Lavinia* is among them; it was painted in 1786, exhibited at Gainsborough's gallery in Schomberg House, then in Liverpool in 1787 under the title *Village Girl with Milk*, before being sold to Macklin and repurposed as *Lavinia* in 1788.[20] These retroactive associations demonstrate complex processes of intermedial adaptation and canon formation, which elevate painters by way of literary classics and cast literature as a retrospective illustration of painting.

Comparing the order of the exhibition catalogue to the sequencing of the print publication reveals divergent priorities. While the exhibition catalogue starts with Gainsborough's rustic scene, which spells out the Englishness of English art, the first number of the British Poets tells a different story. Reproduction opens up Macklin's Poets to a wider visual corpus. The quality of the publication is sanctioned by the choice of the most established engraver of his day: three out of four stipple engravings published in the first number of British Poets are signed 'F.Bartolozzi R.A. & Engraver to his Majesty sculpt.', the fourth by his pupil P. W. Tomkins. Macklin's choice of Bartolozzi invited comparisons between the inventions of the British poets and his corpus of reproductive engravings, going from Raphael, Guercino, Guido Reni, Correggio, and Parmigianino to mythological and allegorical inventions by modern painters. The mediation of print encouraged the dream that such a paper gallery might stand up to Old Master Collections in the Vatican and the Uffizi. Since Macklin's prospectus pointed out that 'Any One Number may be had separate, but no less than a whole Number will be Sold', it is important to pay attention to the juxtaposition of pictures in each number. While the proposals for British Poets had emphasized the Royal Academy titles and Royal appointments of Macklin's painters, the first number does not include Reynolds, nor West, nor Barry, the Professor of Painting. Choosing Angelica Kauffman, Henry Fuseli, and Maria Cosway as the first artists to illustrate the British Poets meant employing foreign artists formed on the Grand Tour and known for a cosmopolitan canon of literary paintings.[21] Their subjects reflect the priorities of the print market. Kauffman's *Selim, or the Shepherd's Moral* from William

Collins's *Continental Eclogues* is not listed in the exhibition catalogue. Showcasing Kauffman in the first number of British Poets meant appealing to a well-established market, since stipple engravings after Kauffman's works were among the most fashionable subjects for furniture prints in the 1770s–80s; her painting tapped into the fashion for oriental themes that she had championed through her portraits of English aristocrats in Turkish dress.[22] Fuseli's *Queen Katharine's Dream* from Shakespeare's *Henry VIII* and *Prince Arthur's Vision* from Edmund Spenser's *Faerie Queene* (1596) exhibited his skills as a painter of dreams and the supernatural associated with the most celebrated writers of the English canon. Cosway was by far the least established of the three. The success of the exhibition depended on the painters' reputation as well as on the choice of fashionable texts. Like Gainsborough's *Lavinia*, Cosway's *The Hours* was retrospectively adapted as an illustration to a British poet. Yet, while Gainsborough's status as a painter clarifies why he might be critical to the success of the enterprise, what qualified Maria Cosway as an ideal ingredient for prospective subscribers to Macklin's series of engravings?

Maria Cosway's trajectory illuminates the cosmopolitan tradition expressed in the first number of The British Poets. Cosway was born in Florence from British parents who 'kept a lodging and boarding-house on a very large establishment, which was the resort of all the nobility and gentry who at that time visited Italy'.[23] In an autobiographical letter written in 1830 Cosway mentions an early passion for drawing, later nourished by the encouragement of Johann Zoffany and Joseph Wright of Derby, and a practice of copying masterpieces at the Uffizi and Palazzo Pitti in Florence. Moving to Rome around 1778, she became part of a circle including the painters James Northcote, Thomas Banks, Prince Hoare, and Henry Fuseli.[24] After her father died, 'she came over to England … filled with the highest expectations of being the wonder of the nation like another Angelica Kauffman',[25] with letters of introduction for all 'the first people of fashion – Sir J. Reynolds, Cipriani, Bartolozzi, Angelica Kauffman'.[26] Apart from the President of the Royal Academy, the other names mentioned indicate a transnational Italian network of artists painting literary and mythological subjects engraved by Bartolozzi and adapted as motifs in interior decoration.

Maria Cosway's exhibition paintings drew on literature as a repository of subjects for painters right from the start. Among the first paintings she exhibited at the Royal Academy in 1781 she chose the subject of Rinaldo from Torquato Tasso's *La Gerusalemme Liberata*, a Renaissance chivalric poem first published in Italian in 1581, which was translated as *Jerusalem*

Delivered by Edward Fairfax in 1600 and John Hoole in 1763. The poem was adapted to music, operas, and paintings by Guercino, Tintoretto, Van Dyck, Poussin, Boucher, and Tiepolo. Subjects from the poem had also been exhibited at the Royal Academy by Kauffman and Richard Cosway in 1772, and provided successful subjects for engravings. Maria Cosway's painting was considered 'in the style of Parmigianino' and got her billed as a 'rising genius'.[27] In 1782 she made her mark with a fancy portrait entered in the exhibition catalogue with a quotation from Spenser's *Faerie Queene*. The *Morning Herald* commented that 'the fair artist has unquestionably a claim to a poetic fancy. In the personification of Cynthia she has evidently introduced the Duchess of Devonshire. The sprightly art which distinguishes that Beauty is admirably hit off in the advancing step of the regent of the night.'[28] Maria Cosway's fancy portrait associates her to the Duchess's fashionable milieu.[29] At the time, the Cosways' residence in Berkeley Square backed onto the Duke of Devonshire's. The painters' dealings with the Devonshires are documented by the many miniatures that Richard Cosway was commissioned to paint of the Duchess. The medium of the fancy portrait combines different exercises in recognition: in addition to detecting the likeness of the Duchess of Devonshire, whom Cosway remembers as 'then the Reigning beauty and fashion',[30] viewers were invited to think about how the sitter embodied the qualities of the literary character taken from the *Fairie Queene*. In turn the iconography of the portrait pointed to the text's circulation within a culture of literary enactments, in which portraiture was part of a spectrum of literary impersonations that included taking on the features of a literary character at a masquerade. Instead of classical or renaissance visual iconographies of Cynthia as an image of the Goddess Diana, Cosway's painting alludes to the attitude of Mercury descending from the sky painted by Raphael in a spandrel fresco of the Villa Farnesina in Rome.[31] The cross-gendering conveys Cosway's bold adaptation and reinvention of the Old Masters for a cosmopolitan London world.

Turning to the work included in the Poets' Gallery, Cosway's *The Hours* was exhibited at the Royal Academy exhibition in 1783, but it is now lost. Although no literary reference was associated to the painting in the title and catalogue entry, its field of allusion was quickly unveiled by Peter Pindar in *More Lyric Odes, to the Royal Academicians* (1783), his parodic homage to the Royal Academy exhibition. To assess Cosway's ambition, Pindar draws on the trope of ineffability in a rhyming couplet: 'No, no! with all my lyric pow'rs / I'm not like Mrs COSWAY's *Hours*'. However, the rhyme aligning 'lyric powers' with Cosway's *Hours* is debunked in the following line, which qualifies her *Hours* as 'red as cock turkeys, plump as barn door chicken', quite unlike the ephemeral grace associated with neoclassical personifications. Pindar's parody continues in a learned footnote, where his act of appreciation mobilizes a fashionable aesthetic vocabulary: 'a sublime picture this! The expression is truly Homerical, – The fair artist hath in the most surprising manner communicated to canvas the old Bard's idea of the *Brandy-fac'd Hours*. – See the Iliad'.[32] Pindar's retitling activates the conventions of literary painting. In Alexander Pope's 'Poetical Index' to Homer the Hours are listed under 'Allegorical and Fictitious Persons' and defined 'Keepers of the Gates of Heaven'.[33] Pindar's writing unveils Homer's airy allegories of time in their fleshly embodiments. Through rustic associations and convivial drinking analogies he brings down their flight to the measure of the everyday, tracing their ephemeral nymph-like steps to the farm yard or the pub. Their survival in the contemporary world is degraded, their performance subjected to innuendo, high art reduced to rustic and comic subjects. Such debasement undermines Cosway's reputation and turns her literary ambition into bathos.

So how would such a painting qualify as an illustration of Macklin's British Poets in 1788? What did Maria Cosway bring to Macklin's enterprise? By the mid-1780s, Cosway's Royal Academy exhibits included literary subjects taken from Spenser, Virgil, Homer, and Ossian. Her academic ambition is ridiculed in a visual satire entitled *Maria Costive. at her Studies* (1786), which features the artist at work in her studio, with a selection of her Royal Academy exhibits arranged chronologically from top to bottom to her right: 'Giants of Ossian' must allude to her 1782 *Darthula, in defending the body of her vanguisued father, discovers herself to Cairbar her lover – Ossian*; beneath it hangs 'Eolus' (1782), while on the easel sits 'Samson' (1784), and 'Deluge' (1785) is cast sideways in the corner, half outside the frame. The painter's dress and stance allude to a portrait made by her husband, Richard Cosway, and engraved by Bartolozzi in 1785, in which she poses in the dress and manner of a Rubens portrait. A drawing resting beneath a bowl on the floor reads 'Dicky Caus', announcing the satire's companion piece, published two days later, entitled *Dicky Causway in Plain English*, which parodies a portrait which presented Richard Cosway in a Raphaelesque pose, sitting next to a biography of Rubens.[34] The Cosway portraits reference the Old Master style of Rubens mediated through the fashion for chalk drawings associated with French eighteenth-century portraits by Boucher and Watteau. Such choices indicate the Cosways' desire to show their cosmopolitan cultural identity as artists and connoisseurs known for their collection of Old Masters, mercilessly debunked by the satires that denounce 'Costive' Mary as a constipated imitator and reveal Dicky 'in plain English'.[35]

In 1784 The Cosways moved to Schomberg House in Pall Mall, where they became neighbours of Gainsborough, and their home backed onto Carlton House, the residence of the Prince of Wales. The new address signalled their social position as artists in a Georgian geography of London's entertainments, since they took over the premises once occupied by John Astley and recently vacated by Dr James Graham, who had turned his suite of rooms into an Aesculapian Temple of Health and Hymen. This classical establishment included a 'Great Apollo Apartment', where fertility cures promised to revive classical pleasures, 'hymenaeal charms' and 'blissful nights' thanks to an 'art of generation' that featured the electromagnetic effects of his famous 'Celestial Bed'.[36] The 'insignia of Dr Graham' continued to mark the premises when the Cosways moved in soon after Graham's practice was shut down.[37] Intrigue also coloured reports of the fashionable gatherings and musical entertainments they hosted at Schomberg House, which were attended by the Prince of Wales and aristocrats that Mary had first met in Italy.[38] Her cosmopolitan networks were expanded in trips to Paris in 1785, 1786, and 1787. Among her new acquaintances was the antiquarian Pierre d'Hancarville, known for his writings about Sir William Hamilton's vases, the art of Pompei and Herculaneum and the uninhibited pleasures of Roman antiquity, who became a long-term correspondent. Her Parisian socializing included the Duke of Orleans and culminated in her Parisian romance with Thomas Jefferson.[39] Horace Walpole ironically captured the international appeal of her soirées at Schomberg House imagining 'the representatives of all the princes of Europe at Mrs Cosway's Diet'.[40] She was styled 'The Goddess of Pall Mall, alias La Decima Musa, alias the Magnetic Muse'.[41] Showcasing her painting alongside works by Kauffman and Fuseli in the first number of the British Poets signalled Macklin's desire to reach out to her cosmopolitan milieu.

Cosway's *The Hours* is entered in the first Poets Gallery catalogue in 1788 under the title 'Ode to Spring'. Instead of Homer, Cosway is associated with Thomas Gray and the first stanza of his poem is reprinted to anchor her invention to a literary source:

> Lo! where the rosy-bosom'd Hours,
> Fair VENUS' train appear,
> Disclose the long-expecting flowers,
>   And wake the purple year!
> The Attic warbler pours her throat,
> Responsive to the cuckow's note,

> The untaught harmony of spring:
> While whisp'ring thro' pleasure as they fly,
> Cool zephyrs thro' the clear blue sky
> Their gather'd fragrance fling.
>   *Vid.* GRAY's *Ode to Spring*.[42]

The alternative, earlier title 'The Hours' is recorded in the caption of the stipple engraving by Bartolozzi published in the first number of Thomas Macklin's Poets Gallery.[43] Using this earlier title as a way into Gray's poem signals the convergence of visual and literary iconographies as the poem became a subject for painters. To compare Cosway to Gray is to identify their subjects' common denominator in a culture of commonplacing. This rhetorical and mnemonical practice of reading and viewing involved collecting, excerpting, and classifying elements of elocution and visual motifs under particular headings ready to be activated in new acts of invention. The poetics of the commonplace is crucial to Macklin's retrofitting of Cosway's painting and Gray's poem. Macklin's curatorial intervention illuminates how a shared classical tradition mediated through different routes, media, and practices of invention can converge in the Poets Gallery.[44]

Originally entitled 'Noon-tide An Ode', Gray's composition was a response to a poem by Richard West.[45] Their poetical exchange was recorded in Gray's Commonplace Book and circulated in correspondence, before being published anonymously in Dodsley's miscellany in 1748.[46] In the Commonplace Book West is identified by the pseudonym Favonius, the Latin equivalent of the Greek Zephyrus, the God of Spring and the West wind. Such a cypher reveals Gray's emotional investment in the allegorical re-enactment of the classical personifications of Spring. Gray's commonplacing offers a rich context for reading the Ode. Under the heading of 'Comparison' Gray entered literary extracts about flowers as fragile symbols of promise, sexual awakening, wasting, and fading away. He started with the famous Chorus of virgins from Catullus's Nuptial Song, which celebrates the flower untouched by the plough compared to the maiden in her prime.[47] In Catullus's poem this image is presented by the Chorus of virgins, to which the male Chorus responds with the alternative image of the vine married to the elm tree, but Gray extrapolated the image of the flower from its nuptial ending and stopped time before the plot could move towards a heterosexual resolution. Within Gray's Commonplace Book the more personal inflection of flowers as symbols of the fragility of time is mediated by a powerfully allusive record of shared reading. Entries transcribing poems and lists of flowers are interspersed with transcriptions and translations from Catullus's erotic poetry. The erotic tempo of Catullus's injunction to 'seize the moment' before the withering of youth acquires a dramatic urgency marked by the inscription of names and dates, which speak of an exchange terminated by death.[48] On the page where he transcribed West's Ode Gray also wrote 'from Catullus: Lesbia, let us (while we may) / Live & love the Time away'. On the following page, he copied Catullus's question: 'Quaeris quot mihi basationes …';[49] below the transcription he added 'Fav: wrote, May 11 1742 He died, the first of June following'.[50] The quotations mobilize Catullus's erotic poetry, opening up the 'ambrosial bed' of Zephyrus and Flora to a homoerotic reading. This possibility is defused in the transition from the privacy of the Commonplace book to the public circulation of print. Fixed in the world of print, entered under the name of the author, Gray's classical personifications become abstractions cut off from the personal histories of the commonplace.

Macklin's retrofitting highlights the versatile gender politics of the commonplace as a shared iconography that could be adapted to different subject positions. Cosway's painting activates the erotic possibilities of the classical Hours, reviving their association with classical rituals of fertility that the Poets Gallery viewers could associate to the classical healing practiced in the Temple of Health and Hymen at Schomberg House in Pall Mall. Gray's 'rosy-bosomed Hours' rhyme with the 'long expecting Flowers'. Literally their expectation refers to the transition from night to day, and winter to Spring, but it also suggests pollination, impregnation, and gestation as key stages in the natural cycle. While the poet is cut out from this promise of Spring, Cosway concentrates on the Hours as an allegory of women's promise of fertility (Figure 9.1). Her composition corresponds to Gray's anatomical detail. Her 'bosomed', scantily clad Hours are suspended in the clouds surrounding a dark sphere symbolizing the earth. Their dance-like procession moves from morning to evening, symbolized by two larger kneeling figures representing Aurora thrusting flowers to the left and Night casting her mantle over them as they leave the scene to the right. As Fuseli pointed out, 'These are said to be the vernal hours of Gray; but the whole is a creation of the fair author.'[51]

Cosway's composition alludes to the Borghese Hours, one of two celebrated bas reliefs from a neo-attic Roman sarcophagus bought by Cardinal Scipione Borghese (1587–1633) and mounted above opposite doors in the great Gallery of Villa Borghese.[52] Engravings of the bas relief appeared under the title 'Nuptiales Chorae' (Nuptial Dances) in Giovanni Pietro Bellori and Pietro Santi Bartoli's *Admiranda Romanorum Antiquitatum ac Veteris Sculpturae Vestigia* (1693), later reproduced under the title 'Danseuses' (dancers) in Bernard de Montfaucon's *Antiquité*

Figure 9.1 Maria Cosway, *The Hours*. Engraved by Francesco Bartolozzi (1788). Yale Center for British Art, Paul Mellon Collection.

expliquée et représentée en figures (1719),[53] and listed as 'dancing hours' in Josiah Wedgwood's 1779 catalogue.[54] As part of a Roman sarcophagus, these classical figures captured the ephemeral, transient life of maidens on the threshold of adulthood. Detached from its physical location and function, this classical composition could be adapted to many uses.

The metamorphosis of maidens into dancers and then hours involved a process of abstraction. Bartoli and Bellori's engravings reduce the three-dimensional bas reliefs on the sarcophagus to two-dimensional works on paper. In the transfer from stone to the page, the design acquires a literary corpus. A caption inserted underneath the engraving identifies the subject as 'Nuptial Dances', and associates it to the epithalamic tradition. A quotation from Claudian's 'Epithalamium of Palladius and Celerina' and a reference to Catullus's *Pervigilium Veneris* bring home the Bacchic implications of the cycle of bloom and procreation.[55] The epithalamic tradition also affects the reproduction of the design, which adds iconographic props not present in the original bas relief: a stick and a puck that Montfaucon interpreted as phallic attributes associated with Bacchic rituals.[56] These references are strengthened when this composition is read as part of a pair representing two moments in the epithalamic ritual. Upon turning the page, the engraving representing the other side of the sarcophagus is titled 'Nuptiale Festum' (Nuptial Feast), followed by a quotation from Statius's Epithalamion, while on the right-hand side, just above the location 'in Hortis Burghesis', another title clarifies the subject as 'Baccha'.[57] When Montfaucon reproduced these plates, he did not include Bellori's captions, and moved the discussion of the Bacchic context to the body of the text, freeing the plates from their association with an epithalamic corpus charged with sexual undertones. Defusing the Bacchic elements of the design meant that the composition could be domesticated to decorate the eighteenth-century interior.

Reproductive media had a significant role in the process of abstraction that freed the iconography of the Dancing Hours. Both Bartoli's and Montfaucon's engravings render the three-dimensionality of the bas relief through cross-hatching. In contrast to their 'baroque shadowy manner', Robert Rosenblum traced the rise of linear abstraction through the choice of techniques that 'reduced' forms 'to completely two-dimensional configuration' in which 'the spatial environment has been completely eradicated'.[58] In a new publication reproducing William Hamilton's Vases in the 1790s, Wilhelm Tischbein advocated classical forms 'confined [...] to the simple outline'.[59] As Thora Brylowe points out, this practice of simplification was part of '"a way of seeing" that idealised and remade the antique'.[60] Freed from the materiality of the originals, classical composition could be reproduced in a range of media, as exemplified in the work of John Flaxman and the Wedgwood factory. Through Flaxman's versions, The Hours became a fashionable model for chimney pieces, table tops, doors, sometimes commissioned directly from artists resident in Rome, sometimes mediated by casts and prints.[61]

Macklin's British Poets has a different print aesthetic: rather than calling attention to the flat medium of paper, Bartolozzi's stipple engraving of Cosway's *The Hours* stands out for the soft volumes and luminosity obtained by the tonal qualities of its dotting technique. Macklin's 1787 proposal announced engravings 'in the manner of Chalk', an intaglio technique that aimed to reproduce the texture of chalk drawings in the crayon manner, to be executed by 'Mr Bartolozzi, his School, and other Eminent Artists'. The first number features stipple engravings, a fashionable technique adopted in furniture prints after Kauffman, which was derived from the crayon manner, but did not attempt to reproduce drawing.[62] In contrast to the flat aesthetic of the outline propounded by publications that turned vases into designs on paper, cross-hatching conveyed a three-dimensional sense of volume, while stipple rendered the soft, sensuous texture of flesh.

Compared to the sources, Cosway's *The Hours* stand out for depth, animation, and a reciprocation of looks that is different from the allegorical hours carved out of marble or traced in outline. The marble hours and their reproductions remain within the confines of their medium; they respect their ornamental roles as allegories, fictitious beings deprived of agency; they do not step out of line. By contrast, Cosway's dancers are engaged in a reciprocation of looks that involves the viewers in the action, inviting them to join the dance. Their performative potential is enhanced when the visual composition is compared to poetry. The literary genres of the epithalamion and the ode call on readers to take on the first and second person pronouns and take part in the action. The epithalamion invites readers to join a ritual of initiation into the life cycle of Spring and fertility. The ode is a means of enthusiasm that traditionally employed music to transport the mind 'above its ordinary state', rendering it fit to address the Gods, or to reach the height of eloquence required to celebrate heroes, while Anacreon and Horace composed 'festive and amorous odes'.[63] Gray's Ode activates such expectations to emphasize the poet's exclusion. His apostrophe takes the form of an injunction to look, but the line of sight predicated by the poem is not reciprocated: his Hours are contained within the third person pronoun, devoid of agency, limited to the function of connotation. Where William Wordsworth would criticize the abstractions of earlier eighteenth-century poetry and discard personifications for the sake of keeping 'the reader in the company of flesh and blood',[64] Cosway turns the Hours into aesthetic subjects endowed with the power of interpellation. Just as Doctor Graham had looked back to 'celestial wives' to restore classical energy to his rituals of fertility, Cosway activates the performative power of the classical ode and the epithalamion to offer a modern cult of fertility that bypasses Gray's sterile inflection. Such potential for agency worked well as an exhibit at the late Mitre Tavern, a site associated with the Society for Free Debate, which had welcomed 'debating ladies' and featured subjects such as 'whether it was not false Delicacy which forbid the fair sex making the first advances to the man they love?', or 'is not the conduct of those parents who abandon their daughters, for the loss of honour, a principal cause of the increase of prostitution?'.[65] At a time when gender boundaries were hotly debated, Cosway reached back to shared classical sources associated with the iconography of the Hours, to Bartoli, Bellori, and Montfaucon, and rearticulated the classical corpus of text and image to revive their incitement to metalepsis, to step outside the frame and transgress the boundary between art and life.

Cosway's invention had a local as well as cosmopolitan circulation in print, which is recorded in a letter that Jefferson sent her from Paris on 27 July 1788:

> With none do I converse more fondly than with my good Maria: not her under the poplar, with the dog and string at her girdle: but the Maria who makes the Hours her own, who teaches them to dance for us in so charming a round, and lets us think of nothing but her who renders them *si gracieuses*. Your Hours, my dear friend, are no longer your own. Every body now demands them; and were it possible for me to want a memorandum of you, it is presented me in every street of Paris. Come then to see what triumph Time is giving you. Come see every body stopping to admire the Hours, suspended against the walls of the Quai des Augustins, the Boulevards, the Palais royal &c. &c. with a 'Maria Cosway delint.' at the bottom.[66]

Sightings of Cosway's engraving trace a geography of the Parisian print market. The engraving's circulation across borders suggests that Macklin's initiative to enlist Cosway among his artists was successful in disseminating the British Poets in the transnational print market before the Revolution.

However, while the works of an Anglo-Italian artist and an Italian engraver capture a cosmopolitan culture of art, a different vision was presented by Reynolds in the discourse to Royal Academicians at the end of the year. Delivered on the anniversary of the founding of the Royal Academy, the annual address was a fitting occasion to evaluate the state of art and acknowledge the contribution of Gainsborough, who had died over the summer: 'if ever this nation should produce genius sufficient to acquire to us the honourable distinction of an English School, the name of Gainsborough will be transmitted to posterity, in the history of the Art, among the very first of that rising name'.[67] Celebrating Gainsborough brought into focus the directions taken by English art since the founding of the Royal Academy. In his comments on Gainsborough, Reynolds seems to return to the agenda he had set out in the inaugural discourse delivered for the opening of the Royal Academy in January 1769, where he had identified the Academy's task to support the study of 'authentick models' and build on the example of past ages, following the model of Raphael – 'all Rome, and the works of Michael Angelo in particular, were to him an Academy'.[68] In 1769 the difference between Rome and London emphasized the need to establish collections of paintings and sculptures, prints and casts. Yet Reynolds presented the predicament of the new generation of English painters in a positive light: 'we shall have nothing to unlearn'.[69] In a marked contrast to that inaugural discourse, retracing his steps in the light of almost 20 years of academic practice in 1788, Reynolds invited painters to 'unlearn much of the common-place method' associated with painters of the Grand Tour.[70] Casting off tradition meant opting for alternative kinds of invention, freeing art from practices of commonplacing that produced a repository of subjects from classical art, literature and history. While in the third discourse he had recommended subjects from literature and history, Gainsborough's achievements lead him in a different direction: 'if Gainsborough did not look at nature with a poet's eye, it must be acknowledged that he saw her with the eye of a painter'.[71] His corpus pointed to an alternative practice of invention, which separated the painter from the poet.

The difference between the exhibition and the print publication might be measured in terms of local and transnational circulation of art, works on view in Pall Mall and prints circulating across national borders as a museum without walls. Macklin's publication of Gainsborough in the second number of the British Poets in 1790 marks the shift from cosmopolitan to English art after the Revolution obstructed the movement across borders that had shaped the field of art and the print market. While the literary galleries had proposed a subscription model to support modern painting through commercial enterprise and the patronage of the people, their demise is symbolically marked by the acquisition of the former Shakspeare Gallery in Pall Mall by the British Institution for Promoting the Fine Arts in the United Kingdom. Founded by aristocrats, collectors, and connoisseurs, the British Institution harked back to an aristocratic model of patronage of the arts. Its decision to exhibit Old Master paintings on loan from aristocratic collections was harshly criticized by British painters as emblematic of the lack of support and patronage for modern painting.[72] In response, in 1813 the British Institution inaugurated a series of posthumous British art retrospectives, which claimed to 'oppose the genuine excellence of modern, to the counterfeited semblance of ancient productions'.[73] The exhibition catalogue for the following year celebrates Hogarth, who 'adopted a new line of art, purely English', claiming that 'the pictures of Gainsborough, as well as those of Hogarth, were drawn entirely from English nature'.[74] Gainsborough's paintings filled the North Room, substituting Boydell's Shakespeare with 'cottage children' and 'rustic scenery'. The painting that Macklin had retitled *Lavinia, from Thomson's Seasons* hung under the earlier title *Girl with Milk*, on loan from the collection of Samuel Rogers. Freeing Gainsborough's rustic subject from its association with Macklin's Poets Gallery and Thomson's *Seasons* sanctioned the divorce of 'the eye of a painter' from 'a poet's eye'.[75]

Notes

1 Sir Joshua Reynolds, *Discourses on Art*, ed. by Robert R. Wark (New Haven, CT: Yale University Press, 1997), 57–8.
2 *PROPOSALS by THOMAS MACKLIN, No. 39 Fleet Street, for Publishing a Series of Prints Illustrative of the Most Celebrated British Poets*, Victoria and Albert Museum, London, 200 B 280. On Macklin's Poets Gallery, see F. R. Boase, 'Macklin and Bowyer', *Journal of the Warburg and Courtauld Institutes* 26: 1–2 (1963): 148–77; Sean Higgins, 'Thomas Macklin's Poets' Gallery: Consuming the Sister Arts in Late Eighteenth-Century London' (unpublished PhD, London: Courtauld, 2002); G. E. Bentley Jr, *Thomas Macklin (1752-1800), Picture-Publisher and Patron: Creator of the Macklin Bible (1791–1800)* (Lampeter: Edwin Mellen Press, 2016), esp. 85–111.
3 *Morning Chronicle and London Advertiser*, Wednesday 9 April 1788; *The Times*, 16 April 1788; *The World*, 17 April 1788.
4 On the Society for Free Debate's move to the Mitre Tavern on 8 September 1785, see Donna T. Andrew, *London Debating Societies, 1776–1799* (London: London Record Society, 1994), 168, no. 1017; for the Society's move from the Mitre to Capel Court, Bartholomew Lane, in February 1788, see *Morning Herald*, 19 February 1788, 1. I am very grateful to Ian Newman for sharing this reference as well as his forthcoming *The Romantic Tavern: Literature and Conviviality in the Age of Revolution* (Cambridge: Cambridge University Press, 2019).
5 *The Morning Post*, 11 April 1788.
6 *The Morning Post*, 11 April 1788; Compare 'Exegi monumentum aere perennius' ('I have finished a monument more lasting than bronze'), Horace, *Odes and Epodes*, ed. by Niall Rudd (Cambridge, MA: Harvard University Press, 2004), 216–17.
7 On print culture's potential to constitute an 'imaginary museum' or 'museum without walls', see André Malraux's *Le musée imaginaire* (1947), translated into English as *Museum Without Walls* (London: Secker and Warburg, 1967), esp. 10–11; Rosalind Krauss, 'Postmodernism's Museum without Walls', in *Thinking about Exhibitions*, ed. Reesa Greenberg, Bruce W. Ferguson, and Sandy Nairne (New York: Routledge, 1996), 341–8; Hal Foster, 'The Archive without Museums', *October*, 77 (1996): 97–119.
8 On Boydell's Houghton Gallery, see Kristin Campbell, '"The Proprietor exerts his utmost Care …": The Commercial and Commemorative Fates and Fortunes of John Boydell's Houghton Gallery Project', in *Agents of Space: Eighteenth-Century Art, Architecture, and Visual Culture*, ed. by Christina Smylitopoulos (Newcastle: Cambridge Scholars Publishing, 2016), 78–100: 79; Luisa Calè, *Fuseli's Milton Gallery: 'Turning Readers into Spectators'* (Oxford: Clarendon Press, 2006), 24–25.
9 *PROPOSALS by THOMAS MACKLIN*; Calè, *Fuseli's Milton Gallery*, 19–20.

10 Rosie Dias, *Exhibiting Englishness: John Boydell's Shakespeare Gallery and the Formation of a National Aesthetic* (New Haven, CT: Yale University Press, 2013).

11 On Fuseli's choice of English subjects to showcase his contribution to the English School, see Calè, *Fuseli's Milton Gallery*, 52–7, 168; Dias, *Exhibiting Englishness*, chapter 3; on the strategic uses of his foreignness to identify the limits of invention, see Calè, *Fuseli's Milton Gallery*, 168; Dias, *Exhibiting Englishness*, 128.

12 *Analytical Review*, 1 (June 1788), 216; Thomas Macklin, *Poetic Description of Choice and Valuable Prints, published by Mr. Macklin, at The Poets' Gallery, Fleet Street* (London: Bensley, 1794), iii.

13 *Analytical Review*, 1 (June 1788), 216.

14 Joseph Warton, *An Essay on the Genius and Writings of Pope*, 4th edn, 2 vols (London, 1782), II: 165; Calè, *Fuseli's Milton Gallery*, 59–60.

15 *A Catalogue of the First Exhibition of Pictures, Painted for Mr. Macklin, by the Artists of Britain, Illustrative of the British Poets* (London, 1788), no. 1, 3.

16 *Analytical Review*, 4 (July 1789), 368.

17 On illustrated editions of Thomson's *Seasons*, see Sandro Jung, 'Print Culture, High-Cultural Consumption, and Thomson's "The Seasons", 1780–1797', *Eighteenth-Century Studies*, 44: 4 (2011): 495–514.

18 William Hazlitt, 'Mr Crabbe', in *The Complete Works of William Hazlitt*, ed. P. P. Howe, 21 vols (London: Dent, 1930–1934), XIX: 53.

19 *AR* (1790). In addition to Lavinia, Fuseli also singled out Maria Cosway's *The Hours*, Gainsborough's *Hobbinol and Ganderetta* associated with Somervile, both of which were published in the second number of the British Poets, published in 1790; Reynolds's *The Vestal*, which recycled as an illustration to Gregory's Ode to Mercy, was not engraved in the British Poets; nor was The Reverend Peters's *The Death-bed of the Just* associated with Young.

20 W. T. Whitley, *Thomas Gainsborough* (London: Murray, 1915), 264–5, 294; Ellis Waterhouse, 'Gainsborough's "Fancy Pictures"', *Burlington Magazine*, 88: 519 (June 1946), 134–41, on 139.

21 Cosway's painting is entered at no. VI; Fuseli's at nos VIII and XI; Kauffman's is not listed, see *A Catalogue of the First Exhibition of Pictures, Painted for Mr. Macklin, by the Artists of Britain, Illustrative of the British Poets*, 7, 9–10.

22 David Alexander, 'Kauffman and the Print Market in Eighteenth-century England', in *Angelica Kauffman: A Continental Artist in Georgian England*, ed. by Wendy Wassying Roworth (Brighton: Reaktion Books, 1992), 140–92; Angela Rosenthal, 'The Inner Orient', *Angelica Kauffman: Art and Sensibility* (New Haven, CT: Yale University Press, 2006), 123–54.

23 Stephen Gwynn, *Memorials of an Eighteenth-Century Painter (James Northcote)* (London: T. Fisher Unwin, 1898), 149.

24 Ibid., 142.

25 Ibid., 149–50.

26 Maria Cosway to Sir William Cosway, Lodi, 24 May 1830, Victoria and Albert Museum, 86 DD Box III, transcribed in G. C. Williamson, *Richard Cosway*

R. A. (London: Bell, 1905), 12–15, 13; see also Gerald Barnett, *Richard and Maria Cosway: A Biography* (Cambridge: Lutterworth Press, 1995), 50.
27 *Gazetteer & New Daily Advertiser*, 12 May 1781.
28 *Morning Herald and Daily Advertiser*, 8 May 1782.
29 Barnett, *Richard and Maria Cosway*, 58–9.
30 Maria Cosway to Sir William Cosway, Lodi, 24 May 1830, Victoria and Albert Museum, transcribed in Williamson, *Richard Cosway*, 13.
31 Raphael's fresco from the Chigi Gallery Spandrel of the Villa Farnesina was engraved by Marcantonio (BM Department of Prints and Drawings, H,2.93).
32 Peter Pindar, *More Lyric Odes, to the Royal Academicians, by Peter Pindar, a Distant Relation to the Poet of Thebes, and Laureate to the Academy* (London, 1783), 4.
33 Alexander Pope, *The Iliad of Homer, translated by Mr Pope*, 6 vols (London: Lintot, 1715–20), VI: 'Poetical Index', identifies Iliad, V.929; see also I: 255; VIII: 534–41; 478–9.
34 Anna Reynolds, Lucy Peter, and Martin Clayton, *Portrait of the Artist* (London: Royal Collection Trust, 2016), 192 and cat. nos 110 and 111.
35 Barnett, *Richard and Maria Cosway*, 66.
36 *The Celestial Beds; or, A Review of the Votaries of the Temple of Health, Adelphi, and the Temple of Hymen, Pall-Mall* (London: Kearsly, 1781); *The Temple of Pleasure: A Poem* (London: Langham, 1783), 3–4; Peter Otto, 'The Regeneration of the Body: Sex, Religion and the Sublime in James Graham's *Temple of Health and Hymen*', *Romanticism on the Net* 23 (August 2001) (accessed 5 March 2018); Peter Otto, *Multiplying Worlds* (Oxford: Oxford University Press, 2011), 68–75.
37 Barnett, *Richard and Maria Cosway*, 66, quoting from *Morning Herald*, 8 August 1785.
38 Barnett, *Richard and Maria Cosway*, 65–6.
39 On Cosway's purported affair with Jefferson, see Barnett, *Richard and Maria Cosway*, 90–9, 103–6.
40 Horace Walpole to Lady Littleton, 28 October 1787, *The Yale Edition of Horace Walpole's Correspondence*, ed. W. S. Lewis, 48 vols (New Haven, CT: Yale University Press, 1937–83), 42: 200, quoted in Tino Gipponi, *Maria e Richard Cosway* (Turin: Allemandi, 1988), 15.
41 Tiberius Cavallo to Prince Hoare, 1788, quoted in Gipponi, *Maria e Richard Cosway*, 15.
42 *A Catalogue of the First Exhibition of Pictures, Painted for Mr. Macklin, by the Artists of Britain, Illustrative of the British Poets* (14 April 1788), 5–6 (No. VI).
43 *The Exhibition of the Royal Academy. The Fifteenth* (London, 1783), No. 261, p. 13.
44 On commonplacing, see Lucia Dacome, 'Noting the Mind: Commonplace Books and the Pursuit of the Self in Eighteenth-Century Britain', *Journal of the History of Ideas* 65: 4 (2004): 603–25; David Allan, *Commonplace Books and Reading in Georgian England* (Cambridge: Cambridge University Press, 2010). On Gray's commonplacing, see John Guillory, *Cultural Capital: The Problem*

of Literary Canon Formation (Chicago, IL: University of Chicago Press, 1993), Chapter 2, esp. 87–89.

45 Richard West to Thomas Gray, 5 May 1742, *Correspondence of Thomas Gray*, ed. by P. Toynbee and L. Whibley, 3 vols (Oxford: Clarendon Press, 1971), I: 201; 'Ode', *Collection of Poems by Several Hands*, 3 vols (London: Dodsley, 1748), II: 265–7; it takes the title 'Ode on the Spring', in *Poems by Mr Gray* (London: Dodsley, 1768), 3–8.

46 Thomas Gray to Richard West, 3 June 1742, *Correspondence*, I: 213, 250–2; Thomas Gray to Horace Walpole, October 1746, HWC, 14, 7.

47 'Ut flos in saeptis secretus nascitur hortis …' ('As a flower springs up secretly in a fenced garden'), Catullus, CIXX.39–47, in *Catullus, Tibullus and Pervigilium Veneris*, trans. by F. W. Cornish (Cambridge, MA: Harvard University Press, 1976), 88–9.

48 Thomas Gray, 'Comparatio', Commonplace Book, Pembroke College, Cambridge, 3 vols, I: 93, 98.

49 'Vivamus, mea Lesbia, atque amemus', Carmen V, *Catullus, Tibullus and Pervigilium Veneris*, 6–7; 'You ask how many kissings of you, Lesbia, are enough for me', Carmen VII, Ibid., 8–9.

50 Gray's Commonplace Book, 'Carmina', I: 256–7.

51 *Analytical Review*, 4 (July 1789), 369.

52 Les danseuses Borghèse, Paris, Louvre, MR 747; Francis Haskell and Nicholas Penny, *Taste and the Antique: The Lure of Classical Sculpture* (New Haven, CT: Yale University Press, 1981), 195–6; Adriano Aymonino, 'The Fortune of the Borghese Dancers in Eighteenth and early Nineteenth-Century European Art and Decoration', *Roma fuori Roma: L'esportazione dell'arte moderna da Pio VI all'Unità (1775–1870)*, ed. by Giovanna Campitelli, Stefano Grandesso, and Carla Mazzarelli (Rome: Campisano, 2012), 477–92.

53 Bernard de Montfaucon, *L'Antiquité expliquée et représentée en figures*, 5 vols (Paris: Florentin Delaulne, Hilaire Foucault, Michel Clousier, Jean-Geoffroy Nyon, Etienne Ganeau, Nicolas Gosselin, et Pierre-François Giffart, 1719), III, part II, pp. 314–5, plates 172–3.

54 'Dancing Hours', *A catalogue of cameos, intaglios, medals, busts, small statues, and bas-relief; with a general account of vases and other ornaments, after the antique, made by Wedgwood and Bentley, and sold at their rooms in Greek Street, Soho, London*, 5th edn with additions (London, 1779), 29, no. 205; Alison Kelly, *Decorative Wedgwood* (London, 1965), 64.

55 'NUPTIALES CHORAE | ET FASTI IUVENUM PLAUSUS MIXTAEQ CHOREIS AUDITAE PER RURA LYRAE. Claudian. Virginum Chorus nuptias celebrat; nec absimilis ritus in Pervigilio Veneris Catulliano – in Hortis Burghesiis', in Giovanni Pietro Bellori and Pietro Santi Bartoli, *Admiranda Romanarum antiquitatum ac veteris sculpturae vestigia anaglyphico opere elaborata ex marmoreis exemplaribus quae Romae adhuc extant. Notis J.P. Bellorii illustrata. Restituit auxit D. de Rubeis* (Rome, 1693), plate 63 (Nuptial

Dances 'and joyous acclamation of youth and the strains of the lyre accompanying dancing in the streets'), see 'Epithalamium of Palladius and Celerina', *Claudian*, trans. Maurice Platnauer, 2 vols (Cambridge, MA: Harvard University Press, 1922), II: 206–7, lines 22–3. The quotation is followed by the comment 'the chorus celebrates the weddings of virgins; nor is a dissimilar rite in Catullus's Pervigilium Veneris – In Villa Borghese' (author's translation).

56 'La premiere & la derniere qui ont une main libre, tiennent l'une une espece de palet, l'autre un petit bâton', Montfaucon, *L'Antiquité expliquée*, III, part II, p. 314.

57 'NUPTIALE FESTUM | FRONDE VIRENT POSTES ET FERVENT COMPITA FLAMMIS SERTA FERUNT. Statius epit. Stellae in Nuptiis ac festis diebus serta arborumq rami prae foribus affigebantur. Martian Capella Claudian. | Baccha. In Hortis Burghesiis', in Bellori and Bartoli, *Admiranda*, plate 64: Wedding Feast | The doorposts are green with foliage, the crossroads ablaze', Statius, 'Epithalamion in honour of Stella and Violentilla', *Sylvae*, ed. and trans. D. R. Shackleton Bailey (Cambridge, MA: Harvard University Press, 2003), 58–9, lines 231–2.

58 Robert Rosenblum, *The International Style of 1800: A Study in Linear Abstraction* (New York: Garland, 1976), esp. 34–35, 51, 120.

59 Quoted in Thora Brylowe, 'Two Kinds of Collections: Sir William Hamilton's Vases, Real and Represented', *Eighteenth-Century Life*, 32: 1 (Winter 2009): 23–56, at 43.

60 Thora Brylowe, 'Antiquity by Design: Re-Mediating the Portland Vase', *Romantic Antiquarianism*, ed. by Noah Heringman and Crystal Lake, Romantic Circles (2014), para 11; Viccy Coltman, 'Sir William Hamilton's Vase Publications', *Journal of Design History* 14 (2001): 1–16.

61 Haskell and Penny, *Taste and the Antique*, 196; Aymonino, 'The Fortune of the Borghese Dancers', cit; Eileen Harris, 'A Tale of Two Tables', *Burlington Magazine*, 155 (June 2013), 390–95.

62 On chalk or crayon manner and stipple engraving, see Anthony Griffiths, *Prints and Printmaking: an Introduction to the History and Techniques* (London: British Museum Publications, 1980), 81–83, 119.

63 Hugh Blair, *Lectures on Rhetoric and Belles Lettres*, 2 vols (London, 1783), II: 354–5.

64 William Wordsworth, Preface to Lyrical Ballads (1800), in *The Prose Works of William Wordsworth*, 3 vols, ed. by W. J. B. Owen and J. W. Smyser (Oxford: Clarendon Press, 1974), I: 150.

65 These subjects were debated at the Mitre Tavern on 19 January 1786 and 26 January 1786; in both cases the outcome was negative, see Andrew, *London Debating Societies 1776–1799*, p. 177, nos 1066–7. Questions tabled by the Society of Free Debate ranged between politics, virtue, and morality, often focusing on gender politics, with subjects such as 'which is the happier State, Marriage, or a single Life?' (16 March 1786, p. 180, no. 1088), 'are the boasted Liberties of

England Real or Imaginary?' (30 March 1786, p. 181, no. 1094), 'is Learning a desirable Accomplishment in a Wife?' (4 May 1786, p. 183, no. 1109), divorce (11 May 1786, p. 184, no. 1112), obedience in marriage (8 March 1787, p. 200, no. 1206), the infidelity of husbands (26 April 1787, p. 206, no. 1234), whether it is 'a Duty incumbent on all Mankind, to enter into the State of Wedlock' (6 December 1787, pp. 213–4, no. 1281).

66 Thomas Jefferson to Maria Cosway, 27 July 1788, *The Papers of Thomas Jefferson*, ed. by Julian P. Boyd (Princeton, NJ: Princeton University Press, 1950–2007), XIII (1956), 423–4, and her response on 19 August 1788, ibid., 524–5. See also Jacques-Louis David: 'On ne peut pas faire une poesie plus ingenieuse et plus naturelle', quoted in Philippe Bordes, 'Jacques-Louis David's Anglophilia on the Eve of the French Revolution', *Burlington Magazine*, 134: 1073 (August 1992), 482–90: 485.

67 Reynolds, *Discourses on Art*, 248.

68 Ibid., 15.

69 Ibid., 16.

70 Ibid., 249.

71 Ibid., 253.

72 Francis Haskell, *The Ephemeral Museum: Old Master Paintings and the Rise of the Art Exhibition* (New Haven, CT: Yale University Press, 2000), 48–50.

73 British Institution, 'Preface', *Catalogue of Pictures by the late Sir Joshua Reynolds, exhibited by the permission of the Proprietors, in honour of the Memory of that Distinguished Artist, and for the Improvement of British Art* (London: Bulmer, 1813), 9. On the institution of posthumous exhibitions of modern British painters, see Haskell, *The Ephemeral Museum*, 50–63.

74 British Institution, 'Preface', *Catalogue of Pictures by the late William Hogarth, Richard Wilson, Thomas Gainsborough, and J. Zoffani. Exhibited by the Permission of the Proprietors in Honour of the Memory of those Distinguished Artists, and for the Improvement of British Art. To which are added etchings distinguishing the names in the Florentine gallery and Royal Academy* (London: Bulmer, 1814), 10–11.

75 British Institution, *Catalogue of Pictures by the late William Hogarth, Richard Wilson, Thomas Gainsborough, and J. Zoffani*, p. 16, no. 71.

10 | Artists' Street: Thomas Stothard, R. H. Cromek, and Literary Illustration on London's Newman Street

MARY L. SHANNON

In the early nineteenth century and into the 1840s, London's Newman Street (off Oxford Street) was popularly known as 'Artists' Street' because of its intense concentration of artistic residents.[1] Many significant names of the late eighteenth- and early nineteenth-century art world had addresses there: Thomas Stothard, Benjamin West, James Heath, and other members and associate members of the Royal Academy. Alongside them were the homes and studios of less well-known artists who worked in many different media: sculptors, engravers, portrait painters, and animal painters, as well as the entrepreneur R. H. Cromek. Of the artists of Newman Street, a significant proportion worked on book illustration or literary subjects, or had close connections to famous nineteenth-century literary figures. They collaborated with, socialized with, and employed one another. They were surrounded by businesses dealing in both visual and print culture, including the printers McQueen and Co., and the Hering family bookbinders. Newman Street provided a geographical place for what we might now call illustration when its cultural 'place' was very much in flux. With its hey-day over by the latter half of the century, Artists' Street was circumscribed by time as well as by place. John Thomas Smith declares Newman Street is still 'full' of artists in 1846, and James Matthew Leigh's School of Art, founded in 1848 at 79 Newman Street, had pre-Raphaelites John Millais and Frederick Leighton (who, among many other achievements, illustrated George Eliot's 1863 novel *Romola*) as pupils. However, the street slipped more down-at-heel after West's death in 1820.[2] This chapter will focus on the networks of Artists' Street c.1800–20 to show how interactions between art and literature played out on the ground and suggest that the place of Artists' Street has implications for the 'place' of the visual within the print culture of the early nineteenth-century, at the transition point between Romantic and early Victorian print culture.

Previous studies of the geography of metropolitan visual culture in the Romantic period have focused on its relationship to the growth of middle-class consumer culture in an age of rising access to both art and literature.

Vic Gatrell argues that the centre of the art world shifted after the 1780s from Covent Garden to Newman Street and the increasingly fashionable addresses of Portland Place or Portland Street by the start of the nineteenth-century.[3] Rosie Dias and Luisa Calè present a similar account of a shift to respectable professionalism by focusing on a very specific type of literary art, the literary gallery: Dias, in her analysis of Josiah Boydell's Shakespeare Gallery in Pall Mall, emphasizes how Pall Mall 'consolidated its reputation as a prominent and thriving artistic locale' to rival that of the Royal Academy during the 1780s and 1790s, due to its location within the fashionable and polite world of St James' and its relative distance from 'the commercial taint of the city'.[4] Dias presents the Pall Mall art world as one which defined the exhibition-goer as a cultured participant in an artistic, literary and historical public sphere. Calè also emphasizes the literary gallery as a place where the reading public became a viewing public, actively participating in this public sphere where readers and viewers 'could join the cultural elite if they performed the right actions, helped by the textual props available at the exhibition'.[5] The increasing professionalization within both print culture and visual culture sees literary art, in these accounts, holding a central and respectable place in the heart of metropolitan culture by the turn of the nineteenth century, while the artist has moved from disreputable Covent Garden garret to Pall Mall exhibition.

A close study of Newman Street offers a new angle, however, on this narrative. Perched on the fringes of fashionable Marylebone, Artists' Street reveals an equally complex but less secure version of metropolitan visual culture where artists working in all kinds of media jostled together in ways which reveal the fluid relationship between art and illustration, between literature and the visual, at the start of the nineteenth century.[6] The term 'artist' was a broad one in the eighteenth and nineteenth centuries: an artist could be a 'person skilled in a practical art', a now-obsolete sense which included engravers and designers.[7] The category of artist stretched all the way from painter to craftsperson or artisan, with illustration work sitting somewhere along this shifting spectrum. The word 'illustration' itself, as the editors point out in the introduction to this book, was not yet fully understood in our modern sense: it could, for example, mean a textual as well as a visual embellishment, or a textual as well as a visual explanation.[8] The language of textual and of visual representation was unstable and being re-defined during what was something of a boom-time for the production of illustrated books and prints.[9] Physical proximity on Artists' Street, then, between the different kinds of artists broadly defined, created the conditions for a fluid understanding of the place of the visual within Romantic print culture, and for the relationship between text and image to be more of a communication circuit than any kind of straightforward binary.

This chapter places Stothard and Cromek, both major yet still relatively understudied figures in Romantic period illustration, back into their context on the ground.[10] Rather than using cultural geography to study networks per se (as I have done in earlier work),[11] this chapter shows how we can use physical proximity to study the very terms of scholarly debate: in this case, the words 'artist' and 'illustration'. Several scholars on nineteenth-century print and visual culture have shown how geographical place has cultural implications.[12] With my focus on Artists' Street, however, I seek to push the relationship between print culture and urban space one step further by showing how it can unite textual criticism, book history, art history, and illustration studies, to create a methodological approach for overcoming the disciplinary boundaries between these areas of inquiry. Julia Thomas argues that digital methodologies enable us to see 'the affiliative interplay between illustrations, their allusions and references to other illustrations', illuminating the ways in which images exist 'as part of a network that shapes and is shaped by culture'.[13] Affiliative relationships exist for Thomas when images echo iconographic details, or create a consistent brand identity for a periodical, or otherwise draw upon 'shared pictorial styles and features'.[14] I would add another category: when images are transmuted into new media (painting to print, print to book plate, plate to textual description of it), the result is a network of images and text. For Thomas:

> […] illustration is an eminently social genre. It makes meanings not just in its (conscious and unconscious) references to other illustrations, but also in the groupings and clusters it generates, the 'networks' that exist within and across the boundaries of the illustrated text.[15]

Thomas's concept has applicability beyond the field of digital humanities: it is not only digital methodologies which highlight such affiliations between image and image, and between image and text. This chapter takes the premise of 'affiliative relationships' further to encompass the affiliations between the artists of Newman Street, as well as those between different types of visual media, and between text and image. There is much recent scholarship on networks in print culture, on the relationship between text and image, and on the relationships between different images: a close geographical study of the locations of production enables us to connect up these areas of scholarly enquiry and bring them into dialogue with each other.[16] Newman Street reveals the link between the 'affiliative interplay between illustrations' and the affiliative relationships ('characterised by a desire to form relationships and associations with others'[17]) among those working at the intersection of print culture and visual culture in the early nineteenth century. The tight focus of the geographical approach enables us to see, paradoxically, how complex the communication circuit of text and image was within Romantic-era print culture.

Given the broad definition of 'artist' in the period, it is striking how much artistic production on Newman Street centred around literary topics. Illustration work allowed artists such as Stothard the opportunity to work with ideas and stories (like the more prestigious but commercially unrewarding genre of history painting) but on a smaller and more commercial scale. The 'most prolific illustrator of his times' (according to Shelley M. Bennett), Stothard was based at no. 28 Newman Street from 1793 until his death in 1834, and Bennett argues that 'Stothard's geographic move represented a material sign' of his artistic success.[18] He produced illustrations for editions of texts such as *The Pilgrim's Progress* (1788), *The Rape of the Lock* (1798), *Robinson Crusoe*, William Cowper's *Poems* (1825), *The Decameron*, and Samuel Rogers's *Italy* (1830), as well as plates for pocket-books, illustrations to almanacs and periodicals, portraits of popular actors, banknotes, and even silverware.[19] He also contributed paintings to Josiah Boydell's Shakespeare Gallery, and Macklin's Poet's Gallery.[20] Encompassing book illustration, plates for literary periodicals, and paintings, the vast amount of Stothard's estimated 5,000 designs were literary subjects.[21] When the cheaper end of the print market was flooded with periodicals and broadsides carrying woodcuts of sensational crimes and bloody murder, the location of Stothard and other literary artists on Artists' Street made an implicit claim for literary images as a valuable and prestigious part of visual culture.

Stothard was by no means the only resident of Artists' Street who worked on literary subjects. In the first two decades of the nineteenth-century, a large proportion of the 40 or so artists on Newman Street did so, and they banded together in mutually supportive networks. Berners Street, Charlotte Street, Rathbone Place, and others within five minutes' walk of Newman Street made up a recognized professional enclave (Figure 10.1), where residence could confer 'social and professional advantages'.[22] Piecing together archival records, historical accounts, and existing research shows us in detail, for the first time, exactly how many artists who worked on literary subjects were in close proximity on Newman Street c.1800–20, and allows us to trace their connections (Figure 10.2)[23] For example, Stothard's neighbour at no. 42 until 1800 was James Heath, the famous engraver, who got his first work from Stothard and with whom he formed a lifelong association.

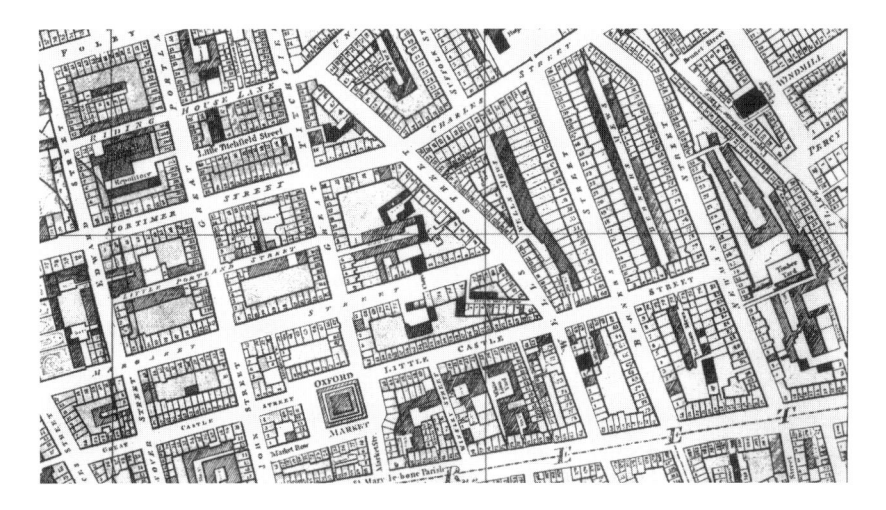

Figure 10.1 The Newman Street area. From *Plan of the Cities of London and Westminster [...] Shewing Every House* (1792–9). A09A3503. City of Westminster Archives Centre.

Heath engraved numerous Stothard designs on literary subjects for books, periodicals, and prints, and produced engravings for Bell's Poets and Boydell's Shakespeare Gallery.[24] Two doors down from Stothard at no. 26 was Henry James Richter, a pupil of Stothard's who moved in radical circles; Richter was hugely in demand as an engraver and illustrator, and produced work for books and annuals. Stothard and Richter remained close friends over the years, with Stothard referring to 'the frequent visits of our friend Richter' in a 1799 letter to his wife.[25] No. 22 was the home of George Dawe, known to Stothard's friend William Godwin. Dawe engraved for Godwin's Juvenile Library, lent money to Godwin via Shelley, and taught young Mary Godwin (later Mary Shelley) drawing and painting.[26] Dawe was notorious for his questionable personal hygiene: Charles Lamb saw 'a crowd of young men and boys following [Dawe] along Oxford Street with admiration' at his dirty face.[27] Further down the street at no. 14 was Royal Academy President Benjamin West: West's paintings were frequently of literary subjects, and the catalogue of his gallery included literary quotations to be read alongside the viewing experience of the painting.[28] West employed Heath's son on a major engraving commission when the boy was only 16, and persuaded Stothard to stand for post of librarian to the Royal Academy.[29]

Robert Hartley Cromek, just across the street from Stothard at no. 64 from 1806, was another important focal point.[30] Cromek was an engraver-turned-entrepreneur who knew everyone there was to know in the world

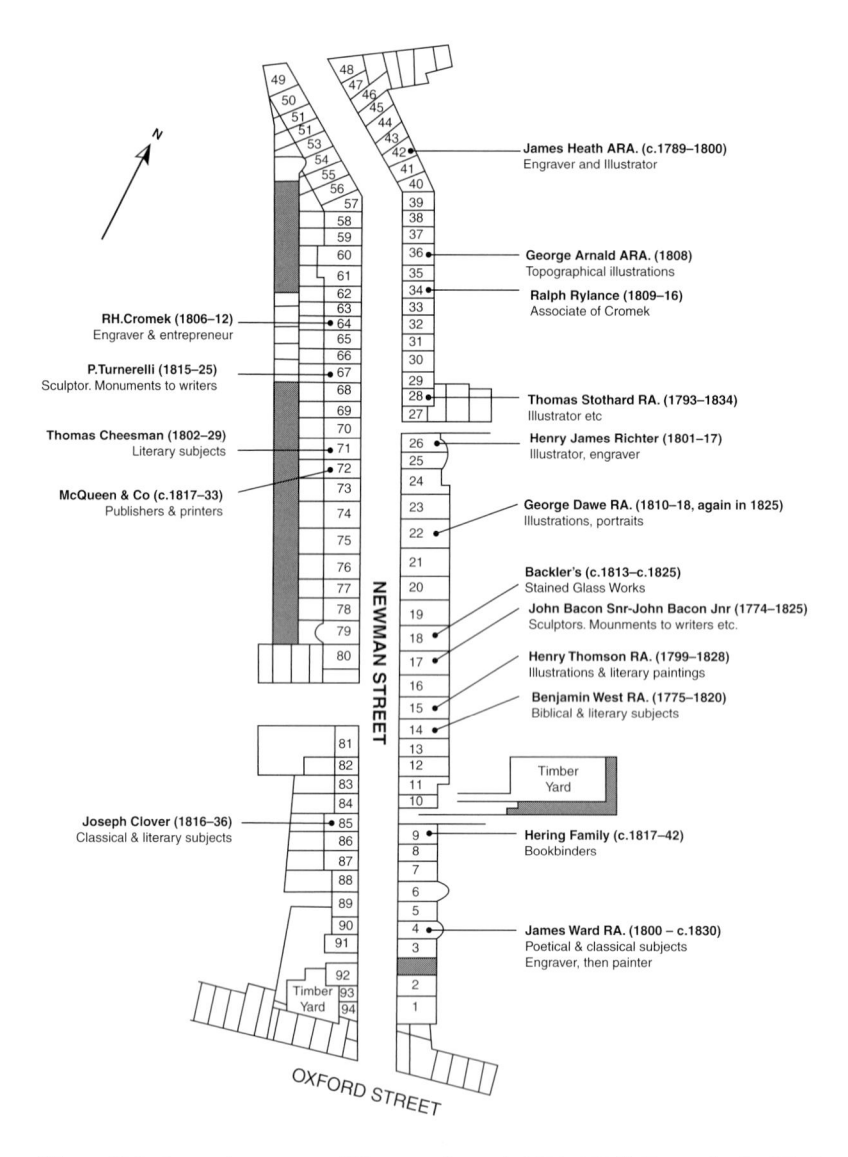

Figure 10.2 Approximate map of Newman Street (c.1800–1820). Drawn by Paul Ingle.

of visual and print culture, including Stothard; John Scholey wrote to Cromek's son on 7 January 1862 that 'your Father appeared to be on very Friendly terms with the Artists, many of whom resided in Newman St and the Neighbourhood'.[31] Thomas Cheesman, down the road at no. 71, who like Cromek trained with Bartollozi, was a subscriber to many of Cromek's ventures, and contributed work to Macklin's Poet's Gallery alongside Stothard.[32] On such a narrow street, little business was private: Ralph Rylance at no. 34 wrote to a friend in 1811 that 'I who live near them, & have heard & seen much, can testify that Cromek's conduct to his wife is most unnatural'.[33] Not all rivalry was friendly: Stothard's friendship with William Blake ended over the design of *The Canterbury Pilgrims*.[34] Newman Street artists collaborated again and again on different ventures, employed each other, competed with each other, and socialized together; Cox-Johnson claims that their children played together.[35] For Gatrell, the turn of the nineteenth-century saw 'a diminished understanding of and need for the old bohemian lifestyles and networks. In an increasingly professionalised art world and a more diversified market, artists followed the money'.[36] But in fact, the Newman Street artists were almost as reliant upon networks and connections as Gatrell's eighteenth-century 'First Bohemians' were.

The desire to cluster together and make use of personal and professional affiliations was understandable when Newman Street's artists used networks to build supportive professional connections. Accounts of the area from the Victorian period emphasize its fall from grace: writing in the 1840s, Thackeray's sketch 'The Artists' depicts Artists' Street as a gothic ruin, as if symptomatic of a gracious civilization in decay:

> Look at Newman Street. Has earth, in any dismal corner of her great round face, a spot more desperately gloomy? The windows are spotted with wafers, holding up ghastly bills, that tell you the house is 'To Let.' [...] here, above all places, must painters take up their quarters, – day by day must these reckless people pass Ahasuerus's treble gate. There was my poor friend, Tom Tickner (who did those sweet things for 'The Book of Beauty'). [...] The street begins with a bailiff's, and ends with a hospital. I wonder how men live in it, and are decently cheerful, with this gloomy, double-barrelled moral pushed perpetually into their faces. Here, however, they persist in living, no one knows why; owls may still be found roosting in Netley Abbey, and a few Arabs are to be seen at the present minute in Palmyra.
>
> The ground-floors of the houses where painters live are mostly make-believe shops, black empty warehouses, containing fabulous goods. [...] A portrait-painter lives on the first floor; a great historical genius inhabits the second. Remark the first-floor's middle drawing-room window; it is four feet higher than its two companions, and has taken a fancy to peep into the secondfloor front. [...] They seem to love solitude, and their mighty spirits rejoice in vastness and gloomy ruin.[37]

The tide of history has moved away from Newman Street; like the owls who roost in a ruined Abbey, or the people who inhabit the ruined splendour of Palmyra, the Victorian residents of Artists' Street are foolishly rowing against that tide. The very buildings of Newman Street function as a 'moral' metaphor for the problems of poverty – the bailiff's and the hospital – and then become personified themselves as if the street is so devoid of human activity that the most lively things on it are brick houses. Newman Street in this sketch paints its own moral:

> The times are changing now, and as authors are no longer compelled to send their works abroad under the guardianship of a great man and a slavish dedication, painters, too, are beginning to deal directly with the public. Who are the great picture-buyers now? – the engravers and their employers, the people.[38]

Art, like writing, has become a proper 'profession', with art and literature democratized and turned into marketable commodities; 'Tom Tickner' produces illustrations for 'The Book of Beauties' rather than high art, and the 'great historical genius' (presumably a history painter) now scrapes by in reduced circumstances. An artist's work is no longer necessarily saleable as such, but passes via the engraver to the public. Morris Eaves points out that '[t]he economic middleman and his systems – whether a mechanical invention in the ordinary sense, like the printing press, or a system of organizing production, sales, and distribution – were firmly in place and beginning to be noticed frequently by artists and authors in Blake's century'.[39] Thackeray, the successful author-illustrator, was the direct beneficiary of this change, but his sketch also mourns the passing of what is suggested was a more glorious age.

In many ways, Thackeray has a point. Newman Street runs north from Oxford Street to the east of Oxford Circus and at the start of the nineteenth century it offered proximity to healthy countryside. The street was only completed around 1770, and in the eighteenth century it was on the literal edge of the city.[40] Two pen and ink drawings by Samuel Grimm from the 1770s show the fields behind what was then the Marylebone hospital, and haymakers worked in the fields near Baker Street even as late as the 1820s.[41] It was also within easy stroll of the fashionable Portland estate, Cavendish Square, and what is now Marylebone High Street. To be 'Respectable' took on a new importance for both artists and writers from the 1790s onwards; Joseph Farrington in his *Diary* comments upon Turner's move to Harley Street (on the west side of Oxford Circus) that '[t]he district is very respectable, and central enough'.[42] Gatrell points out that '"Respectability" had never been an issue in the Covent Garden of Turner's youth, but now it was the coming word'.[43] The founding of the Royal Academy was itself an attempt to bring respectability and status to the artist,[44] so the high proportion of Academicians and Associate Academicians on Newman Street conveyed an aura of gentility to all its inhabitants, and made a statement about the professionalization of art, and by extension, of the kind of literary art which might now be called illustration. Clustering together on Newman Street allowed its artists, whether British or foreign-born, to represent themselves as a coherent community and to build professional networks to convey respectability; Jerry White notes that '[c]ollaboration was one reason for artists to cluster their studios in certain districts of the town'.[45] At the same time, however, it also suggests that such a nebulous quality as 'respectability' had to be constantly defended. Stothard's world of painters and artisans developed partly as a reaction to the kind of Covent Garden 'Bohemianism' of the mid-eighteenth century described by Gatrell, but in important ways it still bore the traces of it.

Indeed, Thackeray's sketch 'The Artists' romanticizes an earlier history for Artists' Street that was much less glamorous than Victorian reminiscences of the street might suggest. West of Oxford Circus was a newly fashionable address, but east of Oxford Circus was much less so, especially by Stothard's day.[46] Although a series of Academicians made their home in Newman Street from the 1770s onwards,[47] it was as close to impoverished St Giles as it was Mayfair or St James, and surrounded by rather more precarious neighbours. Marylebone was well known for its large population of prostitutes.[48] Richardson has shown that neighbouring Norfolk Street was a mixture of middle-, lower-middle-, and working-class inhabitants when the young Dickens spent a portion of his childhood and adolescence there in 1815 and 1829, the exact period of Stothard's residence, while '[j]ust to the south, Newman and Berners Streets preserved a little of their faded gentility, tinted with the raffishness/ of the artists and the professionalism of the doctors who congregated there'.[49] In 1817 Newman Street contained two solicitors, a timber merchant, and a chemist alongside the artists, and in neighbouring Berners Street we find a plumber and a bootmaker.[50] Newman Street residents clearly had enough to be worth stealing from: both West and Stothard were burgled, according to Old Bailey records.[51] However, Stothard bought no. 28 for what was then a 'modest sum' of £1,000 in 1793 (before 1750 large homes in fashionable West End streets could cost £3,000),[52] and his eldest son slept in the attic, perhaps because there were not that many bedrooms.[53] On Newman Street, terrace houses adapted into grand galleries sat alongside tradesmen's homes and subdivided properties; its residents were 'professional men and craftsmen interspersed with other professions and crafts'.[54] This blend of domestic and artisanal space is not in itself unusual in artist's homes;[55] more striking is the way in which Newman Street was awkwardly poised between the public and the private spheres.

Numerous residents opened their home studios as galleries to capitalize on the fashion for exhibitions fuelled by the Pall Mall literary galleries, as lists of open houses published in the *Art Journal* and the *New Picture of London* demonstrate.[56] This reveals the tensions between the literary artist as respectable professional, even celebrated genius, and the artist-illustrator as just another artisan-tradesman, a jack-of-all trades only just one rung up from the Covent Garden 'Bohemian' as described by Gatrell.

The residences of different kinds of literary artists on Newman Street make this tension quite clear. Benjamin West's house and gallery at no. 14 became part of the visual culture tourist trail for well-to-do visitors to London, and accounts of it present it very much as a residence and workplace suitable for the President of the Royal Academy. Samuel Morse recalled in 1811:

> I called in to Mr West's house in Newman/Street one morning, and [...] was shown into his studio. As I entered, a half-portrait of George III stood before me on an easel, and Mr West was sitting with his back toward me copying from it on canvas.[57]

This is the grand Academician at work, with access to royal patronage: we are a long way from Thackeray's impoverished 'Tom Tickner' here. Dorothy Richardson in 1785 describes how:

> From the British Museum we proceeded to Mr West's in Newman Street Oxford Road and were conducted down a long Gallery furnish'd with drawings into a large square Room lighted from the Roof & fill'd with paintings [...] The Door into an inner Room being left a little open, Mr Webber who was with Mr West, heard our voices, & introduced us into Mr West's Painting Room. Here we saw a very large Landscape with a view of Windsor Forest [...]. Mr West was painting a very large Picture for the King's Chapel there.[58]

Again what is emphasized here is royal patronage: West is not painting for just any client. However, Newman Street was mostly made up of terraced houses on narrow plots, not grand residences; the plan of no. 14 shows it was only two rooms deep, each of which were just over 15 feet wide.[59] West's ground floor seems, during his life-time, to have consisted of no more than two parlours, a house-passage which was extended to do service as his gallery, and a studio at the back, all framing a 'very small but elegant' garden.[60] After his death the garden was built on to create a larger gallery for his family to exhibit his works, but this enterprise went bankrupt and the house was sold in 1828.[61] West's house was not so different from the workshop of sculptor John Bacon's, who worked on monuments to Thomas

Gray, John Milton, and Samuel Johnson (among many others) at no. 17. Bacon's business 'required a team of between fifteen and twenty carvers',[62] and the plan of no. 17 shows that the narrow frontage hid a large area behind comprising modelling room, yard, shed, and workshops.[63] Newman Street was not all single family houses: Henry Howard, painter of poetic and classical subjects whose gallery was open to view, shared no. 5 with landscape painter Hugh Irvine, while another artist was a long-term guest.[64] McQueen & Co. publishers were at no. 72 in 1817, but so were the portrait painters J. Tannock and W. Thomas.[65] As Figure 10.3. shows, no. 28 was of similarly modest proportions to West's frontage. When Stothard worked on designs for The Temple of Concord (for the 1814 Peace celebrations), '[t]here was no room in the artist's own house to execute a work on so large a scale' so he painted it at the Mews.[66] Stothard's premises were serviceable, but not luxurious.

At the furthest end of the spectrum from West's premises were the various small businesses which sprang up on and around Newman Street to service the artists. The Artists' Street Academicians may have sought to distinguish themselves from 'the plebian associations with "trade"',[67] but their location on Newman Street placed them just as much in close association with the shops and small businesses upon which they relied, as it did with the wealthy patrons west of Oxford Circus. In 1817 Stothard's neighbours included a carver and gilder at no. 51, and an oil warehouse at no. 94, which may have provided artist supplies.[68] Even as late as 1878 Edward Walford writes that on Newman Street 'half the shops are devoted to the sale of articles subservient to artistic purposes'; the colourmen Sherborn and Tillyer were nearby at 321 Oxford Street.[69] The line between gentleman and tradesman was one the literary artists of Newman Street straddled all the time. An anonymous portrait of Stothard shows him in his studio at no. 28, perhaps the main first-floor reception room, dressed like a fashionable dandy but surrounded by the tools of his trade.[70] West's *Portrait of the Artist and his Family in their Back Garden* (1808–9) emphasizes 14 Newman Street as an elegant and respectable gentleman's residence, not a workplace.[71] Like Stothard's dapper portrait, such representations of the artist are only necessary if their respectability is being undermined by such images as Rowlandson's etching *The Chamber of Genius* (Figure 10.4).[72] The pose of the artist's bare-breasted young wife and the couple's obliviousness to the dangerous antics of their children is a strong contrast to the dignified domesticity of West's painting, or the fashionable professionalism of Stothard's portrait.

The Newman Street artists turned their hands to all kinds of visual media, and illustration work was a sensible commercial choice. Reliant

Figure 10.3 25–28 Newman Street, Westminster LB: front elevations (1956). London Metropolitan Archives, City of London.

upon the commercial market, where wealthy patrons were being overtaken by publishers and printsellers as commissioners of new art,[73] the location of Artists' Street within the commercial space north-east of Oxford Street had a material effect on the ways in which illustrations circulated within early nineteenth-century culture. The potentially precarious nature of artistic and literary professions made such diversification crucial: like the

Figure 10.4 Thomas Rowlandson, *The Chamber of Genius* (1812). © The Trustees of the British Museum.

writers of 'Grub Street', 'forced into a wide versatility to make words pay',[74] the residents of Artists' Street engaged in all kinds of visual forms to capitalize on their talents. This meant that illustrations circulated within print culture in all kinds of material forms, and their affiliations existed between and across different types of media. The work of the Newman Street artists shows how print culture and visual culture worked as more of a communication circuit than the two-way relationship between text and image which much illustration scholarship still assumes, and allows us to see in concrete form why the word 'illustration' had not yet settled into its modern meaning.

The epitome of this diverse approach towards visual work was Stothard, who could 'make the transitions between the similar strictly "design" requirements of the various decorative arts' and 'adapt to the diverse commercial demands of various media'.[75] For example, Stothard designed the commemorative Wellington Shield, paid for by public subscription and presented to the Duke of Wellington for his victory at Waterloo. Stothard made sure to capitalize as much as possible on his work: he had his designs reissued as prints published by his neighbours at no. 72, McQueen and Co., and then these same prints were also reproduced as cut-out-and-keep illustrations in a newspaper.[76] Visual culture from Newman Street circulates here in different forms, as an item for a noble patron but also as a commodity for general purchase and consumption within the lower-middle-class home. Benjamin West employed James Backler and his stained glass workshop at no. 18 to turn several of his literary paintings into stained glass, which were accompanied in the exhibition catalogue by quotes from the relevant texts.[77] Stothard's neighbour Cromek was another commercially minded jack-of-all-trades. Trained as an engraver, Cromek was:

> very much an economic middleman – but not in a conventional way. For most of his professional life he was not a publisher or a bookseller or a printer. He called himself a 'proprietor', that is, someone who owns a property. In Cromek's case the property was always a work of literary or graphic art. In order to promote his property he travelled throughout England and Scotland for long durations of time when such travel was expensive, arduous, and risky […].[78]

Cromek moved with apparent unconcern between literary, artistic, and publishing projects: for instance, he initiated and edited a collection of works by Burns, published by Cadell and Davies at 141 Strand, who had also published engravings by Cromek and editions illustrated by Stothard.[79] Illustration work took place within an environment where visual culture was commercial.

The complex circulation of illustration on Newman Street is further revealed by Stothard's *The Procession of the Canterbury Pilgrims* (1807), which was engraved for a print by Stothard's erstwhile neighbour James Heath in 1817, and instigated and exhibited by his neighbour Cromek.[80] This literary painting was conceived and presented as an illustration of Chaucer's poem, painted by one of the foremost book illustrators of the day, and eventually engraved by another artist well-known for his literary illustrations. Cromek also published a *Critical Description* of the painting by the artist, architect and critic William Carey.[81] It circulated as a painting on public display on Newman Street, as a print available for public purchase to be enjoyed in the privacy of home, and as a printed pamphlet which used letterpress to illustrate the image, and which included extracts from Chaucer's poem.[82] The affiliative relationships between the different versions of the image, and Carey's textual account of it, show that while Stothard the artist sought to locate himself within a concrete professional 'place' in the metropolis, visual material which he produced from this location occupied

Figure 10.5 Louis Schiavonetti and James Heath, after Thomas Stothard, *The Pilgrimage to Canterbury* (1809–17). Engraving. ©Tate, London.

a particularly fluid place within print culture in this period, when the definition of illustration was itself in flux.

The connection of *The Procession of the Canterbury Pilgrims* with Newman Street was emphasized in the advertising material, as a kind of brand marker for literary art. The *Times* announced that:

> PROCESSION OF CHAUCER'S PILGRIMS to CANTERBURY.- The Nobility and Gentry are respectfully informed that a CABINET PICTURE, painted from this most interesting and classical Subject, by Thomas Stothard, Esq. R.A. is now on view at 64, Newman-street. Tickets of admission may be had of Mr. Stothard, 23 [sic.], Newman-street, or of Mr. Cromek, at the place of Exhibition. – it is particularly requested that no money be given to the servant.[83]

Despite the admission charge of one shilling, viewers seem to have flocked to Cromek's home to see the painting. The engraver James Hopwood wrote to an acquaintance in 1807 that:

> Mr Cromek ... has lately had a picture from Chaucer's pilgrims going to Canterbury, by Mr. Stothard; which is considered amongst the greatest productions of the age. He (Mr Cromek) has for nearly two Months been exhibiting it at his House in Newman Street, and the people are still coming by the hundreds in [a] day to see it.[84]

Interest was driven by Cromek's canny promotion strategies: Cromek took the picture on tour around the country. But he also utilized the mechanisms of print culture to emphasize the Newman Street origins of the venture. Locatedness on the street is highlighted in Carey's descriptive pamphlet too: it is 'Published by Cadell and Davies for Mr Cromek, 64 Newman-Street'. Cromek was perhaps very much aware of the commercial value of Newman Street as a brand marker for literary art, as well as arts and crafts in general.

Far from being secure about the status of the image it describes, however, Carey's pamphlet reveals significant unease about the affiliative relationship between text and image. The printed description seems anxious to give illustration the status and dignity of 'high' art. Despite the antiquarian aspect of the picture, which critics including Carey praised for its faithfulness to 'authentic originals in different Museums',[85] Carey is keen to make clear that this image is not history painting, but in fact, illustration – and uses the differences to elevate illustration even higher than the more celebrated genre of history painting.[86] Carey distinguishes it from history painting because of the difficulties of its composition:

> In historical composition the Artist has many advantages in point of grouping and disposition. By placing his principal figure, or main action, anywhere near the centre, he is enabled to introduce his subordinate agents with all due variety of direction, movement, and attitude.

The nature of *The Canterbury Pilgrims*, however, makes this impossible. Stothard has chosen one moment from the poem to stand in for the entire text, making it a challenge to '[exhibit] the characters with a sufficient variety of outline and action'.[87] Stothard answers this challenge, according to Carey, by using the relationship of bodies within space to conjure up relations between them and so a sense of narrative:

> The composition displays several groups, so detached from each other, that each maintains a relative due importance, and yet so judiciously connected, that, altogether, they form one great and well-ordered group, in motion for the attainment/ of a common goal.[88]

Carey reads the string of Pilgrims as made up of four distinct groups of interrelated people, who nonetheless are united by their placement in the landscape into one coherent whole. Stothard's design, and Heath's engraving of it, suggest that the development of an enterprise (whether that is a journey or a story) depends upon the possibility of physical interactions between people. Like the networks of Newman Street, it is physical proximity within space which fosters friendships, affiliations, and rivalries.

Carey also distinguishes *The Canterbury Pilgrims* from history painting because of its subject:

> But this is not the only difficulty. When we survey a general composition from sacred or profane history, we have some important event to excite our interests and exercise our sensibility. Our passions kindle over un-merited sufferings; and we exalt as Virtue triumphs, or Vice is overthrown. Thus, we participate in the acute feelings of Jeptha and his daughter. We glow with Mutius Scevola in the camp of Porsenna. We catch the frenzy of the Conqueror, or we groan over the desolating career of Ambition, on a view of the battles of Alexander, by Le Brun. But the *Procession of the Pilgrims* exhibits no historical event, and unfolds no catastrophe. Abstractedly considered, it neither involves nor excites any individual interest. The Painter must depend upon the resources of his own mind to enrich it with incident, to charm our attention, and to give it value as an imposing spectacle, and a superior work of Art.[89]

Its literary subject presents challenges of emotion and affect. Yet the same difficulties which define the image as illustration also elevate its artistic status to an achievement beyond 'the generality of minds' of artists.[90] The reader-viewer is asked not to understand this as history, but as illustration, and to value it all the more as such. Carey reads the characters directly through the lens of Chaucer's poem: for example, what he sees as the 'sottish drunkenness' of the Miller's face he puts down to the fact that (quoting Chaucer) before the Miller left the Tabard Inn, 'Our Host saw that he was *dronken* of ale'.[91] However, Carey's insistence on how we should 'read' the image serves only to emphasize his uncertainty about the precise relationship between text and image in an increasingly commercialized visual culture in which illustrations circulate within print culture in so many different forms.

The complex circulation of images epitomized by Newman Street practices makes itself felt in the way in which the language of the visual and the verbal is fluid in Carey's account of *The Canterbury Pilgrims*. Carey acknowledges the linguistic difficulties of producing this *Critical Description* when he says of it that:

> It is an attempt to paint excellence in *detail*; to describe a variety of individual Characters, so minutely distinguished by the Poet and Painter, that *the description to be faithful must also be minute*. […] This is attended with a great difficulty; that of giving the reader some general idea of the light, shadow, colouring, and composition of a picture, which he has not seen.[92]

He tries to overcome these challenges by quoting Chaucer several times in an effort to bring the poet's text and his own textual description together, but there is an image-shaped hole in the middle. Carey elaborates on the practical difficulties of producing this *Critical Description*: of not having enough time to do it properly, or to look at the picture properly or for long enough when the printer was waiting for the sheets of copy, so that Carey fears '*In this attempt to follow the* exact *details of the Poet in Stothard's picture, I fear that, like other translators, I have often mistaken my author's meaning* [sic.]'.[93] The language of the visual and verbal is so fluid that it becomes unstable, until it begs the question 'who is illustrating whom?':[94] Stothard is an 'author', the parts of the painting are 'passages', and Carey is his 'translator'.[95] The syntax forces the reader to pay close attention: the 'Poet' could almost be Stothard, just as much as it could be Chaucer. Like Heath the eventual engraver of the print version, Carey is using technology to transpose Stothard's oil painting into a consumable form which can circulate within print culture; the engraver is a kind of 'translator' too, and Carey the writer becomes a kind of engraver.[96] Illustration is both visual and textual here.

Because the place of the visual within print culture is such a fluid and uncertain one in Carey's *Description*, he is keen to guide the reader-viewer to the correct way of seeing. Carey provides the reader with an example of 'a lady who delivered her opinions of the picture to me' with 'lively feeling' and 'good taste' which convinced him of 'the polish of high life in her manner' as well as 'the commercial respectability of her husband'.[97] There is a great concern here to link appreciation of both the visual image and its printed description to a middle-class respectability that is not remotely 'Bohemian', and to emphasize the gentility of the Newman Street world.[98] The reader is guided to proper viewing practices and almost shamed into being as good an audience for the picture as this anonymous lady, an epitome of virtuous femininity who has even written a book for children which Carey plans to pass on to his own family.[99] The circulation of print and the proper appreciation of art are held up together as examples and evidence of good taste and virtue. But the incident also registers an unease about how to define respectability, especially when the public and private spheres are made porous by the entrance of the paying public into Artists' Street homes.

This chapter has argued that working practices on Newman Street created, affected, and epitomized the ways in which visual culture circulated within metropolitan print culture. On Stothard's Newman Street, physical proximity in the city enabled the literary artist to build professional networks. Illustration was just another type of artistic production, and the relationship between text and image was one of a fluid communication circuit rather than a neatly defined binary. Artists' Street represented a moment in the Romantic period when high art, artisan tradecraft, and illustration were inseparable activities. The working practices of the Newman Street artists and their lingering place in the nineteenth-century cultural imaginary suggest that the place of the visual within print culture was constantly in flux. If the Newman Street artists were not exactly tradesman or 'Bohemians', they were definitely engaged in trying to throw off any such connotations; Stothard's world as the respectable literary artist contained more elements of Gatrell's 'First Bohemians' than either Stothard or Cromek might have cared to believe, reliant as they were upon the kinds of networks which Gatrell has shown previously existed in Covent Garden. The etymological roots of the word 'affiliation' lie in the sense of connection to a group of people and to a place, with the hint of tribalism that this carries:[100] the name Artists' Street advertises the importance of its residents' affiliation to place as well as to each other. Newman Street demonstrates how close attention to the location of production of literary images in the Romantic period enables us to see how affiliative relationships between artists, publishers, and middle-men drove the complex cycles of production, re-use, and interpretation of those images.

Notes

1 Cromek's biographer describes how 'Newman Street was popularly called "Artists" street because about 40 painters, scholars, engravers, and others practising the arts lived along its two-block length' (Dennis M. Read, *R.H. Cromek, Engraver, Editor, and Entrepreneur* (Farnham: Ashgate, 2011), 45). Shelley M. Bennett agrees that '*Newman Street was the "Artists Street," inhabited by Benjamin West, John Bacon, John Russell, James Ward, Henry Howard, and many others, amounting to almost forty artists*' (*Thomas Stothard: The Mechanisms of Art Patronage in England c. 1800* (Columbia: University of Missouri Press, 1988), 23).
2 J. T. Smith, *An Antiquarian Ramble in the Streets of London,* ed. Charles Mackay, vol. 1 (London: Richard Bentley, 1846), 126; William Tinsley, *Random Recollections of an Old Publisher*, vol. 1 (London: Simpkin, Marshall, Hamilton, Kent & Co., 1900), 189–201; Kit Wedd, with Lucy Peltz and Cathy Ross, *Artists' London: Holbein to Hirst* (London: Merrell, 2001), 77.
3 Vic Gatrell, *The First Bohemians: Life and Art in London's Golden Age* (London: Allen Lane, 2013), 386; 387.
4 Rosie Dias, *Exhibiting Englishness: John Boydell's Shakespeare Gallery and the Formation of a National Aesthetic* (New Haven, CT: Yale University Press, 2013), 23.

5 Luisa Calè, *Fuseli's Milton Gallery: 'Turning Readers Into Spectators* (Oxford: Clarendon, 2006), 64.
6 Important groundwork on 'London's Quartier Latin' has been done by Kitt Wedd and Anne Cox-Johnson (Ann Cox-Johnson, *Handlist of Painters, Sculptors & Architects associated with St. Marylebone 1760–1960* (London: Borough of St. Marylebone Public Libraries Committee, 1963), i; Wedd, *Artists' London*, 66–81), but neither Wedd nor Cox-Johnson discuss illustration.
7 'artist, n.' OED Online. June 2017. Oxford University Press, www.oed.com/view/Entry/11237?rskey=E44P1T&result=1 (accessed 2 December 2017).
8 See Editors' Introduction, 11–13 above.
9 See William St Clair, *The Reading Nation in the Romantic Period* (Cambridge: Cambridge University Press, 2004).
10 In this I am, of course, following Bruno Latour, *Reassembling the Social: An Introduction to Actor-Network-Theory* (Oxford: Oxford University Press, 2005), 175; 183.
11 Mary L. Shannon, *Dickens, Reynolds and Mayhew on Wellington Street: The Print Culture of a Victorian Street* (Ashgate, 2015).
12 See Rosemary Ashton, *142 Strand: A Radical Address in Victorian London* (London: Chatto & Windus, 2006); Devon Cox, *The Street of Wonderful Possibilities: Whistler, Wilde & Sargent in Tite Street* (London: Frances Lincoln, 2015); Dias, *Exhibiting Englishness*; James Raven Gattrell, *Bookscape: Geographies of Printing and Publishing in London Before 1800* (London: The British Library, 2014); Ruth Richardson, *Dickens and the Workhouse: Oliver Twist and the London Poor* (Oxford: Oxford University Press, 2012).
13 Julia Thomas, *Nineteenth-Century Illustration and the Digital: Studies in Word and Image* (New York: Palgrave, 2017), 97; 101.
14 Ibid., 98.
15 Ibid., 97.
16 See Shannon, *Dickens, Reynolds and Mayhew*; Gerard Curtis, *Visual Words: Art and the Material Book in Victorian England* (Aldershot: Ashgate, 2002); Calè.
17 'affiliative, adj.' OED Online, www.oed.com/view/Entry/3406 (accessed 10 November 2017).
18 Bennett, *Thomas Stothard*, vii, 23; *Johnstone's London Commercial Guide and Street Directory* (London, Johnstone, 1817), 352; *Annals of the Fine Arts* (London: Sherwood, Neely & Jones &c, 1817), 434; Mrs Bray, *Life of Thomas Stothard, R. A.* (London: John Murray, 1851); Cox-Johnson, *Handlist of Painters,* 163.
19 See Bennett, *Thomas Stothard.*
20 For more on these Literary Galleries and their relationships to reading experiences, see Calè and Haywood in this volume.
21 Bennett *Thomas Stothard.*
22 Read, *R.H. Cromek, Engraver, Editor, and Entrepreneur,* 45. Constable, Flaxman, Fuseli, Linnell, Turner, Westall, Northcote, and Opie all lived nearby on the streets surrounding Newman Street: see Edward Walford, 'Oxford Street and its northern

tributaries: Part 2 of 2' in *Old and New London: Volume 4* (London: Cassell, Petter & Galpin, 1878), 441–67. *British History Online*, www.british-history.ac.uk/old-new-london/vol4/pp441-467 (accessed 9 January 2018); David Brandon and Alan Brooke, *Marylebone and Tyburn Past* (London: Historical Publications, 2007), 93 and 143–4; Wedd, *Artists' London,* 63.

23 Street numbering taken from Richard Horwood, *Plan of the Cities of London and Westminster […] Shewing Every House* 1792–9, Westminster Archives Centre. For individual artists see the footnotes below.

24 John Heath, *The Heath Family Engravers 1779–1878*, 3 vols (Aldershot: Scolar Press, 1993); *Exeter Working Papers in Book History: The London book trades 1775–1800: a preliminary checklist of members,* http://bookhistory.blogspot.co.uk/2007/01/london-1775-1800-h.html (accessed 6 October 2017); Cox-Johnson, *Handlist of Painters,* 163. For biographical accounts of Stothard and Heath, which also contain bibliographies of their prolific output, see (as well as Bennett): Bray, *Life of Thomas Stothard*; A. C. Coxhead, *Thomas Stothard, R. A.: An Illustrated Monograph* (London: A. H. Bullen 1906); Heath. *The Heath Family Engravers.*

25 Bennett, *Thomas Stothard,* 14; *Oxford Dictionary of National Biography*; *Annals,* 432; *The Picture of London for 1804* (London: R. Phillips, 1804), 278; *Exeter Working Papers*; Michael Bryan, *Bryan's Dictionary of Painters and Engravers,* ed. George Williamson (London: Macmillan 1903–4), 4: 231; Cox-Johnson, *Handlist of Painters,* 163.

26 Kenneth Neill Cameron, ed., *Shelley and His Circle* (Cambridge: Harvard University Press, 1961–73), 3: 25; Emily W. Sunstein, *Mary Shelley: Romance and Reality* (Baltimore, MD: John's Hopkins University Press, 1989), 50; *ONDB*; *Annals,* 425; *Bryan's Dictionary*, 2: 16, Cox-Johnson, *Handlist of Painters,* 162.

27 Charles Lamb, 'Recollections of a late Royal Academician' (1831), in *Correspondence and Works of Charles Lamb* (London: E. Moxon, 1870), 3: 406.

28 *Johnstone's,* 352; *ODNB*; *Annals,* 435; Cox-Johnson, *Handlist of Painters,* 161; *Catalogue of Pictures and Drawings by the late Benjamin West* (London: C. H. Reynell, 1827).

29 Heath, *The Heath Family Engravers*, 2: 9; Bray, *Life of Thomas Stothard,* 163.

30 See Read, *R.H. Cromek, Engraver, Editor, and Entrepreneur.*

31 Letters Addressed to T. H. Cromek. University of Edinburgh Library. Quoted in Read, *R.H. Cromek, Engraver, Editor, and Entrepreneur,* 45.

32 *ODNB*; *Exeter Working Papers*; *Annals,* 446; Cox-Johnson, *Handlist of Painters,* 164.

33 Letter from Ralph Rylance to William Roscoe, 23 November 1811. Liverpool City Libraries. Quoted in Read, *R.H. Cromek, Engraver, Editor, and Entrepreneur,* 145.

34 See Read, *R.H. Cromek, Engraver, Editor, and Entrepreneur*, 55–69.

35 Cox-Johnson, *Handlist of Painters,* ii. And it was mostly men: although the Cosways lived nearby, and home studios suggest the possibility that wives and husbands worked together, like the Blakes.

36 Gatrell, *The First Bohemians*, 387.
37 W. M. Thackeray, 'The Artists' (from 'Character Sketches').
38 Thackeray, 'The Artists'.
39 Morris Eaves, 'Blake and the Artistic Machine', *PMLA*, 92 (1977): 904.
40 Walford, 'Oxford Street and its northern tributaries', 406–41.
41 London Metropolitan Archives Collage Collection. *Newman Street*. Samuel Grimm; Richardson, *Dickens and the Workhouse*, 55.
42 Joseph Farrington, *The Farington Diary*, 12 November 1798.
43 Gatrell, *The First Bohemians*, 387.
44 Holger Hoock, *The King's Artists: The Royal Academy of Arts and the Politics of British Culture, 1760–1840* (Oxford: Clarendon, 2003), 30–1.
45 Jerry White, *London in the Eighteenth-Century: A Great and Monstrous Thing*, (London: Vintage, 2013), 282; See also Shannon, *Dickens, Reynolds and Mayhew*, 23. On the 'clustering' of trades, see Ronald Abler, John S. Adams and Peter Gould, *Spatial Organisation: The Geographer's View of the World* (Englewood Cliffs, NJ: Prentice-Hall, 1971), 303; 209; 303.
46 Gatrell, *The First Bohemians*, 386–7; Wedd, *Artists' London*, 68; Survey of London draft chapters, *South-East Marylebone*, vols 51 and 52, www.ucl.ac.uk/bartlett/architecture/research/survey-london/current-area-study-south-east-marylebone (accessed 19 January 2018).
47 Hoock, *The King's Artists*, 30.
48 Gordon Mackenzie, *Marylebone: Great City North of Oxford Street* (London: Macmillan, 1972), 94.
49 Richardson, *Dickens and the Workhouse*, 53–4.
50 Johnstone's 1817 Commercial Guide.
51 Old Bailey Proceedings Online, April 1803, trial of SARAH FRANKLIN (t18030420–38); www.oldbaileyonline.org (accessed 6 October 2017); Bray, *Life of Thomas Stothard*, 30–1.
52 Christopher Chalkin, *The Rise of the English Town, 1650–1850* (Cambridge: CUP, 2001), 30.
53 Bray, *Life of Thomas Stothard*, 29; 199.
54 Cox-Johnson, *Handlist of Painters*, ii.
55 On artists' homes see Giles Walkley, *Artists' Houses in London 1764–1914* (Aldershot: Scolar Press, 1994); Angus Whitehead, '"humble but respectable": Recovering the Neighbourhood Surrounding William and Catherine Blake's Last Residence, No. 3 Fountain Court Strand, c.1820–27', *University of Toronto Quarterly*, 80: 4 (Fall 2011): 858–79; Michael Phillips, 'No. 36 Castle Street East: A Reconstruction of James Barry's House and the Making of *The Birth of Pandora*', *The British Art Journal*, 9: 1 (Spring, 2008): 15–27; Gatrell, *The First Bohemians*, 148–53, on Blake's home-cum-studio in Fountain Court, and on squalid artistic 'Bohemia' more generally.
56 See, for example, *The New Picture of London* (London: Samuel Leigh, 1818), 273.

57 Edward Lind Morse, ed., *Samuel F. B. Morse: His Letters and Journals*, vol. 1 (New York: Kraus Reprint, 1972), 42–3.
58 Dorothy Richardson, *Travel Journals*, 5 vols., MS., John Rylands Library, University of Manchester, Ryl. Eng. MS 1123, ff. 311–12, quoted in Wedd, *Artists' London*, 70.
59 George Robins. *Plan of Benjamin West's House*, 1829, engraving and coloured wash. Westminster Archives Centre.
60 Leigh Hunt, *The Autobiography of Leigh Hunt with Reminiscences of Friends and Contemporaries* (London: 1850), 147–8.
61 Wedd, *Artists' London*, 72.
62 Ibid., 73.
63 *Plan of John Bacon's Premises at 17 Newman Street*, 1769, London. London Metropolitan Archives.
64 Cox-Johnson, *Handlist of Painters,* 161; *Annals*, 434.
65 *Johnstone's*, 353; Michael Twyman, *A Directory of London Lithographic Printers 1800–1850* (London: Printing Historical Society, 1976), 40; *Annals*, 434; Cox-Johnson, *Handlist of Painters,* 164.
66 Bray, *Life of Thomas Stothard,* 148.
67 Wedd, *Artists' London,* 31.
68 *Johnstone's*, 352–3.
69 Walford, 'Oxford Street and its northern tributaries', 441–67; Wedd, *Artists' London*, 73.
70 Anon., *Portrait of Thomas Stothard*, c.1800, oil on canvas, 89 x 68.5 cm, Oxfordshire, Roy Davids Ltd, reproduced in Wedd, *Artists' London,* 73.
71 Benjamin West, *Portrait of the Artist and his Family in their Back Garden* (1808–9), oil on canvas. Smithsonian Institution, Washington, DC. Reproduced in Wedd, *Artists' London*, 71.
72 Wedd, *Artists' London,* fig. 64; Gatrell, *The First Bohemians,* fig. 64.
73 'By the end of the eighteenth-century, the print-seller publisher had become a major source of patronage for British artists.' Bennett, *Thomas Stothard,* 44.
74 White, *London in the Eighteenth-Century,* 259.
75 Bennett, *Thomas Stothard,* 44.
76 Balmanno Collection. Vol. 4. British Museum Prints & Drawings. 1849,0721. 1812-18.
77 *Catalogue of Pictures Painted on Glass […], Now Exhibiting at Mr. Backler's Stained Glass Works* (London: John Tyler, 1818); *Johnstone's*, 352; www.backlers.com (accessed 3 November2017).
78 Read, *R.H. Cromek, Engraver, Editor, and Entrepreneur,* 148.
79 Read, *R.H. Cromek, Engraver, Editor, and Entrepreneur*, 107; see, for example, Sir Nicholas Crisp, Bt. by Robert Hartley Cromek, published by T. Cadell & W. Davies, after Unknown artist, line engraving, published 1 May 1795, 10 5/8 in. x 8 in. (270 mm x 203 mm) paper size. National Portrait Gallery. NPG D8724, www.npg.org.uk/collections (accessed 20 July 2017).

80 For a full account of the rather tortuous genesis of the painting and the engraving, see Read, *R.H. Cromek, Engraver, Editor, and Entrepreneur*, 45–69.
81 William P. Carey, *Critical Description of the Procession of Chaucer's Pilgrims to Canterbury* (London: Cadell and Davies for R. H. Cromek, 64 Newman-street, 1808). See, as a comparison, William Blake's *Descriptive Catalogue* of his own version of *Canterbury Pilgrims* in David V. Erdman, ed., *The Complete Poetry and Prose of William Blake* (Berkeley: University of California Press, 1982).
82 Technological developments enabled this: steel engraving allowed for more reproduction of images than copper engraving, because copper plates were softer and wore out quicker. See Gary Kelly in *The Oxford Handbook of the Eighteenth-Century Novel*, ed. J. A. Downie (Oxford: OUP, 2016), 512.
83 'PROCESSION OF CHAUCER'S PILGRIMS to CANTERBURY', *Times*, 5 March 1807.
84 Letter from James Hopwood to James Montgomery, 3rd April 1807, Sheffield City Libraries, SLPS 36–95, quoted in Read, *R.H. Cromek, Engraver, Editor, and Entrepreneur*, 48.
85 Carey, *Critical Description*, 11.
86 Ibid., 9.
87 Ibid., 9–10.
88 Ibid., 76–7.
89 Ibid., 10.
90 Ibid., 9.
91 Ibid., 15.
92 Ibid., 14.
93 Ibid., 77.
94 Martin Meisel, *Realizations: Narrative, Pictorial, and Theatrical Arts in Nineteenth-Century England* (Princeton, NJ: Princeton University Press, 1983), 248.
95 Carey, *Critical Description*, 77; 75; 77.
96 On the relationship between writing and engraving see J. Hillis Miller, *Illustration* (London: Reaktion Books, 1992), 93, and Curtis, *Visual Words*, 7–49.
97 Carey, *Critical Description*, 76.
98 Although it would not have taken place on Newman Street, as Carey saw the painting in Liverpool (Read, *R.H. Cromek, Engraver, Editor, and Entrepreneur*, 53).
99 Carey, *Critical Description*, 76.
100 'affiliation, n.' OED Online, www.oed.com/view/Entry/3405 (accessed 10 November 2017).

11 | The Development of Magazine Illustration in Regency Britain – The Example of *Arliss's Pocket Magazine* 1818–1833

BRIAN MAIDMENT

Despite its modest appearance and content, *The Pocket Magazine* offers much of interest to the print historian (see Figure 11.1). Indeed, its ordinariness is in many ways exemplary of the ways in which significant developments within print culture take place quietly beyond well-known and frequently cited experimental publications. The *Pocket Magazine* was, by contemporary standards and under a variety of publishers' imprints and different names, long lived (1818–1833), certainly long enough to suggest a shift from Regency assumptions about the nature and readership of periodicals towards something more obviously Victorian. As its title implies, *The Pocket Magazine* was self-consciously proud of its small size which certainly allowed the magazine to be accommodated in a relatively capacious pocket. The miniaturizing of the format of many print genres at this time is widely apparent. The shift towards wood engraving as a major form of illustration perhaps suggested that the ideal page should be something close in size to the dimensions of a box wood vignette. Cheapness of production may also have been a factor. More substantially, the changes in scale, again expressed in the title of *The Pocket Magazine*, posit the 'pocket' against the library table underlining the dialogue between the vernacular and the genteel that animates the development of a wide range of Regency print culture. Put another way, the life of *The Pocket Magazine* coincides precisely with the historical moment that saw the genteel monthly or weekly miscellany, primarily illustrated by metal engraving, give way to a new wave of cheap weeklies making much wider use of the wood engraving that sought to combine the informative with the entertaining.[1] *The Pocket Magazine* demonstrates exactly these shifts in emphasis and address, retaining aspects of established magazines like *The Gentleman's Magazine* while at the same time reaching out to a broader and perhaps less sophisticated readership with only limited leisure time. *The Pocket Magazine* sat half-way between genteel monthlies like *The Gentleman's Magazine* and the new informational miscellanies like *The Mirror of Literature* in terms of its content (predominantly fiction). The emphasis on size ('the pocket' rather than 'the library' or 'the drawing room') suggested that its aim was to combine cheapness and handiness.

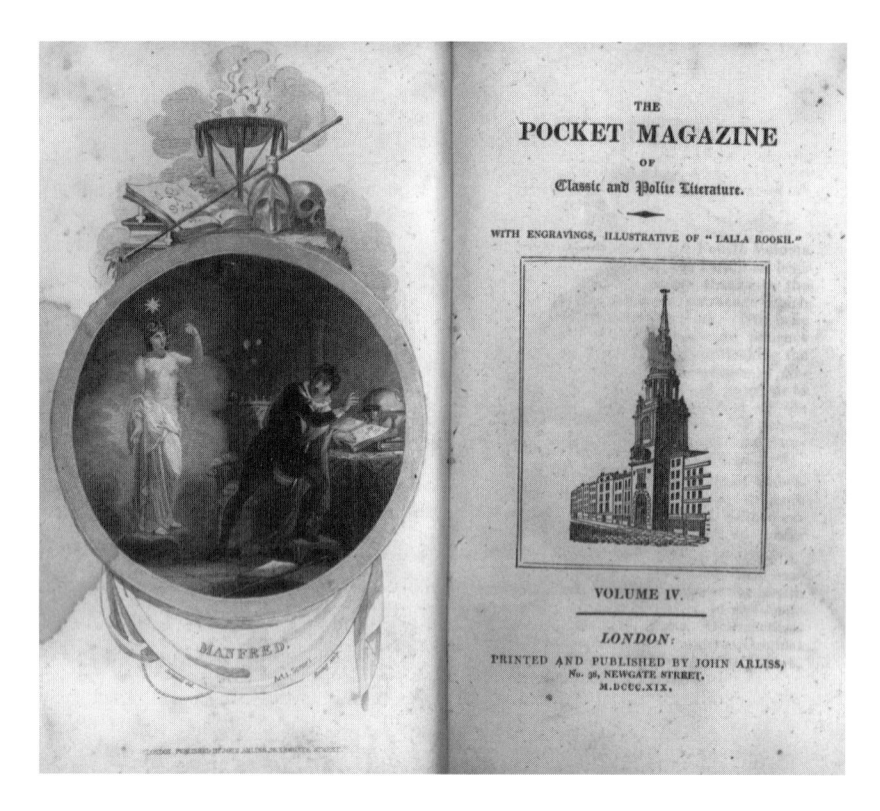

Figure 11.1 Title opening to volume IV of *The Pocket Magazine* (John Arliss 1819). Author's collection.

These shifts in format, readership, and taste were underpinned by access to the newly available representational media of wood engraving and lithography. Unusually for such a modest publication, *The Pocket Magazine* used, in its 15 years of publication, metal engraving (Figure 11.1), wood engraving (Figure 11.2) and lithography (Figure 11.3) to supply its illustrations, and the most interesting print historical narrative that the magazine has to tell concerns the various ways in which it endeavoured to assimilate new reprographic technology, aesthetic ambition, and cheapness into a single format that would attract both established readers of periodicals and a new, less-known class of less affluent but culturally ambitious consumers.

In the course of its quite lengthy history, *Arliss's Pocket Magazine of Classic and Polite Literature* was successively issued as a monthly magazine by three publishers. The first series was published by John, and later Henry Arliss, and its run comprised 13 half yearly volumes published between 1818 and to 1824, when it was passed on to, or purchased by, Knight and Lacey, and re-launched as a New Series under the full title of *Arliss's Pocket Magazine*

THE
POCKET MAGAZINE

OF

Classic and Polite Literature.

WITH ENGRAVINGS ILLUSTRATIVE OF THE RECENT WORKS
OF THE REV. G. CRABBE.

VOLUME VII.

LONDON:

PRINTED AND PUBLISHED BY JOHN ARLISS,
STAINING-LANE, CHEAPSIDE.
M.DCCC.XXI.

Figure 11.2 Title-page to volume VII of *The Pocket Magazine* (John Arliss 1821). Author's collection.

Figure 11.3 Lithographed illustration by Robert Seymour from volume 5 of the Knight and Lacey 'New Series' of *The Pocket Magazine* (1826). Author's collection.

of Classic and Polite Literature thus maintaining the magazine's association with its first publisher despite the change of ownership. Five volumes were published by Knight and Lacey between 1824 and 1826, when the title was taken over by James and later Joseph Robins, who published 14 more half yearly volumes between 1827 and 1833 under the title of *The Pocket Magazine – Robins's Series*.[2] As its title suggested, one defining feature of the magazine was its small size,[3] but illustration was also central to its definition of what a well-developed miscellany should be offering its readers especially by bringing art produced by established artists to a broader reading public in however miniaturized a form.[4] It is the aim of this chapter to suggest some of the ways in which the small scale shifts in the nature of *The Pocket Magazine's* illustrations are indicative of wider changes in the development of cheap mass circulation magazines in the Regency period and point to the volatile, experimental, and fraught nature of publishing and the market place for print in this period. It is also an attempt to think through the role of illustration in magazines which were 'low' in content costs, but relatively ambitious in terms of production costs.

i

All three of *The Pocket Magazine's* publishers were interesting, and their combined business histories form almost a paradigm of the high risk opportunism that characterized the market place in London in the 1820s and 1830s. John and later his son Henry Arliss essentially ran a printing business that used its commercial resources to venture on out into publishing when an appropriate opportunity arose. The printer/publisher/entrepreneur combination is of course crucial to the development of early Victorian print, and underpinned publications such as *Punch* and *The Illustrated London News* which were capitalized in this way. Arliss published a number of serial publications that drew on the new opportunities offered by an expanding market place – song-books (*The Melodist: and Mirthful Olio* ran for at least three volumes in the late 1820s, and other serialized Arliss song-books include *The Pegasus* (1832)[5]), children's primers and educational textbooks gathered under the general designation of the 'Juvenile Library', and other relatively low risk ventures. According to the obituary notice published in *The Gentleman's Magazine* Arliss was 'celebrated as one of the most elegant printers of his time' and 'possessed a considerable taste in embellishing juvenile works with wood engravings'.[6] The obituary goes on to link Arliss's name with Whittington as having 'largely contributed to the revival of the beautiful in the art of printing', and he worked in collaboration with Whittingham on a number of publications, including a long satirical poem called *Paddy Hew* that featured a hand-coloured wood-engraved frontispiece. Their major joint project seems to have been the 26 volumes of *The London Theatre*, a collection of play texts collected and edited by Thomas Dibdin that was begun in 1815 thus forming one of several such ventures that were simultaneously competing for customers. In 1822, as well as *The Pocket Magazine*, John Arliss was simultaneously issuing an even smaller sized monthly journal, *The Gem*, which was differentiated by containing only fiction, or, as the subtitle put it: 'Select and Entertaining Tales. Prose and Verse. From recent Works of Merit'[7] – piracies, in short. Each issue was prefaced by a full-page engraving, and the opening page offered two tiny wood engravings enclosed in ruled frames – the first of these, which gave the journal's title, grew more elaborate as the publication continued. More varied and sophisticated use of small-scale wood engraving was shown in *Arliss's Literary Collections: Original and Selected*, reprinted in volume form by Houlston & Sons around 1830 from a run of original 12 page issues.[8] This work made a title-page claim to be 'illustrated with numerous superb wood engravings by the most eminent artists' and it does show considerable decorative sensibility in assimilating a broad range of variously shaped and framed illustrations into the text. The appeal of bringing 'the most eminent artists' to readers through even small-scale and relatively unsophisticated engraved versions of their works was one that was widely acknowledged across the cheap miscellanies produced in the 1820s. As interesting as this scattering of images is, the publication's slide in content from an anthology of literary texts towards a general interest magazine, with topographical descriptions and historical anecdotes taking over from album poetry as its central interest, is clearly visible.

These kinds of publications suggest that, while remaining a relatively small-scale publisher, Arliss was willing to engage in the production of modest texts, and especially illustrated books and magazines, across a wide spectrum of forms and genres. In practice his chosen kinds of ventures – song-books, play texts, serialized miscellanies, and children's books – were exactly those unambitious but increasingly popular genres that were underpinning the expansion of the print market at this time and making illustration an essential element in attracting a broader reading public. The cheapness and versatility of the wood engraving formed an essential element in the production of these print genres, and had clearly begun to outlive its reputation as a largely vernacular reprographic medium associated with 'low' cultural forms such as the song-sheet or broadside. Publications like

The Gem and *Arliss's Literary Collections* showed the firm's genuine ability to use wood engravings in a highly effective and decorative way, making a virtue of the smallness of scale implied by the use of boxwood blocks, and giving tininess in book production considerable aesthetic power. *Arliss's Pocket Magazine* was to some extent visionary in giving 'pocket-sized' literature a shape, form, and status of its own. John Arliss died in April 1825, and his son Henry took over and continued the business, though perhaps without his father's ability to foster successful projects.

Knight and Lacey operated at a much higher level of visibility and risk, and their business ambitions eventually led to their downfall. Knight and Lacey's specialism, an important one in the history of print culture at this time, was that of finding a variety of ways of turning small units of information – the 'snippet' or the 'anecdote' – into book-length publications that worked through accumulation, miscellaneity, and profusion rather than narrative drive or overall cohesiveness. Loosely organized by topic or subject, such books of accumulated information looked to the emergence of niche markets and interest groups which were big enough to return profits on bulky and often quite sustained multi-volume projects. In this mode, Knight and Lacey published a three-volume *Dramatic Table Talk* (1825) that assembled together a mass of theatrical anecdotes and gossip. *Celebrated Trials* (6 volumes 1825) and *Anecdotes of the Schools of Painting* (3 volumes 1825) performed similar functions for the law and for fine art. *Public Characters: Biographical and Characteristic Sketches with Portraits, of the Most Distinguished Personages of the Present Age*, with engraved portraits, was published in three volumes in 1828.

Of high significance for the wider history of print culture was the firm's interest in magazines of popular information that brought three factors to bear on the assembling of nuggets of information – seriality, wood-engraved illustration and, in many cases, a narrowly defined niche readership. Three of Knight and Lacey's magazines were of major importance in the democratizing of specialist knowledge in the 1820s and 1830s – *The Lancet* (1823 to date), *The Chemist* (1824–5), and *The Mechanics' Magazine* (1823–73). *The Mechanics' Magazine* was Knight and Lacey's most significant magazine, and was pioneering in its translation of technical processes into visual information by means of small-scale wood engraving aimed at a new artisan readership. *The Pulpit* (1823–71) was another significant element in the firm's portfolio of journals. The firm also published in the mid-1820s (1826–7) *The Library for the People*, a pre-*Penny Magazine* weekly serial encyclopaedia aimed at a broad-based artisan readership. In 1827 this magazine morphed into *The Chimney Corner Companion*, a compilation of miscellaneous information published in 24-page monthly parts. Each issue was led by a wood cut or engraved first page, and also contained a range of small-scale images dropped into the text. Early numbers had combined wood-engraved vignettes with full-page copper engravings, but the convenience and cheapness of wood engraving gradually ousted the need for the more expensive metal-engraved images. In style, the wood engravings comprised highly finished vignettes, detailed framed crudely engraved images, and simple line drawings, thus drawing on the full range of stylistic possibilities offered by the medium. Other of the firm's publications of this kind included a project of William Cobbett's called *The Housekeeper's Magazine* (1825–6) which was an early version of such successful early Victorian magazines as *The Family Economist*, and *The Adventurer of the Nineteenth Century* (1823–4), an early journal of travel reportage.

In all these projects, the illustrated magazine can be seen moving away from a general interest publication into much more precisely defined niche interests. The widely diverse magazines published by Knight and Lacey suggest the extent to which the wood engraving had by this time been assimilated into widespread use for both decorative and explanatory purposes. While these publications of the late 1820s acknowledged that wood engraving had a crucial role in developing not just Knight and Lacey's list but print culture more widely, the firm nonetheless showed considerable willingness to experiment with different kinds of illustration not all aimed at the mass market. Several of their multi-volume collections, like *Public Characters*, used traditional engraved portraits as a form of illustration, and the linear simplicity of these full-length portraits was effective. As a firm widely interested in publishing Byron's works, Knight and Lacey published early biographical studies of the poet, the most significant being William Parry's *Last Days of Lord Byron* (1825), which was illustrated with three coloured aquatints and an engraved frontispiece by the firm's house artist Robert Seymour, suggesting both the firm's willingness to reach out to a genteel market for expensive books when appropriate and their recognition of Seymour's ability in more ambitious artistic genres than wood engraving.

Another sign of Knight and Lacey's interest in the genres, forms, and reprographic variety becoming available to the print market in the 1820s was their exploitation of complex engraved title-pages to give weight and dignity to volumes that were subsequently more modestly illustrated elsewhere. The volume reissue of the first two volumes of *The Mechanics' Magazine* provide two notable examples of elaborately engraved emblematic title-pages of this kind, although nothing in this idiom could be more impressive than the title-page of Robert Stuart's *A Descriptive History of the Steam Engine* (1823). Such a deep engagement with the wide range of available reprographic media available, and equally intense acknowledgement of the drive towards cheaper illustrations were crucial to Knight and Lacey's stewardship of *The Pocket Magazine* between 1824 and 1826.

While Knight and Lacey's ambitions outran their commercial flair (the firm went temporarily bankrupt in 1826), *The Pocket Magazine*'s third publisher, Joseph Robins, enjoyed sustained success as a specialist in publishing illustrated books, particularly humorous works, and especially works by the rising star of book illustration, George Cruikshank. Cruikshank's biographer, Robert Patten, describes Joseph Robins's firm as 'solid' and 'diversified', and describes in some detail Cruikshank's happy alliance with Robins on many projects at a key moment in Cruikshank's career.[9] Robins came from a long family line that had been involved with the print trades not just as printers and publishers but also as booksellers, stationers and sellers of paper hangings. His importance in relation to the history of periodicals is two-fold. First, he pioneered the use of coloured illustrations in a number of periodicals, including two – the *Ladies Pocket Magazine* (1824–36) and the *Gentleman's Pocket Magazine* (1827–30) – that used 'pocket' in their title. These two magazines drew on Robins's previous experience with another periodical that included Cruikshank colour illustrations, *The Humourist*, which ran in 40 6d. parts between 1819 and 1820.[10] The presence of Cruikshank makes clear Robins's second major contribution to the history of periodical illustration – he was one of the first publishers to take full advantage of an emerging taste in the late 1810s and early 1820s for comic illustration, and his wider publishing activities gave him access not just to Cruikshank's work but also to a mass of humorous illustrations being published in volume form under his name.

Robins launched a more up-market illustrated magazine, *The Dublin and London Magazine*, with some Cruikshank illustrations, in 1825, and it ran until 1827. But he was well aware of the need for a diversified and broad-based list of periodical titles if his firm was to take full advantage of the newly available range of readers who might be persuaded to subscribe to attractive and well-illustrated magazines. The genteel end of his market was substantially catered for – in addition to the two magazines already cited, Robins launched the *Young Gentleman's Magazine of Amusement and Information* (in 1826), and published the long-running *Ladies Museum* (1798–1832) throughout the 1820s. But Robins had not neglected the market for miscellanies, although his *Repository of Modern Literature*, which ran for two volumes in 1823, had been a more complex and expensive publication than most titles published in this fashionable but largely down-market mode. Robins had illustrated the *Repository* with both elaborate full-page metal engravings and carefully wrought wood-engraved vignettes. In volume I the wood engravings are largely of the kinds of topographical subjects widely found in the miscellanies, but volume II launched a long series of Shakespeare illustrations to accompany descriptions of scenes from the plays. The full-page engravings were mostly portraits of eminent individuals in a wide variety of styles, but all with some sense of aesthetic ambition. In many cases these portraits were imported from other of Robins's publications, which gave the plates in the *Repository* a somewhat miscellaneous appearance. The rather weird depiction of the renowned London street sweeper Charles Mackey, with its surreally detailed head imposed on a crudely sketched background (vol. II, 306) was taken from *Wonderful Characters*, a three-volume publication that Robins had published in 1821. It was Robins's ability to draw on the considerable stock of images, and especially comic images, held elsewhere in his publications together with his experience of publishing a wide range of differing types of illustration that made him an obvious person to take over the struggling *Pocket Magazine* from the bankrupt Knight and Lacey.

Robins, despite having *The Pocket Magazine* to manage, extended his interest in publishing a popular informative/entertaining illustrated weekly miscellany throughout the 1820s. In August 1829 he took over *The Portfolio of Amusement and Instruction in History, Science, Literature, the Fine Arts, & c.*, a 3d. weekly magazine published by John Duncombe since 1823 that had reached a 'new series' with its 168th issue on 25 July 1829. A feature of Duncombe's version of *The Portfolio* had been the quality of the illustrations which were set in a more spacious page with larger type than usual for such a type of publication. The illustrations, used as part of the issue title-page, featured tonally quite sophisticated lithographs which, while replicating the formal qualities and Gothic tropes of the wood-engraved illustrations for serially published popular fiction at this time, were distinctly more ambitious. This ambitiousness was acknowledged by publishing each illustration within a ruled frame to suggest its pictorial qualities, thus distinguishing these illustrations from the mass of vignette wood engraving that was the usual reprographic form for such miscellanies. The first issue of the magazine published by Robins, no. 177,[11] made immediate changes to *The Portfolio*, replacing Duncombe's ambitious images, which had sought to give weight to the Gothic commonplaces of fictional illustration, with lively, quite large-scale but crudely drawn wood-engraved vignettes. Some of Robins's title-page vignettes drew on comic graphic tropes rather than the more familiar theatrical melodrama and gothic settings more frequently used to illustrate the short fictions published in the miscellanies, thus introducing an obvious modal shift from literary seriousness to a more boisterous humour. Robins continued to tinker with illustrative possibilities through the next few issues of the magazine, dropping small topographical vignettes into the text to preface short, descriptive articles, and occasionally offering an issue with a separate full-page engraved plate. The 17 October 1829 issue, for example, accompanied its lead article on 'Death of the King's Giraffe', with an engraving of 'The King's Cameleopard' that seems to have been imported from another publication. Other issues offered portraits of well-known actors like T. P. Cooke and Charles Keane. But as the magazine endured, Robins's illustrative repertoire began to narrow, and by the summer of 1830 many title-pages for issues of *The Portfolio* were displaying 'Topographical Illustrations' and then 'Metropolitan Illustrations' comprising small-scale wood engravings rather obviously reused from the multi-volume surveys of London topography that Robins was publishing elsewhere in volume form. Such a retreat from full-page metal engravings to comic vignettes and small-scale topographical wood engravings suggests lowered expectations for the graphic content of the magazine. Or it may be that the unambitious wood engraving had become so commonplace by this time in the early 1830s as an illustrative medium that relatively down-market publishers felt little pressure to maintain the aesthetic and technical ambitiousness of the previous decade. Under Robins's guidance not just *The Portfolio* but also *The Pocket Magazine* certainly celebrated the humorous wood engraving in an unapologetic way as appropriate for its readers.

ii

Superficially, all the various series of *The Pocket Magazine* subscribed to the same pattern of illustration. Each issue of the magazine ran a full-page (though of course small in size) engraved plate either borrowed from other 'pocket' editions of literary classics or commissioned for use in the magazine.[12] These plates were used to give dramatic graphic shape to extracts from the well-known literary works that formed the central content of the magazine. Other similar engraved plates were used as frontispieces for the volume republication of the magazine. These relatively sophisticated engravings were combined with small-scale wood-engraved vignettes used to mark the opening page of each issue. The tiny wood engravings varied enormously in manner and level of finish, some having the crudeness of vernacular woodcuts for crude broadside publications while others had the compact microcosmic energy and high finish of the emblem, thus recalling the graphic decoration that accompanied the publication of many volumes of eighteenth-century poetry. Such a combination of metal engraving and wood engraving clearly mediated between the conflicting cultural alignments implicit in the miscellany – genteel against vernacular, the need for cheapness against traditional aesthetic ambitions, and, perhaps, decorative effectiveness against both naturalism and the informational. As already suggested, some of the full-page engravings, often by distinguished painters and illustrators like Richard Westall and Henry Corbould,[13] both prolific draughtsmen widely commissioned to produce illustrations in the early nineteenth century, were probably imported from previously published illustrated editions of British writers such as Byron, Moore, and Scott.

The Pocket Magazine, in its successive iterations, was thus deeply entrenched within the experiences of publishers of illustrated serial publications at a moment of both opportunity and difficulty. The opportunities were largely the outcome of a rapidly increasing potential readership for diverting and instructive literature, the recognition of seriality as a valuable mode of publication, and the widespread introduction of reprographic methods, especially the wood engraving and lithography, which could provide, speedily, relatively cheap illustration. The difficulties were perhaps less obvious, but nonetheless powerful formative influences, and the remainder of this chapter seeks to elaborate the complex problems that confronted publishers, editors, and illustrators at this time, difficulties that were substantially re-enacted on a much bigger scale by the widely known and celebrated journals of the late Regency period such as *The Mirror of Literature*, *The Penny Magazine* and *The Saturday Magazine*.

iii

The first difficulty was one of content – the relentless demands of periodicity meant that fresh material needed to be found for each weekly or monthly issue of a magazine. Verbal content could be relatively easily solved through a combination of unashamed piracy from other periodicals with the reprinting of widely available literary texts. Illustrations were more difficult to find on a regular basis. Some use could be made of the stock of decorative blocks that could serve as end-pieces or textual embellishment held by many printers and publishers. Such small wood blocks had proved a valuable means of filling out the spaces left on the page by, for example, the layout of poems, and, of course, could be conveniently printed off at the same time as the type-set elements of the page. Engraved plates, that required separate printing from type-set text, and which were therefore usually ascribed to a page of their own, were more demanding both in terms of the time and expense required for their making and in the need to be aligned closely to the texts they were illustrating. A shift from 'decoration' or 'embellishment' to 'illustration' was consequently widely accelerated, if not initiated by, the periodical press in the 1820s and 1830s, especially in accompaniment to extracts from well-known literary texts. Blocks or plates could undoubtedly be commissioned by the editor or proprietor of a journal from artists and engravers, but delays seem to have been frequent and increasingly frustrating for *The Pocket Magazine*.

Until the title went to Robins, with his considerable back catalogue of blocks and access to Cruikshank's output, Arliss and Knight and Lacey had found themselves under constant pressure to sustain the promised level of illustration in the magazine. The central issue concerned the production of the engraved plates – wood-engraved blocks were widely available from stock or could be quickly made to fill a particular space, but the production of metal-engraved plates was more difficult. Arliss found this a particularly irritating problem. The Preface to Volume III (1819) offers apologies for 'the plates not having been regularly given in some of the recent numbers'. Further comments refer specifically to the wish to ensure the aesthetic quality of the plates and not allow them to become 'hasty scratches from obscure spoilers of copper'. But the problem did not go away. The Preface to Volume VII (1821) talks of the 'considerate patience' with which readers have 'borne the delay that has taken place in giving the plates' and promises 'the utmost regularity in future'. But, alas, even by Volume XI from 1823 'it is once more the painful duty of the Proprietor to apologize for his being still in arrears with the plates'. By this point it would be 'tedious' and 'irksome' to 'enumerate all the causes which have combined to prevent him from performing his promises'. It is an interesting comment on the way magazines at this time, especially miscellanies that reprinted much material from other already published sources, that it was the proprietor and not the editor who was forced to apologise, and it seems to be the case that it was part of the proprietor's or the publisher's agreed role to take responsibility for the illustrations and design of the magazine. The Preface to Volume II of Arliss's series of *The Pocket Magazine* (1819) makes such a division of oversight clear:

> The Proprietor has spared neither expence [sic] nor trouble, to procure such embellishments as may prove not unworthy of the approbation of

persons of taste; and has paid no trifling, and, it is hoped, no fruitless, attention to typographical accuracy and beauty. The Editor, on his side, has endeavoured to make the literary part of the Magazine a source of amusement and instruction to all its readers.

It is no wonder that with these difficulties Arliss was keen to sell on his title to Knight and Lacey. Yet Knight and Lacey, despite their considerable resources, fared little better. In an Announcement that prefaced Volume V of their 'New Series' (1826) the publishers stated that:

> The Subscribers to Arliss's Pocket Magazine are respectfully informed that the work will in future be published by James Robins and Co. ... by whom arrangements are made for furnishing an *uninterrupted* series of splendid engravings, with considerable novelty in the literary department. Messrs. Knight and Lacey cannot take leave of their numerous subscribers without expressing their regret that the pressure of unavoidable circumstances has compelled them so frequently to omit the engravings, but they feel happy in being able to state that no such disappointment is likely to occur in the future.

It seems that the writer of the Announcement was aware of Robins's large backlist of illustrated publications which gave the firm a substantial resource from which to fill the pages of *The Pocket Magazine*.

One potential solution to the problems of gathering illustrations from over-pressed engravers and previous publications, tried by Knight and Lacey during their relatively brief ownership of the title, had been to employ a 'house artist'. Robert Seymour had been trained as a draughtsman for wood engraving by the firm but had shown talents beyond expectation, and had been used to produce a range of more ambitious illustrations for Knight and Lacey's publications, becoming a friend of Henry Lacey's in the process.[14] For a brief stint, Seymour produced lithographs for *The Pocket Magazine*, in an attempt to boost the status of the magazine's graphic content (Figure 11.3). For the first three volumes of Knight and Lacey's Second Series of *The Pocket Magazine* the firm had stayed faithful to the tried and tested illustrative formula established by Arliss, using in particular a sequence of engravings produced by Corbould to illustrate an edition of Scott's poetic works. These were printed opposite extracts from the poems and must have formed a cheap and useful way of establishing an aura of gentility for a magazine essentially comprising serialized short fiction, brief historical and topographical articles and miscellaneous anecdotes and snippets mainly drawn in from other magazines. But in Volume IV of Knight and Lacey's 'New Series' (1826) something more interesting happens. The 'Prefatory note' to the volume offers the by this time familiar editorial apologies for the magazine's failure to maintain the advertised run of plates with any consistency.[15] Despite, or perhaps because of, its cheapness, small-scale and scrappy content, *Arliss's Pocket Magazine* clearly felt a compulsion to retain its most culturally ambitious element – the full-page, highly finished decorative engraving. Its solution was an innovative one. Perhaps already well aware of Seymour's abilities to produce something more sophisticated than an endless stream of small-scale descriptive wood engravings, the magazine began to commission the firm's house artist to produce original images to include alongside its literary offerings. Startlingly, given the date, these were produced by means of the unexpected medium of lithographs. While without the ability to reproduce lithographs themselves, Knight and Lacey must have calculated that having their own artist draw direct on to stones which could then be printed on a jobbing basis by the leading firm of Hullmandel was in the long term both cheaper than buying in plates or images already made for other publications and interesting and original enough artistically to attract readers to their publication.[16] It is a mark of the very particular relationship that Seymour had established with his employers that they felt confident enough in his abilities to commission him for this important task.

Robins's solution to the difficulties of supplying illustrations on a regular basis was perhaps a more realistic one. Much of the illustrated content of the Robins series of *The Pocket Magazine* came from blocks that had already been commissioned or owned by Robins for other publications, and for which he held the copyright (Figure 11.4). While this was an economically and logistically obvious way to provide a magazine with a stream of visual content, it also had widespread consequences for the content of the magazine. In Robins's case the obvious illustrations to use were the stock of wood-engraved vignettes that had been drawn by the likes of George or Robert Cruikshank for various humorous publications in the late 1820s. In using these illustrations, Robins was inevitably making a major modal change to the content of his magazine, bringing the comic into play against the Romantic intensity of the previous illustrative practices of the magazine (Figure 11.5). In the reuse of previously published small-scale comic wood engravings, Robins was following an important trend. *Bell's Life in London* had initiated this practice with the introduction of its 'Gallery of Comicalities' in 1827,[17] although legal and copyright difficulties had forced the magazine to move towards commissioning illustrations from relatively little-known artists. Over the next few years it became clear to publishers and editors that the blocks that carried comic images, however small and

Figure 11.4 Double-page spread from volume II of the 'Robins Series' of *The Pocket Magazine* (1828) 109. Author's collection.

unambitious, were a valuable commercial asset that enabled the republication of images in differing print contexts for widely varied readerships. In short, the comic image became a commodity that could be re-ascribed to a wide variety of print outlets. By 1835, for example, Seymour's illustrations for *Figaro in London* had been re-published within almanacs and as large-scale sheets of images without textual annotation. The legitimation of the wood-engraved comic image as something attractive and culturally challenging enough to form a major attraction for a miscellany like *The Pocket Magazine* was an important moment in the development of nineteenth-century periodical illustration that looked forward to *Punch* and its many competitors.

iv

A second major difficulty confronting the illustration of *The Pocket Magazine* concerned the widely differing cultural status of the different reprographic methods and the graphic styles they permitted or encouraged. None of the

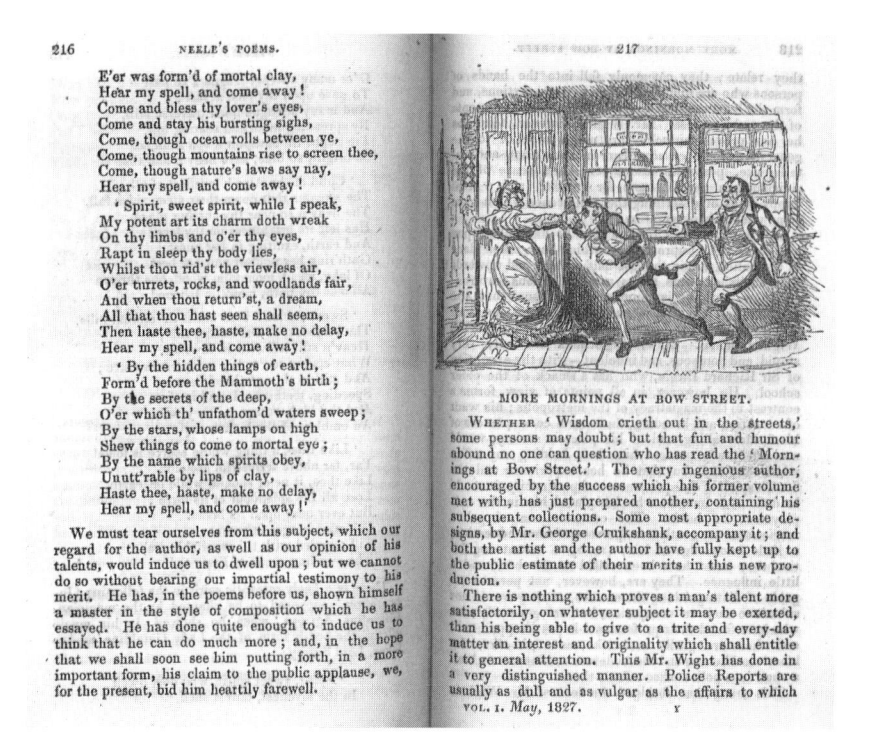

Figure 11.5 Double-page spread from the 'Robins Series' of *The Pocket Magazine* (vol. 1, May 1827, 216–7). The illustration and text are borrowed from John Wight's *More Mornings at Bow Street* with a wood engraving by George Cruikshank. Robins had recently published Wight's book. Author's collection.

three publishers of *The Pocket Magazine* felt able to dispense with full-page engravings of literary topics despite their increasing reliance on various wood-engraved elements within each issue. Many of these interpellated wood engravings harked back to a vernacular broadside or school book tradition of simplified linear graphic representation despite being situated in the magazine alongside sophisticated full-page metal engravings and more traditional decorative elements. Apparent discrepancies in cultural levels between metal-engraved and wood-engraved illustrations were exacerbated by the extremely elaborate and emblematically dense frames that were used to contain the single page plates (see Figure 11.1). Some sense of the anxiety caused by the disparate cultural registers offered by the illustrations can be gauged from the magazine's persistent efforts to pictorialize wood engravings through various framing devices. But there were obvious attempts to give even the simplest wood engraving an increased pictorial presence. Framing was one key chosen device to increase the status of the wood engraving (see Figure 11.2). The simple vignette, a topographical caprice, used here to illustrate the title-page for volume VII of the Arliss series is contained within both a single line and a double line that together turn the image into a crude simulacrum of a framed print hanging on a wall. Such framing is widely used in the magazine to offset the linear simplicity of the wood-engraved illustrations. The central characteristic of the vignette form – its lack of a clearly defined 'edge' so that the image fades or bleeds into the white page – is thus sacrificed in an attempt to enhance the status of the tonal and compositional simplicities traditionally associated with the wood engraving. It is characteristic of the increasing status of the wood engraving that when Robins introduces the comic vignette to his series of *The Pocket Magazine* (see Figure 11.5) the humorous energy and high spirits of the image are allowed to formulate themselves into an unframed space that relegates the type-set textual content of the page to a secondary role, and can even compete for visual attention with a full engraved plate printed on the other side of the double-page opening.

v

In all three series of *The Pocket Magazine* the illustrations sought to maintain the cultural status of the engraved full-page plate while also exploiting the simplicity, graphic immediacy, and decorative potential of the wood engraving. In this, the magazine was using visual elements to underpin its wider cultural claim. *The Pocket Magazine* was trying to present a miscellany of borrowed, pirated, and otherwise accumulated content as something more than diversionary entertainment to fill in an evening in a gentleman's drawing room. Despite the aim of the magazine to reach beyond the traditional readership for literary miscellanies through the use of a smaller format and the use of content largely imported at no cost from already printed texts, the full-page engraved frontispiece remained a continuing statement of the magazine's claims to gentility and cultural status. Its importance was affirmed by the elaborate framing of the main image within an accumulation of linear and emblematic devices. While the full-page frontispieces served the ostensible purpose of illustrating episodes from texts printed in the magazine, they also displayed a considerable aesthetic autonomy that went beyond the merely decorative. The *Pocket Magazine*'s issue frontispieces showed artistic ambition and brought an aura of sophistication to the relatively modest literary and social aspirations of the journal.

The cultural resonances of the cheaper, handier wood engraving were more of an issue. Some wood engravings, in the tradition of eighteenth century books of poetry, were used as page fillers, largely with a decorative function and with the additional aim of asserting a certain level of cultural sophistication as emblematic devices. Other wood engravings were essentially illustrative, offering visual information in order to expand articles on topography or history. In these instances, very simple images were often subject to modes of framing that sought to replicate more ambitious 'pictures'. Such images predate, but resonate with, the great informational project of the wood engraving to be found a decade later in *The Penny Magazine*, *The Saturday Magazine*, and *Pinnock's Guide to Knowledge*. The comic illustrations drawn across by Robins from his extensive list of publications to fill out *The Pocket Magazine*, however, brought a new level of aesthetic and cultural ambition into the illustration of the magazine. The use of comic modes, derived from caricature but formulated into sophisticated wood-engraved vignettes, suggested ways in which even modest literary miscellanies could undertake a major modal shift away from the traditionally genteel. In this way, as well as in its experiments with lithography, *The Pocket Magazine* remains alert to, and to some extent shaped by, the shifting illustrative potentialities becoming available in the 1820s, potentialities that would be widely exploited by the mass circulation illustrated journals of the 1820s and 1830s.

Notes

1 For discussions of the development of cheap weekly periodicals between 1820 and 1840 see Jon Topham, '"The Mirror of Literature, Amusement and Instruction" and Cheap Miscellanies in Early Nineteenth-Century Britain' in G. Cantor et al. eds., *Reading the Magazine of Nature: Science in the Nineteenth Century Periodical* (Cambridge: Cambridge University Press, 2004): 37–66; Jon Topham, 'Thomas Byerley, John Limbird, and the Production of Cheap Periodicals in Regency Britain', *Book History* 8 (2005): 75–106; Brian Maidment, 'Dinners or Desserts? – Miscellaneity, Knowledge and Illustration in Magazines of the 1820s and 1830s', *Victorian Periodicals Review* 43 (Winter 2010): 353–87.

2 Later called 'Robins's New and Improved Series of Arliss's Pocket Magazine'. The Robins series did not use consecutive numbering for the volumes but rather gave the year together with 'volume 1' or 'volume 2'.

3 There were other similar miscellanies that made a point of their miniature format. See, for example, *The Miniature Magazine or Monthly Epitome* published by John Bysh, which launched its second series in 1820 using an extremely

similar pattern of content and illustration to *Arliss's Pocket Magazine*. The same combination of occasional decoratively framed engraved illustrations of literary subjects and clumsy title-page wood-engraved vignettes was used by both magazines. Arliss also published an even smaller periodical, *The Gem*, which ran for four volumes between 1820 and 1822. *The Gem* was a largely fiction-based magazine, drawing its content unashamedly from what its title-page calls 'recent works of merit'.

4 One difficulty of describing the illustration of such journals is that the full-page plates are often missing from volumes, presumably cut out for use in albums or scrapbooks.

5 Henry Arliss later published *The Funny Library of Wit, Satire and Humour* in 16 parts between July and November 1832 which contains some illustrations by Cruikshank, and provides further evidence of the ways in which magazines at this time reprinted images from previous publications.

6 This obituary was reprinted in *The Annual Register* for 1826 and by C. H. Timperley in his 1837 *A Dictionary of Printers and Printing* (London, 1837), 896. The issue title-page for Arliss's *The Gem* in 1820 gives his address as 'John Arliss, Juvenile Library, Newgate Street'. Publishers of childrens' literature were necessarily well-acquainted with the demands of illustration.

7 *The Gem* was reprinted as a four-volume set in 1822 with each volume comprising six 32-page part issues from the original publication.

8 *Arliss's Literary Collections* is undated in all its published forms, although the British Library ascribes the Houlston & Sons volume to c.1830. My feeling is that the original issue is c.1821/2.

9 Robert L. Patten, *George Cruikshank's Life Times and Art* (London and Cambridge: The Lutterworth Press, 2 vols, 1992 and 1996), 1: 269.

10 Patten, 1, 190–2.

11 Re-designated by Robins as 'issue 10 of the 'New Series', vol. 1.

12 I have tried to find precise sources for illustrations in *The Pocket Magazine* among previously issued pocket editions of well-known literary texts published by Cooke and others without much success despite obvious similarities in the size, framing, and engraving technique. But there is internal evidence from illustrations in the magazine that they had previously been published elsewhere. In volume II of the original Arliss series, for example, the text on p. 51 prints a verse extract under the heading 'Subject of the plate. From Lord Byron's Poems XX', with Vol. IV, page 20 as a subscript. Opposite is a framed engraving entitled 'Byron's Poems' with 'Poem 20 Line 9' added. Such allusions to a pre-existing publication are replicated throughout the Arliss volumes suggesting that the engravings were being reused from previous volumes. They certainly have the form and manner of late eighteenth-century re-issues of literary classics.

13 Richard Westall (1765–1836) is described by Houfe as 'popular and prolific' and specialized in working 'chiefly for publishers of poetry, decorating their pocket editions with vignettes and "conversation piece" subjects within decorative

borders. His drawing are … firmly in the 18th. century tradition'. Simon Houfe, *The Dictionary of 19th Century British Book Illustrators and Caricaturists* (Woodbridge: Antique Collectors' Club, revised ed. 1996) 345. Richard Corbould formed part of an artistic dynasty that included his third son Henry, and had worked on Cooke's miniature editions of classic literature published between 1795 and 1800. See Houfe *Dictionary* 99–100.

14 For Seymour as a magazine artist see Brian Maidment, 'The Draughtsman's Contacts – Robert Seymour and Periodical Illustration in 1832', *The Journal of European Periodicals Studies* (online journal 2016): 37–52.

15 'It has been a subject of much regret to the proprietors of *The Pocket Magazine*, that circumstances, arising out of the unprecedented distress of the commercial world, have prevented them from strictly fulfilling those engagements into which they originally entered … the Plates not having been regularly given … One of the wood cuts not being procurable in time for this number, the Publishers have added twelve pages of letter press …' 'New Series', vol. 4, Preface (1826).

16 Seven of Seymour's lithographs appear in Volumes IV and V of the Knight and Lacey 'New Series' interspersed with more conventionally produced metal engravings. The title-page of both volumes is also lithographed, although the plate is not signed. Previous volumes had used metal engravings.

17 For *Bell's Life in London* see David Kunzle, 'Between Broadsheet Caricature and *Punch*: Cheap Newspaper Cuts for the Lower Classes in the 1830s', *Art Journal* 4: 43 (1983): 339–46; Brian Maidment, 'The Gallery of Comicalities: Graphic Humour, Wood-Engraving, and the Development of the Comic Magazine, 1820–1841', *Victorian Periodicals Review* 50: 1 (Spring 2017): 214–27.

Coda: Romantic Illustration and the Privatization of History Painting

MARTIN MYRONE

The second painting to be formally accessioned into the collection of the newly forming National Portrait Gallery in London was, in 1857, a portrait of Thomas Stothard.[1] Given that the purpose of the new national institution was to establish 'a collection of the portraits of distinguished men, who had themselves risen by such an incentive to exertion and to fame' in 'the hope that the likeness of him who gazed upon them might hereafter be found worthy to stand beside them' the choice may well surprise many modern readers.[2] Although he enjoyed a long and high-profile career, achieving commercial success and professional standing as a Royal Academician, Stothard's is not a familiar name today, even among art historians. Where he has been given attention, it has often been as a kind of foil, a straight man whose apparently numberless oil paintings and drawings of literary and historical scenes produced mainly to provide illustrations for books aimed at the general market, lack the intellect or invention of works in the same genre by his old friend William Blake, or the scale and ambition of literary and imaginative works by Henry Fuseli or James Barry, or the formal precision of John Flaxman's linear designs. Stothard's work has been seen as just too small, too conventional, too commercial, and too popular to merit serious scholarly interest. So his early appearance in the canon of 'distinguished' men who could be expected to inspire the next generations of Britons charged with manning the growing British Empire hardly seems natural. Nor was the painter of the portrait, originally identified as George Henry Harlow but then established to be James Green, of a rank likely to fulfil that sort of role. That the very first portrait accessioned into the National Portrait Gallery was the Chandos portrait of William Shakespeare risks lending the subsequent appearance of Stothard a high degree of bathos. That the following accession, the third, was Sir Thomas Lawrence's magnificent unfinished portrait of William Wilberforce, which for its obvious aesthetic interest as a portrait and the pre-eminence of both sitter and painter would seem to be beyond reproach, risks condemning the choice of Stothard as absurd.

It is worth introducing a note of caution at this point. The National Portrait Gallery's acceptance of the gift of the portrait of Stothard may not have been an unequivocal statement of faith in that figure's cultural pre-eminence. It looks like there was a degree of wrangling in play, with the donor, James Hughes Anderdon, wanting to claim precedence as a supporter of this new institution. According to a note by Anderdon, Lord Stanhope, the Chairman of the Trustees, had to ask who Stothard was which hardly indicates that the painter and illustrator had an established place in art history even at this relatively early date. Stothard does not after all loom large in the various sculptural pantheons that adorned the major cultural institutions of the late Victorian era. Nonetheless, his work was relatively well represented in the forming national collection of British art, what later became the Tate collection, with a cluster of paintings in the foundational bequest of Robert Vernon (1847) and several important acquisitions in the later nineteenth century. His paintings and drawings were well represented at the Victoria & Albert Museum, and his graphic works at the British Museum. He had received a full monograph, in the form of A. E. Bray's *Life of Thomas Stothard* (1851), as well as featuring in the major biographical surveys of British art. The portrait by James Green had been shown at the Royal Academy in 1830, and had been published in Arnold's *Library of the Fine Arts*, 1833 and *Magazine of the Fine Arts*, 1833. Notwithstanding Lord Stanhope's reported bemusement, the inclusion of this portrait in the canon of British cultural figures was not entirely outlandish, even if it was not as predictable as the addition of its neighbours, showing Shakespeare and Wilberforce.

That situation did, though, change. In the context of the national art collection, the literary and illustrative character of Stothard's works meant that they were quite quickly relegated as works of art. They were among the pictures that, as Judy Egerton has observed, represented 'Certain realms of subject matter, especially subjects drawn from history, literature and imagination [which] were perceived as the province of the Tate rather than the National Gallery', and were rather promptly transferred from Trafalgar Square to the new gallery of British art at Millbank in its first decades.[3] At the Tate, Stothard's pictures have not been shown regularly or extensively. The general neglect of Stothard and his art, and the dismissal of the kind of small-scale book illustration of which he was the acknowledged master, has been almost complete. He was, at best, considered a commercial artist, a purveyor of a fashionable re-purposing of Neoclassicism, perhaps draining history painting of formal ambition and moral purpose and rendering it as merely ornamental and commodified.[4]

Considering the chapters collected here, the National Portrait Gallery's early admission of Stothard among the pantheon of great Britons may however start to make more sense. It may even look rather prescient. For Stothard's name seems to appear more frequently in this volume than that of any other individual artist or publisher. He is flagged up in the editors' introduction, re-elevated alongside Turner as an illustrator of Samuel Rogers by Maureen McCue, located by Mary L. Shannon as a 'key nodal point' in the productive networks centred on Newman Street, while his 'illustrative-interpretive' work is foregrounded by Sandro Jung. There is, perhaps, an element of reparative justice involved in this collection of chapters, and not just regarding Stothard. Here, literary scholars and cultural historians could be seen as correcting the prejudice of generations of art historians to rediscover what the editors term a 'lost culture of illustration'. If we look away from the canonical cultural institution of the Royal Academy exhibitions, or the established narratives of heroic artistic achievement directed towards the grand progression of British art towards naturalism and imaginative experimentation – the modernist teleology that lends Turner and Constable and Blake such incredible dominance in the art history of this period – and turn instead to the dense and complex networks of social, commercial, and professional connections that underpinned cultural production in a broader sense and for a broader viewership during the Romantic period, we are, surely, led quite naturally to recover the reputations of a figure like Stothard or indeed the poet who originally owned the James Green portrait, Samuel Rogers. The same might be said to other key players in the stories set before us in the chapters above – R. H. Cromek, Thomas Macklin, Thomas Kirk, Maria Cosway, and others. Even the familiarly heroic (or at least pseudo-heroic) Henry Fuseli is offered to us in new lights in Susan Matthews's account, renewing our understanding of him as more adapted to commercial realities than we usually allow. And what is involved is not merely the revaluation of overlooked figures from British art history, giving them back pedestals so that they can sit alongside more familiar artists, but a reconsideration of what 'illustration' might mean, how the function of the engraved image designed to sit alongside text might be valued and interpreted. As lucidly established by the editors at the head of this volume, the illustrative image had a manifold role in the context of the Romantic literary text publication, as dynamically involving 'typification, enhancement and textual accompaniment'.

Across these chapters we are presented with interlocking cultural worlds where Stothard can be considered as a major player, not a minor figure. If there is nothing of the patriotic boasting which accompanied the formation of the National Portrait Gallery, there is also a sense of an understanding of the national culture being set right by putting Stothard in the limelight.

There is a sense of democratic representation, or representativeness, in the generation and circulation of book illustration at the accelerated pace, more extensive number, and more accessible cost, exposed as a major feature of Romantic literary culture in these chapters. From the high-ground perspective of Shaftesburian civic humanism the story of history painting through the late eighteenth and into the early nineteenth century was one of terminal, sorry decline.[5] That James Barry, Henry Fuseli, and Benjamin Robert Haydon placed such emphasis on sheer physical scale in their bucking against the privatization of history painting is important. Size did matter, if history painting was to be preserved as a masculine activity with a living relationship to classical traditions of thought and the virtuous actions these would mobilize. If the commercial galleries of Boydell and Macklin in the 1790s represented an attempt to combine the academic Grand Manner at full scale with marketable publications, they faltered as business enterprises. The elite aesthetic of the Sublime was now to be achieved at a more domestic scale, pocket-sized even: Romantic book illustration provided for a Sublime-in-little.[6]

The contributors to this volume together offer a different set of possible narratives about this decline of history painting. They can seem often to actively relish the dissolution of the hierarchies of scale, medium, and aesthetic attention which accompanied the flourishing of literary illustration. Dustin Frazier Wood points to the 'cross-fertilization that influenced literary and historical works that sought to define English stories in visual terms'. Resurrecting Martin Meisel's important, still rather under-used text *Realizations* (1983), Sophie Thomas sets out illustration as 'the extension of one medium or mode of discourse by another'.[7] It was, to re-quote Julia Thomas, 'an eminently social medium', and the social relations involved had a democratic potential.[8] This in turn opened up possibilities for a more equitable engagement with high culture across the genders, with present-day resonances. Luisa Calè considers the cosmopolitan circulations, symbolic and material, that were put in motion by Maria Cosway's *Hours* as constituting a 'museum without walls', a buzz-phrase capturing the twin contemporary aspirations for the globalization and democratization of art.[9] And Ian Haywood is right, surely to offer the tantalizing prospect of a new line of enquiry into 'female agency across both Macklin's and other literary galleries'.[10] This would extend existing work on the liberatory potential of female participation in the bourgeois public sphere, and the forging of 'first wave' feminism.[11] There are hints here of egalitarian or even rhizomatic connections between texts and images, readers and viewers, consumers and producers. Given the liberal, humanistic, democratic, even demotic, ethos that pervades modern literary studies, such are likely to be enthralling. As Mary L. Shannon notes, bringing figures like Stothard and Cromek into play is a radically egalitarian prospect, putting artists 'on the ground' in Latourian terms, and making networks, not individual agents, do the work. The 'museum without walls' has been envisaged as a liberation from history, universalizing art and establishing 'the common heritage of all mankind'.[12] Something of this is anticipated by Blake in his *Descriptive Catalogue* (1809), as quoted by Sophie Thomas:

> Shall Painting be confined to the sordid drudgery of fac-simile representations of merely mortal and perishing substances, and not be as poetry and music art, elevated into its own proper sphere of invention and visionary conception? No, it shall not be so!

As Peter Otto expands, it is Blake who promises the most expansive form of illustration, expansion beyond 'explanation' towards a generative 'critique, renarration or re-envisioning'. The liberation of the illustrative image from its strictly illustrational function can generate, in these accounts, a promise of a democratic, open-ended, and imaginative engagement with both text and image.

Overall, there is the sense that re-examining Romantic illustration opens out new understandings of the literary text, new possibilities for literary consumption, and the social and political engagements these may entail. But if the purpose of a coda is not merely to conclude by rounding up, but to offer something in the way of critique, renarration, and re-envisioning, there are questions here as well. The micro-historical detail pursued by many of the authors here is richly rewarding, and illuminates a complex, mobile, pervasive environment for the production, marketing, and consumption of illustration that is only approximately and partially recovered if we adhere too closely to conventional distinctions of national school and national contexts, genre, and the evaluative judgements typically brought into play by art history. But in the absence of a synoptic survey of book illustration in this period, can our analysis be sufficiently systematic? And having returned certain figures to the fore, like Stothard, we are still left with the larger question of who, generally, were the book illustrators? Mary L. Shannon may be right to point to the dictionary definition of 'artist' as accommodating a range of identities, including engravers and designers. But how the figure of the 'artist', or indeed 'illustrator' (if that is different) was constituted needs deeper consideration. Pierre Bourdieu mischievously pointed out: 'I believe that it is anachronistic to say that Michelangelo was an artist', emphasising 'the problems of the genesis, not of an individual, but of a space in which this individual can exist as an artist'.[13] In fact 'illustrator' was not available as an identity alternative to 'artist'. Although the OED indicates that the term 'illustrator' was available in the sense that we might expect of it in the eighteenth century, it is also the case that it was not in routine use. Those artists who we know were busy providing illustrations for literary publications were routinely identified as 'Artists' with the qualifying generic terms 'Historical', 'Fancy', or 'Literary' – but not illustration. Stothard was typically included in an artists' listing as specializing in 'History, Domestic Life, &c'.[14] The task of designing for illustration was undertaken by individuals whose professional identities led away from the world of publishing, and faced towards the Academy and artistic tradition.

What were the economics and social costs of the proliferation of illustration? Antony Griffiths notes that physical proximity between book publishers and print publishers in the eighteenth century did not necessarily entail closer forms of working.[15] Blake's comment in 1800 that he had seen London's cultural world transform, so that there were now 'as many Booksellers as there are Butchers & as many Printshops as of any other trade' is on the one hand an observation about the new urgency and extent of the print market, but it is also to point to the commercialization of culture.[16] Books were now trades as much, and perhaps in the same way, as meat. I am less certain than the editors that the artists employed by Boydell or Macklin did not need feel demeaned by producing works destined to be reproduced as illustrations. There was in these arrangements an economic dependence, stipulations about the sizes of canvases, choices of subject and aesthetic styles that some of the most pig-headed artists contested or ignored. It is important that artists sought out independent exhibiting opportunities in order, quite explicitly, to break from this dependence – Fuseli most spectacularly with his ill-destined Milton Gallery. As Griffiths and others have emphasized, the introduction of printed images into books in greater numbers and with greater refinement was a complicated, expensive, time-consuming and risky business, involving different skill-sets and commercial practices.[17] While assertions about the accelerated speed, and growing extent and impact of the printed illustration in the Romantic decades are doubtless strictly accurate – and there is proof aplenty in the chapters collected here – they may also be a risk of losing sight of the conflict, division, inefficiencies, and contradictions involved. We are, collectively, still some way from having a comprehensive sense of the commercial logic of book illustration seen from the by no means wholly compatible perspectives of artists, engravers, publishers, printers, booksellers, and consumers. To privilege the artists' point of view, the proliferation of Romantic illustration might often be registered as representing an opportunity, but we would do well to note the accompanying note of regret or equivocation which often appears. As James Northcote wrote in his autobiography, quoted by Dustin Frazier Wood here, 'small historical and fancy subjects from the most popular authors of the day' were sure to sell.[18] Henry Fuseli wrote of the smaller, more domesticated picture which he invented as commercially expedient and a means of supporting less marketable but more ambitious works: 'Small pictures to make the Large ones go on', as he put it.[19] These artists were at the top end of the cultural marketplace. For numberless others scraping a living in urban centres across the country, the reality was probably more like that testified by David Barber (1795–1848), a very obscure drawing master and artist originally from Dewsbury in Yorkshire. David Barber's career as an artist is generally obscure, but he seems characteristically to have maintained a profile in his home town while also seeking out work in London. The struggles he faced were illuminated when he was called to Bow Street, in 1823, accused of withholding goods by the picture dealer Dyson:

> Mr Barber, when called upon to answer the charge, said, the Magistrate then saw before him one of the numerous class of unfortunate fellows in this metropolis who, having embraced the profession without adequate means of supporting themselves in respectability until (supposing they had talent) their works brought them into notice and patronage, were obliged to earn a bare subsistence in the miserable drudgery of supplying print-shops or dealers in pictures.[20]

As Antony Griffiths has detailed in his important chapter on book illustration in his magisterial recent history of print, there was scope for outright conflict between publishers and artists.[21] Even Thomas Stothard, who on the face of it profited enormously for his work as an illustrator, was pessimistic when he advised an aspiring younger artist, John Wood (1801–1870). The latter recalled of his youthful ambitions:

> In my early career in Art, I was employed to make a few illustrations to Swift's and other works: this kind of occupation although it kindled my ambition, and pleased my notions at the time, seeing my name in print, yet, I did not feel ambitious to continue in this particular province of employment, my attention was already beginning to be much engaged in Portrait-painting; a course that I was recommended to follow in preference.
>
> My friend Mr Stothard told me, employment would be much more likely to be obtained than I might ever hope for by making book illustrations: he

quoted some painful allusions to his own ill-requited reward for continued efforts, and the very small remuneration in general received for his designs.[22]

The aged Stothard – whose portrait Wood would take (Dulwich Picture Gallery) – advised the younger painter to stick with portrait painting. If not dismissed as 'miserable drugdery', book illustration was not necessarily an elevating, or even remunerative, activity. As an early guide to the National Portrait Gallery asserted, of Stothard: 'Historical painter, chiefly, however, in ornamental decoration and illustration for books.'[23] That qualification is routine and telling. If Kay Dian Kriz set out how the energies committed to history painting were in a manner sublimated into landscape painting in this period, we might want also to consider how the moral ambitions of history painting were in parallel scaled down in the form of book illustrations.[24] The history painting which was rendered in an engraving fitted into a book suitable for the littlest hand and most modest pocket was history painting without 'context'. The editors of the present volume assert, interestingly, that 'Purchasing an illustrated book was the equivalent of visiting the Royal Academy and acquiring a work of art, albeit on a reduced scale.' But the context for these experiences are different in ways which involved much more than physical dimensions. What was involved was a public (albeit regulated) space, a social event, royal prestige and press notice on the one hand, established a ritual context conducted in public view; on the other, the private, the domestic, the consumable, with the illustrated book featuring in the minute rituals of everyday life in the home. There was, we might say, a loss of context, which equates to the familiar – perhaps all too familiar – process of privatization and the loss of community this entails.

As I venture to suggest below, we might do well to consider that loss of 'context' for literary and historical images as having a moral bearing. But there are immediate and literal ways in which illustration was 'decontextualized'. There was, as several of the authors here set out in fine detail, scope for illustrators to depart from, interpret, and expand on the literary source. The relationship between text and image is everywhere here shown to be complex, dynamic, manifold, unresolved. There are of course the insights of recent work on the manipulation and reworking of images, through collecting, cutting, pasting, and extra-illustration.[25] Even in the context of ostensibly standard commercial publications, there were variations and deviations in the use and placing of plates: 'for many an illustrated book it is very difficult to identify such a thing as a standard copy'.[26] There was the cannibalization of imagery, which could also involve outright abuse or invention. Plates were sold and exchanged, reworked and repurposed.[27]

The teasing open of the relationship between text and image might then become more volatile, even more radically dissociative, than is acknowledged here. The absence of a corpus of Romantic illustration, which would anyway need to be set against a corpus of source images in the form of paintings and designs, makes room for these misreadings and reuses to be silently reproduced. A couple of examples will suggest what may be in play here. There is the painting by the portrait and history painter (and only occasional illustrator) Henry Perronet Briggs of *Juliet and the Nurse* (Tate), exhibited at the Royal Academy with the title and Shakespearean source explicitly stated in 1827. This was subsequently engraved as an illustration to 'The Mortal Immortal' by Mary Shelley, when that fantastic tale was published in the literary annual *The Keepsake* at the end of 1833. This, 'the most frequently anthologized of Mary Shelley's stories' has received some attention from literary historians.[28] Modern commentators have seemed to simply accept the plate as an illustration of Shelley's text, with Brigg's figure matched to 'the scene in which Bertha and her benefactoress argue about Albert Hoffer'.[29] What may have occurred here was that the publisher provided Shelley with the print, in the form of an unlettered proof or with the title removed, as a prompt for her literary endeavour. But while for instance Bertha Sonia Hofkosh acknowledges the primacy of the image, like other literary commentators she seems unaware of the image's original framing narrative, asserting a close relationship between print and text.[30] So does the reordering of the process of illustration matter, does the transformation of the image's contents matter? Do we, in interpreting the image now, need to know about these transformations?

A different disjunction is to be found in the case of a painting of a black African man being attended to by a young blonde white girl, by Henry Meyer.[31] When it was first shown in public, in 1827, it was accompanied by a sentimental poem by Charles Lamb, entitled 'The Young Catechist'.[32] On that occasion Meyer also showed his portrait of Lamb (now passed by all readers entering the Rare Books & Music Room at the British Library, London), which presented the writer in his capacity as a Clerk at East India House. Lamb and Meyer were schoolboys together at Christ's Hospital school in London, and Lamb provided the poetic accompaniment as an act of friendship. The writer was, though, scathing about Meyer's painting: 'an artist who painted me lately, had painted a blackamoor praying, and not filling his canvas, stuffed in his little girl aside of Blackey, gaping at him unmeaningly; and then didn't know what to call it', prompting him to provide the poetic accompaniment: 'When I'd done it, the artist (who had clapt in Miss merely as a fill-space) swore I exprest his full meaning'.[33] So it appears from this account that the black figure was initially conceived as independent, the sentimentalized white girl was an ungraceful addition by the artist, and the narrative content provided by Lamb's poem a complete afterthought. The painting was then at a later date also engraved several times, under different titles and on one occasion to accompany a completely different poem. Do these transformations matter? They surely do, given the way racial and gender difference are played out in the original painting. But how readily can we trace such transformations, given the still limited state of knowledge about Romantic illustration as a total field of activity?

The Sublime art of history painting was thus brought down to ground, down to earth, and into the hands of, if not the masses (yet, although Brian Maidment points to what was to come), at least an expanding middle-rank of society. Romantic book illustration opened up new forms of social identification and cultural performance, more porous and accommodating perhaps, but also more thoroughly privatized, in the full senses of that term. Might it be, as Fuseli seems to have apprehended in his Lectures on Painting, that the accommodation of bourgeois civility necessarily and inevitably led to the commercialization of culture and the loss of even the possibility of heroic, virtuous action?[34] Illustration might be, as the editors here assert, 'a democratization of British art', matching the chronology of political revolutionary agitation and reform. But we might ask of the story of art as much as of the story of political representation, at what cost, and in whose interests? As 'neither exactly satire or celebration', Fuseli's addresses to the spaces between public and private in which certain kinds of domesticated history painting might thrive was, as Susan Matthews sets out, profoundly equivocal.[35] His may, perhaps, be the most just and ethically coherent position.

It is at that point that art historians, certainly, or even the kind of theoretically informed and politically alert literary and cultural historians who have populated this present volume, might need to look beyond even their field of study. We need, surely, to venture the kind of larger, wider historical claims which have been more usually the territory of philosophical critics of modernity. In considering the costs as well as the benefits of the 'democratization of British art', insofar as this also, surely, involved the privatization of history painting, these critics of liberal individualism and the market society may have some unexpected pertinence. The relevance of Charles Taylor's rather generously balanced view of the 'malaise of modernity' for our understanding of the epistemological or even moral uncertainty of eighteenth-century consumer society and its literary representation has been explored by Paul Keen.[36] There may even be merit in reflecting on the lessons of the rather more abrasive and pessimistic critic of liberal modernity, Alasdair MacIntyre. In his famously (perhaps infamously) contentious work *After Virtue* (1981), MacIntyre identifies in the liberal modernity which took shape during the early nineteenth century a decisive stage in the catastrophic breakdown of morality which we still live with: 'What we possess [now, he writes] are the fragments of a conceptual scheme, parts which now lack those contexts from which their significance derived. We possess indeed simulacra of morality, we continue to use many of the key expressions. But we have – very largely, if not entirely – lost our comprehension, both theoretical and practical, of morality'.[37] We are left, instead, with consumer choices, a market society absorbed by the pursuit of personal pleasures and interests without self-understanding. What is at stake in MacIntyre's account is the possibility of moral action at all, in the context of a culture so evacuated of commonly agreed values. Dare we suggest that history painting's privatization and de-contextualization in the form of Romantic literary illustration falls chronologically into precisely the same historical framework provided for the ascent and triumph of the liberal free market in Karl Polanyi's classic account, one of the foundations of MacIntyre's analysis?[38] Is the precise coincidence of the material covered in this volume with the dates of this ascent – the 'great transformation' that takes us from Adam Smith to David Ricardo, and through the duration of the Speenhamland System (1790–1834), a last blast of paternalism whose expiry marked the final triumph of market society – really to be treated as merely coincidental? Or only somehow, mysteriously, deterministically related? That there was some form of 'democratization' involved in both the ascent of the market society and the proliferation of Romantic illustration is hardly to be argued. But whether democratization is all that it seems, or fulfils all that it promises, may be among the great questions of our post-Trump, post-Brexit era. If the neoliberalism of our time has been, as Nancy Fraser proposes, really the 'second coming' of the nineteenth-century liberalism installed through the 'great transformation' of around 1790–1830, the analysis of the cultural transformations of that moment, not least the proliferation of literary texts and their illustration given such careful consideration here, may have gained a new and unexpected urgency.[39]

Notes

1 For the details of the portrait and its provenance provided here see Richard Walker, *Regency Portraits* (National Portrait Gallery, London 1985) now available

online at www.npg.org.uk/collections/search/portraitExtended/mw06075/Thomas-Stothard. The portrait and its history was brought to my attention by Lucy Peltz of the National Portrait Gallery.
2 Earl Stanhope in the House of Commons, 4 March 1856, 'Gallery of National Portraits', Hansard vol 140 cc1770-89, available online at https://api.parliament.uk/historic-hansard/lords/1856/mar/04/gallery-of-national-portraits.
3 Judy Egerton, *National Gallery Catalogues: The British Paintings* (National Gallery, London, distributed by Yale University Press 1998), 14. Sixteen of the 18 pictures originally given to or purchased by the National Gallery were transferred to the new Tate Gallery in 1919; the remaining two pictures were transferred in 1929.
4 See Shelley Bennett, *Thomas Stothard RA* (Ann Arbor, MI; London: University Microfilms International, 1982) and *Thomas Stothard: The Mechanisms of Art Patronage in England circa 1800* (Columbia: University of Missouri Press, 1988). More recently, see Cora Gilroy-Ware, 'Marmorealities: Classical Nakedness in British Sculpture and Historical Painting, 1798–1840', Ph.D. Thesis, University of York, 2013, who focuses with renewed seriousness on Stothard's paintings while also setting aside his book illustrations (see esp. 197–8).
5 See John Barrell's hugely influential account, *The Political Theory of Painting from Reynolds to Hazlitt: the Body of the Public* (New Haven, CT; London: Yale University Press, 1986).
6 For the art historical context of these shifts, see David H. Solkin, *Art in Britain 1660–1815* (Yale University Press/Pelican History of Art: Paul Mellon Centre for Studies in British Art, 2015), esp. 306.
7 See above, p. 38, quoting Martin Meisel, *Realizations: Narrative, Pictorial, and Theatrical Arts in Nineteenth-Century England* (Princeton, NJ: Princeton University Press, 1983), 30.
8 Julia Thomas, *Nineteenth Century Illustration and the Digital: Studies in Word and Image* (New York: Palgrave, 2017), quoted here by Mary L. Shannon, p. 49.
9 Stemming from André Malraux's influential essay on the democratizing transformations of art through reproduction, 'Museum without Walls', in *Voices of Silence*, trans. Stuart Gilbert (St Albans: Paladin, 1974).
10 See above, p. 133, n. 47.
11 Carla Hesse, *The Other Enlightenment: How French Women Became Modern* (Princeton, NJ; Oxford 2001); see also Elizabeth Eger, *Bluestockings: Women of Reason from Enlightenment to Romanticism* (Houndmills: Palgrave Macmillan, 2010).
12 Malraux, *Le musée imaginaire*, 46.
13 Pierre Bourdieu and Roger Chartier, *The Sociologist and the Historian*, trans. David Fernbach (Cambridge, UK; Malden, MA: Polity Press, 2015), 64.
14 James Elmes ed., *Annals of the Fine Arts*, vol. 1 (London, 1817), 434.
15 Antony Griffiths, *The Print before Photography: An Introduction to European Printmaking 1550–1820* (London: The British Museum Press, 2016), 181.
16 Letter to George Cumberland, 2 July 1800, quoted here by Susan Matthews, p. 81.

17 For counter-narratives focusing on the laboriousness and craft of engraving, as opposed to its modernity, see Morris Eaves, *The Counter-Arts Conspiracy: Art and Industry in the age of Blake* (Ithaca, NY: Cornell University Press, 1992); also Martin Myrone, 'Engraving's Third Dimension', in Mark Hallett, Nigel Llewellyn and Martin Myrone, eds, *Court, Country, City: British Art and Architecture, 1660–1735* (New Haven, CT: Yale Center for British Art, 2016).
18 See above, 50.
19 To William Roscoe, 22 October 1791, in David H. Weinglass ed., *The Collected English Letters of Henry Fuseli* (Millwood, NY: Kraus International Publications, 1982), 74.
20 *Evening Mail*, 21 April 1823.
21 Griffiths, *The Print before Photography*, 181–94.
22 British Library, Add MS 37,159, 133–5.
23 [George Scharf], *Catalogue of the National Portrait Gallery* (London: National Portrait Gallery, 1859), 37.
24 Kay Dian Kriz, *The Idea of the English Landscape Painter: Genius as Alibi in the Early Nineteenth Century* (New Haven, CT; London: published for the Paul Mellon Centre for Studies in British Art by Yale University Press, 1997).
25 Most recently, Lucy Peltz, *Facing the Text: Extra-illustration, Print Culture, and Society in Britain, 1769–1840* (San Marino: The Huntington Library, Art Collections, and Botanical Gardens, 2017).
26 Griffiths, *The Print before Photography*, 185.
27 Ibid., 189–90.
28 Charles E. Robinson, *Mary Shelley: Collected Tales and Stories* (Baltimore, MD; London: John Hopkins University Press, 1976), 390.
29 Lucy Morrison and Staci L. Stone, *A Mary Shelley Encyclopedia* (Westport, CT; London: Greenwood Press, 2003), 293.
30 'Disfiguring Economies: Mary Shelley's Short Stories', in Audrey A. Fisch, Anne K. Mellor, and Esther H. Schor eds, *The Other Mary Shelley: Beyond Frankenstein* (New York and Oxford: Oxford University Press, 1993), 204–19.
31 Currently with Ben Elwes Fine Art, London.
32 Alfred Ainger ed., *The Letters of Charles Lamb*, 2 vols (London: Macmillan & Co., 1897), 2: 194.
33 Ainger, *The Letters of Charles Lamb*, 193–4.
34 Barrell, *The Political Theory of Painting*, 279–83.
35 Ibid., 258–307.
36 Paul Keen, *Literature, Commerce, and the Spectacle of Modernity, 1750–1800* (Cambridge University Press 2012), esp. 206–7, citing Charles Taylor, *The Ethics of Authenticity* (Harvard University Press, 1992).
37 Alasdair MacInytre, *After Virtue: A Study in Moral Theory*, 3rd edn (Notre Dame, Indiana: University of Notre Dame Press 2007), 2.
38 Karl Polanyi, *The Great Transformation: The Political and Economic Origins of Our Time* (Boston: Beacon Press, 1957). On Polanyi and MacIntyre, see Peter

McMylor, *Alasdair MacIntyre: Critic of Modernity* (Abingdon: Routledge 1994), 77–108 and *passim*; Terry Pinkard, 'MacIntyre's Critique of Modernity', in Mark C. Murphy ed., *Alasdair Macintyre* (Cambridge University Press, 2003), 176–200.

39 Nancy Fraser, *Fortunes of Feminism: From State-managed Capitalism to Neoliberal Crisis* (London: Verso Books, 2013), 229.

Bibliography

Primary Works

A catalogue of cameos, intaglios, medals, busts, small statues, and bas-relief; with a general account of vases and other ornaments, after the antique, made by Wedgwood and Bentley, and sold at their rooms in Greek Street, Soho, London, 5th edn with additions. London, 1779.

Allgemeiner Litteratur-Anzeiger (14 October 1799).

'An Account of Elfrida', *London Chronicle* (21–24 November 1772).

Analytical Review, 1 (June 1788).

Annals of the Fine Arts. London: Sherwood, Neely & Jones &c, 1817.

Annual Review, 6. 1808.

Anon. 'BOOKS PUBLISHED THIS DAY: Rogers's *Italy*', in *The London Literary Gazette and Journal of Belle Lettres, Arts, Sciences, &c.*, No. 713 (18 September 1830).

Anon. 'Literary Criticism [*Fifty-Six Engravings Illustrative of Italy. A Poem.* By Samuel Rogers, Esq. London. Jennings and Chaplin. 1830. (*Unpublished.*) *Pompeiana, or Observations of the Topography, Edifices and Ornaments of Pompeii*. By Sir William Gell, F.R.S., &c. New Series. Parts 1, 2, 3. London. Jennings and Chaplin. 1830.]', in *The Edinburgh Literary Journal; or, Weekly Register of Criticism and Belles Lettres*, 92 (14 August 1830), 101–4.

Anon. 'PROCESSION OF CHAUCER'S PILGRIMS to CANTERBURY', *Times* (5 March 1807).

Arliss, John. *Pocket Magazine of Classic and Polite Literature* (1818–1827).

Baker, David Erskine, Isaac Reed and Stephen Jones. *Biographia Dramatica; or, a Companion to the Playhouse*. 3 vols. London: Longman, Hurst, Rees, Orme and Brown, 1812.

Baker, Robert. *Observations on the Pictures Now in Exhibition at the Royal Academy, Spring Gardens, and Mr. Christie's*. London: John Bell, 1771.

Barnard, Edward. *The New, Comprehensive and Complete History of England, from the Earliest Period of Authentic Information, to the Middle of the Year MDCCLXXXIII*. London: Alexander Hogg, 1783.

Barruel, Abbé Augustin. *Histoire du Clergé pendant la Révolution Francoise; Ouvrage dédié à la Nation Angloise*. London: Debrett, 1793.

Barry, James (Professor of Painting to the Royal Academy). *A Letter to the Right Honourable the President, Vice-Presidents, and the Rest of the Noblemen and*

> *Gentlemen, of the Society for the Encouragement of Arts, Manufactures and Commerce, John-Street, Adelphi.* London: Thomas Davison: 1793.

Bell, John (ed.). *Bell's British Theatre*. 34. London: John Bell, 1797.

Bellori, Giovanni Pietro and Bartoli, Pietro Santi. *Admiranda Romanarum antiquitatum ac veteris sculpturae vestigia anaglyphico opere elaborata ex marmoreis exemplaribus quae Romae adhuc extant. Notis J.P. Bellorii illustrata. Restituit auxit D. de Rubeis.* Rome, 1693.

Bible: Authorized King James Version. Ed. Robert Carroll and Stephen Prickett Oxford; New York: Oxford University Press, 1997.

Blair, Hugh, *Lectures on Rhetoric and Belles Lettres*, 2 vols. London, 1783.

Blake, William. *Descriptive Catalogue* in David V. Erdman (ed.). *The Complete Poetry and Prose of William Blake*. Berkeley: University of California Press, 1982.

Bray, Anna Eliza. *Life of Thomas Stothard R. A.* London: John Murray, 1851.

British Institution, 'Preface', *Catalogue of Pictures by the late William Hogarth, Richard Wilson, Thomas Gainsborough, and J. Zoffani. Exhibited by the Permission of the Proprietors in Honour of the Memory of those Distinguished Artists, and for the Improvement of British Art. To which are added etchings distinguishing the names in the Florentine gallery and Royal Academy.* London: Bulmer, 1814.

British Institution, *Catalogue of Pictures by the late Sir Joshua Reynolds, exhibited by the permission of the Proprietors, in honour of the Memory of that Distinguished Artist, and for the Improvement of British Art.* London: Bulmer, 1813.

Carey, William P. *Critical Description of the Procession of Chaucer's Pilgrims to Canterbury.* London: Cadell and Davies for R. H. Cromek, 64 Newman Street, 1808.

Catalogue of Pictures and Drawings by the late Benjamin West. London: C. H. Reynell, 1827.

Catalogue of Pictures Painted on Glass [...], Now Exhibiting at Mr. Backler's Stained Glass Works. London: John Tyler, 1818.

Catullus. *Catullus, Tibullus and Pervigilium Veneris*, trans. by F. W. Cornish. Cambridge, MA: Harvard University Press, 1976.

'Chorus of the Dramatic Poem of *Elfrida*. As performed at Covent-Garden', *Critical Review* 35, 1773.

'Chorus of the Dramatic Poem of Elfrida. As Performed at the Theatre-Royal in Covent-Garden', *Monthly Review* 47, 1772.

Collins, William *Odes on Several Descriptive and Allegoric Subjects*. London: A. Millar, 1747.

Darwin, Erasmus. *The Loves of the Plants*. London: J. Johnson, 1789.

> *The Botanic Garden, Part One: The Economy of Vegetation; Part Two: The Loves of the Plants*. 1st and 5th editions. London: J. Johnson, 1791, 1799.
>
> *The Temple of Nature, or The Origin of Society*. London: J. Johnson, 1803.
>
> *The Temple of Nature by Erasmus Darwin*, ed. Martin Priestman, Romantic Circles, 2006. www.rc.umd.edu/editions/darwin_temple/index.html, last accessed 09.10.2017.

Elfrid: or the Fair Inconstant. London: Bernard Lintott, 1710.

Essays by Leigh Hunt. London: Edward Moxon, 1840.

Extracts from the Journals and Correspondence of Miss Berry from the year 1783 to 1852, ed. by Lady Theresa Lewis, 2nd edn, 3 vols. London: Longmans, Green and Co., 1866.

Free Society of Artists, *Catalogue*. London, 1761.

Fuseli, Henry (ed. John Knowles). *Lectures on Painting, delivered at the Royal Academy, now first printed from the original manuscripts, second series*. London: Colburn and Bentley, 1830.

Garlick, Kenneth and Angus Macintyre (eds). *The Diary of Joseph Farington, Vol V. August 1801–March 1803*. New Haven, CT; London: Yale University Press, 1979, 1822.

Garrick, David. *The Private Correspondence of David Garrick with the Most Celebrated Persons of His Time*, 2nd edn, 2 vols. London: Henry Colburn, 1835.

Geddes, Alexander. *Critical Remarks on the Hebrew Scriptures: Corresponding with a New Translation of the Bible*. London, 1800.

The Holy Bible, or the Books Accounted Sacred by Jews and Christians, trans. Geddes. London, 1792.

Gentleman's Magazine, 78. 1808.

Gloucester Journal, 29 October 1804.

Gray, Thomas. *Poems by Mr Gray*. London: Dodsley, 1768.

Commonplace Book, Pembroke College, Cambridge, 3 vols.

Correspondence of Thomas Gray, ed. by P. Toynbee and L. Whibley, 3 vols. Oxford: Clarendon Press, 1971.

The Complete Poems of Thomas Gray, ed. by H. W. Starr and J. R. Hendrickson. Oxford: Oxford University Press, 1966.

Gwynn, Stephen. *Memorials of an Eighteenth-Century Painter (James Northcote)*. London: T. Fisher Unwin, 1898.

Hampshire Chronicle, 1 January 1810.

Haydon, B. R. *Painting*. Edinburgh: Adam and Charles Black, 1838.

Hayley, William. *Essay on Painting*. London: J. Dodsley, 1781.

Hazlitt, William. 'Mr Crabbe', in *The Complete Works of William Hazlitt*, ed. by P. P. Howe, 21 vols. London: Dent, 1930–1934, 19, 53.

Hegel, Georg Wilhelm Friedrich. *Phenomenology of Spirit*, trans. A. V. Miller. Oxford: Oxford University Press, 1977.

Hill, Aaron. *The Dramatic Works of Aaron Hill*, 2 vols. London, 1760.

Hope, Thomas. *Household Furniture and Interior Decoration Executed from Designs by Thomas Hope*, printed by T. Bensley. London: Longman, Hurst, Rees and Orme, 1807.

Hunt, Leigh. *The Autobiography of Leigh Hunt with Reminiscences of Friends and Contemporaries*. London: held by the British Library, 1850.

Hunt, Robert, 'Royal Academy Exhibition', in *The Examiner* (21 May 1809).

Ipswich Journal, 25 October 1800.

Jacob, Simon. 'The Account Book of James Northcote', *Walpole Society*, vol. 58, 1996 [C. R. Smith], 'Pictorial Illustrations of Shakespeare', *Quarterly Review* 142 (1876): 457–79.

Jerningham, Edward. 'The Ancient English Wake: A Poem', in *Poems by Mr Jerningham* 2 vols. London: J. Robson, 1786.

Johnstone's London Commercial Guide and Street Directory. London, Johnstone, 1817.

Jones, Edward. *Musical and Poetical Relicks of the Welsh Bards*. 1784.

Lamb, Charles. 'Recollections of a late Royal Academician' (1831), in *Correspondence and Works of Charles Lamb*. London: E. Moxon, 1870.

Langbaine, Gerard. *An Account of the English Dramatic Poets*. Oxford: George West and Henry Clements, 1691.

Leslie, C. R. and T. Taylor, *Life and Times of Sir Joshua Reynolds*, 2 vols. London: 1865.

Locke, John. *An Essay Concerning Human Understanding* [1690]. Ed. Raymond Wilburn. London: Dent Everyman, 1947.

Lockman, John. *A New History of England, by Question and Answer. Extracted from the Most Celebrated English Historians, Particularly M. Rapin de Thoyras, for the Entertainment of our Youth of both Sexes*, 8th edn. London: T. Astley, 1752.

Macklin, Thomas. *A Catalogue of the First Exhibition of Pictures, Painted for Mr. Macklin, by the Artists of Britain, Illustrative of the British Poets*. London, 1788.

Poet's Gallery: A Catalogue of the Second Exhibition of Pictures, Painted for Mr. Macklin, by the Artists of Britain, Illustrative of the British Poets. London, 1789.

Poetic Description of Choice and Valuable Prints, Published by Mr Macklin at the Poets Gallery, Fleet Street. London: T. Benson, 1794.

PROPOSALS by THOMAS MACKLIN, No. 39 Fleet Street, for Publishing a Series of Prints Illustrative of the Most Celebrated British Poets, Victoria and Albert Museum, London, 1787.

Malone, Edmund. *The Works of Sir Joshua Reynolds* 3 vols. London: T. Cadell and W. Davies, 1801.

Mason, William. *Elfrida: A Dramatic Poem, Modelled on the Ancient Greek Tragedy*. London: John and Paul Knapton, 1752.

Montfaucon, Bernard de. *L'Antiquité expliquée et représentée en figures*, 5 vols. Paris: Florentin Delaulne, Hilaire Foucault, Michel Clousier, Jean-Geoffroy Nyon, Etienne Ganeau, Nicolas Gosselin, et Pierre-François Giffart, 1719.

Monthly Review 6. 1752.

Morgenblatt für gebildete Leser, 12. 1818.

Morning Chronicle and London Advertiser, Wednesday 9 April 1788.

Morning Post, 16 December 1801.

Mortimer, Thomas. *A New History of England, from the Earliest Accounts of Britain, to the Ratification of the Peace of Versailles, 1763*, 3 vols. London: J. Wilson and J. Fell, 1764.

Oracle and Public Advertiser, 13 November 1797.

Paine, Thomas. *The Age of Reason. Part the Second. Being an Investigation of True and Fabulous Theology*. London, 1796.

Pindar, Peter. *More Lyric Odes, to the Royal Academicians, by Peter Pindar, a Distant Relation to the Poet of Thebes, and Laureate to the Academy*. London, 1783.

Poems by William Cowper of the Inner Temple, Esq, in two volumes, A New Edition London, J.Johnson, in St Paul's Church Yard, by T. Bensley, 1806.

Pope, Alexander, *The Iliad of Homer, Translated by Mr Pope*, 6 vols. London: Lintot, 1715–20.

Pye, John. *Patronage of British Art, an Historical Sketch*. London: Longman, Brown, Green, and Longmans, 1845.

Rapin-Thoyras, Paul. *Histoire d'Angleterre*. The Hague: Alexandre de Rogissart, 1724–7.

Raymond, George Frederick. *A New, Universal and Impartial History of England, from the Earliest Authentic Records, and Most Genuine Historical Evidence, to the Winter of the Year 1784*. London: J. Cooke, 1785.

Reynolds, Sir Joshua, *Discourses on Art*, ed. by Robert R. Wark. New Haven, CT: Yale University Press, 1997.

Rogers, Samuel. *Italy*. London: Edward Moxon, 1838.

The Italian Journals of Samuel Rogers, ed. by J. R. Hale. London: Faber and Faber, 1956.

Royal Academy of Arts. *The Exhibition of the Royal Academy*. London: W. Griffin, 1774.

Russel, William Augustus. *A New and Authentic History of England, from the Most Remote Period of Genuine Historical Evidence, to the Present Important Crisis*. London: J. Cooke, 1777.

Salisbury and Winchester Journal, 23 November 1801.

Salisbury and Winchester Journal, 8 February 1802.

Seward, William. *Supplement to the Anecdotes of Some Distinguished Persons, Chiefly of the Present and Two Preceding Centuries*. London: Cadell Jun. and Davies, 1797.

Smith, J. T. *An Antiquarian Ramble in the Streets of London*, ed. Charles Mackay, vol. 1. London: Richard Bentley, 1846.

Staffordshire Advertiser, 14 February 1802.

Swedenborg, Emanuel. *A Treatise concerning Heaven and Hell, and of the Wonderful Things Therein*. London, 1784.

Sydney, Temple. *A New and Complete History of England, from the Earliest Period of Authentic Intelligence to the Present Time*. London: J. Cooke, 1773.

Temperly, C. H. *A Dictionary of Printers and Printing*. London: H. Johnson, 1839, 896.

Thackeray, W. M. 'The Artists', in *The Works of William Makepeace Thackeray*, 24 vols. London: Smith, Elder & Co., 1869, 15: 423–40.

The Celestial Beds; or, A Review of the Votaries of the Temple of Health, Adelphi, and the Temple of Hymen, Pall-Mall. London: Kearsly, 1781.

'The Competition of Bell, Boydell, and Macklin', *The Times* (13 December 1790).

The Descriptive Sketch of the Storming of Seringapatam, as Exhibited in the Great Historical Picture Painted by Robert Ker Porter [Edinburgh], [1800?].

The Exhibition of the Royal Academy. The Fifteenth. London, 1783.

The History of England, trans. Nicholas Tindal, 2nd edn, 2 vols. London: James, John and Paul Knapton, 1732.

The Life and Writings of Henry Fuseli, the former written and the latter edited by John Knowles, 3 vols. London: Colburn and Bentley, 1831.

The Odyssey of Homer translated into English Blank Verse, by William Cowper, Esq, with a preface by his kinsman J.Johnson, LLB and illustrated with engravings from the paintings and designs of Fuseli, Howard, Smirke, Stothard, Westall &c. &c. members of the Royal Academy, 4 vols. London: J. Johnson, 1810.

The Picture of London for 1804. London: R. Phillips, 1804.

The Pocket Magazine, Robins's Series (1827–1833).

The Rape of the Lock, an Heroi-Comical Poem by A. Pope. Adorned with Plates. London, Printed by T. Bensley, for F. J. du Roveray, 1798.

The Temple of Pleasure: A Poem. London: Langham, 1783.

The Vauxhall Affray; or, the Macaronies Defeated. London: J. Williams, 1773.

'Theatrical Intelligence', *The Covent-Garden Magazine; or, Amorous Repository: Calculated Solely for the Entertainment of the Polite World* (November 1772).

Thomson, James. *The Seasons. Embellished with Fourteen Plates.* London: John Stockdale, 1794.

Tinsley, William. *Random Recollections of an Old Publisher*, vol. 1. London: Simpkin, Marshall, Hamilton, Kent & Co., 1900.

Vertue, George. *The Heads of the Kings of England, Proper for Mr. Rapin's History, Translated by N. Tindal M. A. viz. Egbert First Monarch of England, Alfred the Great, Canute the Dane, William the Conqueror, First of the Norman Line, And all the Succeeding Kings and Sovereign Queens, to the Revolution; with Some of the most Illustrious Princes of the Royal Family. Collected, Drawn, and Engraven, with Ornaments and Decorations, by George Vertue.* London: James, John and Paul Knapton, 1736.

Volney, Constantin-François, *The Ruins, or a Survey of the Revolutions of Empires.* Trans. Anon. London: J. Johnson, 1795.

von Schwarzkopf, Joachim. *Über Staats- und Adress-Calender. Ein Beitrag zur Staatenkunde.* Berlin: Heinrich August Rottmann, 1792.

Walford, Edward. 'Oxford Street and its northern tributaries: Part 2 of 2', in *Old and New London: Volume 4.* London: Cassell, Petter & Galpin, 1878, 441–67. British History Online, www.british-history.ac.uk

Warton, Joseph, *An Essay on the Genius and Writings of Pope*, 4th edn, 2 vols. London, 1782.

Weinglass, D. H. *Prints and Engraved Illustrations By and After Henry Fuseli: A Catalogue Raisonné.* Aldershot: Scolar Press, 1994.

Whincop, Thomas (ed). *Scanderbeg: Or, Love and Liberty. A Tragedy Written by the late Thomas Whincop, Esq. To which are added A LIST of all the DRAMATIC AUTHORS, with some Account of their Lives; and of all the DRAMATIC PIECES ever published in the English Language, to the Year 1747.* London: W. Reeve, 1747.

Wordsworth, William. *The Prose Works of William Wordsworth*, 3 vols, ed. by W. J. B. Owen and J. W. Smyser. Oxford: Clarendon Press, 1974.

Secondary Works

Abler, Ronald, John S. Adams and Peter Gould. *Spatial Organisation: The Geographer's View of the World.* Englewood Cliffs, NJ: Prentice-Hall, 1971.

Ackroyd, Peter. *Blake.* New York: Knopf, 1996.

Acosta, Ana M. *Reading Genesis in the Long Eighteenth Century: From Milton to Mary Shelley*. Aldershot, Hampshire: Ashgate, 2006.

Alexander, David. 'Kauffman and the Print Market in Eighteenth-century England', in *Angelica Kauffman: A Continental Artist in Georgian England*, ed. by Wendy Wassying Roworth. Brighton: Reaktion Books, 1992, 140–92.

Altick, Richard D. *Paintings from Books: Art and Literature in Britain 1760–1900*. Columbus: Ohio State University Press, 1985.

The Shows of London. New Haven, CT; London: Harvard University Press, 1978.

Anderson, Benedict. *Imagined Communities: Reflections on the Origin and Spread of Nationalism*. London: Verso, 1983.

Andrews, Malcolm. *The Search for the Picturesque: Landscape Aesthetics and Tourism in Britain, 1760–1800*. Aldershot: Scolar Press, 1989.

'A Neglected Classical Phase of Turner's Art: His Vignettes to Rogers's *Italy*', *Journal of the Warburg and Courtauld Institutes*, 32 (1969): 405–10.

Ashton, Rosemary *142 Strand: A Radical Address in Victorian London*. London: Chatto & Windus, 2006.

Aymonino, Adriano. 'The Fortune of the Borghese Dancers in Eighteenth and early Nineteenth-Century European Art and Decoration', *Roma fuori Roma: L'esportazione dell'arte moderna da Pio VI all'Unità (1775–1870)*, ed. by Giovanna Campitelli, Stefano Grandesso and Carla Mazzarelli. Rome: Campisano, 2012, 477–92.

Balfour, Ian. *The Rhetoric of Romantic Prophecy*. Stanford, CA: Stanford University Press, 2002.

Barnett, Gerald, *Richard and Maria Cosway: A Biography*. Cambridge: Lutterworth Press, 1995.

Barrell, John. 'Spectacles for Republicans', in *Sensation and Sensibility: Viewing Gainsborough's 'Cottage Door'*, ed. by Ann Bermingham. New Haven, CT; London: Yale University Press, 2005.

The Dark Side of the Landscape: The Rural Poor in English Painting, 1730–1840. Cambridge: Cambridge University Press, 1983.

The Political Theory of Painting from Reynolds to Hazlitt: The Body of the Public. New Haven, CT: Yale University Press, 1995.

'Thomas Banks and the Society for Constitutional Reform', in *Living with the Royal Academy: Artistic Ideals and Experiences in England, 1768–1848,* ed. by Sarah Monks, John Barrell and Mark Hallett. Farnham: Ashgate, 2013, 131–52.

Baudino, Isabelle. 'Works of Historical Fancy? Samuel Wale's illustrations for Thomas Mortimer's "New History of England"', paper presented at Fancy-Fantaisie-Capriccio, Toulouse, 2015. https://hal.archives-ouvertes.fr/hal-01663098

Bennett, Shelley M. *Thomas Stothard: the Mechanisms of Art Patronage in England c.1800*. Columbia: University of Missouri Press, 1988.

Bentley, G. E. Jr. 'Coleridge, Stothard, and the First Illustration of "Christabel"', *Studies in Romanticism* 20: 1 (1981): 111–16.

——— 'F.I. Du Roveray, Illustrated-Book Publisher 1796–1806: III: Du Roveray's Artists and Engravers and the Engravers' Strike', *Bibliographical Society of Australia and New Zealand Bulletin*, 12: 3 (1988, issued May 1990): 97–145.

——— *The Stranger from Paradise: A Biography of William Blake*. New Haven, CT: Published for the Paul Mellon Centre for Studies in British Art by Yale University Press, 2001.

——— *Thomas Macklin (1752–1800), Picture-Publisher and Patron: Creator of the Macklin Bible (1791–1800)*. Lampeter: Edwin Mellen Press, 2016.

Black, Jeremy. *The English Press in the Eighteenth Century*. 1987; London: Routledge Revivals, 2011.

Blake, William, Thomas Gray and Geoffrey Keynes, *William Blake's Water-Colour Designs for the Poems of Thomas Gray*. Introduction and commentary by Geoffrey Keynes. London: Eyre Methuen Ltd; Paris: Trianon Press, 1972.

Bloomfield, B. C. 'The Publication of *The Farmer's Boy* by Robert Bloomfield', *The Library* 15: 2 (1993): 75–94.

Boase, T. S. R. 'Macklin and Bowyer', *Journal of the Warburg and Courtauld Institutes*, 26: 1–2 (1963): 148–77.

Bonnell, Thomas Frank. *The Most Disreputable Trade: Publishing the Classics of English Poetry 1765–1810*. Oxford: Oxford University Press, 2008.

Bordes, Philippe. 'Jacques-Louis David's Anglophilia on the Eve of the French Revolution', *Burlington Magazine*, 134: 1073 (August 1992), 482–90.

Brandon, David and Alan Brooke, *Marylebone and Tyburn Past*. London: Historical Publications, 2007.

Brown, David Blayney (ed.). *J. M. W. Turner: Sketchbooks, Drawings and Watercolours* (Tate Research Publication, December 2012), www.tate.org.uk/art/research-publications/jmw-turner/project-overview-r1109225 (accessed 9 May 2018).

Bryan, Michael. *Bryan's Dictionary of Painters and Engravers*, ed. George Williamson. London: Macmillan 1903–4.

Brylowe, Thora. 'Antiquity by Design: Re-Mediating the Portland Vase', in *Romantic Antiquarianism*, ed. by Noah Heringman and Crystal Lake. Romantic Circles, 2014.

——— 'Two Kinds of Collections: Sir William Hamilton's Vases, Real and Represented', *Eighteenth-Century Life*, 32: 1 (Winter 2009): 23–56.

Burden, Michael. *Garrick, Arne and the Masque of Alfred: A Case Study in National, Theatrical, and Musical Politics*. Lampeter: Edwin Mellen, 1994.

Burke, Edmund. *A Philosophical Enquiry into the Sublime and Beautiful*, ed. James T. Boulton. New York: Routledge, 2008.

Burnim, Kalman A. and Philip H. Highfill Jr., *John Bell, Patron of British Theatrical Portraiture*. Carbondale: Southern Illinois University Press, 1998.

Burwick, Frederick. 'The Romantic Reception of the Boydell Shakespeare Gallery: Lamb, Coleridge, and Hazlitt', in *The Boydell Shakespeare Gallery*, ed. by Walter Pape and Frederick Burwick. Bottrop, Essen: Verlag Peter Pomp, 1996.

Butler, Marilyn. *Mapping Mythologies: Countercurrents in Eighteenth-Century Poetry and Cultural History*. Cambridge: Cambridge University Press, 2015.

Romantics, Rebels and Reactionaries: English Literature and its Background 1760–1830. Oxford: Oxford University Press, 1981.

Butlin, Martin. *The Paintings and Drawings of William Blake*, 2 vols. New Haven, CT: Yale University Press, 1981.

Calè, Luisa. 'Blake and Literary Galleries', in *Blake and Conflict*, ed. by Sarah Haggarty and Jon Mee. Houndmills: Palgrave Macmillan, 2009.

Fuseli's Milton Gallery: 'Turning Readers into Spectators'. Oxford: Clarendon, 2006.

Cameron, Kenneth Neill (ed.). *Shelley and His Circle*. Cambridge: Harvard University Press, 1961–73.

Campbell, Kristin. '"The Proprietor exerts his utmost Care …": The Commercial and Commemorative Fates and Fortunes of John Boydell's Houghton Gallery Project', in *Agents of Space: Eighteenth-Century Art, Architecture, and Visual Culture*, ed. by Christina Smylitopoulos. Newcastle: Cambridge Scholars Publishing, 2016, 78–100.

Carruthers, Gerard and Alan Rawes (eds.). *English Romanticism and the Celtic World*. Cambridge: Cambridge University Press, 2003.

Chalkin, Christopher. *The Rise of the English Town, 1650–1850*. Cambridge: Cambridge University Press, 2001.

Clayton, Timothy. *The English Print 1688–1802*. New Haven, CT; London: Yale University Press, 1997.

Cochran, Peter. *The Farmer's Boy' by Robert Bloomfield: A Parallel Text Edition*. Newcastle: Cambridge Scholars Press, 2014.

Cohn, Norman. *Cosmos, Chaos and the World to Come: The Ancient Roots of Apocalyptic Faith*, 2nd edn, 2001; rpt. New Haven, CT; London: Yale University Press, 1999.

Colley, Linda. *Britons: Forging the Nation 17807–1837*. London: Pimlico, 1992.

Coltman, Viccy. 'Sir William Hamilton's Vase Publications', *Journal of Design History*, 14 (2001): 1–16.

Connerton, Paul. *How Modernity Forgets*. Cambridge: Cambridge University Press, 2009.

Cox, Devon. *The Street of Wonderful Possibilities: Whistler, Wilde & Sargent in Tite Street*. London: Frances Lincoln, 2015.

Cox, Oliver J. W. 'Frederick, Prince of Wales, and the First Performance of "Rule, Britannia!"', *The Historical Journal*, 56 (2013): 931–54.

Coxhead, A. C. *Thomas Stothard, RA.: An Illustrated Monograph*. London: A. H. Bullen, 1906.

Cox-Johnson, Ann. *Handlist of Painters, Sculptors & Architects Associated with St. Marylebone 1760–1960*. London: Borough of St. Marylebone Public Libraries Committee, 1963.

Crabbe, George. *The Complete Poetical Works*, ed. Norma Dalrymple-Champneys, 3 vols. Oxford: Clarendon Press, 1988.

Crosby, Mark and Robert N. Essick (eds). *Genesis: William Blake's Last Illuminated Work*. San Marino, CA: Huntington Library, Art Collections, and Botanical Gardens, 2012.

Curtis, Gerard. *Visual Words: Art and the Material Book in Victorian England*. Aldershot: Ashgate, 2002.

Damon, S. Foster. *William Blake: His Philosophy and Symbols*. 1924; rpt. London: Dawsons of Pall Mall, 1969.

Deleuze, Gilles and Félix Guattari, *Anti-Oedipus: Capitalism and Schizophrenia*, trans. Robert Hurley, Mark Seem and Helen R. Lane. Minneapolis: University of Minnesota Press, 1983.

Dias, Rosie. '"A World of Pictures": Pall Mall and the Topography of Display', in *Georgian Geographies: Essays on Space, Place and Landscape in the Eighteenth Century*, ed. by Miles Ogborn and Charles W. J. Withers. Manchester: Manchester University Press, 2004.

Exhibiting Englishness: John Boydell's Shakespeare Gallery and the Formation of a National Aesthetic. New Haven, CT; London: Yale University Press, 2013.

Dillard, Leigh. 'Drawing Outside the Book: Parallel Illustration and the Creation of a Visual Literary Culture', in *Book Illustration in the Long Eighteenth Century: Reconfiguring the Visual Periphery of the Text*, ed. by C. Ionescu and R. Schellenberg. Newcastle: Cambridge Scholars Publishing, 2011, 195–242.

Downie, J. A. (ed.), *The Oxford Handbook of the Eighteenth-Century Novel*. Oxford: Oxford University Press, 2016.

Draper, John. *William Mason: A Study in Eighteenth-Century Culture*. New York: New York University, 1924.

Easson, Kay Parkhurst. 'Blake and the Art of the Book', in *Blake in his Time*, ed. by Robert N. Essick and Donald Pearce. Bloomington and London: Indiana University Press, 1978, 35–52.

Eaves, Morris. 'Blake and the Artistic Machine', *PMLA*, 92 (1977): 904.

'The Sister Arts in British Romanticism', in *The Cambridge Companion to British Romanticism*, 2nd edn, ed. by Stuart Curran. Cambridge: Cambridge University Press, 2010.

Edgecombe, Rodney Stenning. *Leigh Hunt and the Poetry of Fancy*. London and Toronto: Associated University Press, 1994.

Erdman, David V. *Blake, Prophet against Empire: A Poet's Interpretation of the History of His Own Times*. Princeton, NJ: Princeton University Press, 1969.

(ed.). *The Complete Poetry and Prose of William Blake*, comm. by Harold Bloom. New York: Anchor-Doubleday, 1986.

Essick, Robert N. *William Blake's Commercial Book Illustrations: A Catalogue and Study of the Plates Engraved by Blake after Designs by Other Artists*. Oxford: Clarendon Press, 1991.

Essick, Robert N. and Rosamund A. Paice, 'Newly Uncovered Blake Drawings in the British Museum', *Blake: An Illustrated Quarterly*, 37.3 (Winter 2003/2004), 84–100.

Ezell, Margaret J. M. *Social Authorship and the Advent of Print*. Baltimore: Johns Hopkins University Press, 2003.
Favret, Mary A. *War at a Distance: Romanticism and the Making of Modern Wartime*. Princeton, NJ; Oxford: Princeton University Press, 2010.
Fine John, V. A. *The Ancient Greeks: A Critical History*. Cambridge, MA: Belknap Press of Harvard University Press, 1983.
Finlay, Nancy. 'Parnell's "The Hermit": Illustrations by Stothard', *The Scriblerian and the Kit-Cats*, 18 (1985): 1–5.
  'Thomas Stothard's Illustrations of Thomson's *Seasons* for the *Royal Engagement Pocket Atlas*', *The Princeton University Library Chronicle*, 42 (1981): 165–77.
Frayling, Christopher. 'Fuseli's *The Nightmare*: Somewhere between the Sublime and the Ridiculous', in Martin Myrone, Christopher Frayling and Marina Warner, *Gothic Nightmares: Fuseli, Blake and the Romantic Imagination* (London: Tate Publishing, 2006), 9–40.
Fulford, Tim and Lynda Pratt (eds). *The Letters of Robert Bloomfield and his Circle*, www.rc.umd.edu/editions/bloomfield_letters/HTML/letterEEd.25.70.html
Garlick, Kenneth. and Angus Macintyre (ed.), *The Diary of Joseph Farington, Vol V. August 1801–March 1803*. New Haven and London: Yale University Press, 1979.
Gatrell, Vic. *The First Bohemians: Life and Art in London's Golden Age*. London: Allen Lane, 2013.
Genette, Gerard. *Paratexts: Thresholds of Interpretation*. Cambridge: Cambridge University Press, 1997.
Gipponi, Tino, *Maria e Richard Cosway*. Turin: Allemandi, 1988.
Godfrey, Richard T. *Printmaking in Britain: a General History from its Beginnings to the Present Day*. Oxford: Phaidon, 1978.
Gordon, N. P. J. 'The Murder of Buondelmonte: Contesting Place in Early Fourteenth-Century Florentine Chronicles', *Renaissance Studies*, 20: 4 (2006): 459–77.
Gowan, Donald E. *From Eden to Babel: A Commentary on the Book of Genesis 1-11*. Grand Rapids, MI: William B. Eerdmans and Edinburgh: Handsel Press, 1988.
Graver, Bruce. 'Illustrating *The Farmer's Boy*', in *Robert Bloomfield: Lyric, Class, and the Romantic Canon*, ed. by Simon White, John Goodridge and Bridget Keegan. Lewisburg, PA: Bucknell University Press, 2006, 49–69.
Graves, Algernon. *The Society of Artists of Great Britain 1760–1791, The Free Society of Artists 1761–1783*. London: George Bell, 1907.
Graves, Robert. *The Greek Myths*, 2 vols. Harmondsworth: Penguin, 1955.
Griffin, Dustin. *Patriotism and Poetry in Eighteenth-Century Britain*. Cambridge, Cambridge University Press, 2002.
Griffiths, Anthony. *Prints and Printmaking: An Introduction to the History and Techniques*. London: British Museum Publications, 1980.
  The Print Before Photography: An Introduction to European Printmaking 1550–1820. London: British Museum, 2016.
Hagstrum, Jean H., *The Sister Arts: The Tradition of Literary Pictorialism and English Poetry from Dryden to Gray*. Chicago and London: University of Chicago Press, 1958.

William Blake: Poet and Painter. Chicago, IL: University of Chicago Press, 1964.

Hale, J. R. 'Samuel Rogers the Perfectionist', *The Huntington Library Quarterly*, 25: 1 (1961): 61–7.

Hammelmann, Hanns. *Book Illustrators in Eighteenth-Century England*, ed. by T. S. R. Boase. New Haven, CT: Yale University Press, 1975.

Hargraves, Matthew. '*Candidates for Fame*': *The Society of Artists of Great Britain 1760–1791*. New Haven, CT: Yale University Press, 2005.

Harris, Eileen. 'A Tale of Two Tables', *Burlington Magazine*, 155 (June 2013), 390–5.

Haskell, Francis. *The Ephemeral Museum: Old Master Paintings and the Rise of the Art Exhibition*. New Haven, CT: Yale University Press, 2000.

History and its Images: Art and the Interpretation of the Past. New Haven, CT: Yale University Press, 1993.

Haskell, Francis and Penny, Nicholas. *Taste and the Antique: The Lure of Classical Sculpture*. New Haven, CT: Yale University Press, 1981.

Hawkins, Anne. 'Reconstructing the Shakespeare Boydell Gallery', in *Shakespeare and the Culture of Romanticism*, ed. by Joseph M. Ortiz. Aldershot: Ashgate, 2013.

Haywood, Ian. *Romanticism and Caricature*. Cambridge: Cambridge University Press, 2013.

Heath, John. *The Heath Family Engravers 1779–1878*, 3 vols. Aldershot: Scolar Press, 1993.

Higgins, Sean. 'Thomas Macklin's Poets' Gallery: Consuming the Sister Arts in Late Eighteenth-Century London'. Unpublished PhD, London: Courtauld 2002.

Hogan, Charles Beecher (ed.). *The London Stage 1660–1800: Part 5: 1776–1800*. Carbondale: Southern Illinois University, 1968.

Holcomb, Adele M. 'Turner and Rogers's *Italy* Revisted', *Studies in Romanticism*, 27: 1 (1988): 63–95.

Hollander, Anne. *Moving Pictures*. Cambridge, MA: Harvard University Press, 1991 [originally published 1986].

Hoock, Holger. *The King's Artists: The Royal Academy of Arts and the Politics of British Culture, 1760–1840*. Oxford: Clarendon, 2003.

Houfe, Simon. *The Dictionary of 19th Century British Book Illustrators and Caricaturists*. Woodbridge: Antique Collectors' Club, revised ed. 1996.

Hunnisett, Basil. *An Illustrated Dictionary of British Steel Engravers*. Aldershot: Scolar Press, 1989.

Hutton, Ronald. 'Robert Bowyer and the Historic Gallery: A Study of the Creation of a Magnificent Work of Art', unpublished PhD dissertation, 4 vols. University of Chicago, 1992.

Hyde, Sarah. 'Printmakers and the Royal Academy Exhibitions, 1780–1836', in *Art on the Line: The Royal Academy Exhibitions at Somerset House 1780–1836*, ed. by David H. Solkin. New Haven, CT; London: Yale University Press, 2001.

Ionescu, Christina and R. Schellenberg (eds). *Book Illustration in the Long Eighteenth Century: Reconfiguring the Visual Periphery of the Text*. Newcastle: Cambridge Scholars, 2011.

Jackson, H. J. *Those Who Write for Immortality: Romantic Reputations and the Dream of Lasting Fame*. New Haven, CT: Yale University Press, 2014.

Jefferson, Thomas. *The Papers of Thomas Jefferson*, ed. by Julian P. Boyd. Princeton, NJ: Princeton University Press, 1950–2007.

Jestin, Loftus. *The Answer to the Lyre: Richard Bentley's Illustrations for Thomas Gray's Poems*. Philadelphia: University of Pennsylvania Press, 1990.

Joshua, Essaka. *The Romantics and the May Day Tradition*. London: Routledge, 2016.

Jung, Sandro. 'Illustrated Pocket Diaries and the Commodification of Culture', *Eighteenth-Century Life*, 37: 3 (2013): 53–84.

——— *James Thomson's 'The Seasons': Print Culture, and Visual Interpretation 1730–1842*. Bethlehem: Lehigh University Press, 2015.

——— *Kleine artige Kupfer: Buchillustration im 18. Jahrhundert*. Wiesbaden: Harrassowitz, 2018.

——— 'Packaging, Design and Colour: Form Fine-Printed to Small-Format Editions of Thomson's *The Seasons*, 1793–1802', in *British Literature and Culture*, ed. by Sandro Jung. London: Derek S. Brewer, 2013, 97–124.

——— 'Print Culture, High-Cultural Consumption, and Thomson's "The Seasons", 1780–1797', *Eighteenth-Century Studies*, 44: 4 (2011): 495–514.

——— *The Fragmentary Poetic: Eighteenth-Century Uses of an Experimental Mode*. Bethlehem: Lehigh University Press, 2009.

——— *The Publishing and Marketing of Illustrated Literature in Scotland, 1760–1825*. Bethlehem, PA: Lehigh University Press, 2017.

——— 'Thomas Stothard's Illustrations for *The Royal Engagement Pocket Atlas*, 1779–1826', *The Library*, 12: 1 (2011): 3–22.

——— 'Thomas Stothard, Milton and the Illustrative Vignette: The Houghton Library Designs for *The Royal Engagement Pocket Atlas*', *Yearbook of English Studies*, 45 (2015): 137–58.

——— 'Thomson, Macpherson, Ramsay, and the Making and Marketing of Illustrated Scottish Literary Editions in the 1790s', *Papers of the Bibliographical Society of America*, 109: 1 (2015): 5–61.

Kelly, Alison, *Decorative Wedgwood in Architecture and Furniture*. London: Country Life, 1965.

Kerslake, J. F. (ed.). *Catalogue of Theatrical Portraits in London Public Collections*. London: Society for Theatre Research, 1961.

Keynes, Geoffrey. *William Blake's Water-Colour Designs for the Poems of Thomas Gray*. London: Eyre Methuen Ltd; Paris: Trianon Press, 1972.

Keynes, Simon. 'The Cult of King Alfred', *Anglo-Saxon England*, 28 (1999): 292–318.

King-Hele, Desmond. *Erasmus Darwin: A Life of Unequalled Achievement*. London: de la Mare, 1999.

Kunzle, David. 'Between Broadsheet Caricature and *Punch* – Cheap Newspaper Cuts for the Lower Classes in the 1830s', *Art Journal*, 4: 43 (1983).

Latour, Bruno. *Reassembling the Social: An Introduction to Actor-Network-Theory*. Oxford: Oxford University Press, 2005.

Lewis, W. S., Grover Cronin Jr. and Charles H. Bennett (eds). *Horace Walpole's Correspondence with William Mason*, The Yale Edition of Horace Walpole's Correspondence, vols. 28–29. New Haven, CT: Yale University Press, 1955.

Lipking, Lawrence. 'Quick Poetic Eyes: Another Look at Literary Pictorialism', in *Articulate Images: The Sister Arts from Hogarth to Tennyson*, ed. by Richard Wendorf. Minneapolis: University of Minnesota Press, 1983, 3–25.

Lippincott, Louise. *Selling Art in Georgian London: The Rise of Arthur Pond*. New Haven, CT: Yale University Press, 1983.

Lord, Peter. *Gwenllian: Essays on Visual Culture*. Llandysul, Dyfed, Wales: Gomer, 1994.

McCarthy, F. I. '*The Bard* of Thomas Gray: Its Composition and its Use by Painters', *National Library of Wales Journal*, 14: 1 (Summer, 1965): 105–13.

McClellan, Andrew. *Inventing the Louvre: Art, Politics, and the Origins of the Modern Museum in Eighteenth-Century Paris*. Cambridge: Cambridge University Press, 1994.

McCue, Maureen. *British Romanticism and the Reception of Italian Old Master Art, 1793-1840*. Farnham, Surrey: Ashgate, 2014.

McGann, Jerome J. 'The Idea of an Indeterminate Text: Blake's Bible of Hell and Dr. Alexander Geddes', *Studies in Romanticism*, 25 (1986): 303–24.

Mackenzie, Gordon. *Marylebone: Great City North of Oxford Street*. London: Macmillan, 1972.

McPhee, Constance Curran. 'The Exemplary Past? British History Subjects in London Exhibitions, 1760–1810', unpublished PhD dissertation. University of Pennsylvania, 1995.

Maidment, Brian. 'Dinners or Desserts? – Miscellaneity, Knowledge and Illustration in Magazines of the 1820s and 1830s', *Victorian Periodicals Review*, 43 (Winter 2010): 353–87.

— 'The Draughtsman's Contacts – Robert Seymour and Periodical Illustration in 1832', *The Journal of European Periodicals Studies* (online journal 2016): 37–52.

— 'The Gallery of Comicalities: Graphic Humour, Wood-Engraving, and the Development of the Comic Magazine, 1820–1841', *Victorian Periodicals Review*, 50: 1 (Spring 2017): 214–27.

Malmesbury, William of. *Gesta Regum Anglorum*, ed. and trans by R. A. B. Mynors, R. M. Thomson and M. Winterbottom. Oxford: Clarendon Press, 1998.

Matthews, Susan. *Blake, Sexuality and Bourgeois Politeness*. Cambridge: Cambridge University Press, 2011.

Meisel, Martin. *Realizations: Narrative, Pictorial, and Theatrical Arts in Nineteenth-Century England*. Princeton, NJ: Princeton University Press, 1983.

Miller, J. Hillis. *Illustration*. London: Reaktion Books, 1992.

Milton, John. *Paradise Lost*, ed. by Alastair Fowler, rev. 2nd edn. London and New York: Longman, 1998.

Mitchell, W. J. T. *Iconology: Image, Text, Ideology*. Chicago, IL; London: University of Chicago Press, 1987.

Mitchell, Rosemary. *Picturing the Past: English History in Text and Image 1830–1870*. Oxford: Clarendon, 2000.

Morse, Edward Lind (ed.). *Samuel F. B. Morse: His Letters and Journals*, vol. 1. New York: Kraus Reprint, 1972.

Myrone, Martin (ed.). *'Seen in My Visions': A Descriptive Catalogue of Pictures by William Blake*. London: Tate Publishing, 2009.

Bodybuilding: Reforming Masculinities in British Art 1750–1810. New Haven, CT; London: Yale University Press, 2005.

with Christopher Frayling and Marina Warner, *Gothic Nightmares: Fuseli, Blake and the Romantic Imagination*. London: Tate Publishing, 2006.

Henry Fuseli. London: Tate Gallery Publishing, 2001.

Seen in my Visions. Tate, 2009.

Myrone, Martin and Lucy Peltz (eds). *Picturing the Past: Aspects of Antiquarian Culture and Practice 1700–1850*. Aldershot: Ashgate, 1999.

Nanavutty, Piloo. 'A Title-Page in Blake's Illustrated Genesis Manuscript', *Journal of the Warburg and Courtauld Institutes,* 10 (1947): 114–22.

Nenadic, Stana. 'Print Collecting and Popular Culture in Eighteenth-Century Scotland', *History*, 82: 266 (1997): 203–22.

Nichol, D. 'J. J. and P. Knapton', in *The British Literary Book Trade, 1700–1820*, vol. 154, *Dictionary of Literary Biography*, ed. by James K. Bracken and Joel Silver. London: Gale, 1995, 170–5.

Niles, John D. *The Idea of Anglo-Saxon England 1066–1901: Remembering, Forgetting, Deciphering and Renewing the Past*. Oxford: Blackwell, 2015.

Noble, Percy. *Anne Seymour Damer: A Woman of Art and Fashion, 1748–1828*. K. Paul, Trench, Trübner, 1908.

Norton, Elizabeth. *Elfrida: The First Crowned Queen of England*. Stroud: Amberley, 2013.

Oleksijczuk, Denise Blake. *The First Panoramas: Visions of British Imperialism*. London: University of Minnesota Press, 2011.

Otto, Peter. '"A Pompous High Priest": Urizen's Ancient Phallic Religion in *The Four Zoas*', *Blake: An Illustrated Quarterly,* 35 (2001): 4–22.

Blake's Critique of Transcendence: Love, Jealousy, and the Sublime in 'The Four Zoas'. Oxford: Oxford University Press, 2000.

Multiplying Worlds. Oxford: Oxford University Press, 2011.

'The Regeneration of the Body: Sex, Religion and the Sublime in James Graham's Temple of Health and Hymen', *Romanticism on the Net*, 23 (August 2001) (accessed 5 March 2018).

Paley, Morton. *The Traveller in the Evening: The Last Works of William Blake*. Oxford: Oxford University Press, 2003.

Parker, Joanne. *'England's Darling': The Victorian Cult of Alfred the Great*. Manchester: Manchester University Press, 2007.

Patenaude, Troy. '"The Glory of a Nation": Recovering William Blake's 1809 Exhibition', *The British Art Journal*, 4: 1 (2003): 55–63.

Patton, Robert L. *George Cruikshank's Life Times and Art*. London and Cambridge: The Lutterworth Press, 2 vols., 1992 and 1996.

Phillips, Mark Salber. *On Historical Distance*. New Haven, CT: Yale University Press, 2013.

Phillips, Michael. 'Blake and the Terror 1792–3', *The Library*, Sixth series, vol. XVI: 4 (December 1994): 263–97.

'No. 36 Castle Street East: A Reconstruction of James Barry's House and the Making of *The Birth of Pandora*', *The British Art Journal*, 9: 1 (Spring, 2008): 15–27.

Piggot, Jan. *Turner's Vignettes: 29 September 1993–13 February 1994*. London: Tate Gallery, 1993.

Piper, Andrew. *Dreaming in Books: The Making of the Bibliographic Imagination in the Romantic Period*. Chicago and London: University of Chicago Press, 2009.

Pollard, Arthur (ed.). *George Crabbe: The Critical Heritage*. London: Routledge, 1972.

Postle, Martin. *Reynolds: The Subject Pictures*. Cambridge: Cambridge University Press, 1995.

Powell, Nicolas. *Fuseli: The Nightmare*. London: Penguin, 1973.

Presbrey, Frank. *The History and Development of Advertising*. New York: Doubleday, 1929.

Pressly, William L. *The Artist as Original Genius: Shakespeare's 'fine Frenzy' in Late Eighteenth-Century British Art*. Newark: University of Delaware Press, 2007.

Priestman, Martin. *Romantic Atheism: Poetry and Freethought, 1780–1830*. Cambridge University Press, 1999.

Rad, Gerhard von. *Old Testament Theology: The Theology of Israel's Historical Traditions*, trans. D. M. G. Stalkes. London: S. C. M. Press, 1975.

Rancière, Jacques. *The Politics of Aesthetics: The Distribution of the Sensible*, trans. Gabriel Rockhill. Continuum, London & New York, 2004.

Raven, James. *Bookscape: Geographies of Printing and Publishing in London Before 1800*. London: The British Library, 2014.

The Business of Books: Booksellers and the English Book Trade. New Haven, CT: Yale University Press, 2007.

Read, Dennis M. *R. H. Cromek, Engraver, Editor, and Entrepreneur*. Farnham: Ashgate, 2011.

Renier, Anne. *Friendship's Offering: An Essay on the Annuals and Gift Books of the Nineteenth Century*. London: Private Library Association, 1964.

Reynolds, Anna, Lucy Peter and Martin Clayton. *Portrait of the Artist*. London: Royal Collection Trust, 2016.

Richardson, Ruth. *Dickens and the Workhouse: Oliver Twist and the London Poor*. Oxford: Oxford University Press, 2012.

Rogers, Samuel, *The Italian Journals of Samuel Rogers*, ed. by J. R. Hale. London: Faber and Faber, 1956.

Roman, Cynthia. 'Pictures for Private Purses: Robert Bowyer's Historic Gallery and illustrated edition of David Hume's *History of England*', unpublished PhD dissertation. Brown University, 1997.

Rosenblum, Robert. *The International Style of 1800: A Study in Linear Abstraction*. New York: Garland, 1976.

Rosenthal, Angela. *Angelica Kauffman: Art and Sensibility*. New Haven, CT: Yale University Press, 2006.

Rovee, Christopher Kent. *Imagining the Gallery: The Social Body of English Romanticism*. Stanford, CA: Stanford University Press, 2006.

Rowland, Christopher. *Blake and the Bible*. New Haven, CT: Yale University Press, 2010.

Roworth, Wendy Wassyng (ed.). *Angelica Kauffman: A Continental Artist in Georgian England*. London: Reaktion, 1992.

Saklofske, Jon. 'A Fly in the Ointment: Exploring the Creative Relationship Between William Blake and Thomas Gray', *Word & Image: A Journal of Verbal/Visual Enquiry,* 19: 3 (2003): 166–79.

Schiff, Gert. *Johann Heinrich Füssli, 1741–1825: Text und Oeuvrekatalog*, 2 vols. Zürich: Verlag Berichthaus, 1973.

and Werner Hoffmann, trans. Sarah Twohig, *Henry Fuseli*. London: Tate Gallery, 1975.

Seward, William. *Supplement to the anecdotes of some distinguished persons, chiefly of the present and two preceding centuries*. 1797.

Shanes, Eric. *The Life and Masterworks of J. M. W. Turner*. New York: Parkstone Press, 2008.

Shannon, Mary L. *Dickens, Reynolds and Mayhew on Wellington Street: The Print Culture of a Victorian Street*. Aldershot: Ashgate, 2015.

Shaw, Philip. *Suffering and Sentiment in Romantic Military Art*. Aldershot: Ashgate, 2013.

Shawe-Taylor, Desmond. *Dramatic Art: Theatrical Paintings from the Garrick Club*. London: Dulwich Picture Gallery, 1997.

Sillars, Stuart. *Painting Shakespeare: The Artist as Critic 1720–1820*. Cambridge: Cambridge University Press, 2006.

Simmons, Clare A. *Popular Medievalism in Romantic-Era Britain*. New York: Palgrave Macmillan, 2011.

Simon, Jacob. 'The Account Book of James Northcote', *Walpole Society*, vol.58, 1996 [C.R.Smith], "Pictorial Illustrations of Shakespeare," *Quarterly Review* 142 (1876): 457–79.

Sivertsev, Alexei M. *Judaism and Imperial Ideology in Late Antiquity*. Cambridge: Cambridge University Press, 2011.

Society and Sentiment: Genres of Historical Writing in Britain, 1740–1820. Princeton, NJ: Princeton, 2000.

Solkin, David. *Painting for Money: The Visual Arts and the Public Sphere in Eighteenth-Century England*. New Haven, CT: Yale University Press, 1993.

Stafford, Pauline. 'Ælfthryth', in *The Blackwell Encyclopedia of Anglo-Saxon England*, ed. by Michael Lapidge et al. Oxford: Blackwell, 1999.

— 'The King's Wife in Wessex', *Past and Present*, 91 (1981): 3–27.

— 'The Portrayal of Royal Women in England, Mid-Tenth to Mid-Twelfth Centuries', in *Medieval Queenship*, ed. by Janet Parsons. Stroud: Sutton, 1993, 143–67.

St Clair, William. *The Reading Nation in the Romantic Period*. Cambridge: Cambridge University Press, 2004.

Stewart, Susan. *On Longing: Narratives of the Miniature, the Gigantic, the Souvenir, the Collection*. Baltimore and London: Johns Hopkins University Press, 1984.

Sullivan, M. G. 'Stothard, Thomas (1755–1834)', *Oxford Dictionary of National Biography* (Oxford University Press, 2004; online edn, September 2012), www.oxforddnb.com/view/article/26603.

Sunstein, Emily W. *Mary Shelley: Romance and Reality*. Baltimore, MD: Johns Hopkins University Press, 1989.

Tattersfield, Nigel. *Thomas Bewick: The Complete Illustrative Work*, 3 vols. London: The British Library, The Bibliographical Society, Oak Knoll Press, 2011.

Tayler, Irene. *Blake's Illustrations to the Poems of Gray*. Princeton, NJ: Princeton University Press, 1971.

— 'Two Eighteenth-Century Illustrators of Gray', *Fearful Joy; Papers from the Thomas Gray Bicentenary Conference at Carleton University*, ed. by James Downey and Ben Jones. Montreal: McGill-Queen's University Press, 1974, 119–26.

Temple, Nigel. 'Humphry Repton, Illustrator, and William Peacock's "Polite Repository," 1790–1811', *Garden History*, 16: (1988): 161–73.

Thomas, Julia. 'Illustrations by Belsey', *Textual Practice*, 24: 6 (2010): 1073–1090.

— *Nineteenth-Century Illustration and the Digital: Studies in Word and Image*. New York: Palgrave, 2017.

Thomas, Sophie. 'Poetry and Illustration: "Amicable Strife"', in *A Companion to Romantic Poetry*, ed. by Charles Mahoney. Oxford: Blackwell, 2011.

Thompson, E. P. *The Making of the English Working Class*. London: Penguin, 1977.

Thompson, Hilary. 'Narrative Closure in the Vignettes of Thomas and John Bewick', *Word & Image*, 10: 4 (1994): 395–408.

Tomory, Peter. *The Life and Art of Henry Fuseli*. London: Thames & Hudson, 1972.

Topham, John. '"The Mirror of Literature, Amusement and Instruction" and Cheap Miscellanies in Early Nineteenth-Century Britain', in *Reading the Magazine of Nature: Science in the Nineteenth Century Periodical*, ed. by G. Cantor et al. Cambridge: Cambridge University Press, 2004, 37–66.

'Thomas Byerley, John Limbird, and the Production of Cheap Periodicals in Regency Britain', *Book History,* 8 (2005): 75–106.

Toynbee, Paget and Leonard Whibley (eds). *Correspondence of Thomas Gray*, corrections and additions by H. W. Starr, 2nd edn, 3 vols. Oxford: Clarendon, 1971.

Trumpener, Katie. *Bardic Nationalism: The Romantic Novel and the British Empire.* Princeton, NJ: Princeton University Press, 1997.

Twyman, Michael. *A Directory of London lithographic printers 1800–1850.* London: Printing Historical Society, 1976.

Vaughan, Frank A. *Again to the Life of Eternity: William Blake's Illustrations to the Poems of Thomas Gray*. Selinsgrove: Susquehanna University Press; London: Associated University Press, 1996.

'Blake's Illustrations to Gray's "The Bard."' *Colby Quarterly,* 17: 4 (December, 1981): 211–37.

Walkley, Giles. *Artists' Houses in London 1764–1914.* Aldershot: Scolar Press, 1994.

Walpole, Horace. *The Yale Edition of Horace Walpole's Correspondence*, ed. by W. S. Lewis, 48 vols. New Haven, CT: Yale University Press, 1937–83.

Warner, Marina. 'Invented Plots: The Enchanted Puppets and Fairy Doubles of Henry Fuseli', in Myrone, Frayling and Warner, *Gothic Nightmares: Fuseli, Blake and the Romantic Imagination.* London: Tate Publishing, 2006, 23–9.

Waterhouse, Ellis, 'Gainsborough's "Fancy Pictures"', *Burlington Magazine,* 88: 519 (June 1946).

Watkin, David and Philip Hewat-Jaboor (eds). *Thomas Hope, Regency Designer.* New Haven, CT; London: Yale University Press, 2008.

Wedd, Kit, Lucy Peltz and Cathy Ross. *Artists's London: Holbein to Hirst.* London: Merrell, 2001.

Weeks, Donald. 'Samuel Rogers: Man of Taste', *PMLA,* 62: .2 (1947): 472–86.

Whibley, Leonard (ed.). *The Correspondence of Richard Hurd & William Mason, and Letters of Richard Hurd to Thomas Gray. With Introduction and Notes by Ernest Harold Pearce.* Cambridge: Cambridge University Press, 1932.

White, Jerry. *London in the Eighteenth-Century: A Great and Monstrous Thing.* London: Vintage, 2013.

Whitehead, Angus. '"Humble but respectable": Recovering the Neighbourhood Surrounding William and Catherine Blake's Last Residence. No. 3 Fountain Court Strand, c.1820–27', *University of Toronto Quarterly,* 80: 4 (Fall 2011), 858–79.

Whittaker, Jason. *William Blake and the Myths of Britain.* Houndmills, Basingstoke, Hampshire: Macmillan Press; New York: St. Martin's Press, 1999.

Wiggins, Alison and Rosalind Field (eds). *Guy of Warwick: Icon and Ancestor.* Rochester: D. S. Brewer, 2007.

Williamson, G. C. *Richard Cosway R. A.* London: Bell, 1905.

Wilson, Nigel (ed.). *Encyclopedia of Ancient Greece.* New York and London: Routledge, 2006.

Winchester Stone, George Jr (ed.). *The London Stage 1660–1800: Part 4: 1747–1776*. Carbondale: Southern Illinois University, 1962.

Wood, Gillian D'Arcy. *The Shock of the Real: Romanticism and Visual Culture, 1760–1860*. New York: Palgrave, 2001.

Woodworth, Mary K. 'Blake's Illustrations for Gray's Poems', *Notes and Queries* (August, 1970), 312–13.

Archival

Advertisement, 'Barnard's New and Complete History of England' (1790), BL HS.74/1987(12)

Balmanno Collection. Vol. 4. British Museum Prints & Drawings

City of Westminster Archives Centre

London Metropolitan Archives Centre

Mason, William, commonplace book, mid-18th century. York Minster Archive, MS Add 25

Royal Academy of Arts, 'Royal Academy Critiques &c. Vol. I, 1769–1793'

Web Resources

Backler Family. www.backlers.com

Blake Archive. www.blakearchive.org.

Edward Walford's Old and New London vol. 4 (1878). British History Online. www.british-history.ac.uk/old-new-london/

Exeter Working Papers in Book History: The London book trades 1775–1800: a preliminary checklist of members. http://bookhistory.blogspot.co.uk/2007/01/london-1775-1800-h.html

http://godwindiary.bodleian.ox.ac.uk/diary/1800-05-17.html

National Portrait Gallery Online. www.npg.org.uk/collections

Old Bailey Proceedings Online. www.oldbaileyonline.org

Survey of London. Draft chapters, *South-East Marylebone*, vols 51 and 52. www.ucl.ac.uk/bartlett/architecture/research/survey-london/current-area-study-south-east-marylebone

Tate. www.tate.org.uk

The Oxford Dictionary of National Biography. www.oxforddnb.com

The Oxford English Dictionary Online. www.oed.com

Thomas Gray Archive. www.thomasgray.org

Yale Center for British Art. www.britishart.yale.edu

Index

Æthelred, 72, 85
Analytical Review, 25
Anglo-Saxon England, 14, 71, 72, 90, 315, 317, 320
Anglo-Saxonism, xi, 78
Anubis, 103, 104, 105, 107, 108
Artaud, William,
　Mercy Stopping the Rage of War, 209, 214, 215
Astley, Thomas, 23
astronomy, 107
Athelwold, 76, 77, 78, 79, 80, 81, 83, 84, 85

Backler, James, 256
Bacon, John, 261
Bage, Robert, 205
Barnard, Edward, 303
Bartolozzi, Francesco, 201, 205, 223
Bell, John, 304
　Bell's British Theatre, 82, 87, 89, 92, 304
　Bell's British Poets, 55, 174, 247
Bellori, Giovanni Pietro, 304
Bewick, Thomas, 10, 12, 13, 15, 145, 147, 150
Bible, 3, 20, 25, 30, 31, 33, 38, 42, 44, 45, 175, 202, 203, 204, 216, 219, 221, 237, 304, 305, 310, 316, 319
　Acts, 32, 35, 212
　Creation, the, 35, 39
　Exodus, 32
　Ezekiel, 41, 65
　Genesis, v, vii, 14, 25, 26, 27, 28, 29, 30, 31, 33, 34, 35, 36, 38, 42, 43, 44, 45, 46, 111, 309, 312, 313, 317; Chapter 1 *passim*
　Luke, 42
　Revelation, 32, 41
Birchall, James, 81
Blake, William, Chapters 1 and 2 *passim*, 310
　A Vision of The Last Judgment, 38
　America, 83
　First Book of Urizen, 25, 26, 33, 106
　Illustrations to Enoch, 26
　Jerusalem, 26, 32, 37, 39, 42, 226
　Marriage of Heaven and Hell, 35
　Visions of the Daughters of Albion, 106, 117
botany, 6, 100, 108
Bowyer, Robert, 10, 61, 144, 199, 249
　Historic Gallery, 14, 87, 202, 204

Boydell, John, 13, 25, 76, 81, 106, 150, 212, 222, 226, 290
　Shakespeare Gallery, 15, 19, 20, 98, 139, 200, 201, 216, 217, 218, 238, 244, 246, 247, 261, 311, 312
British Institution, 236, 242, 304
Bunbury, Henry, 202
Burke, Edmund, 310
Butlin, Martin, 311
Byron, Lord George Gordon, 6, 15, 150, 161, 162, 163, 164, 166, 189, 274, 278

Cadell, Thomas, 124, 132, 149, 256, 258
Carey, William P., 304
Casali, Andrea, 80, 84, 85
Catullus, 230, 232, 240, 241, 304
Cheesman, Thomas, 248
classical mythology, 106
Claudian, 232, 240, 241
Cochran, Peter, 311
Collins, William, 304
　'Ode to Mercy', 205, 209, 214
Colman, George, 79
commonplaces, 276
communication circuit, 5, 17, 199, 245, 246, 255, 261
Cooke, Charles,
　Pocket Edition of Select British Poets, 3, 56, 88, 200, 201, 217, 221, 222, 223, 225, 226, 228, 229, 233, 235, 236, 237, 238, 239, 306
Cosway, Maria,
　Chapter 9 *passim*
Covent Garden, 79, 81, 84, 86, 244, 250, 252, 261
Crabbe, George, 312
Critical Review, 79, 92, 304
Cromek, Robert Hartley, 15, 243, 248, 290;
　Chapter 10 *passim*
Cupid, 114, 115, 117, 217

Darwin, Erasmus
　The Botanic Garden, 94, 100, 105, 107
　Economy of Vegetation 100, 101, 103, 107
　The Loves of the Plants, 96, 97, 100, 102
　The Temple of Nature, 94, 108, 109
Dickens, Charles, 4
Dione, 114, 115

drama, i, v, xi, 14, 48, 49, 52, 57, 58, 70, 71, 72, 77, 86, 163, 182, 183
dreams, 96, 97, 116, 128, 226
Drury Lane, 79

Eaves, Morris, 312
Edward the Martyr, 71, 76, 84, 85, 89, 93
Egypt, 103, 104, 105, 107, 108, 111
Eichhorn, Johann Gottfried, 30
Elfrida, 14, 71, 72, 73, 75, 76, 77, 78, 79, 80, 81, 82, 83, 84, 85, 87, 88, 89, 90, 91, 92, 303, 304, 306, 317
engraving, 1, 2, 6, 7, 8, 9, 12, 14, 15, 17, 47, 60, 70, 75, 85, 88, 100, 122, 131, 134, 142, 174, 175, 182, 189, 219, 222, 223, 230, 232, 233, 235, 241, 247, 258, 265, 266, 267, 268, 272, 273, 274, 276, 278, 280, 283, 284, 285, 286, 295, 300
Erdman, David V., 312
Eros, 114, 115
etching, 131
evolution, 65, 71
exhibitions, xii, 61, 121, 138, 174, 176, 201, 215, 221, 242, 252, 290

femininity, 44, 215, 260
Flaxman, John, 10, 47, 57, 64, 132, 233, 262, 288
Flora, 100, 101, 102, 108, 117, 231
Florence (city), ix, 114, 172, 177, 184, 185, 186, 187, 190, 192, 226
folio prints, 202
four elements, 100, 101
Free Society of Artists, 84, 92, 93, 305, 313
French Revolution, 130, 141, 242, 310
Fuseli, Henry, 305; Chapters 4 and 5 passim
  The Nightmare, 95, 96, 98, 100, 108, 113, 116, 128
  Milton Gallery, 150, 174, 175

Gainsborough, Thomas, 201, 223, 224
Garden of Eden, 29, 38, 39, 40
Gay, John, 33
Geddes, Alexander, 305
Gessner, Salomon, 144
Gillray, James, 213
Goldsmith, Oliver, 144, 158
gothic, 81, 85, 249, 277
Graham, James, 229
Gray, Thomas, 305; Chapters 2 and 9 passim
  Elegy in a Country Churchyard, 210
Grignion, Charles, 75

Hamilton, William, 80, 205, 229, 233
  The Antient English Wake, 205, 207, 210, 220
Hartley, Elizabeth, 79, 81, 87

Heath, James, 243, 246, 256
Hill, Aaron, 305
Hirschfeld, Christian Lorenz, 147
history painting, vi, xii, 84, 175, 214, 246, 258, 259, 289, 291, 295, 297 Coda passim
Hogarth, William, 70, 115, 203
Hogg, Alexander, 76
Homer, 119, 124, 125, 130, 134, 228, 229, 239, 307
Horace, 91, 92, 234, 237, 239, 240, 316, 321
Hume, David,
  History of England, vii, viii, 70, 72, 75, 81, 85, 87, 88, 89, 90, 91, 93, 303, 306, 307, 309, 319, 322
Hurd, Richard, Bishop of Worcester, 83

Italy, v, 7, 15, 62, 120, 144, 171, 172, 173, 174, 176, 177, 179, 182, 183, 185, 186, 189, 192, 193, 194, 226, 229, 246, 303, 307, 309, 314
Italy (poem), see Rogers, Samuel

Jacobinism, 209
Jerningham, Edward,
  The Antient English Wake, 205, 207, 210, 220
Johnson, Joseph, 96, 105, 107, 113, 119, 122, 124, 132

Kauffman, Angelica, 80, 201, 223, 225, 226
Kearsley, George, 76
Kent, William, 144
Knapton, John and Paul, 73, 76, 90, 91, 306, 307, 308, 317

Linnell, John, 35
literary galleries, 13, 25, 40, 54, 163, 205, Chapters 8 and 9 passim.
  See also Shakespeare Gallery; Thomas Macklin's Poets Gallery; Henry Fuseli's Milton Gallery
Locke, John, 119, 123
Lockman, John, A New History of England, 5, 87, 105, 123, 243
Loutherbourg, Philip James de, 14, 120, 121, 125

Macklin, Thomas, 290, 306, Chapters 8 and 9 passim
  Poets' Gallery, see Macklin, Thomas
Mallet, David, 78
Marylebone, 244, 250, 251, 262, 263, 264, 310, 311, 316, 322
Mason, William, 306, 322
medievalism, xi, 71, 72, 80, 90, 212
mezzotint, 81
Milton, John, 6, 9, 14, 16, 18, 20, 26, 34, 45, 46, 47, 65, 93, 113, 116, 118, 121, 122, 134,

166, 167, 170, 186, 187, 189, 199, 214, 216, 237, 238, 253, 262, 309, 311, 315, 317
Milton Gallery, see Fuseli, Henry
Montfaucon, Bernard de, 306
Monthly Review, 77, 78, 79, 91, 92, 128, 141, 304, 306
More, Hannah, 205, 207
Morning Chronicle, 203, 205, 218, 237, 306
Morning Post, 169, 204, 205, 218, 237, 306
Mortimer, Thomas, 306

Newman Street, Chapter 10 *passim*
Nixon, James, 81

Opie, John, 166, 202
Oracle, 97, 169, 204, 218, 306
Ossian, 50, 228

Paine, Thomas, 306
Pall Mall, 45, 113, 120, 202, 204, 206, 217, 218, 229, 231, 236, 244, 252, 312
Paracelsus, 100
pastoral, 152, 155, 157, 158, 205, 213, 214, 224
Pindar, Peter, 306
Pluche, Abbé Noël-Antoine, 103
portraiture, 70, 147, 227
print culture, xi, xiii, 3, 9, 13, 56, 149, 150, 199, 200, 204, 237, 243, 244, 245, 248, 255, 257, 258, 259, 260, 267, 273, 274
printing, 12, 60, 68, 123, 150, 223, 250, 271, 279
prints, i, v, xii, 9, 10, 12, 13, 14, 16, 19, 70, 71, 72, 73, 83, 96, 123, 143, 175, 194, 200, 201, 202, 203, 215, 217, 219, 220, 222, 223, 226, 233, 235, 236, 244, 247, 256, 286
Chapter 4 *passim*
Psyche, 114
public sphere, 222, 244, 291

Repton, Humphry, 153
respectability, 193, 250, 253, 260, 294
Reynolds, Joshua, 307
The Cottagers, 205, 208, 210, 212, 214
Richter, Henry James, 247
Rigaud, Jean François, 81
Rogers, Samuel, 307, Chapter 7 *passim*
Italy (poem), see Chapter 7 *passim*
Rovee, Christopher Kent, 9, 200
Royal Academy, 3, 8, 9, 19, 52, 57, 61, 65, 66, 80, 81, 85, 92, 107, 115, 120, 128, 141, 174, 193, 200, 216, 219, 221, 223, 225, 226, 227, 228, 235, 239, 242, 243, 244, 247, 250, 252, 264, 290, 295, 296, 303, 304, 305, 307, 309, 314, 322
Royal Engagement Pocket Atlas, v, viii, ix, 15, 143, 145, 149, 151, 152, 154, 155, 156, 157, 158, 160, 161, 163, 164, 165, 166, 167, 168, 169, 170, 175, 313, 315, Chapter 6 *passim*
Rubens, Peter Paul, 214, 228

Schomberg House, 229, 231
science, 14, 98, 100, 105
Shakespeare, William, 288
Shakespeare Gallery, 15, 19, 20, 98, 139, 200, 201, 216, 217, 218, 238, 244, 246, 247, 261, 311, 312
Shenstone, William, 205
Sillars, Stuart, 319
Smirke, Robert, 87, 128
Spenser, Edmund, 226
St Clair, William, 148
Stothard, Thomas, 194, 320, Chapter 7 and 10 *passim*
The Procession of the Canterbury Pilgrims, 256, 257
Wellington Shield, 255
subscription, 76, 162, 236, 255
Swedenborg, Emanuel, 307

Tasso, Torquato, 226
Temple Bar, 201
Thomson, James, *The Seasons*, xii, 6, 16, 17, 18, 150, 151, 155, 157, 166, 169, 170, 205, 208, 212, 219, 224, 238, 308, 315

Venice, ix, 172, 177, 178, 179, 180, 182, 183, 184, 186, 192
Vernor and Hood, 150, 157
Vertue, George, 308
viewing practices, 260
Virgil, 126, 171, 228
virtue, 49, 78, 79, 190, 241, 260, 273
Volney, Constantin-François, 107

Wale, Samuel, 73, 85
Walpole, Horace, 15, 39, 121, 203, 225, 226
Watson, Richard, 31
Wedgwood, Josiah, 100, 103, 232
West, Benjamin, 52, 201, 221, 243, 248, 252, 256
Wheatley, Francis, 201, 205, 215
William of Malmesbury, 73, 77
Wordsworth, William, 308